An Introduction to Philosophy: A Christian Guide to the Things That Really Matter is an excellent step into the world of philosophy. It leads the beginning student step by step from the basics into the deeper world of philosophical thought. It is clear and thorough in its treatments of the wide variety of topics in philosophy. This book is filled with helpful sidebars, illustrations, and explanations. The authors show how philosophical thinking informs how we inhabit the world and can contribute to a better life. Chapter 2, "Can I Control My Thought Life? Mental Exercises for Maintaining Good Mental Hygiene," alone is worth the price of the book.

—**Gregory E. Ganssle,** PhD, professor of philosophy,
Talbot School of Theology, Biola University

This book is a wonderful, practical, insightful, and balanced introduction to philosophy. It brings together the intellectual and the practical, the bigger picture and personal application. If you are a newcomer to philosophy—or even if you've been at it for a while—you'll find this a helpful guide to steer you into the way of wisdom. The book is quite comprehensive, but not daunting. Since every human being has a worldview or philosophy of life (and, so, we are all philosophers), this book will assist you in "taking every thought captive to the obedience of Christ."

—**Paul Copan,** Pledger Family Chair of Philosophy and Ethics,
Palm Beach Atlantic University, West Palm Beach (Florida);
author, *Loving Wisdom: A Guide to Philosophy and Christian Faith*

For those who love wisdom, philosophy bears tremendous potential for making sense of knowledge, reality, and meaning. Yet philosophy as a discipline can seem inaccessible and irrelevant for those who have just begun to think deeply about the nature of the world and their place in it. By contrast, *An Introduction to Philosophy* by Drs. Sherman, Holland, Osmundsen, and Rasor rewards the reader with access to the discipline and a compelling case for the relevance of philosophy "to the things that really matter." This work draws deeply on the historical philosophical tradition, but it is an introduction for today. From start to finish, its authors demonstrate the relevance of philosophy for perennial questions about meaning, purpose, and human flourishing, ultimately leading the mind upward to the wisdom of God in Christ. I highly recommend it as a textbook for introductory philosophy courses and as an excellent resource for the church.

—**Jason S. Hiles,** dean, College of Theology and
Grand Canyon Theological Seminary, Grand Canyon University

Impressive in scope. Accessible. Engaging. This book represents everything you want in an introduction to philosophy. None of these features are the book's chief virtue, however. Its greatest achievement is its powerful demonstration of how faith and philosophy go together. This book will equip readers to love God with all their being, including their minds, as they become conversant with critical conversations in the academy, church, and culture.

—**Paul M. Gould,** professor of philosophy of religion, and director, MA in philosophy of religion, Palm Beach Atlantic University

Many introduction to philosophy textbooks for a Christian audience are too demanding for newcomers, or are largely superficial, or are irrelevant to the fundamental doctrines of Christian theology. This textbook strikes a difficult balance, being both accessible and useful to Christians who want to utilize philosophy in service of their faith. The authors efficiently survey the primary issues in philosophy with charity, insight, and an eye toward philosophy's relevance to the gospel of Jesus Christ. An earnest reading will satisfy certain curiosities, raise new questions, challenge previously unexamined ideas, and encourage devotion to the Lord.

—**Sanjay Merchant,** professor of theology, Moody Bible Institute

To ask what really matters is already to philosophize. You cannot fully avoid thinking about life's big questions in the long run. Such questions—those that inform and animate the chapters of this book—will come unbeckoned at various points in your life, whether or not you are prepared for them. Even now, you have implicit assumptions about them, if not conscious answers to them. Wouldn't it be worth it to have *good* answers to the questions that really matter?

The authors of this new introductory text in philosophy have judiciously selected a number of issues of central importance to the human condition that demand our attention. Along the way, they skillfully guide the reader in thinking through them carefully, thoroughly, and *Christianly*—sensitive to the claim that God has spoken.

—**Joshua W. Seachris,** associate teaching professor of philosophy, University of Notre Dame

A comprehensive and accessible introduction to philosophy. A guide to an intellectually robust Christian faith, designed to help the individual develop an integrated Christian worldview engaging science, logic, and the deepest questions of life.

—**Eric J. Silverman,** Christopher Newport University

A splendid book. Sherman, Holland, Osmundsen, and Rasor tackle the core issues of philosophy with clarity, alacrity, and sensitivity to the ways Christianity informs and is informed by philosophical reflection.

—Tim Pickavance, professor of philosophy,
Talbot School of Theology, Biola University

What an accomplishment! This is the most thorough introduction to philosophy from a distinctly Christian perspective of which I'm aware. The book's treatment of concepts is thoughtfully curated for the true beginner with a dynamic teacher's voice throughout. It's a master class in philosophy.

—Travis Dickinson, PhD, professor of philosophy,
Dallas Baptist University

An Introduction to Philosophy: A Christian Guide to the Things That Really Matter is a comprehensive but accessible textbook filled with wisdom for Christian life and thought.

—Keith Hess, associate professor of philosophy and apologetics,
Oklahoma Baptist University

What an outstanding new introduction to philosophy! Sherman, Holland, Osmundsen, and Rasor have done the church a tremendous service by providing an accessible, thorough, contemporary, engaging, and truly Christ-honoring on-ramp to the study of life's most important and enduring questions. Excellent for students of philosophy, pastors, and other church leaders who are rightly serious about critical thought, and really any Christian eager to responsibly steward their mind for Christ, in service to his kingdom.

—Dr. John Y. Kwak, associate professor of pastoral theology,
Western Seminary

AN INTRODUCTION TO
Philosophy

AN INTRODUCTION TO
Philosophy

A CHRISTIAN GUIDE TO THE THINGS
THAT REALLY MATTER

Steven B. Sherman, Richard A. Holland Jr.,
Gary S. Osmundsen, and Peter J. Rasor II

ZONDERVAN ACADEMIC

An Introduction to Philosophy
Copyright © 2025 by Steven B. Sherman, Richard A. Holland Jr., Gary S. Osmundsen, and Peter J. Rasor II

Published in Grand Rapids, Michigan, by Zondervan. Zondervan is a registered trademark of The Zondervan Corporation, L.L.C., a wholly owned subsidiary of HarperCollins Christian Publishing, Inc.

Requests for information should be addressed to customercare@harpercollins.com.

Zondervan titles may be purchased in bulk for educational, business, fundraising, or sales promotional use. For information, please email SpecialMarkets@Zondervan.com.

ISBN 978-0-310-11173-3 (hardcover)
ISBN 978-0-310-11174-0 (ebook)

Cover design: Emily Weigel
Cover art: © Minimallista / Shutterstock
Interior design: Kait Lamphere

Printed in the United States of America

25 26 27 28 29 30 31 32 33 34 35 36 37 /TRM/ 17 16 15 14 13 12 11 10 9 8 7 6 5 4 3 2 1

Contents

Part 1: Introduction to Philosophy

Part 2: Logic, Reasoning, and Arguments

Part 3: Epistemology
What, How, and Why We Can Know

Part 4: Metaphysics
Exploration into the Nature of Reality and Human Persons

Part 5: Philosophy and Science
Complementary and Conflicting

Part 6: Philosophy of Religion and Philosophical Theology
The Relation between Philosophy and Faith

Part 7: Ethics
Theory and Application

Part 8: The Meaning of Life

Foreword

This book is a visible result of something wonderful. But to understand this, we need to reflect on one of Jesus' key parables about the nature of the Kingdom of God and how it typically works in the world. In Matthew 13:33, Jesus provided a crucial and brilliant analogy between the way leaven—usually yeast—transforms an entire loaf of bread. Leaven has a transformative influence on something that changes it for the better. Here's the punch line: The leaven was *hidden* in the bread; its presence and progressive influence remains hidden until a certain stage of transformation is reached. In the same way, God's Kingdom usually moves quietly and in a covert way.

What does all this have to do with the book before you? In the 1920s, American culture increasingly began to regard Christianity as an irrational superstition with science replacing it as the authority of culture. By the 1960s, science was viewed as the only, or at least the vastly superior, way to know reality. The result? By the end of the twentieth century, all the things that matter to us—for example, Does God exist and how can we know? Is there objective meaning to life? Is there such a thing as objective right and wrong?—came to be regarded as issues that no one could know the truth of the matter one way or another. So people chose what they believed about these issues by blind faith and by how they felt about them. Our culture and individual lives have been greatly harmed by this development.

But God has been at work in a hidden, leavening way not visible to most people until quite recently. In the 1970s, he raised up a group of academic philosophers who were committed Christians that wanted to bring Christian ideas back to the university and, as a result, to the broader culture. Like leaven, a movement aimed at developing the Christian mind, especially in philosophy, began to grow.

There is a way to tell if the leaven of this movement has transformed the culture in a noticeable way. This would become evident not only when more and more professors of philosophy were openly Christians but, even more important, when the growth in Christian philosophy filtered down to the person in the street, including the undergraduate classroom. *An Introduction to Philosophy* is a major indication that the resurgence of Christian philosophy, including the general value among Christians of learning how to think well, has arrived. I celebrate its release.

This wonderful work by Steven B. Sherman, Rich Holland, Gary Osmundsen, and Peter J. Rasor II is not just another textbook. It is a symbolic capstone of a movement that provides quality Christian thinking about important philosophical topics.

But why would God raise up a movement in philosophy to recapture the relevance of the gospel and a Christian worldview in the church and broader culture? The answer: God is a God of reason, and he invites us to reason together with him. Thus, learning to think philosophically is a core aspect of loving God and growing in Christlikeness. Christians who study the history of revival note that a revival and its impact do not last long unless it is eventually combined with a renewal of Christian thought, especially in philosophy and theology.

As you will see in the pages to follow, these observations make a lot of sense. You will learn that philosophy is the attempt to think well about things that really matter. Some people think that philosophy is one of the most impractical fields taught in the university. Nothing could be further from the truth. It is the most practical of all fields, since it involves learning to think well about the most important issues that define us as human persons. To see this, look at this book's table of contents. Here are just some of the topics covered in *An Introduction to Philosophy*:

1. How can philosophy help me control my thoughts, deal with anxiety and depression, and make me less vulnerable to making decisions based on my up-and-down emotions?
2. How can I learn to think more logically and carefully?
3. What is knowledge, and can I know things that can't be tested with my five senses? What are some examples of this? How can I know God exists?
4. What does it mean to say something is real? What kinds of things are real?
5. What is a human person? Do they have souls and commonsense free will? Are human persons really responsible for their actions?

6. What are some intelligent ways to integrate science with biblical/theological claims?
7. Is there such a thing as objective right and wrong, and how do we know one way or the other?
8. How can I improve my ethical reasoning and think well about current troubling moral controversies?
9. Is there meaning to life? If so, what is it and how do we know?

I don't know about you, but I can't think of anything more practical than learning to think carefully about these kinds of questions, and this book will help you in this task.

One final thought: More and more young adults are leaving the church and abandoning belief in God because they have never been taught why they should believe. They fear Christianity is false and irrational, and they don't know how to think about all this. In an important interview in *Leadership* journal, Barna Group president David Kinnaman lists six reasons young people leave the church and Christianity itself. Four are especially relevant to the importance of this book: the church's shallowness of thought, including its biblical teachings and practices; an unsafe place to express doubts and get answers to questions; isolationism, a failure to interact intelligently with the surrounding culture; and, last but not least, the church's anti-science attitude, including being out of step with scientific developments and debate.[1]

I wish these people who were surveyed could have read *An Introduction to Philosophy*. It would have stopped so many from abandoning Christianity. However, you have the opportunity to read this book. Take advantage of it. And spread the word about it to others.

—*J. P. Moreland,* Distinguished Professor of Philosophy,
Talbot School of Theology, Biola University, and
author of *Love Your God with All Your Mind.*

NOTES

1. Eric Reed, compiler of information from David Kinnaman, "Six Reasons Why Young People Leave the Church," *Leadership* (Winter 2012), www.christianitytoday.com/le/2012/winter/youngleavechurch.html.

Preface

Writing this book started with a lunch meeting discussing how to better teach philosophy to our undergraduate students. Of course, the genesis of the idea came long before that meeting, as each of us came to that conversation already seeing a need for an introduction to philosophy that would serve our students well—perhaps other students and readers, too. We saw a need for an accessible introduction that would be helpful to those students who had never heard of these ideas before, and we also saw a need for an introduction that was more friendly to the Christian worldview than were those that we had used previously in our classes. We believe this book fills that need. This book truly is an introduction, as it is designed to be the reader's first exposure to the ideas we present here. We also wrote the book as *Christian* philosophers. We wanted to avoid the hostility toward the Christian worldview that often appears in many introductory philosophy texts, and we wanted to instill into the presentation a deliberately Christian way of looking at the topics, which necessarily entails fairly and consistently engaging with alternative worldviews. Thus, we think that students from other religious perspectives, those with no religious affiliation ("nones"), or even committed atheists will still be able to learn much from the contents of the book, as our presentation is neither focused on polemics nor a distinct work in apologetics. We present the philosophical issues as best we can, and we do it as Christians.

We knew the process of writing this book would be difficult. How do you write just one book with four separate authors? It isn't easy, especially when we each have our own strengths and weaknesses, and we each tend to speak about the issues in a slightly different way. We decided to have Steve act as our managing editor, as he had already spent quite a bit of time thinking about how a project like this could come to fruition. He worked diligently to develop plans and schedules, to keep us on task, and to make sure we were producing a book that met our stated goals. To leverage our own individual strengths and areas of interest, we began the process of assigning specific chapters to an author. As each one of us prepared a draft of a chapter, we shared it among the others, who then provided substantive feedback and suggestions for changes or revisions. Where consensus couldn't be reached, we left open live options that we agreed were reasonable ones to hold. This was a lengthy, difficult process. We thought it was worth it, though, and we happily committed to seeing the project through to completion, setting aside time during our weekends and summer breaks to write it. What you see in this book is the product of decades of teaching philosophy to undergraduate students and a heart for explaining philosophical ideas to non-philosophers (although in a sense, any person who thinks deeply about something is already a philosopher). We are grateful to Matt Estel at Zondervan, who patiently worked with us throughout the entire process of developing the manuscript and provided helpful guidance along the way. His editorial talents contributed to the overall clarity in our writing. We also want to thank Brian Phipps, who oversaw the editorial process, as well as the entire Zondervan team for helping bring this project to completion.

Each of us would like to speak to you personally about our roles in this project:

Steven B. Sherman

My first philosophy class came as a shock. My "practical atheist theism" at the time meant that I believed in God, but it really didn't matter to my "you do you" life. Philosophical questions like "Is this chair really there?" seemed wacky to me as a multi-sport athlete and "party hardy" beach boy. My mediocre grade in the class showed everyone I was "too cool" for this egghead stuff. But then life hit the fan. With a heartfelt cry, I began asking God to reveal himself and to help me with my twenty-year-old mess of a life. Three hours later on that Sunday morning (during my first time attending a church service held in a high-school gym in Orange County, CA) came my conversion; trusting in myself was transformed to trusting in God and the Good News (gospel), forever changing things. My whole view of reality began to morph into a *Christian* worldview. Education took on new meaning, particularly after learning that Jesus and the historic Christian faith placed a premium on loving God with all your mind (and whole self). Reading became fuel for my soul: consuming the Scriptures and studying theology, apologetics, philosophy, ethics, and the spiritual life. Eventually, I embraced the powerful claim that "all truth is God's truth," which expanded my understanding of God's design and purpose for creation: human beings in particular. Several formative books helped guide my life and calling, including philosophy and apologetics works like Francis Schaffer's *The God Who is There*, Walter Martin's *Kingdom of the Cults*, and John Courtney Murray's *The Problem of God*, plus superb Christian fiction by C. S. Lewis, namely *The Chronicles of Narnia* and *The Screwtape Letters*.

Writing this book has been much more than just labor; it's been a labor of love: and not just love for philosophy (the pursuit of wisdom) but, more important, love for God (to whom we owe everything) and love for others (including you, our reader). We had you in mind when we began thinking and collaborating on what content should be included, what we sensed was most important to introduce and discuss, and what topics might make the greatest positive impact on your life (like they have on ours). We want you to know that you matter to God. We believe the Lord desires you to experience the best life possible, which in part involves loving God with your mind. Besides serving as managing editor, I wrote chapters that included areas I have strong interests in: chapter 5 on hermeneutics, trying to explain what it means and why it's important for understanding texts; chapter 19 on philosophical theology, seeing how philosophy and theology interrelate; chapter 21 (with Rich) on theological ethics and morals; chapter 23 on the crucial and controversial matter of sexual ethics; and chapter 24 on the existentially-relevant and related topics of communication and information ethics.

Rich Holland

Sometime in the early 1990s, while I was studying Mechanical Engineering at Virginia Tech and preparing to enter the US Army, a close friend handed me a copy of C. S. Lewis's *Mere Christianity*. I devoured it! Never had I been exposed to such ideas and I found myself overwhelmed with what seemed to me to be both an alien mode of thinking about the world and the right way of thinking about the world. That book awakened in me a passion to pursue truth and highlighted my need for some significant epistemic house-cleaning in my own mind. My motivation to participate in this project arises from a deep desire to help others enjoy the pursuit of truth, as reading *Mere Christianity* did for me. Of course, I cannot aspire to have the kind of impact on the world of ideas that Lewis has had; but perhaps in some small way, I can make some positive impact in the lives of those who will read this volume.

My most significant contribution to this book comes in chapters 6, 7, 8, and 9, the chapters on logic, argumentation, and reasoning. In those chapters, I tried to focus on providing clear and simple explanations of the key ideas. In my own experiences in the past, I have been exposed to overly complex explanations that were inaccessible to most beginning philosophy students. So in these chapters, I tried to do the opposite: provide a clear, accessible introduction to logic, with special focus on helping our readers see why good reasoning really matters. I also made a significant contribution in a few of the chapters on ethics. This is another passion of mine and an area of study that I think is increasingly important in the world today. Peter and I partnered together to craft an introduction to ethics in chapter 20, and Steve and I worked together to introduce theological ethics in chapter 21. I also wrote chapter 22 on bioethics. In each of these chapters, my goal was to help highlight the most important issues in ethics, so that our reader might get a sense of what it means to live a good life.

Gary Osmundsen

After embracing Christianity in my early twenties, I faced immediate challenges from family, friends, and professors. In my quest for answers, I discovered *Love Your God with All Your Mind* by JP Moreland—the author of the foreword to this book. Moreland's book was transformative: it provided reasonable answers to my vexing questions, leading me to delve further into studying philosophy. Four years later, I was studying under Moreland at Biola University and serving as his teaching assistant. JP's friendship, influence, and writings were pivotal in this journey. I dedicate the chapters I've written to him. It's truly humbling—surreal, in fact—to witness the philosopher that inspired me to study philosophy recommend this book to others. Deep gratitude extends to him and other philosophers, professors, colleagues, family, and friends who shaped my philosophical explorations. Developing the skill of thinking Christianly about life's profound questions and embracing philosophy as a lifestyle has, indeed, enriched the meaning, purposes, and values I see in life. I hope this book gives readers a mere fraction of what studying philosophy has given to me. At the very least, I hope it reignites the flame of curiosity that once burned bright in them as children.

The chapters I wrote for this book are ones I really enjoy thinking about. I took an irenic approach to these chapters while also staying committed to a commonsense approach toward thinking Christianly about these topics. In chapters 1 and 2, I tried to motivate readers to see both the value and practical benefits of studying philosophy, for Christians and non-Christians alike. Chapter 4 looks at four main subdisciplines of philosophy. I explain how they are foundational to any method of inquiry—quite often sharing interdependency amongst each other. Chapter 10 addresses some major questions involving epistemic goods like truth, knowledge, and understanding. Chapter 11 uses skepticism as a heuristic device to better understand these goods. Chapter 12 addresses how these epistemic goods relate to "the God question." Various positions are laid; some positions are recommended over others. Chapters 13, 14, and 15 address some major metaphysical questions involving the nature of reality, persons, and free will. Again, various positions are given, but the ones recommended receive additional reasons in support of them. In chapter 25, I provide a way to think about framing the meaning-of-life question, and in chapter 26, I offer some reasons why the Christian answer is arguably better than an attractive non-theistic alternative.

Peter J. Rasor II

I grew up in a Christian home. I went to church every week. I became a Christian at age ten. I was highly involved with my youth group as a teenager. I never questioned whether God existed, who Jesus was, or much about the core teachings and practices of Christianity. I did, however, think a lot. It often caused me problems in school, where I would be caught daydreaming. My high-school German teacher would often draw on the chalk board a stick figure and what was presumably planet Earth, write my name over the stick figure, and sing, "Come back, Peter." Thinking. It was a hobby, a preoccupation of mine, and it often got me into trouble. But thinking got me into trouble in the church, as well. I often probed pastors and teachers with questions I had about Christianity and life in general. The replies were typically the same: silence or half-baked sentimental cliches. Finding a place in the church to cultivate the mind was non-existent. Then I found C. S. Lewis while in college. Then I found Lee Strobel and his first book *The Case for Christ*. One author led to another. I found myself engulfed in philosophy. I had found my thinking partners—people who were just like me—Christians who thought all the time.

My hope is that the students of this book will fall in love with thinking about the important questions of life, not just for the sake of thinking but to find truth and the good life (which, by the way, is found only in Christ). Perhaps you are not a habitual thinker. That's okay. Everyone has different talents, personalities, dispositions, and the like. At least begin to think more deeply. For this book, fortunately, I had the opportunity to write the chapters in the areas of philosophy that I most enjoy: the history of philosophy (chapter 3), philosophy of science (chapter 16), scientism (chapter 17), and philosophy of religion (chapter 18). I also contributed to chapter 15 on free will and determinism and chapter 20 on ethics. I consider these as some of the most important subjects to think about. I hope the reader begins to ponder these topics deeply. Go ahead. Think. Get into trouble.

PART 1

Introduction to Philosophy

CHAPTER 1

Why Does Philosophy Matter?

Some of you might be thinking, "What am I getting myself into? I don't even know what philosophy is." If this is you, we can empathize with what you're thinking and feeling. At first, we didn't really understand philosophy either. But we loved the questions it asks and the way it attempts to answer them.

Let's start off by recognizing that "philosophy is not," as philosopher J. P. Moreland likes to joke, "psychology spelt funny." Regrettably, our decades of experience teaching philosophy to college students have taught us that more people believe something like this than you might think. This is largely because most versions of K–12 education neglect to offer students the opportunity to study philosophy. That is unfortunate for a number of reasons, not the least of which is the fact that virtually anyone reading this chapter is already a philosopher.

You don't believe it? Have you ever thought hard about things that really matter? For example, have you ever asked the following kinds of questions: Does God exist? Why does the universe exist? Do humans have free will? Who is a good person? What is truth? What is the meaning of life? Is there life after death? Why is there so much pain and suffering in the world? How can I find true happiness in life? Why do experts disagree over answers to these questions? If you ever thought about any of these big-ticket questions, then guess what? You're doing philosophy! The next question is: Are you any good at it?

Philosophy Defined

We've already arrived at a rough-and-ready definition of *philosophy*: thinking hard about things that really matter. This book will primarily use that definition.

But there are, of course, other definitions that help us better understand what philosophy is. For example, the history of the word *philosophy* comes from the Greek words *phileo* ("to love") and *sophia* ("wisdom"). So philosophy means "to love wisdom."

Another definition of philosophy is this: Philosophy is a second-order discipline that assesses, analyzes, and critiques the assumptions, key concepts, methods, and arguments used by first-order disciplines.[1] First-order disciplines are fields like math, physics, chemistry, biology, psychology, anthropology, history, literature, law, sociology, economics, astronomy, and so on. Much of the work done by first-order disciplines is descriptive—they describe the characteristics and events that constitute facts about some level of reality. Philosophy, however, is a second-order discipline because it takes its own unique tools and methods and applies them to first-order disciplines. Moreland likes to say, "Philosophers keep the books on everyone, including themselves." This is because as a normative discipline, philosophy explains why some method ought to be used over another; it attempts to explain why some key concept ought to be clarified and defined this way instead of that; it argues for why some statement, model, or theory ought to be seen as more accurate than alternatives, in light of the evidence and arguments in support of them. Philosophy tries to make first-order disciplines better at getting truth, even by challenging key assumptions made in philosophy itself. Furthermore, philosophy aims to show how truths from different first-order disciplines can better cohere with each other and shed light on philosophical questions.

Of course, philosophy has its own subdisciplines, such as logic, epistemology, metaphysics, and value theory. They influence other subdisciplines in philosophy, which is why these four are often treated as the main subdisciplines of philosophy. Logic investigates, among other things, the kind of laws governing rational thought. Logic provides tools to formulate good arguments and methods for diagnosing bad ones. Epistemology aims to provide adequate accounts of good things like truth, justification, rationality, knowledge, understanding, and wisdom. Metaphysics aims to provide an adequate account of the fundamental nature of reality and what specific kind of things furnish the world. Value theory investigates the kind of values appealed to in judgments or arguments involving what is right, wrong, good, bad, beautiful, ugly, and so on.

Other subdisciplines of philosophy are more specifically focused on a particular subject matter that can be subsumed under one or more of the four we've listed. They arguably fall outside the core four subdisciplines but are dependent upon them, given that some of their assumptions involve metaphysics, epistemology, value theory, and logic. Philosophy of science, philosophy of religion, philosophy of language, philosophical theology, philosophical hermeneutics, aesthetics, meta-ethics, normative ethics, applied ethics, philosophy of time, philosophy of mind, skepticism, and social epistemology are all examples of other subdisciplines of philosophy. If this is the first time you have ever studied philosophy, these terms may sound very strange to you. But don't feel overwhelmed! Our task in this book is to help you understand these concepts so that they don't seem so strange.

Human Curiosity, Questions, and Psychological Stability

It shouldn't be surprising that you and I have already thought about some of these philosophical questions. After all, humans are naturally curious and want answers to big-ticket questions. Indeed, Plato said, "Philosophy begins with wonder," and Aristotle—Plato's student—said, "All humans desire to know." Given humans' natural curiosity and desire for answers to their questions, you might think philosophy would sit comfortably next to math, science, and history in a high school curriculum. Unfortunately, the curiosity and desire to know about things that really matter doesn't get fostered in many peoples' education. The good news is that this introduction to philosophy can help remedy that![2]

What's more, this exploration into philosophy can address another human desire: a desire for a harmonious thought life. Don't we like it when our thoughts, beliefs, desires, bits of knowledge, and understanding all seem to live in harmony? Of course we do! This is because humans naturally desire to avoid pain— sometimes at all costs! And physical pain isn't the only kind of pain. We also want to avoid pain that comes from cognitive dissonance. Cognitive dissonance is the mental anguish that comes from discovering two mental states in tension with each other. Perhaps a belief is now in tension with a newly acquired belief, or a belief is now in tension with a thought about some newly acquired evidence that indicates one's belief is false.

For example, consider a case involving a college student named Jamie. One day after Jamie's sociology class, she finds herself believing (a) "Human actions are determined by historical, social, economic, and structural forces." Later, however, Jamie reflects on (a) and finds herself believing (b) "Environmental factors can influence a human action, but they do not determine human actions in all cases because humans have free will. Sometimes we can act differently than what we did—we could have done otherwise." After recognizing (a) and (b) are in tension with each other, Jamie experiences mental anguish. She experiences the pain that accompanies cognitive dissonance. She realizes that something has to give. Either (a) is false, or (b) is false, or both (a) and (b) are false. Clearly, they both can't be true. These incompatible beliefs prevent Jamie from experiencing the harmony we all long for within our thought life. In an effort to regain it, she has to decide how to respond to it.

This leads us to some good news about philosophy. Philosophy can provide Jamie and others the tools needed to resolve this tension and achieve a harmonious thought life. But unless we know how to think better about things that really matter by putting to work the tools of philosophy, we will not achieve this harmony. Nor will we achieve other good things that we naturally desire—things like truth, knowledge, understanding, and happiness. Because unless we learn how to think better, we will not get better at acquiring these goods. Philosophy provides important resources that improve our ability to think well. Indeed, philosophy offers tools that enable one to better evaluate and assess arguments and evidence, analyze key concepts and definitions, and employ certain principles and laws, all by employing specific intellectual, moral, and theological virtues, which enable one to think better and thus live generally better. Philosophy, therefore, is a practice that can assist one to become a better thinker. More specifically, philosophy offers us ways to become better at evaluating evidence, arguments, and forming more reasonable beliefs—indeed, beliefs that can enjoy more justification because of philosophy's assistance.

Imagine you are in a situation like Jamie's. How are you going to resolve the tension brought about by two incompatible beliefs about human freedom? Will you appropriately respond with the right attitude, seeking to resolve the tension through proper rational analysis? Or are you going to alleviate the cognitive dissonance irresponsibly? Will you seek relief from this pain by purposefully ignoring the incompatible beliefs by, say, listening to music or having a snack? Or perhaps you suppress the evidence in support of belief by employing some type of informal fallacy.[3] You attack the motives or intentions of the professor who argued that humans don't have free will. (After all, that's what most people do these days on news networks and social media.) The question of whether you respond responsibly or irresponsibly raises an additional question of how much you value truth, assuming you already know what truth is. (The question "What is truth?" is itself an inherently philosophical question.) The irony is that you use the term *truth* all the time. But do you know what it is? Do you have a definition or theory of truth that can withstand scrutiny? Philosophy is uniquely equipped—unlike any other discipline—to assist you in thinking better about and forming better answers to important questions.

Of course, cognitive dissonance can be generated in countless ways. Once we start considering inherently philosophical questions—such as, What is a human person? Who is a good person? How does one become a good person? How does one become happy in a world like this?—we start to see how cognitive dissonance can rear its ugly head, as we see how often our family, friends, and intellectual authorities disagree on answers. (This isn't even taking into consideration all the disagreement we are bombarded with once we consider what shows up in social media.) To better achieve a harmonious thought life and reduce unnecessary stress and anxiety, we want you to consider how philosophy can, perhaps, be a key ingredient to the remedy you need.

To satisfy our natural desire to be curious, to have our questions answered, and to have a healthy and harmonious thought life, philosophy can be an important vehicle to get you there. Put simply: our hope is that you see how philosophy can help you live better. Philosophy can equip you to form better beliefs. Forming better beliefs can result in increasing your ability to get things like truth, knowledge, and understanding. And acquiring more of these goods contributes toward living a better life.

How Philosophy Addresses Specific Christian Values

Everything so far in this chapter appeals to values that we believe almost everyone shares. After all, don't we all get a little intellectually curious sometimes and want our meaningful questions answered? Don't we want our thoughts to be in harmony with one another? But there is a chance that you are a Christian or have some interest in the Christian worldview. If that's you, then please consider the following reasons for why philosophy is vitally important to living life well as a Christian.

First, when Jesus was asked, "Which is the greatest commandment in [God's] Law?" he answered, "Love the Lord your God with all your heart and with all your soul and with all your mind. This is the first and greatest commandment" (Matt. 22:36–38). Well, to better understand and obey this commandment, don't we need to think hard about it? Don't we need to think hard about who God is, what God is like, what love is, how one loves God with heart, mind, and soul, and what the human heart, soul, and mind are?

See what is going on? We are beginning to think hard about the greatest commandment. Which is to say, we are doing philosophy. Since philosophy is thinking hard about things that really matter, the practice of philosophy is vital to being a Christian. For, in order to love God with all your heart, soul, and mind,

Does Colossians 2:8 warn Christians not to study philosophy? Some mistakenly believe that Paul's letter to the Colossian church is a warning against studying philosophy. Paul says to make sure "no one takes you captive through hollow and deceptive philosophy." What Paul was warning against is different human traditions that teach "hollow and deceptive" philosophical teachings that are heretical. Paul was addressing the false teachings that had infiltrated the local assembly and undermined the gospel he preached: a gospel rooted in the teachings of Jesus, not human speculation or some competing religion. What's more, in Acts 17 Paul showed familiarity with certain philosophers to build on common ground with his audience in order to justify claims found in Christ. So Paul studied and practiced philosophy.

and to love your neighbor as yourself, we need to think well on how to properly go about obeying these commands.

Second, becoming a mature Christian requires thinking hard about Christianity's history, doctrine, theology, anthropology, ethics, and description of reality, as well as our relation to both reality and God. If there are true statements comprising these subjects, then there are false statements, theories, theologies, and worldviews in opposition to them too. So philosophy, as C. S. Lewis pointed out, "must exist, if for no other reason, because bad philosophy needs to be answered."[4] Therefore, philosophy is vital for us to continue growing in our capacity and maturity to love God with all of our hearts, souls, and minds by not being led astray by false teachings, current trends, movements/causes, theories, political ideologies, idols, and arguments that compete for our allegiance (2 Cor. 10:5). This suggests another important reason.

Third, whether or not you realize it, you and virtually everyone else have some kind of worldview. A worldview is a mental map we use to interpret evidence, form beliefs, and understand reality. It is composed of specific assumptions, commitments, norms, standards, values, principles, beliefs, and theories that filter and process information. Sometimes we are even unaware of the ways our worldview is filtering, processing, "coloring," and assisting us when forming beliefs and interpreting reality. All you need to do to learn more about your worldview is to consider if you already have answers to the following questions:

- Does God exist?
- If God exists, what is God like? Does God have a character?
- If God exists, is God personal or impersonal? And is God interested in relating to human beings?
- Do only physical things exist?
- Do humans have free will and make free choices?
- Is determinism true?

- Do humans have an essence or a nature?
- Are humans naturally good, bad, or something in between?
- Are there objective moral values in the world?
- What is equality? What do people mean when they say a just society requires it?
- Can humans have knowledge about the way the world really is? Do humans have the ability to get truth, knowledge, and understanding—at some level—about reality?
- Is there objective meaning and purpose in the world, and can humans discover them?
- Is there an objective way for humans to flourish and be happy at both an individual and collective level?
- Is there life after death?

This list of questions is by no means exhaustive. But it does capture the kind of ingredients that go into forming a worldview. (By the way, if you don't understand some of these questions, then that's another reason why philosophy is valuable. Studying philosophy will help you understand and think better about why these big-ticket questions matter and how to form reasonable answers to them.)

The state of one's worldview not only filters and processes the information and evidence from the external world at the subconscious level, but it also governs how likely one is to consciously take some idea, statement, or belief to be true or false, depending on how well it coheres with other things one already believes. For example, Sam Harris (a well-known atheist) and Moses (a well-known theist) could be looking at the burning bush, hear an audible voice emanating from it, and form two entirely different beliefs about what's happening. Even though Sam Harris and Moses share the same evidence, they are committed to two different worldviews. This will help explain why Moses forms beliefs like "God exists" and "God spoke to me," whereas Sam Harris might form the belief "I just had a very strange hallucination." Their worldviews help explain why they disagree about what happened.[5] This is partly because Harris's worldview is one wherein God doesn't exist, so that will significantly influence his perceptual experience. Moses' worldview is a theistic one, which will significantly influence his perceptual experience.

Your worldview affects the fluctuating number of true beliefs and false beliefs you have. So don't we want to continue living in such a way that we increase the number of true beliefs we have and decrease the number of false beliefs we have? Of course we do! This is another reason, then, why philosophy is so important:

the practice of philosophy helps us to actively monitor, refine, and maintain a more accurate, coherent worldview. The more true beliefs we have, the more accurate our worldview will be. The more accurate our worldview, the more reliable we will be at perceiving reality and forming true beliefs. Indeed, a more accurate worldview will contribute toward how reliable we are at getting knowledge, understanding, wisdom, and a harmonious thought life.

The last reason for why philosophy is important for Christians is this: Jesus was a philosopher![6] Jesus thought hard about things that really matter, not the least of which is thinking well about how to love God and others while living within the reality of God's kingdom. Indeed, Jesus addressed many falsities that prevented people from being able to know God and live in communion with God in his kingdom. Since one of the purposes of life is to know God and develop Christlike character, Christians do well when seeing how Jesus thought about important topics, life experiences, and arguments. Then they can learn how to do likewise. Jesus is, after all, an exemplar for Christians to follow and emulate (Matt. 11:28–30; 1 Cor. 11:1; 1 Jn. 2:6).

Take, for example, a case involving Jesus interacting with the Sadducees in Luke 20:27–40. The Sadducees were a group of intellectuals who thought they had an argument that shows why the doctrine of bodily resurrection (i.e., life after death) is absurd and, thus, must be false. The Sadducees reasoned like this: If the resurrection is true, then people will be married in heaven. But if a woman's husband dies and she remarries, and that husband dies and she remarries again, and that husband dies and she remarries again, then that woman would be in a polygamous marriage in heaven. But that's absurd, because the law of Moses does not endorse polygamous marriage. So the doctrine of bodily resurrection must be false.

In response, Jesus addressed at least two false assumptions supporting the Sadducees' argument: the resurrection entails (1) humans will have bodies designed for sexual intercourse and reproduction, and (2) the institution of human marriage will continue in the new heaven and new earth just like it does here and now. Jesus addressed these false assumptions by pointing out two things. First, the resurrected body will not be exactly like the bodies we have now, which are, among other things, mortal and designed to reproduce. Second, the Sadducees already believed in something that entails the resurrection/life after death: God testified to Moses that he is the one, true, living God of Abraham, Isaac, and Jacob. One of their beliefs (God's testimony to Moses) conflicts with God's word to Moses (which entails that the patriarchs are alive and well despite their bodies decomposing in the ground).

Do you think you can respond to people with whom you disagree like Jesus did? Can you provide a winsome, reasonable, and loving defense of why you believe Christianity is true (1 Pet. 3:15; Jude 3)? Do you have the philosophical tools along with the moral and intellectual virtues that Jesus had to think hard about things that matter? Regardless of how you answer, this book can contribute to further cultivating the kind of heart, mind, soul, and character we believe Christians should strive to obtain. Philosophy, then, can play a significant role in the sanctification process—cultivating Christlike character.

Conclusion

Everyone is a philosopher. Whether you are a good philosopher depends on how well you can utilize the tools and methods of philosophy. We assume that all humans are curious, desire their questions answered, and want a harmonious thought life. Philosophy can address this natural inquisitiveness. As Christians, we believe philosophy is vital toward getting the truth about God and reality. More specifically, philosophy aids and assists one in obeying the two greatest commandments, responding to bad philosophy and theology, constructing and maintaining an accurate and coherent worldview, and growing in Christlike character.

Questions for Reflection

1. After learning that philosophy is "thinking hard about things that matter," does it surprise you to learn that virtually everyone is a philosopher? What are some of the first philosophical questions you asked or spent time thinking about growing up as a child? Did your elementary and high school education assist you in finding answers to these questions?
2. What practical benefits are there to studying philosophy? Can you think of any that were not mentioned in the chapter?
3. Why should Christians study philosophy? What other reasons can you think of that were not provided in the chapter?
4. Is philosophy better equipped to address worldview questions than other disciplines? Or do you think other disciplines are better equipped to answer these big questions? Why?
5. Have you ever thought of Jesus as a philosopher? Is that a good description of him? In what ways is he like a philosopher? In what ways is he not?

For Further Reading

General Level Readers

Baggini, Julian, and Peter S. Fosl. *The Philosopher's Toolkit: A Compendium of Philosophical Concepts and Methods.* 2nd ed. Oxford: Wiley-Blackwell, 2010.

Copan, Paul. *Loving Wisdom: A Guide to Philosophy and Christian Faith.* 2nd ed. Grand Rapids, MI: Eerdmans, 2020.

Cowan, Steven B., and James Spiegel. *The Love of Wisdom: A Christian Introduction to Philosophy.* Nashville: B&H, 2009.

DeWeese, Garrett J., and J. P. Moreland. *Philosophy Made Slightly Less Difficult: A Beginner's Guide to Life's Big Questions.* Downers Grove, IL: IVP Academic, 2021.

Dickinson, Travis. *Logic and the Way of Jesus.* Nashville: B&H Academic, 2022.

Moreland, J. P. *Love Your God with All Your Mind: The Role of Reason in the Life of the Soul.* Colorado Springs: NavPress, 2012.

Morris, Dolores G. *Believing Philosophy: A Guide to Becoming a Christian Philosopher.* Grand Rapids: Zondervan Academic, 2021.

Morris, Tom. *Philosophy for Dummies.* 2nd ed. Hoboken, NJ: Wiley, 2022.

Advanced Level Readers

Dew, James K., Jr., and Paul M. Gould. *Philosophy: A Christian Introduction.* Grand Rapids: Baker Academic, 2019.

DeWeese, Garrett. *Doing Philosophy as a Christian.* Downers Grove, IL: IVP Academic, 2011.

Inman, Ross D. *Christian Philosophy as a Way of Life: An Invitation to Wonder.* Grand Rapids: Baker Academic, 2023.

Moreland, J. P., and William Lane Craig. *Philosophical Foundations for a Christian Worldview.* 2nd ed. Downers Grove, IL: IVP Academic, 2017.

NOTES

1. This definition is inspired by J. P. Moreland's and William Lane Craig's definition in *Philosophical Foundations for a Christian Worldview* (Downers Grove, IL: IVP Academic, 2017), 15.

2. Ross Inman points out how psychologists have discovered some of the benefits of wonder. Some psychological benefits are (1) increasing one's awareness of the world or nature and decreasing unhealthy levels of self-importance; (2) cultivate greater degrees of humility—that is, a healthier self-estimation of one's strengths and weaknesses and gratitude toward others, especially extending credit where credit is due; (3) increased measures of a sense of connectedness with family, friends, and one's roots or community; and (4) increased measures of intellectual exploration and understanding. See Ross Inman, *Christian Philosophy as a Way of Life: An Invitation to Wonder* (Grand Rapids: Baker Academic, 2023), chap. 1.

3. For an in-depth analysis into the anatomy of this kind of informal fallacy, see Robert K. Garcia and Nathan L. King, "Getting Our Minds out of the Gutter: Fallacies That Foul Our

Discourse (and Virtues That Clean It Up)," in *Virtues in Action: New Essays in Applied Virtue Ethics*, ed. Michael W. Austin (New York: Palgrave-MacMillan, 2013), 190–206.

4. C. S. Lewis, *The Weight of Glory* (New York: HarperCollins, 2001), 58.

5. Relatedly, worldviews contain beliefs about values, which contribute to the formation of many moral beliefs. People generally weight some values heavier than others. Depending on what values one believes are true and get weighted heavier (i.e., taken as more significant and important) can arguably—in part—explain one's intuitive responses to evidence, statements, questions, and various cases involving morality. Further support for one's belief sometimes comes from reasoning, which will, then, often be informed by these values. Some of these values, according to Johnathan Haidt, are even "sacred values," which partly explain one's political affiliations. They are as follows: care/harm; liberty/oppression; fairness/cheating; loyalty/betrayal; authority/subversion; sanctity/degradation. See Jonathan Haidt, *The Righteous Mind: Why Good People Are Divided by Politics and Religion* (New York: Pantheon, 2012).

6. One way to consider Jesus in this new light is to read Dallas Willard, "Jesus the Logician," in *Christian Scholar's Review* 28, no. 4 (1999): 605–14. We also recommend reading Travis Dickinson, *Logic and the Way of Jesus* (Nashville: B&H Academic, 2022).

CHAPTER 2

Can I Control My Thought Life?

Mental Exercises for Maintaining Good Mental Hygiene

Any sports fans out there? We love to watch and read about different athletic achievements. We take them to be, among other things, admirable, inspiring, and often beautiful events to behold. Consider these two athletic achievements. In 2002, Cael Sanderson won his fourth consecutive NCAA Division I wrestling championship. That win capped off a perfect, undefeated career—compiling 159 wins and zero losses. He is the only Division I wrestler to ever go undefeated all four years, acquire *more than* 100 wins, and win four National Championships. Another incredible athletic feat took place October 12, 2019: Eliud Kipchoge ran a marathon in under two hours. To put this into perspective, Kipchoge maintained an average pace of 4 minutes and 35 seconds per mile over the 26.2-mile grind. When you get a chance, go see how long it takes to run a mile as fast as you can. Compare your time to a 4:35 mile, and then imagine sustaining that pace for another 25.2 miles.[1]

In addition to athletic achievements, there are intellectual achievements. Unfortunately, modern American culture doesn't value intellectual achievements like it values athletic achievements. When is the last time you saw the price of a ticket to an academic debate come close to the price of a ticket to a professional sporting event? We believe, however, that intellectual achievements should also inspire us.

Like athletic achievements, intellectual achievements don't come easy. Learning to think well requires years of cultivating specific abilities and skills just like athletes train to master their craft. These abilities and skills are sometimes called virtues:

- *Moral virtues,* like love, courage, temperance, and prudence.
- *Intellectual virtues,* like conscientiousness, curiosity, open-mindedness, autonomy, intellectual humility, charity, intellectual perseverance, and love of truth, knowledge, understanding, and wisdom.
- *Theological virtues,* like faith, hope, and love.

These virtues function as dispositions, abilities, or skills that enable you to successfully achieve good goals. Intellectual achievements are as varied as athletic ones. Examples of intellectual achievements include getting the truth because you exercised conscientiousness and perseverance, or getting understanding from someone you disagree with because you exercised intellectual courage, humility, open-mindedness, and charity. Thus, we take getting truth, knowledge, understanding, or wisdom to be achievements that require the cultivation and exercise of certain virtues—just like Cael Sanderson and Eliud Kipchoge exercised certain virtues to achieve their athletic feats.

Just as Sanderson and Kipchoge had to train to replace their bad athletic habits with good ones, so too must we uproot some bad habits of thought and replace them with better ones if we want to be intellectually virtuous. These bad habits of thought or unreliable patterns of reasoning are common intellectual vices that injure our psyche and prevent us from getting the truth. Indeed, these vices can prevent us from having the kind of psychological stability needed to think well.

Just what are these vices? They are bad habits of thought. More specifically, they are formerly called *cognitive distortions,* which are irrational thought patterns and/or behavior patterns. They contribute toward inaccurate interpretations of reality; unjustified beliefs; irresponsible behaviors; and irrational thoughts, feelings, and emotions. Unless we learn how to discover these culprits, our psychological well-being will suffer and our ability to get truth weakens. We do well, then, to learn about cognitive distortions. The reason why is this: cognitive distortions can cause much preventable stress, anxiety, and/or depression we are all vulnerable to experiencing. This is not to deny the existence of other causes that are outside of our control. The vicissitudes of life ranging from chemical events to geological ones can partly cause various kinds and degrees of stress, anxiety, and/or depression. But we want to concentrate our attention on the ways in which we have formed certain habits of thought that can contribute to this. Because the good news is that we do have some control over them if we're willing to put forth the time, effort, and practice, just as good athletes are accustomed to doing.

Cognitive distortions deserve to be in a philosophy book because they are a frequent barrier to becoming a good philosopher—one who is able to think well about things that matter. Furthermore, we believe introducing you to cognitively distorted ways of thinking can provide a key ingredient to the kind of remedies needed for maintaining good mental hygiene.[2] As a result, you will have some tools to combat versions of anxiety and depression. Indeed, the ones we explore are the most common ones that psychologists and psychiatrists alike have witnessed and diagnosed in their patients.

If you haven't already heard, the statistical data on the mental health of Americans is not good. The National Institute of Mental Health (NIMH) reported in 2021 that more than one in five of all US adults (57.8 million) experiences mental illness, whether mental, behavioral, or emotional, which can vary from mild to severe.[3] After collecting data from 373 college campuses nationwide, the Healthy Mind Study discovered that more than 60 percent of college students satisfied criteria for one mental health problem.[4] And according to the Center for Collegiate Mental Health (CCMH) 2019 Annual Report, which collects data from 163 college and university campuses, approximately 20–35 percent of college students might need mental health treatment in a given year. The rates of non-suicidal self-injury (28.7%), serious suicidal thoughts (36.7%), and suicide attempts (10.6%) have increased over the last nine years. And the average rate of self-reported anxiety and depression has increased over the last eight years. The percentage of students seeking mental health treatment from counselors for anxiety increased from 55 percent in 2013 to 63 percent in 2019, making it the most common concern. Depression and stress were the second and third highest concerns amongst college students, respectively.[5] These are disconcerting trends, to say the least.[6]

We want to emphasize that merely learning about cognitive distortions will *not* provide a magical cure for someone suffering from poor mental health. Nevertheless, it is an important exercise toward becoming more intellectually virtuous, which can contribute to a healthier thought life. What's more, you cannot think well about things that really matter if you are frequently engaging in these distorted ways of thinking. It's the point of this chapter, then, to identify these cognitive distortions so we can become more intellectually virtuous and, thus, become better at thinking well about things that matter. The healthier your thought life is, the better you will be at practicing philosophy.

Cognitive Distortions
(Unreliable Patterns of Thought That Are About You)

The following are definitions and examples for twelve of the most common cognitive distortions.[7]

1. *All-or-Nothing Thinking.* You see things in black-and-white categories. For example, when your performance falls short of perfection, you respond by seeing yourself as a total failure. This mental rut often forms the basis for perfectionism. Unfortunately, setting up unrealistic expectations ultimately sets one up for failure. For example, someone who takes second or third place in an event interprets this achievement as a complete failure and identifies as a loser! "If you aren't first, you're last!" has become a meme. Or consider a case wherein one receives friendly, helpful advice on how to do action A. In response, this person thinks he or she is the worst person at doing A. "Fine! I'm the worst student ever! I'm going to drop out of this class!"

2. *Overgeneralization.* You see a single negative event as a never-ending pattern of defeat. You take a specific event and invalidly infer from it that the same outcome will always keep happening to you despite lacking adequate evidence to support it. For example, you ask someone out on a date, and that person turns you down. From that event, you invalidly infer there's no use asking anyone else out on a date because no one will ever go out with you.[8]

3. *Negative Filtering.* You discover some negative detail in an event and/or person and obsess over it. By obsessively dwelling on it, you allow it to distort your perception of reality. For example, you take a test and are confident you missed four out of twenty questions. You validly infer that if that's true, you'll get a B- (80%) on the test. But from that evidence, you invalidly infer that you will certainly fail the class. Worse, you now obsess over all the bad things that will happen because of failing. (See item 6.) Or consider this case. You had a blessed time catching up with family and friends at a holiday gathering. Then, as you are saying your goodbyes, your uncle makes an indecent joke. During the ride home you obsess over the joke. By obsessing over it, you ignore everything else that was good about the evening. Now you're convinced the holiday gathering was a complete disaster, and you wish you never went.

4. *Discounting Positives.* You reject positive experiences by insisting they "don't count" for some reason or other. You take an event that most reasonable people will see as harmless, and you interpret it as malicious. Worse, you might even take offense to it and seek revenge. This way, you can maintain a negative belief that you want to be true despite the available evidence from everyday experience that falsifies your belief. For example, take Jones, a colleague of yours. He compliments you on a recent success. But you want to believe that you're not good at

what you do. So you resist this evidence by dismissing it as something people just say to feel good about themselves. Notice how this pattern of thinking serves as a strategy to protect your belief from being falsified.

5. *Jumping to Conclusions.* You take some event and invalidly infer from it a negative interpretation despite lacking evidence, let alone conclusive evidence. This cognitive distortion comes in two forms.

   a. *Mind Reading.* You arbitrarily conclude that someone is reacting negatively to you, and you don't bother to verify if it's true. For example, you send a harmless text message to a friend and don't get an immediate response. Because you haven't heard back yet, you infer this person must be upset with you or, worse, doesn't like you anymore.

   b. *Fortune Telling.* You anticipate that things will turn out badly, and you feel certain your prediction will be true. For example, go back to the case involving your friend not returning your text message. You engage in *mind reading* by believing this person is mad at you. But now you won't verify whether this is true, because if you call, you're certain this person will think you're too intrusive. Again, you're assuming something to be true on inadequate evidence.

6. *Catastrophizing.* You take some everyday experience or event and turn it into a nightmarish monster. This involves taking your errors, fears, or imperfections and exaggerating their importance. For example, you make an honest mistake and blow it up by saying something like this: "Oh, no! I made a mistake. This will spread all over social media. My reputation is ruined, and I will be left friendless and jobless." Parents are vulnerable to taking some everyday event and quickly running through all the possible outcomes that can result in the harm or death of their child. The sooner we recognize what we're doing and begin changing our thought patterns, we can alleviate the level of anxiety we've brought upon ourselves.

7. *Emotional Reasoning.* You assume your negative emotions necessarily reflect the way things really are. You allow your feelings to guide your interpretation of reality. The idea behind emotional reasoning is simple: "I feel it; therefore it must be true." Mere feelings are taken as undeniable evidence for the truth of something. Emotional reasoning holds our faculty of reason hostage, making it work for our feelings rather than the other way around. We often ask people, "How are you feeling today?" But we should be asking them "How are you thinking today?"[9] This is because much of how we feel is directly the result of what we continue

thinking about. Examples of emotional reasoning include "I feel overwhelmed and hopeless. Therefore, my problem is impossible to solve"; "I feel something bad will happen to me today. Therefore, I'd better stay home and not go to work"; "I feel upset because of your success. Therefore, your success is bad and must be discredited."

8. *Inability to Disconfirm.* You consult only sources that deliver information that will confirm your belief. You suppress or ignore any evidence that may falsify your belief. This is sometimes called *confirmation bias.*[10] But when it's used to reinforce unhealthy thoughts about yourself, it's a cognitive distortion since it can lead to anxiety and depression. For example, you may believe that you're unlovable. In order to maintain and protect this belief, you suppress or ignore any counterevidence that suggests otherwise. "Ha! Jones's 'act of love' toward me was done because Jones wanted to feel good about himself, not because I'm lovable."

9. *Labeling and Mislabeling.* This is an extreme form of overgeneralization. You take some mistake or error you've made and then attach a negative label to yourself. You allow a mistake or error you've made to be justification for creating a negative, categorical self-image. You're personally labeling whenever you make a mistake and respond by saying things like, "I'm a born loser," or "I'm such an idiot," or "I'm such a screw-up." Mislabeling involves describing an event with language that is highly colored and emotionally overloaded.

10. *Personalization.* You see yourself as responsible for some bad event even though your actions did not bring it about. For example, a child's parents get divorced, and the child infers this must have happened because he doesn't always do his weekly chores. Or, perhaps a parent learns his twenty-year-old son is addicted to opioids and infers, "This must have happened because I could have been a better parent." This overbearing sense of guilt for something you're not responsible for has crippling effects on one's mental health.[11]

11. *Blaming.* Speaking of divorce and severed relationships, this cognitive distortion has the potential to destroy virtually any relationship. It involves invalidly inferring from your negative feelings or moods that your feelings are directly caused by another person. Blaming fixates on attributing causal responsibility to anyone but yourself. For example, perhaps the most important thing you believe about yourself is that you are a victim. Your identity is reduced to victimhood. "I'm a victim of circumstance" is a common meme. Perhaps you perceive yourself as

a victim because of some flaw in your parents. You believe, say, your parents loved your sibling more than you. Now you blame your parents for all your problems and never take any responsibility for consequential choices you have made. Even if a parent did treat a child unfairly, that doesn't necessarily determine that the child will later become an adult and cheat on his spouse or rob a bank or murder his neighbor. No, cases of infidelity—like other moral actions—are usually caused by the agent's decision to do so.

12. *What If?* This cognitive distortion typically occurs when someone tries to falsify or provide counterevidence for the thing you're catastrophizing about. Upon hearing the reasons someone provides, you repress it by manufacturing a new hypothetical scenario: "Well, what if X happens instead?" Coaches commonly address their athletes who engage in catastrophizing with counterevidence only to hear them respond by reiterating the what-if-this-happens response: "But then what if this happens? . . . but then what if this happens? . . . but then what if this happens? . . ." For example, a cross country coach reminds an athlete what pace to run for each mile after the anxious athlete expresses his fear "What if I forget my pacing strategy?" Moments later the same athlete asks the coach, "What if my hamstring cramps?" After that concern is addressed, the athlete then asks, "What if I get diarrhea?" Notice, too, how this kind of what-if thinking not only provides a means of sustaining the mental rut of catastrophizing but can increase anxiety levels by making the catastrophe feel inevitable and causing new ones.

"Taking the Reins of a Runaway Thought Life": Practical Steps toward Healthier Thinking

It's not the point of this chapter to address all the relevant psychology and treatments associated with cognitive distortions. We do think introducing the reader to them is necessary for becoming more intellectually virtuous and maintaining good mental hygiene. What's more, the rise in the number of college students seeking counseling for their mental health is alarming. Addressing these cognitive distortions may help someone reading this by giving them tools to recognize and name the potential culprit. Unfortunately, many people don't even know these patterns of thought are pathological. Trained psychologists and psychiatrists, however, know better. They include them in their diagnosis of why a patient is, perhaps, suffering from some version of anxiety or depression.

We hope readers will take better care of their thought lives and see why these bad habits of thought need to be uprooted and replaced with healthier ones.

Here is a mental workout program we encourage you to practice.[12] Training your mind this way will contribute toward becoming more intellectually virtuous and maintaining good mental hygiene. The good news is that you have already learned the first exercise: learning the names and patterns of these common cognitive distortions.

Mental Exercise 1: Know the List of Potential Culprits. Learn the names of the cognitively distorted patterns of thoughts and behaviors. Understand why they are unreliable means to get truth or interpret reality, so you become convinced they're irrational, unhealthy ways of thinking and acting. Further, understand how they can cause levels of anxiety and depression.

Mental Exercise 2: Identify the Culprit. Once you find yourself thinking in a cognitively distorted way, then name it. This is what it means to self-monitor your thought life. Trace back the chain of thoughts you believe is responsible for the current anxiety, depression, or anger you're currently experiencing. Once you discover the cognitive distortion that's responsible, name it—call it out for what it is. "Oh, no. I'm catastrophizing again," or "I see what I'm doing—I'm emotionally reasoning," or "I see what I'm doing. I'm participating in mind reading again. This is irrational!"

Mental Exercise 3: Reassess Your Evidence. First, practice thinking more critically. Ask yourself, "What evidence do I have to support this thought that's making me anxious, worried, fearful, angry, or depressed?" Think hard about what good evidence you have to support your current mental state. Consider alternative hypotheses, explanations, or interpretations of an event that are better supported by good evidence and reasons— not your irrational thoughts, feelings, desires, or anger. Then choose the best available hypothesis, explanation, or interpretation in light of your reevaluated evidence and reasons. Remember, the goal is to get the truth and perceive reality more accurately. Second, if you find yourself thinking in distorted ways again, disrupt the habit by doing something else. Go call a friend, or go exercise, or go listen to music—do something to get out of this mental rut. After you've disempowered the cognitive distortion by discovering it and naming it, you will want to create a new habit so that it is harder for you to jump back on that cognitively distorted merry-go-round pattern of thinking.

Mental Exercise 4: Reassess Your Response. Once enough time has passed and you're at a healthy distance from that episode, think about how effective your response was. Ask yourself what other ways you can improve. For example, how much time lapsed before you began thinking about whether you were participating in a cognitive distortion? Were you able to identify and name the exact culprit or culprits? How willing were you to question the validity of your emotional response and reassess your evidence and reasons? How strong of an effort was made to consider alternative explanations, conclusions, or interpretations? How effective was your method for jumping off the cognitively distorted merry-go-round pattern of thinking? Do you think if you tried something else, you could have broken that pattern of thinking sooner?

Mental Exercise 5: Dive Deeper into Maintaining Good Mental Hygiene. What we offer here is just the beginning of learning about cognitive distortions and, briefly, how cognitive behavioral therapy is a way to respond to them. We highly recommend J. P. Moreland's book *Finding Quiet: My Story of Overcoming Anxiety and the Practices That Brought Peace*. It interacts with some of the best current literature on neuroscience, psychology, psychiatry, and medicine from a Christian worldview. What's more, it incorporates good mental hygiene practices framed within the sanctification process (i.e., learning how to cultivate Christlike character). Moreland supports these practices with biblical principles and references. Two other books we'd also recommend (neither written from a Christian perspective) are David D. Burns, *Feeling Good: The New Mood Therapy*, and Robert L. Leahy, Stephen J. F. Holland, and Lata K. McGinn, *Treatment Plans and Interventions for Depression and Anxiety Disorders*.

Conclusion

One way we defined philosophy in chapter 1 is thinking hard about things that matter. In this chapter we thought hard about specific ways we think about ourselves. Hopefully, at this point, you are seeing how thinking in a cognitively distorted way is an unreliable way of getting truth. Indeed, it can contribute to stress, anxiety, and depression. And it's a frequent barrier to becoming a good philosopher. Furthermore, we believe introducing you to cognitively distorted ways of thinking and some proactive steps one can take to address them is a part of maintaining good mental hygiene.

Questions for Reflection

1. How strong is your conviction that we really do have some control over what we decide to do when thoughts, ideas, feelings, emotions, desires, or some combination thereof show up in our minds? Can you see the connection between this belief and whether one will try practicing these mental exercises?

2. Do you think some people will resist the idea of actively taking steps to uproot these cognitively distorted patterns of reasoning? More carefully, do you think some people might believe that how one naturally thinks or responds to events is good and valuable because it's "their way of thinking" and thus doesn't need correction?

3. After reading this chapter, what kind of cultural slogans foster cognitively distorted patterns of reasoning? For example, how do popular phrases like "Follow your heart" or "I'm a victim of circumstance" or "If I'm not first, I'm last" or "If it feels good, it can't be bad" exacerbate cognitively distorted ways of thinking?

4. Do you believe improving one's intellectual abilities through practice and training is similar to athletes having to practice and train to improve their athletic ability?

5. Do you believe this chapter is a way to further tease out some of the implications behind the apostle Paul's words when he said Christians need to "take captive every thought" (or pattern of reasoning) for Christ (2 Cor. 10:5) or when he said Christians should "not conform to the pattern of this world, but be transformed by the renewing" of their minds (Rom. 12:2)?

For Further Reading

Burns, David D. *Feeling Good: The New Mood Therapy*. New York: HarperCollins, 1980.

Byerly, T. Ryan. *Introducing Logic and Critical Thinking: The Skills of Reasoning and the Virtues of Inquiry*. Grand Rapids: Baker Academic, 2017.

Cohen, Elliot D. *Logic-Based Therapy and Everyday Emotions: A Case-Based Approach*. Lanham, MD: Rowman and Littlefield, 2016.

Haidt, Jonathan. *The Anxious Generation: How the Great Rewiring of Childhood is Causing an Epidemic of Mental Illness*. New York: Penguin Publishing Group, 2024.

King, Nathan L. *The Excellent Mind: Intellectual Virtues for Everyday Life*. Oxford: Oxford University Press, 2021.

Leahy, Robert L., Stephen J. F. Holland, and Lata K. McGinn. *Treatment Plans and Interventions for Depression and Anxiety Disorders*, 2nd ed. New York: Guilford, 2012.

Little, Sabrina B. *The Examined Run: Why Good People Make Better Runners*. Oxford: Oxford University Press, 2024.

Lukianoff, Greg, and Jonathan Haidt. *The Coddling of the American Mind: How Good Intentions and Bad Ideas Are Setting Up a Generation for Failure*. New York: Penguin, 2019.

Moreland, J. P. *Finding Quiet: My Story of Overcoming Anxiety and the Practices That Brought Peace*. Grand Rapids: Zondervan, 2019.

Willard, Dallas. *Renovation of the Heart: Putting on the Character of Christ*. Colorado Springs: NavPress, 2002.

NOTES

1. These feats were, to be more precise, accomplishments that expanded the athletic boundaries for what is possible for athletes to achieve.

2. Back in 1893, the founder of the American Psychiatric Association, Isaac Ray, defined mental hygiene as "the art of preserving the mind against all incidents and influences calculated to deteriorate its qualities, impair its energies, or derange its movements. The management of the bodily powers . . . , the government of the passions, the sympathy with current emotions and opinions, the discipline of the intellect—all these come within the province of mental hygiene."

3. See National Institute of Mental Health, "Mental Illness," updated March 2023, www.nimh .nih.gov/health/statistics/mental-illness.

4. See Zara Abrams, "Student Mental Health Is in Crisis. Campuses Are Rethinking Their Approach," *Monitor on Psychology* 53, no. 7 (October 2022), www.apa.org/monitor/2022/10 /mental-health-campus-care.

5. See Center for Collegiate Mental Health, 2019 Annual Report, January 2020, Publication No. STA 20–244.

6. We highly recommend Jonathan Haidt's book *The Anxious Generation*. In this book Haidt offers some explanations for why adolescent mental health has worsened since the early 2010s. One important culprit is how outdoor playing and play in general have been substituted or replaced with electronics and social media. See Jonathan Haidt, *The Anxious Generation: How the Great Rewiring of Childhood Is Causing an Epidemic of Mental Illness* (New York: Penguin, 2024).

7. We borrow this list from Greg Lukianoff and Jonathan Haidt, "The Coddling of the American Mind," *The Atlantic*, September 2015. Lukianoff and Haidt adopted their list from two books: David D. Burns's classic book *Feeling Good: The New Mood Therapy*, and Robert L. Leahy, Stephen J. F. Holland, and Lata K. McGinn's popular textbook *Treatment Plans and Interventions for Depression and Anxiety Disorders*, 2nd edition, which we also appeal to, making slight amendments and providing additional examples to their original entries. We recommend reading Lukianoff's and Haidt's article in the *Atlantic* and their book length treatment of it—*The Coddling of the American Mind: How Good Intentions and Bad Ideas Are Setting Up a Generation for Failure* (New York: Penguin, 2019).

8. By a "valid inference," we mean an inference from strong evidence (i.e., reliable evidence that has what it takes) to reasonably support a conclusion. In chapter 7 we will discuss a form of

an argument that uses a valid pattern of reasoning that guarantees a true conclusion if all the premises are true.

9. See Dallas Willard for how he expounds upon this piece of wisdom involving the relation thoughts have to feelings and vice versa. See Dallas Willard, *Renovation of the Heart: Putting on the Character of Christ* (Colorado Springs: NavPress, 2021), 119.

10. English psychologist Peter Wason coined the term "confirmation bias," which is when one is motivated to protect and/or further support a cherished belief or value one wants to be true by only consulting sources that reconfirm it. One who engages in confirmation bias will only read or listen to testimony that's comforting to hear. Ingesting information from biased sources is like one's motivation for eating certain foods: both the information and food are used as a means toward comfort. Those engaged in confirmation bias purposefully consult sources that will protect one's cherished belief or value.

11. There is a critical distinction that we'll revisit later in chapter 15; it's the difference between (a) that which influences versus (b) that which determines. The subject suffering from personalization sees his or her influential role as the determining cause of something bad. We know the importance of this distinction first-hand as parents: namely, we can influence our children to make wise decisions, but we can't determine what decision they'll make, the way a puppeteer determines the actions of a puppet by controlling its strings. This is why we have the old adage: You can bring a horse to water, but you can't make it drink.

12. Most versions of cognitive behavioral therapy (CBT) follow these steps. First, identify the significant event or personal condition that's generating the challenge. Second, monitor what thoughts, beliefs, and affective states accompany one's engagement with the targeted event or condition. Third, diagnose what cognitive distortions one's pattern of thinking most closely aligns with. Fourth, reprogram or practice new patterns of thoughts that are more reliable at getting to the truth and accurately interpret reality. See Mayo Clinic Staff, "Cognitive Behavioral Therapy," Mayo Clinic, March 16, 2019, www.mayoclinic.org/tests -procedures/cognitive-behavioral-therapy/about/pac-20384610. We have borrowed what we call "mental exercises" from J. P. Moreland's book *Finding Quiet*. Instead of framing them as a remedy within cognitive behavioral therapy, for the purposes of this chapter, we treat them as mental exercises one can practice in efforts toward becoming more intellectually virtuous. Moreland's Four-Step solution is adapted from Jeffrey M. Schwartz and Rebecca Gladding, *You Are Not Your Brain: The Four-Step Solution* (New York: Avery, 2011). Moreland testifies from experience that this four-step remedy is effective, but he makes sure to incorporate the work and role the Trinity plays within a Christian framework of sanctification.

CHAPTER 3

When and Where Did Philosophy Begin?

A Brief History of Its Timeline and Masterminds

Philosophy is difficult. It is especially difficult for the introductory student. An introductory course can seem like numerous topics thrown together without much correlation between them. What does God (philosophy of religion) have to do with how we know things (epistemology)? What is this odd and often confusing discussion called metaphysics, and what does it have to do with my life? Why, just why, are there so many strange and made-up terms?

If you feel like this after just a few chapters, you are not alone. We need to keep in mind, however, what twentieth-century philosopher Frederick Copleston stated: "The history of philosophy is certainly not a mere congeries of opinions, a narration of isolated items of thought that have no connection with one another."[1] It is really a narration of one long discussion between philosophers on different topics. Thus, this chapter is essential for the beginning student. By briefly surveying the history of philosophy, we can better grasp what philosophy is all about. By the end of this chapter, you should be able to see more clearly how philosophy is like one long threaded discussion.

The Popular Pre-Socratics

The history of western philosophy begins in ancient Greece in the sixth and fifth centuries BC. These philosophers are designated as the "Pre-Socratics" because they chronologically come before the very influential Greek philosopher Socrates. We will be looking briefly in this section at four major pre-Socratic figures or movements: Thales, Pythagoras, Heraclitus, and "the atomists."

Thales (ca. 620 BC–ca. 546 BC)

Thales is one of the earliest Greek philosophers, born in Miletus in Greek Ionia. Thales' philosophy was primarily concerned with understanding the underlying make-up of the universe, or what came to be known as *metaphysics*.

The primary question he formulated that continues to be pondered today is, "How does the one relate to the many?" By this, Thales recognized that the world appears to be divided yet united—there is a oneness and a diversity to everything that exists. For example, there are things such as trees that make them what they are (trees). Trees, however, also have a diversity among them. Some are tall; some are short. Some are healthy; some are not. Some have flowers; others do not.

In connection to this observation, Thales noted how the world appears to be in transformation, or change. Trees bloom in the spring; they die in autumn. Humans are born, and then humans eventually die.

Underlying the diversity and change, Thales, along with the other Pre-Socratics, concluded that there must be some underlying "element" that unites the world, yet gives rise to all its diversity and change. Thales' answer? Water! Water, he reasoned, can be in three different states—solid, liquid, or gas—yet they are in essence the same thing. In a very real sense, he viewed water as the ultimate reality.

Pythagoras (ca. 570 BC–ca. 490 BC)

Pythagoras, as you could probably guess by his name, has traditionally been associated with the Pythagorean theorem. (Whether he proved this theorem is debated among philosophers.) In fact, it is quite difficult to ascertain his exact philosophy since he never committed any of it to writing. Most of what we know about Pythagoras's philosophy has come down through his disciples.

Like his Greek predecessors, Pythagoras appeared to have been interested in the problem of the "one and the many." For him,

LOGOS IN CHRISTIANITY

The Greek term *Logos* becomes very significant in first century Christianity. The term is used to refer to Jesus Christ in the New Testament book of the Gospel of John: "In the beginning was the Word [*Logos*], and the Word [*Logos*] was with God, and the Word [*Logos*] was God" (John 1:1). Many biblical commentators believe that this term was used to bring to the reader's mind the Greek *Logos* idea. The difference is that the Gospel of John says the *Logos* is a person—Jesus. He is the ground of reason in the world. Later, other Christians like Justin Martyr (ca. AD 100–ca. AD 165) used the term to connect all rationality to Jesus.

however, *Number* is what unifies all reality. Number is what gives diversity to the physical objects in the world; number organizes and orders the material world. Here we find the beginning of the philosophical idea of *Form*, which finds its thorough development in the philosophy of Plato, which we will discuss.

Heraclitus (ca. 544 BC–ca. 480 BC)

Heraclitus, from the city of Ephesus, was more concerned with the concept of change. Change, he argued, was an intrinsic part of the world. Everything is in constant flux, so much so that he became famous for his phrase, "You cannot step twice into the same river. . . . They scatter and combine . . . and approach and separate."[2] Because a river is by nature flowing water, no one can actually step into the same river twice: the water that was flowing when she stepped into it is no longer there. Because of this constant change, he believed that ultimate reality consisted merely of a perpetual process of change and not of any particular element or substance that maintains the same identity over time.

Another teaching he was known for was his *fiery Logos*. The Logos (from the Greek *logos*, meaning "reason," "word," or "rationality") was the universal law, or rational principle, that undergirded or drove all change. This Logos was innate in all things, ordering and giving rationality to the universe. It is similar to the Eastern religious pantheistic idea that everything is God. It is something most anyone can tap into, it is impersonal, and it brings about the destiny of the world. It is "fiery" because Heraclitus thought fire was the one element that drove the change in the world. We can understand why Heraclitus would view fire as the agency of change: fire consumes and destroys, yet its effects allow trees and other plants to grow again and bring about new life. Wildfires, for example, although destructive, are known for also allowing regrowth of forests.

The Atomists (5th Century BC)

The final philosophers to be focused on in this section are Leucippus (ca. 5th century BC) and Democritus (ca. 460–ca. 370 BC), referred to as the "Atomists" (from the Greek word *atomos*, meaning "indivisible"). They developed the idea that physical reality is composed of very tiny moving particles, or *atoms*. This is where contemporary science derives its term "atoms" that we are familiar with today.

For the atomists, these tiny particles are eternal and indestructible. They are solid and have various shapes and sizes, and they move rapidly in what they called "the void" (think of a big container, or space). As these atoms swirl in the void, they collide into each other, creating the larger material objects we see. Note how this is a continuation of the interest in the one and the many. The "one" are the atoms that give rise to the "many" diverse physical objects in the world.

It is often said that the atomists developed this doctrine of atoms to counter a paradox proposed by Leucippus's teacher, Zeno the Eleatic (born about 489 BC):[3] the paradox of motion. Motion, said Zeno, seems impossible and possible at the same time. The thought experiment that Zeno used to illustrate this paradox was traveling from, say, point 1 (P1) to point 2 (P2). (See Fig. 3.1.)

In order to move from P1 to P2, one must travel half the distance from P1 to P2 (what we can call P3). Upon further contemplation, in order to get to P3, we must travel half the distance from P1 to P3 (what we can call P4). Such a course of action, said Zeno, could be done infinitely, thus making it (in theory) impossible to actually travel from P1 to P2. However, in reality we know that we can and do travel from P1 to P2. But how is this possible if there is an infinite number of points between P1 and P2? The atomists attempted to resolve this paradox by postulating that there really are not an infinite number of points between P1 and P2. Rather, the distance is composed of the finite atoms. Whether this solves Zeno's paradox of motion is certainly up for debate. It does, however, show us the type of problems the early Pre-Socratics attempted to solve about the nature of the world.

FIG. 3.1

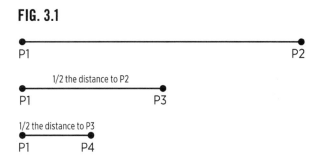

The Three "Greek Greats"

We now turn to the three greatest philosophers of ancient Greece: Socrates, Plato, and Aristotle. These three "Greek Greats" of philosophy turned to developing philosophical *systems* rather than attempting to resolve one philosophical problem, such as the "one and the many." In a real sense, we could call these systems "worldviews." They spoke on the numerous topics that make up a worldview: ultimate reality (metaphysics), ethics (moral right and wrong), epistemology (knowledge), politics, and much more. Because of this, a chapter such as this cannot possibly do justice to their systems. We can highlight only some important features of their philosophies.

Socrates (469–399 BC)

Socrates is understood as setting the bedrock for philosophy. It is, therefore, interesting that none of his writings still exist. Everything we know about his

SOPHISM

Sophism was a movement contemporary with Socrates in the fifth century BC. Some of the more popular Sophists included Protagoras, Gorgias, and Thrasymachus. Sophism (from *sophia*, meaning "wisdom") was characterized by relativism, skepticism, and rhetoric. Sophists were known for offering their wisdom to the average person just to make money. Socrates is viewed as responding and interacting with the Sophists' denial of objective truth. The English term "sophistry" is derived from the Sophist school.

thought comes through those who came after him, especially his pupil Plato. In fact, most of what we know about Socrates comes through the mouths of Plato's characters in his philosophical dialogs, like *Phaedo* and the *Euthyphro*. Secondarily, we gain some insight into Socrates' thoughts through his contemporaries Xenophon and Aristophanes. We can also learn some from Aristotle, Plato's pupil, whom we will meet later.

Philosophical Method

To get a sense of Socrates' philosophy, we must first understand the philosophical methodology for which he became famous. His approach to philosophy was to use *dialectic*, that is, a conversation that continually asks questions to ascertain the exact definition of words and come to a definitive answer to a philosophical question. Today, philosophers often refer to this method as the *Socratic method.*

This method often irritated Socrates' contemporaries. Some thought Socrates was playing dumb or trying to be unreasonable. Others thought he was just a clown or fool. None of these, however, were true. His method was used to obtain truth, which was in contrast to another philosophical school of the time known as Sophism. (See sidebar.) To obtain truth, Socrates believed one must continually dig and probe by following up one question with another. Only by accurately defining terms and having clarity of thought could a person come to a solid philosophical conclusion. Undoubtedly, the constant and numerous questions Socrates asked his interlocutors often annoyed and irritated them. His dialectic frequently revealed their ignorance and exasperated them because they were unable to answer precisely to satisfy Socrates.

Ethics

Socrates' methodology was intimately intertwined with his overall philosophical pursuit of the moral life, or *ethics*. Socrates wanted to think clearly and define terms precisely so that he (and others) could know the truth and then live the truth. He thought that if one knows the truth, then it naturally leads one to live it.

Socrates' objective of the moral life was *eudaimonia* (Greek), or happiness. This goal was unique to Socrates' thought and novel to the philosophical endeavor. Up to this point, the idea that humanity had a purpose and design was not pursued or considered. Socrates thus introduced the idea of *teleology* (Greek, *teleos*), meaning "design" or "goal," to philosophy.

We must, however, be careful to understand what Socrates meant by "happiness." It is tempting to think of happiness as a pursuit of a life that is carefree, free of difficulties, or filled with physical pleasures and lack of needs, possibly even hedonism (i.e., a life filled with gratuitous pleasure and self-fulfillment). In contrast, Socrates believed that such a view of happiness would ultimately lead to a person's unhappiness. In order to obtain true happiness, Socrates believed that one must discern rationally what is ultimately best for humanity. For Socrates, justice was better than injustice; self-control better than no self-control; courage better than cowardice. The moral life, therefore, was achieved through rational pursuit of discerning what would bring ultimate happiness to humanity. It was not achieved by pursuing one's feelings and passions but perfecting the state of one's soul through acquiring virtues.

Universal Definitions

A primary element in Socrates' philosophy was the pursuit of precise universal definitions. This pursuit was accomplished by his dialectic method. One question after another, he would ask his interlocutor to provide a more precise definition of a term (especially an ethical term) until one was reached that could be applied universally.

For example, in Book 1 of Plato's *Republic*, Socrates converses with an elderly man, Cephalus, on the nature of justice. Cephalus begins by saying justice is "truthtelling and paying back what one has received from anyone."[4] Socrates challenges this definition. If one were, for example, to come into possession of a person's weapons who is initially in his right mind but then goes mad, the weapons should not be returned, although justice (as defined by Cephalus) demands it. Who would return weapons to a person who has gone mad and may thus use them for harmful purposes?

Cephalus agrees with Socrates' observation. But then Cephalus's friend, Polemarchus, takes up the discussion and offers an alternative definition of justice: "to render each his due."[5] Socrates, again, finds this definition insufficient, for the previous example illustrates that the man's weapons are in some sense "due to him," but it would surely be unjust to return them if he is mad. Polemarchus agrees, and the search continues for a precise definition of justice, without success.

This exercise in the *Republic* demonstrates well Socrates' dialectical method and passionate pursuit of definitional precision. It also shows why some would find conversing with Socrates to be frustrating. Pursuing definitional precision for a lengthy time that often concluded with no success would leave some disgusted. Such an exercise also led some to think Socrates was undermining ethics and poisoning youth's minds with immorality. Socrates questioned and required precise definitions of terms that typically were taken for granted to be known. This eventually led the Greek state also to accuse Socrates not only of corrupting youth but also of undermining the Greed gods that were worshiped by the state. This ultimately led to Socrates' death by execution.

Trial and Death

Socrates' trial is perhaps one of the most well-known events of his life. Plato's *Apology* records much of Socrates' testimony in light of the accusations brought against him. As summarized in Socrates' own words, the court indicted him for "criminal meddling in that he inquires into things below the earth and in the sky, and makes the weaker argument defeat the stronger, and teaches others to follow his example."[6] More specifically, he was accused of "corrupting the minds of the young, and of believing in deities of his own invention instead of the gods recognized by the state."[7] Socrates, although strenuously and calmly denying the accusations, was condemned to death by hemlock.

In Plato's dialog *Phaedo*, Socrates is presented as a brave, resolute, and confident man ready and willing to die for his unjust conviction. With several friends at his side in his personal home and just before sunset, Socrates took the cup of hemlock "cheerfully" and "quite calmly and with no sign of distaste . . . drained the cup in one breath."[8] As the hemlock filled his veins, making him cold, Socrates spoke his last words: "Crito, we ought to offer a cock [rooster] to Asclepius. See to it, and don't forget."[9]

This final scene of Socrates' life, although its verity is questioned by some, provides an accurate depiction of how many philosophers, especially Plato, viewed Socrates. He was seen as the philosopher par excellence, a man with a sober mind, values, and courage to face the injustice of even the great Greek society.

Plato (ca. 429 BC–347 BC)

If Socrates' thought is the seedbed, or beginning, for philosophical "system building," Plato's work could certainly be viewed as the epitome of a completely full-orbed philosophical system. His work included discussion and analysis upon every philosophical question imaginable: metaphysics, epistemology, ethics, religion, politics, and even aesthetics (what is "the beautiful?"). Because of this, we will highlight just a few aspects of his metaphysics and epistemology.

The Forms

The foundation of Plato's metaphysics is his idea of the *Forms*. To understand this concept, think of a physical object in the world, like a chair. Chairs, as we know, come in all shapes, sizes, and colors. Although characteristics vary from one chair to another, there is something that makes a chair *a chair*. If one were to eliminate all the chairs in the world, we could and would still have an idea of a chair in our minds. This idea or concept of a chair that can be conceived apart from particular chairs in the world would be known as a universal. A universal is that which makes an object what it is apart from its physical characteristics in the world, including things like size, shape, and color.

Everything in the world has a universal: trees, desks, stars—everything. These physical objects in the world are merely copies of a non-physical or "spiritual" world known as the *Forms*. (We can think of the universals as existing in the realm of the Forms.) As such, there is a Form of a tree, and all the trees in the physical world are merely copies of that one tree Form. Likewise, think of planets: there is Mercury, Venus, Earth, Mars, and so on. These are the particular planets found in our galaxy, but there is a planet Form that they all are copied from and that makes them planets.

Interestingly, Plato argued that even abstract ideas like justice, goodness, and other moral virtues have Forms. Therefore, if one were simply to give examples of acts of justice in the world to understand justice, Plato would respond by saying that these are merely instances or copies of the Form justice, not justice itself. In order to grasp what justice really is, we would need to ask ourselves what is common to every instance of justice that ties them altogether. What makes justice *justice*? We need a precise, formal definition that holds in every case that we would consider just.

One aspect of the Forms that is of interest and significance in a theistic context is the question of how these Forms ultimately relate to the world. In the dialog *Timaeus*, Plato depicts a divine-like figure, the Demiurge, as fashioning the world after the Forms, like a potter does clay. The material from which the world is formed seems to be pre-existent, as the Demiurge takes it from a sort of cosmic receptacle.

The identification of Plato's Demiurge has been much debated. Is it God, or is it just a symbol, representation, or metaphor of how the world is a copy of the true one, the Forms themselves? Although its identification may be difficult to resolve, it is interesting to note that one of the greatest philosophers of the Greek tradition posited at least a quasi-like creator of the universe. The creator depicted in the *Timaeus* certainly has significant dissimilarities to the Creator of orthodox Christianity. It is, nevertheless, a creator who fashions and molds the universe.

Allegory of the Cave

Plato's *epistemology* (philosophy of knowledge) overlaps and is interwoven with his metaphysics of the Forms. The best way to understand it is to consider Plato's Allegory of the Cave (see Fig. 3.2) that he presents in his famous work *The Republic*.

FIG. 3.2

As Fig. 3.2 illustrates, a group of prisoners are bound on the floor of the cave, oriented toward the cave's back wall. They can see nothing else and have been that way their entire lives. Unbeknownst to them, a fire rages behind them, and a group of men passes in front of the fire on a pathway toward the mouth of the cave. As this group passes in front of the fire, their shadows are cast upon the back wall of the cave so the prisoners can see them. If you were one of the lifelong bound prisoners, what would you know about reality? What would you take reality to consist of? According to Plato, you would know only a world of shadows and not the actual world itself. This is how Plato views knowledge and reality. The shadows represent the physical objects of the world, which are really copies of the true reality, the Forms.

The analogy of the cave relates to epistemology in the following way. Plato views humanity as the bound prisoners, and humanity's goal is to come to the knowledge of the Forms. Most of humanity, however, are blinded and cannot and do not realize they are seeing mere copies of the Forms. But there is a way of escape if a human desires to see, understand, and gain knowledge. As Fig. 3.2 shows, there is an ascent that leads to the mouth of the cave and to the genuine sunlight (which represents the Forms). As one begins and continues to gain knowledge, she ascends to the sunlight of knowledge.

But how does one gain knowledge, and what exactly is it? According to Plato, knowledge is defined as "justified true belief," which today generally continues to hold sway in philosophy. (More will be explored on this topic in chapter 4 on epistemology.) Such knowledge, says Plato, is gained through rational contemplation, just thinking about things. Plato's epistemology is what we call *rationalistic*. Mere human cognition, contemplation, and reflection bring one to knowledge of the Forms and, therefore, what is true reality. As such, Plato's epistemology affirms that there is a true, objective reality to be known, and humans discover, not create, reality.

The Pre-Existent Soul

One primary element of Plato's philosophy that ties his rationalist epistemology with his metaphysics is his understanding of the pre-existence of the human soul. Plato believed that human nature consists of both physical (corporeal) and non-physical (non-corporeal) elements. The corporeal element is the body; the non-corporeal is the soul. The soul is superior to the body because it is eternal and seeks that which is real, the Forms. The body, on the other hand, is inferior. It weighs down the human as it focuses upon the mere shadows of the Forms, the physical world.

According to Plato, the aim of the true philosopher is for the soul to ascend to the light of knowledge (recall the allegory of the cave), the Forms. This is possible only because the soul pre-existed in the presence of the Forms. It should be noted that, because the soul pre-existed in the presence of the Forms, the soul already has knowledge of the Forms. The soul innately contains this knowledge. It is, therefore, through recollection that the soul is able to know the true reality of the Forms. In actuality, then, a person does not come to knowledge in the sense of learning. The soul must merely remember. This exercise is difficult since the body continuously distracts the soul by focusing on the copies of the Forms rather than the Forms themselves. The body clouds reality, and only the true philosopher can break through the fog and the weight of the body to be lifted to see reality clearly.

The Philosopher King

Plato's epistemology and metaphysics also come together to inform his political philosophy. To ascertain the foundation of Plato's politics, it must be remembered that Plato regarded his teacher, Socrates, as the wisest of all philosophers. The problem was that the democratic Greek state executed this fine sage. Because of this, as one could guess, Plato thought lowly of the Greek state. If such a political system, which was assumed to be great by many, put to death the most revered philosopher of all time, certainly something was wrong with the system. Plato concluded, therefore, that democracy was in fact insufficient for human flourishing.

What was needed to govern a people rightly was a king who was a philosopher. It was, after all, the philosopher who could attain the surest knowledge and be the most virtuous. In other words, a philosopher king would be the best to govern a people. He would have the ability to discern between reality and the mere copies of reality, know what true justice is, and make the ascent out of the cave to its mouth where the realm of the Forms shone the brightest. The people, on the other hand, who focus entirely upon representations of reality, would be unwise in decision-making. The philosopher king would lead the people as a shepherd does foolish, wandering sheep.

The Moral Life

Plato's ethics, like Socrates', was focused upon *eudaimonia*, or happiness. Again, happiness should not be confused with hedonism or the belief that one's self-interests and pleasures are the goal of life. Rather, happiness for Plato was about controlling the passions and developing the rational soul, or mind. There must be a balance between these two, for either extreme will lead to unhappiness.

Plato illustrates this balance using a charioteer driving two horses. In his work *Phaedrus*, Plato describes one horse as good. He is white and is a "lover of glory, but with temperance and modesty." [10] He "needs no whip" to drive him. He is driven by the mere command of the charioteer. This horse can be said to represent virtue, like justice and temperance. In contrast to this, the other horse is black, "hot-blooded, consorting with wantonness and vainglory." He is controlled only by a whip. It is the duty of the rational soul, the charioteer, to control these two horses. The passions may be served or fulfilled, but only by balancing them out by driving the virtues. The passions, if not bridled and driven appropriately, will ruin the philosopher and be a cause of his unhappiness.

The rational soul, however, could also be a cause of the philosopher's unhappiness. In fact, it is the rational soul that is the ultimate cause of evil. As already mentioned, the rational soul pre-existed in the presence of the Forms. As such, the soul knew the virtues well. But with the soul's advent of embodiment, it lost its knowledge of the virtues. The body, as physical, is naturally drawn to the physical objects of the world, which are mere copies of the Forms. The body, then, drags down and clouds the soul from remembering the Forms of the virtues. This ignorance of the virtues is therefore the ultimate cause of evil in the world. It is the soul's ignorance that brings evil into existence. It simply cannot remember what is morally right and wrong. The true philosopher's aim is to recollect, or gain knowledge of, these Forms of virtue.

Aristotle (384 BC–322 BC)

If Plato was *the* "Greek giant" of philosophy, Aristotle was not too far behind him. This is not surprising, considering Aristotle was a pupil of Plato for twenty years. Aristotle is also famous for becoming Alexander the Great's teacher. Aristotle, in contrast with Plato, was more of an empiricist, one who believed that knowledge was obtained by empirical observation. Although his metaphysics, particularly concerning the Forms, was consistent with Plato's philosophy early on, Aristotle came to repudiate the theory. It could be said that Aristotle was one of the last great Greek philosophers who had profound impact upon generations of philosophers and continues to do so.

Logic and Reasoning

One significant contribution Aristotle made to philosophy is his discovery of the basic laws of thought, or the Laws of Logic. Later in this book, you will learn the most basic Laws that Aristotle discovered: the laws of non-contradiction, identity, and excluded middle. Additionally, you will learn some of the fundamentals of rational argumentation using Aristotle's development of the syllogism. For now, we note that Aristotle was the first to develop the system of logic known as the *syllogism*. The syllogism is an argument arranged in multiple premises followed by a conclusion. If the premises are true, the conclusion necessarily follows. The most famous syllogism is as follows:

Major premise: All humans are mortal.
Minor premise: Socrates is a human.
Conclusion: Therefore, Socrates is mortal.

Aristotle's primary purpose of the syllogism was to show the nature of particular relationships of things in the world. In this example, the relationship between Socrates and mortality is demonstrated: what makes Socrates mortal is that he is human.

Bear in mind that the syllogism, for Aristotle, was not merely about relating words and propositions. The syllogism was in fact a demonstration of what reality is actually like. His primary concern was to use the syllogism to show what could be demonstrated empirically, or what was the case scientifically. The major and minor premises are substantiated inductively, or through observation of the real world. As Copleston has so aptly stated, the syllogism for Aristotle "is an analysis of human thought *in its thought about reality.*"[11]

Metaphysics

Aristotle's work *Metaphysics*, in which he lays out his metaphysical philosophy, is notoriously difficult to read. As such, we will lay out only some basic ideas to grasp his general outlook.

To begin, Aristotle disagreed with his teacher, Plato, concerning the doctrine of the Forms.[12] To recall, Plato believed that the Forms existed in some spiritual world, and these Forms were the archetypes for all objects in the world. In contrast, rather than being "otherworldly," Aristotle argued that the essences of what made things are located in this actual world. He described the essence of an object (that which is essential for something to be what it is) as "substance" and the different variations among similar objects "predicates" (sometimes called "accidents"). To use the example of trees again, whatever makes a tree *a tree* is the substance, while the shapes and sizes would be the predicates.

Why did Aristotle posit the substance of objects in the world rather than in the spiritual world of Plato's Forms? He provides numerous reasons, but we will focus upon only three here. First, Aristotle believed that postulating the Forms added just more substances that could not be explained. It is one thing to recognize that universals (like "tree-ness," for example) exist as the Forms illustrated, but it was quite another to provide the Forms with actual, separate existence. To grant them such simply created the problem of their existence. How do the Forms exist? The Forms, therefore, did not really explain the existence of objects in the world.

Second, the Forms were to explain the existence of substances of real-world sensible objects. But if this is so, how is it that the Forms which are insensible give rise to sensible objects? If the objects of the world were to be a copy of and participate in the Forms, then reason would dictate that the Forms themselves would also have to be sensible. Plato, however, clearly indicated that the Forms were not. Coincidentally, the Forms could not even explain the existence of objects in the world. The Forms were a spiritual existence unto themselves.

Third, Aristotle struggled to discern what it meant for the world's sensible objects to participate in the Forms. What does this exactly look like? How does this occur? How are sensible objects reflections or shadows of the Forms? Plato did not seem to give an explanation.

If, according to Aristotle, the Platonic Forms did not exist, then how did he explain the concept of universals? As already mentioned, Aristotle affirmed the idea of universals: there is something that similar objects in the world share (substance) that makes them what they are and able to be categorized together. An oak tree and a maple tree are both trees, after all. Aristotle attempted to solve the problem by arguing that universals are a concept of the mind and not a separate existence in a spiritual realm. We must be careful to note that the concept of the universal in the mind corresponds to the substance of the sense object. Otherwise, we would be bereft of any true knowledge of the world.

The Unmoved Mover

An integral part of Aristotle's metaphysics is the theological concept known as the *Unmoved Mover* that moves, or actualizes, all other substances or material objects. To understand how Aristotle comes to this conclusion, we begin by observing that he takes the primary concern of metaphysics to be the study of being, or existence. What emerges from this study is the ultimate question of what gives rise to the existence of objects in the world, or how substances come into being.

For Aristotle, all substances owe their existence to some other type of substance. For example, a block of wood owes its existence to a tree, which in turn owes its existence to things like water and sunlight. But water and sunlight owe their existence to other substances, like hydrogen or oxygen, which again owe their existence to atoms and then subatomic particles. We can say that all substances in the world rely or depend upon another substance for their existence, or, in Aristotle's words, their movement or actuality.

This tracing of dependency of existence, however, cannot go on forever since this would entail an infinite series, which cannot exist. It is for this reason that Aristotle postulates that there must be an unchangeable, unactualized substance that gives rise to all other substances in the sensible world. There must be an Unmoved Mover that moves (actualizes or gives rise to) all other substances. This Unmoved Mover is designated as the Divine, or God. This Aristotelean argument is later coopted by Thomas Aquinas in the Middle Ages as one of his Five Ways to demonstrate the existence of God. (See sidebar.)

THOMAS AQUINAS

Thomas Aquinas (AD 1225–AD 1274) was a Roman Catholic theologian and philosopher. He is considered one of the greatest thinkers of the Middle Ages. He is known for using Aristotelean philosophy to expound upon theological concepts, such as the Eucharist. His "Five Ways," or arguments for God's existence, remain today a staple in the philosophy of religion. One of Aquinas's Five Ways incorporates Aristotle's idea of motion to show that God exists. Aquinas's Five Ways are discussed more in chapter 18 on the philosophy of religion in this text.

Ethics

Like his forebearers, Aristotle viewed the moral life as *eudaimonia*, or happiness. This is the chief end of man. But what did this happiness look like? What did it exactly entail? The answers to such questions are not definitive for Aristotle. Happiness is not mathematics. There is no definitive correct answer, only generalized principles.

The best way to describe Aristotle's view is by referring to his now famous *Golden Mean*. The Golden Mean is the way to describe that the morally right action, or that which will bring happiness, is the one that avoids two extremes (which are considered vices): one of excess and the other of deficiency. To take a popular example, courage is a virtuous action because it avoids the extremes of foolishness (taking an action that is too bold or rash) and cowardness (not taking any action because of fear).

Interestingly, the virtuous act is not always the Golden Mean. It may be one of the extremes, depending upon other factors, like the situation. How would one know? Ultimately, it would be discerned by the wise man, or philosopher. Here we see an echo of Plato's philosopher king as the only one capable of truly ruling a people and understanding the world.

The "Modern Movers"

Space limits us from looking at other Greek philosophers—like the Epicureans, Stoics, and Skeptics—three centuries before Christianity arrived on the world scene. We must also jump over the prominent philosophers of the Middle Ages, like Augustine, Anselm, and the giant Thomas Aquinas. On a positive note, some key thoughts of the Epicureans, Skeptics, Anselm, and Aquinas will be discussed in later chapters. We now turn to two very significant philosophers of the Modern period, what we can call the "Modern Movers": René Descartes and John Locke. Their impact upon Western thought is monumental.

René Descartes (AD 1596–1650)

Descartes is known as the "Father of Modern Philosophy." He is the first philosopher to give pride of place to human rationality for obtaining certainty of knowledge. Pursuing the certitude of knowledge has been the focus of what has become known as Modernism.

In order to come to 100 percent certainty, Descartes approached pursuing knowledge by *methodic doubt*, by doubting any and every claim of knowledge that could be doubted. Through this method, he believed he could come to a bedrock foundation of truth (or truths) absolutely and certainly knowable. From there, he would be able to deduce other certain truths. In essence, Descartes attempts to tear down everything he knew and then build it back up again so he would have certitude of what he claimed to know.

Descartes doubted his knowledge of everything. He even went as far as explaining that an evil genius could be fooling him into thinking that he and the external world existed (think of the movie *The Matrix* here, where humans are merely plugged into a computer system that makes them think they are living in a real world). How would anyone know if he was being deceived into thinking he existed?

Descartes finally concludes in his work *Meditations on First Philosophy* that, even if he is being deceived by an evil genius, he is at least thinking. If he is thinking, he argues, then he exists. This is the phrase that Descartes became famous for: "I think, therefore, I am" (*cogito ergo sum* in Latin). Descartes believes this is the bedrock truth that he can know for certain. From here, he goes on to deduce that an external world exists, and even God.

John Locke (AD 1632–1704)

John Locke is known as "The Father of British Empiricism." Locke believed, contrary to Descartes, that certitude of knowledge was via *empiricism*, or observation through the five senses. His *Essay Concerning Human Understanding* became the definitive work for seventeenth-century empiricism in Great Britain. From that point forward, empiricism has largely reigned in the Western world.

Locke's epistemology begins with the concept that humans do not have any innate ideas, or knowledge of any kind in the intellect. Rather, the human mind comes into the world as a *tabula rasa* ("blank slate"). As humans perceive objects in the world, they gain knowledge as the objects impress upon their intellect via sensations. Humans, therefore, are passive (not active) in gaining knowledge. Nevertheless, Locke argues that humans have the intellectual power of reflection—a kind of inborn mechanism endowed by God that enables humans to manage and reason about the sensations taken into the mind through observation.

Before concluding with Locke, we would be remiss if we did not mention the popularity of his political philosophy. His thought on this subject had profound influence upon the founding documents of the United States. The idea of separation of powers was unique to him. He argued for this "balance of power" because he had a mistrust of governing authorities, which reflects his Christian conviction that humans are sinners and will abuse their power. One particular abuse of power that Locke was concerned about was the usurpation of the intrinsic power of the people to govern themselves. If this occurred, Locke argued, the people have the right to rebel against the governing authorities and establish a better one that protects their property and rights. This idea clearly grounded the argument for America declaring independence from England.

Conclusion

As we conclude this chapter, note what we can glean from this brief history: each philosopher stands on the shoulders of those who came before him. The Pre-Socratics attempted to resolve the issue of "the one and the many." The three Greek Greats also dealt with this issue, but they observed that all of life must be a coherent whole, or system, in order to make sense of the unity and diversity of the world. In the Modern period, philosophers like Descartes and Locke turned to the question of knowledge. How can we know for certain what we claim to know? How do we discern if the worldviews of Socrates, Plato, and Aristotle are correct? These types of questions are still the focus of philosophers today. Although we did not have space to mention some of the influential thinkers during and after the Modern period—like David Hume, Immanuel Kant, Ludwig Wittgenstein, Jacques Derrida, Alvin Plantinga, and William Lane Craig—their contributions to philosophy will be touched upon in the forthcoming chapters. As we move forward, keep in mind that you are entering into a discussion that has roots in ancient Greece!

Questions for Reflection

1. What might be some ways John Locke's empiricism influenced western cultures?
2. The Pre-Socratics observed that the world was governed by reason. In what ways might this be a touchpoint with the Christian worldview?
3. In what ways is the history of philosophy one long, threaded discussion?
4. The modern philosophers, like Locke and Descartes, turned their attention to epistemology. Do you think this was a good idea? Why or why not?

For Further Reading

Copleston, Frederick. *A History of Philosophy.* 9 vols. New York: Doubleday, 1993.
Evans, C. Stephen. *A History of Western Philosophy: From the Pre-Socratics to Postmodernism.* Downers Grove, IL: IVP Academic, 2018.

Kenny, Anthony. *A New History of Western Philosophy*. Repr. Oxford University Press, 2012.

Russell, Bertrand. *The History of Western Philosophy*. New York: Simon and Schuster, 1967.

Stumpf, Samuel Enoch, and James Fieser. *Philosophy: History and Problems*. 7th ed. Boston: McGraw-Hill, 2007.

NOTES

1. Frederick Copleston, *A History of Philosophy*, vol. 1: *Greece and Rome, from the Pre-Socratics to Plotinus* (New York: Doubleday, 1993), 4. Copleston's history of philosophy spans nine volumes and is considered a classic in the history of philosophy. Every student who desires to learn more about the history of philosophy is strongly encouraged to obtain this great work.

2. Heraclitus, fragment 91, in Kathleen Freeman, *Ancilla to the Pre-Socratic Philosophers: A Complete Translation of the Fragments in Diels*, Fragmente der Vorsokratiker (Cambridge: Harvard University Press, 1983), 31.

3. This estimated date is taken from Copleston, *A History of Philosophy*, 1:54.

4. Plato, *Republic* 331c, in *Plato: The Collected Dialogues including the Letters*, ed. Edith Hamilton and Huntington Cairns, Bollingen Series LXXI (Princeton: Princeton University Press, 1989), 580.

5. Plato, *Republic* 331e, 580.

6. Plato, *Socrates' Defense (Apology)*, 19b, in Hamilton and Cairns, *Plato*, 5.

7. Plato, *Socrates' Defense (Apology)*, 24b, 10.

8. Plato, *Phaedo*, 117b–c, in Hamilton and Cairns, *Plato*, 97.

9. Plato, *Phaedo*, 118, 98.

10. Plato, *Phaedrus*, 253d-e in Hamilton and Cairns, *Plato*, 499–500.

11. Copleston, *History of Philosophy*, 1:278, emphasis added.

12. For a more thorough discussion on Aristotle's analysis of Plato's Forms, see Copleston, *History of Philosophy*, 1:292–305. Some of Aristotle's critiques of the Forms given by Copleston are reproduced paraphrastically here.

CHAPTER 4

What Is Philosophy Exactly?

The Big Picture and Its Interrelated Parts

One of the most important contributions philosophy can provide is this: the tools needed to develop a better worldview than the one you currently have. As a reminder, a worldview is a mental map we use to interpret evidence and form beliefs to help us better navigate through reality. More specifically, a worldview consists of existing assumptions, commitments, and beliefs about rules, standards, and principles that filter evidence and process it when forming beliefs about the nature of reality and answers to life's most profound questions.[1] These beliefs, then, inform the decisions and commitments we make and orient us toward reality in a certain way.

Understanding your own worldview is vital for the following reasons. First, your worldview helps determine how successful you will be at increasing your stock of true beliefs (and decreasing your stock of false beliefs). Second, your worldview explains a lot about what you see as the meaning and purpose of life. Third, it helps explain your values, which influences the person you want to be. If that's all true, then your worldview will largely contribute to your ability to live a happy, successful, well-lived life. So we think philosophy plays a vital role in everyone's life because it can help us get truth, knowledge, understanding, and wisdom. Indeed, it is hard to take seriously the idea that a well-lived life can be severely lacking in these goods. Lacking just one can result in experiencing much unnecessary pain, suffering, and even death. Indeed, children often learn the pain that comes from not knowing what surfaces can burn their hand, as do adults lacking wisdom of what kind of actions foster healthy relationships.

We listed some significant worldview questions in chapter 1. It turns out that these questions are inherently philosophical. Philosophy alone is uniquely equipped to address them because they fall outside the scope of other disciplines like science, history, and math. Regardless of which worldview question you attempt to answer, your answer ultimately depends on assumptions (i.e., beliefs we have but are not currently thinking about) and presuppositions (i.e., beliefs we have and are currently thinking about) that one or more of the subdisciplines of philosophy specifically addresses. Take the question we'll call the meaning-of-life question. Any answer to this question likely depends on inherently philosophical assumptions and presuppositions. Let's see how the subdisciplines of philosophy might help us answer this question.

The meaning-of-life question entails that there are humans who care about its answer. But what exactly is a human person? That is a *metaphysical* question. The meaning-of-life question assumes humans can or can't get knowledge to answer it. But what is knowledge? That is an *epistemic* question. The meaning-of-life question presupposes that some values make a life more meaningful and purposeful than others. But what values do that? That is a *value theory* (or axiological) question involving *ethics*. Suppose we offered an argument for the meaning of life. The question of whether the argument is good assumes arguments can be properly evaluated. But can arguments be properly evaluated? That is a question of *logic*. Thus, attempting to answer one philosophical question quickly requires relying upon a number of metaphysical, epistemic, axiological (value-based), and logical assumptions and presuppositions. We do well, then, to begin exploring what these subdisciplines of philosophy are about.

DEFINITION OF METAPHYSICS

The term *metaphysics* is difficult to define. The origins of this word trace back to an editor of Aristotle's (384–322 BC) philosophical works who used it to refer to fourteen unnamed books Aristotle wrote after his works titled *Physics*. Aristotle's *Physics* is a collection of books that studied physical things furnishing the natural world. Aristotle's *Metaphysics* is a collection of books that studied the first cause of things and aimed to discover what things do not change and are eternal. For our purposes, we are going to define metaphysics as the philosophical study of the fundamental nature of reality and categories that make up the world.

Metaphysics

Have you ever worn a virtual reality headset? Perhaps you've played a video game that requires the use of them. If not, imagine wearing computer-goggles that projected a digital environment for you to explore. This technology is already impressive. But now imagine technology becoming so good that your eyes can't discriminate the difference between the real world and a virtual world. Let's take this a step further: imagine the outlandish scenario wherein the only world you interact with is a manufactured, virtual world. Since birth, this is the only "world" you know. Your eyes—indeed, your entire nervous system—are closed off from accessing the real world. Your environment, relationships, vocation, and even your body are entirely made up of ones and zeros—after all, it's a virtual reality, not the real world.

We don't need to consider the kind of people and their motivations for making you the hapless victim of this deceitful trick. (We'll just refer to them as mad scientists.) What is of interest to us is what it would be like from your first-person point of view living here. For the sake of clarity, mad scientists are using technology to directly stimulate your nervous system and brain to generate the appearance of a world. Your real—flesh and blood—body is, say, encased in a pod of chemicals.[2] Thus, everything you perceive is part of a virtual world (i.e., a computer simulation of a world composed of ones and zeros like a video game)—not the real world (i.e., a world composed of quarks and strings, and carbon-based, flesh-and-blood human beings). Let us call this kind of case Virtual Reality.

Now imagine being rescued from living in Virtual Reality. Your rescuer—let's call her Ms. Aletheia—is tasked with convincing you that you're now in the real world. But as you can imagine, it might be difficult for Ms. Aletheia to convince you that you've been living in a make-believe world constructed by mad scientists for your entire life. So Ms. Aletheia uses a strategy that involves placing you back into another version of Virtual Reality called Virtual Reality 2.0 by plugging your brain into it. She does this so you can experience what it's like to perceive and interact with a virtual world. Here's how the conversation might go between you and Ms. Aletheia after entering Virtual Reality 2.0:

> **You:** "This body I have, this floor I'm walking on, this flower I'm seeing—none of it is real?"
>
> **Ms. Aletheia:** "What does it mean for something to be 'real'?"
>
> **You:** "I'm not sure. But I think it has something to do with experiencing it with my senses. If I can see it, taste it, smell it, feel it, or touch it, then that's evidence it is real—it exists."
>
> **Ms. Aletheia:** "Yes, but what if what you're experiencing through your senses is the result of electrical signals stimulating your nervous system and your brain interpreting them as real objects when, in fact, they are mere projections—like the way things appear to you in a dream?"

Notice this exchange of questions is of a unique sort. They are what philosophers call "metaphysical questions." They are questions centered around what makes a virtual world different from the real world. These questions can be reduced to a more fundamental one: What is the nature of reality? Is there one fundamental thing that has always existed, does exist, and will continue to exist? Is that fundamental thing matter, abstract objects, or mind?

Another related metaphysical question is this: Can reality be carved up into specific abstract categories or classifications, such as substances, property-things, properties, relations, events, states of affairs, and so on? Let's briefly consider these metaphysical categories.

- A *substance* is the thing that has parts, attributes, and characteristics; it has a unifying power that gives properties their genuine purposes and identity, according to its nature.
- A *property* can be a type of quality, attribute, or characteristic.
- A *natural kind* is a classification for a substance based on its essential properties, constituting an essence.
- A *property-thing* is a collection of qualities, attributes, and/or characteristics that lacks an additional unifying power (unlike substances) that gives properties a purpose and identity. Property-things don't have properties; they are the sum of their properties.
- A *relation* is the metaphorical glue used to describe how two or more things relate to each other.
- An *event* is a segment of time involving change, say, a substance losing a property (hair) and gaining an additional property (weight).
- A *state of affairs* refers to facts about an event in the world or facts about a state of the world, or different possible events or states about the way the world could have been otherwise.

If any of these categories really do exist, does it follow, then, that there are now things that exist in the world (e.g., abstract, nonphysical things like categories) beyond what exists in the universe (e.g., physical things discovered via science)? Asking these kinds of questions is one way of thinking about the role metaphysics plays in the pursuit of acquiring truth.

Metaphysics, then, is a philosophical enterprise that tries to provide reasonable and justified answers to specific questions like these. Metaphysicians aim to discover and then utilize fundamental abstract structures and categories of reality to simplify, systematize, and justify our beliefs and practices in other domains of inquiry (e.g., science, math, ethics, medicine, law, etc.). For example, in science, should we place atoms in the category of a property-thing or substance? Does the negative charge and spin of an electron go into the category of a property? Should we place water, gold, and the dog Fido into the category of natural kinds? Is the essence or nature of water H_2O? Is the essence or nature of gold atomic number 79? Is the essence or nature of Fido canineness? See how these metaphysical questions begin informing how we think about science and the scientific approaches and methods used to discover truths about physical things?

What about humans? Are we individual substances that retain the same identity over time or merely a collection of atoms arranged humanly and thus a property of the one substance? Or are we a bundle of properties and thus nothing above and beyond a property-thing? Which category better describes the kind of thing humans are? And what are the implications of placing us in one of these categories? What does it say about our identity, agency, and value? These metaphysical questions inform how science and ethics will be practiced and how data get interpreted.

Metaphysical concepts like property, property-thing, substance, essence, nature, and natural kind are just some of the conceptual tools metaphysicians debate over; moreover, metaphysicians will use some or all of these concepts to describe and understand at a deep level (beyond the physical) the nature of reality and the things that exist in it. But make no mistake: every discipline outside of metaphysics is committed to certain metaphysical assumptions and presuppositions—whether practitioners in those disciplines admit it or not. These assumptions carry significant implications on how that discipline is practiced. All the more reason to study metaphysics, to ensure better metaphysical views are informing the discipline and more justified parameters employed to work within.

Epistemology

We live in the information age. Indeed, each day most of us find ourselves swimming in a sea of information. At the touch of a screen, we can access the internet and get more information than we will ever have time to sift through. Indeed, claims about God, justice, politics, ethics, health, cultural norms, and so on are made daily on our social media feeds, televisions, podcasts, and online lectures. We also hear much about misinformation, disinformation, malinformation, and news sources that are unabashedly biased (at best) and gaslighting us (at worst). It is common to feel intellectual dizziness in this churning sea of information, especially given all the disagreement. What's more, many of us feel frequently pressured from various sources to take a position on some topic. Help! Where's the Dramamine?

So what does all this have to do with epistemology?

Epistemology is a subdiscipline of philosophy that cares about important things involving the life of the mind. In general, epistemology is the subdiscipline that explains how our minds can connect to reality and get the truth. More specifically, epistemologists analyze important epistemic goods like justification, truth, knowledge, understanding, and wisdom. These epistemic goods assist us in better explaining how our minds can cognitively connect with reality.[3] Many epistemologists are also interested in what sort of skills and abilities contribute to cultivating an intellectually virtuous character, which assists in getting epistemic goods. Developing the kind of skills, abilities, and character needed to navigate through this sea of information to reach the shores of truth is vital. So we think that not studying epistemology weakens our mind's "immune system," which can weaken or distort our connection with reality. By not staying epistemically fit, we are more vulnerable to forming false beliefs, being manipulated by specious arguments, or failing to achieve the harmonious thought life we need to succeed and flourish.

To those holding a Christian worldview, specific claims leveled against their views can sometimes generate some intellectual dizziness. This sea of information includes claims such as these:

DEFINITION OF EPISTEMOLOGY

Episteme is the Greek word for "knowledge." *Logos* is the Greek word for "reason," "word," or "account." When combined, these two words form the word *epistemology*, which means the study of knowledge. Epistemologists search for answers to questions like these: What is knowledge? How can humans get knowledge? What is the value of knowledge? What makes knowledge better than mere true belief or opinion? Epistemology arguably traces its origins back to Plato's *Theaetetus*, which pursues an answer to the question, "What is knowledge?" There is also the question of "What do we know?" which traces back to ancient *skepticism*, specifically academic skepticism and Pyrrhonian skepticism.

1. Faith is in conflict with reason, evidence, and science.
2. Reasonable belief in God requires justification from cogent arguments.
3. There is no good evidence or arguments for God's existence.
4. It is bigoted to believe Christianity's conception of God is true and all other conceptions of God are inaccurate or false.
5. Evil and the lack of an experiential awareness of God's presence justifies atheism.

6. Christians wouldn't believe Christianity is true if they were born at a different time and in a different place.

We believe epistemology is a vital discipline that provides the kind of training needed to learn how to sail through these rough seas of information and disagreement. What's more, we believe epistemology can assist us to know better the kind of epistemic goods we desire and how intellectual virtues can make us more successful at getting them.

Ethics

If you take a class in anthropology or sociology, you will encounter studies that describe certain behaviors common within a culture. In some cultures, for example, it is disrespectful for students to look into the eyes of their teachers; in other cultures, it is a sign of respect. In some cultures, it is morally permissible to consume alcohol; in other cultures, it is not. In some cultures, it is morally permissible to arrange a marriage for one's child; in other cultures, it is not. There is a difference, however, between describing what humans do and prescribing what one ought to do. This is the difference between *descriptive* analysis and *normative* analysis. A normative analysis aims to make accurate moral evaluations, to claim why some moral beliefs or actions are right or wrong, good or bad, praiseworthy or blameworthy. And numerous ethical theories aim to justify these moral evaluations. Different ethical theories assist us in mining for virtues, principles, or consequences (or some combination thereof) that we believe the right moral decision or action should secure.

One thing I like to do during the Christmas season is play a prank on Santa. Before my kids sit on Santa's lap, I tell them, "When he asks you if you have been a good boy or girl, respond this way: 'Santa, can you please first define goodness?'"[4] Then I tell them to watch him squirm in his chair. The reason why Santa usually squirms a bit is that defining the good

ETHICS OR MORALITY?

It's not uncommon to hear people use the terms *ethics* and *morality* to mean different things. For example, code of conduct policies at companies and colleges—the dos and don'ts—are taken as ethics or ethical policies, whereas one's personal code of conduct, which is informed by the moral values and principles informing one's moral reasoning, is often associated with morality. Accordingly, one's morality may not line up with a company's ethical policies. In this book, we typically use the term *ethics* to refer to moral philosophy—theories used to justify a moral belief. *Morality* or *morals* refer to specific principles or values informing one's judgement.

is not easy. Many experts, for thousands of years, have attempted to define the good, and yet there is still no consensus.

One way to think about ethics is to see it as that subdiscipline of philosophy aiming to give an account of goodness. More specifically, ethics has three branches, and one of those branches, *metaethics*, aims to give an account of the fundamental nature of morality, including goodness. So my daughter asks Santa a metaethical question. Santa's definition of goodness may trace back to a specific ethical theory. Ethical theories use a definition of goodness to justify why a moral belief is better than another or why an action is morally permissible or impermissible. This branch of ethics is called *normative ethics*. Finally, *applied ethics* takes a specific moral theory and shows how it can assist in making a moral decision in a real-world situation, especially when there is no obvious action that secures all the good things one would like to see happen. Ethics, then, is about discovering what the good is so that we can learn both how to become a good person and how to build a just and good world together.[5]

Logic

In light of this turbulent sea of information we live in, it is high time we explore some important skills to navigate through it. The tools of logic can help us sift through the claims made by others in an effort to discern fact from fiction, counterfeit from authentic. Indeed, given all the warnings of misinformation, disinformation, malinformation, and propaganda competing for our allegiance, we need to think critically and even be skeptical toward all these claims daily thrown our way. When we encounter a claim, we need to get in the habit of demanding evidence in support of it. This evidence will typically be expressed in a statement—what logicians call a *premise*. Additional evidence might be added, resulting in more premises. The premises are then used to support a claim—what logicians call a *conclusion*. The reasoning used to defend this conclusion is called an *argument*.

When we encounter an argument, do we know how to evaluate it? Can we discern whether it is good or bad? When we try to convince ourselves or someone else that a conclusion is true by using an argument, are *we* using good arguments? Logic, then, is primarily concerned with establishing methods for determining whether an argument's premises adequately support its conclusion. Strictly speaking, it is not the job of logicians to determine whether each premise is true. A responsible thinker must evaluate an argument by determining whether the premises are true. Logic assists a responsible thinker by helping him or her determine whether the premises support the conclusion.

We should care about logic because we all use reason to form new beliefs. Sometimes we use arguments to discover the truth for ourselves. Other times we use arguments to persuade ourselves (or others) to perform some action or dissuade ourselves (or others) not to perform an action. Since reason is a common source that we use to form beliefs, it is important to be able to locate an argument from a lineup of mere assertions, explanations, illustrations, or reports. And when we do discover an argument, we need to know how to evaluate it. Noted philosopher Dallas Willard said too many people judge an argument based on its conclusion, rather than judging the conclusion based on the argument. College students are far too often not given the tools and training needed to properly evaluate arguments.[6] Indeed, nowadays it seems as if far too many people consult their stomachs to determine whether an argument is good—relying upon how the conclusion makes them feel. This approach works well for deciding which flavor of ice cream to order, but not for assessing the merits of an argument.

The good news is that you already practice logic. *Logic* is using specific methods and tools to evaluate whether an argument is any good. And we all take ourselves to be rational—logical thinkers—thereby making us logicians. The question is: Are we any good at logic? There is even more good news: you are already good at logic (at some level). But we want you to be better at it. We want you to increase the number of concepts, tools, and methods you possess for evaluating arguments. For example, we take it that you already can see some important differences in these arguments:

Case 1: Cassius Clay is Muhammad Ali. Muhammad Ali is the father of Muhammad Ali Jr. Therefore, Cassius Clay is the father of Muhammad Ali Jr.

Case 2: Captain Sigvald's home is called The Sea Chest. The Sea Chest is located in Cape May, New Jersey. If Mr. Garofola visits Captain Sigvald at the Sea Chest, we may infer that Mr. Garofola is in Cape May, New Jersey.

Case 3: During the months of June, July, and August the consumption of ice cream increases by 25 percent compared to the other nine months. More people die from drowning in the months of June, July, and August than the other nine months. Therefore, the consumption of ice cream is causing more people to die from drowning.

We assume that after reading these three cases you think the reasoning is good in Cases 1 and 2 but bad in Case 3. Do you know why? Can you see why your nonsense-detector went off after reading Case 3? Further, do you have the proper terminology to articulate why it went off? Training in logic will enable you to better calibrate your nonsense-detector and understand what sets it off so you can explain it better to yourself and others.

In Case 1, for example, premise one makes an *identity claim*. It says Cassius Clay is Muhammad Ali. In this case, two names are referring to the *same* person. Premise two says Muhammad Ali is the father of Muhammad Ali Jr. Well, then, if premises one and two are true, then inferring that Cassius Clay is Muhammad Ali Jr's father preserves the truth in premises one and two. The inference used in this pattern of reasoning is valid, thereby guaranteeing the truth of the conclusion (assuming the premises are true). That's the beauty of validity! It's a pattern of reasoning that preserves truth through valid inferences.

Invalid inferences do not preserve truth, nor do they adequately support a conclusion. Consider Case 3. The inference made from the first two premises doesn't adequately support the conclusion. Just because ice cream consumption increases at the same time drownings increase, it doesn't support the conclusion that ice cream consumption *causes* drownings. Just because two things co-occur with each other, it doesn't support the further claim that one causes the other. For example, itchy eyes typically co-occur with sneezing. But does it follow that itchy eyes cause sneezing or sneezing causes itchy eyes? Of course not! Rather, allergies cause both itchy eyes and sneezing. Let us return to Case 3. There can be multiple part-causes that explain why each victim of drowning experienced respiratory impairment from liquid filling the lungs. Case 3, then, uses premises that don't adequately support the conclusion. Furthermore, logicians have given this kind of bad argument a name: *the false cause fallacy*—specifically, the fallacy of thinking correlation is the same thing as causation.

One way of thinking about logic is seeing it as a way to train yourself to reason better in an effort to get truth. If reasoning well is an achievement, then reasoning well requires special training. We believe training in the discipline of logic will assist your reasoning abilities—specifically, constructing and evaluating arguments. In the chapters that follow, you will gain additional skills to help determine whether the premises of the arguments you encounter are true.

Conclusion

We've given you a brief overview of the four main subdisciplines of philosophy. In other chapters, we will look more in depth at metaphysics, epistemology, ethics, and logic. Other chapters will build from one or more of these four subdisciplines, extending philosophical inquiry into other areas like free will, science, and the philosophy of religion, to mention a few. By better understanding metaphysics, epistemology, ethics, and logic, you will be better equipped to see how they can shed light on different topics in the chapters that follow.

Questions for Reflection

1. In this chapter, we discussed how an answer to a philosophical question (e.g., What is the meaning of life?) can often be evaluated from a metaphysical, epistemological, ethical, and logical point of view. Can you come up with other examples of how metaphysical, epistemological, ethical, and/or logical assumptions are made in other disciplines?
2. What are some metaphysical assumptions in play whenever anyone claims to know something, especially about the external world?
3. Since virtually everyone uses the terms *true* and *truth*, why is it important to know what truth is? Do you think people have a difficult time converging on truth or agreeing on some matter because the disputants are using different definitions of truth?
4. Do you see any connection between metaphysics and ethics? How about this: Do you see why it's important to first know what a human person is (metaphysical question) before prescribing what is good for humans (ethical statement)?
5. How can the benefits of logic inoculate you from bad arguments? Do you think people are vulnerable to manipulation because they lack training in logic?

For Further Reading

Austin, Michael W., and R. Douglas Geivett. *Being Good: Christian Virtues for Everyday Life.* Grand Rapids: Eerdmans, 2022.

Dickinson, Travis. *Logic and the Way of Jesus: Thinking Critically and Christianly.* Nashville: B&H Academic, 2022.

Horner, David A. *Mind Your Faith: A Student's Guide to Thinking and Living Well.* Downers Grove, IL: IVP Academic, 2011.

Moreland, J. P. *Love Your God with All Your Mind: The Role of Reason in the Life of the Soul.* Colorado Spring: NavPress, 2012.

Pickavance, Timothy. *Knowledge for the Love of God: Why Your Heart Needs Your Mind.* Grand Rapids: Eerdmans, 2022.

Rasmussen, Joshua. *How Reason Can Lead to God: A Philosopher's Bridge to Faith.* Downers Grove, IL: IVP Academic, 2019.

NOTES

1. Some profound questions are these: Does God exist? Does God personally interact with humans? Do objective moral values exist? What is the meaning of life? How did life originate? Do humans have free will? Is there life after death? What is knowledge and can humans get it? What happens when humans die? Who is a good person?

2. Some of you may be familiar with the movie *The Matrix*. This scenario is inspired by the character Neo living in a pod of chemicals wherein his nervous system is directly connected to a super-computer directly stimulating it, which is controlled by malevolent, conscious machines. See the Wachowskis (directors), (1999), *The Matrix*, Warner Brothers production company.

3. Linda Zagzebski is the first to coin the phrase that knowledge is when someone has "cognitive contact with reality" because of "acts of intellectual virtue." See Linda Zagzebski, *Virtues of the Mind: An Inquiry into the Nature of Virtue and the Ethical Foundations of Knowledge* (Cambridge: Cambridge University Press, 1996), xv.

4. Credit to J. P. Moreland for creating this fun holiday activity.

5. Another way of thinking about ethics is considering C. S. Lewis's analogy involving a fleet of ships. There are three things we care about regarding a fleet of ships. First, how do we keep the ships from sinking? Second, how do we keep the ships from crashing into each other? Third, what destination should the captains plot their course toward? Similarly, we care about how to get one's character in good working order—cultivating virtuous character (individual component); justly and harmoniously relating to other people (social component); and discovering the meaning and purpose of life (metaphysical component). These three components are interdependent because, even if good ethical principles get ratified into laws, without people of good character, no one will have the power and ability to obey them. Furthermore, is the purpose and meaning of life simply to maintain a holding pattern of different social interactions, enabling us to live in harmony with each other? Or is there something more to the meaning and purpose of life? See C. S. Lewis, *Mere Christianity* (New York: HarperCollins, 2001), 69–75.

6. This point was made during a lecture given at the University of California Los Angeles (UCLA) in the Spring of 2003. Willard was lecturing on "The Nature and Necessity of Worldviews" under the auspices of the *Veritas Forum*.

CHAPTER 5

What Is Hermeneutics?

Factors Shaping Our Beliefs and Interpretations

Hermeneutics. Herman who? Her menu ticks? What in the world does it (hermeneutics) mean? It actually does have a lot to do with what is going on in the world. In fact, hermeneutics is always involved in your thought life and daily activities. You might be thinking, "Are you kidding? If I don't even know what the word means, how can it be a huge part of my life? That seems ridiculous." Before you dismiss this claim outright, let's first find out what hermeneutics is.

Hermeneutics is the theory and practice of interpretation.[1] As such, it's both a science and an art that focuses on understanding. This basic definition confirms why we think hermeneutics is vital to life—particularly life lived well. Throughout this chapter, we'll unpack "all things hermeneutics," encouraging you to consider this often overlooked yet critical topic. Our method will be to engage five important questions pertaining to hermeneutics:

1. When, where, how, why, and from whom did we get the term?
2. What are some good and appropriate ways of defining and explaining hermeneutics?
3. What are the main branches of hermeneutics, and who are some key "hermeneuts"?
4. What unifies and what divides hermeneutical thinking?
5. What difference does hermeneutics make to our daily lives?

We hope this chapter provides some important tools to benefit your own hermeneutical journey. Remember: it is all about understanding! It matters that we understand what we mean—and what others think we mean—when we communicate. For instance, if I respond to someone's text message with "That's ridiculous!" am I meaning to communicate that what they said was "crazy" or that it was "great"? This "ridiculous" problem actually occurred in a Philosophy of Religion class several years ago. A student had been listening intently to the lecture and discussion when he burst out, "That's ridiculous!" At first, it seemed he was voicing opposition to an insight being presented as especially important, meaning that he thought it was stupid or silly. However, his follow-up comments made it clear how impressed or amazed he was with what he had just learned! Surely, what we mean with what we communicate matters more than we may think. Just as important is understanding what influences our communication— existing at a deeper, more basic level than what we actually articulate—verbally or nonverbally.

Maybe you've heard this saying before: "It all depends on who you talk to." At first glance, it seems to be true to life. Take, for instance, Major League Baseball. Which is the best baseball team? Ask any New York Yankees fan, and they're sure to tell you, "the Yankees, hands down!" The same is true for Los Angeles Dodgers fans or pretty much any other baseball club, although it's more likely if theirs is a winning team. Let's say a team finished in last place three years in a row (we'll call them the Turkeys). It seems probable that fans of the Turkeys would be less likely to say their team is the best. But wait just a minute! What about the fact that the Turkeys won two World Series back-to-back before the recent lean years? Or what if some team has fallen on hard times for the last decade, but overall has won more total World Series than any other team? Wouldn't that qualify the team as the best ever? I hope you can see from this MLB illustration just how challenging it is to pin down what we mean—or intend to mean—when we use words: in this case, the word *best*. That is where hermeneutics may offer us help.

When it comes to favorite baseball teams, ice cream flavors, or hair styles, it seems to be a matter of personal or community tastes or opinions (like those of families or friends or culture) than some objective standard. (We probably won't write a scholarly paper on why chocolate is indisputably the best ice cream flavor, even if we think so.) For more important issues—relational or ethical or theological or philosophical—we need something more substantial than mere feelings, conjectures, or guesses. We need a baseline, to start, plus understanding about the larger context or scope involved. More than merely "it all depends on who you talk to," explaining, understanding, and skillfully attending to hermeneutics depends on various factors we'll be discussing shortly.

Understanding hermeneutics begins with seeing how the term came about and how it's been used over time. We begin with a brief history of hermeneutics, noting some key "hermeneuts" (experts in the field) along the way.

Brief History of "Hermeneutics"

The term *hermeneutics* has been around a long time—going all the way back to ancient Greece. In Greek, it's spelled (technically, transliterated) *hermeneuein*. It seems to have been used first by scholars who "discussed how divine messages or mental ideas are expressed in human language."[2] Until about the beginning of the nineteenth century, hermeneutics was mostly concerned with three academic disciplines: legal (study of or relating to law), theological (study of God or divinity, revelation, religious knowledge and belief), and philological (study of language in written or oral sources). Hermeneutics, then, was mainly a method for finding and explaining the one and only meaning of the subject matter being studied. Even though different interpretations permeated these disciplines, most thinkers believed that one true answer existed; all other answers simply were insufficient or incorrect. Some weakness of thought or application was to blame. Perhaps you can see the underlying assumption: there just could not be more than one possible answer. It's an all or nothing, zero-sum approach. One interpretation wins and all others lose.

The nineteenth century witnessed a major shift in the meaning and application of hermeneutics when German scholar F. D. E. Schleiermacher (1768–1834) began using the term in much broader ways. Raised in both the Christian faith (especially from his parents, religious community, and spiritual ideals) and Enlightenment culture (mainly focused on human discovery and achievement), Schleiermacher broadened the scope of hermeneutics to include every academic discipline and all of life's experiences. It became an all-encompassing theory of interpretation: "a set of rules that provide the basis for good interpretive practice no matter what the subject matter."[3]

While Schleiermacher's hermeneutical approach emphasized the psychological level and thus individual experiences (even if understood as a "community of individuals"), Wilhelm Dilthey (1833–1911) turned his hermeneutical attention to social psychology, focusing on corporate experiences and shared worldviews.[4] Whereas Schleiermacher focused on both the *theological* (God/spiritual realm-oriented) and *anthropological* (human-oriented) levels, Dilthey addressed almost exclusively the anthropological condition. Both hermeneuts were intensely interested in human experience. Both thinkers opened new and helpful ways of understanding ourselves and others, even if incompletely.

Significantly more radical changes in hermeneutics would develop in the twentieth century. Philosophers Edmund Husserl (1859–1938) and his apprentice Martin Heidegger (1889–1976) focused philosophy on *phenomenalism*: a movement arguing that "phenomena are the only objects of knowledge, or . . . phenomena are the only realities."[5] Heidegger argued that hermeneutics is less about the science of phenomena and more about the phenomena of "being-there" in one's situation—in deeper ways than just analyzing biological data or other scientific information. Human beings are unique among all other beings: most important, since they have the capacity to think and ask questions about meaning and meaningfulness—and to live life meaningfully in the world. To lose this capacity to technology, or reducing people to mere objects, is just wrong.

Heidegger's philosophical work has profoundly influenced many thinkers, including Hans-Georg Gadamer (1900–2002), arguably the most influential hermeneut of the twentieth century.[6] Gadamer's detailed hermeneutical philosophy runs very deep. For our introductory purposes, we'll summarize his primary hermeneutical contributions and impact:[7]

- The *scope* of hermeneutics is widened, and interpretation is made universal to include virtually all texts (beyond legal, theological, and philological).
- *Tradition and language* are viewed as necessary for human thought (rather than something opposed to it or to be rejected or overcome).
- *Truth* is seen as nonreducible to a set of criteria (criteria such as promoted by the scientific method).
- *Phronesis* (practical wisdom) and open dialogue serve as central means to coming to understand (recognizing the finite nature of human knowledge/knowing, while *not* necessitating subjectivism or relativism).
- All philosophy begins from *praxis* (human practice), and hermeneutics is essentially practical philosophy (rather than merely theoretical).
- *Knowing* is more than conceptual (because it emerges from our practical quest for meaningful human existence).

Thanks in large part to Gadamer (and those who follow after[8]), this is where hermeneutics is today. It has become integrated within virtually all academic curricula, programs, and courses, even if more implicitly than explicitly, and even if less in the natural sciences than in the human sciences. Hermeneutics is integrated into all of our everyday contexts, too, including our thought life and actions. If this is so, perhaps first we ought to consider some definitions and explanations of hermeneutics that move beyond our earlier introductory definition.

Defining and Explaining Hermeneutics

While we can see that the scope of hermeneutics is extensive, the following descriptions should give us a good overall understanding of what hermeneutics involves: (a) critically reflecting on what is going on when we interpret, including presuppositional, situational, motivational, and related factors; (b) primarily focusing on the theory and practice of interpretation; (c) engaging oneself in trying to get to the meaning of things; (d) working to understand others while also trying to be understood; (e) exploring "how we read, understand, and handle texts, especially those written in another time or in a context of life different from our own"[9]; (f) serving as "a science, since it provides a logical, orderly classification of the laws of interpretation," as "an art, for it is an acquired skill demanding both imagination and an ability to apply the 'laws' to selected passages or books," and "when utilized to interpret Scripture is a spiritual act, depending on the leading of the Holy Spirit."[10]

You might have noticed the final explanation involves a distinctly Christian understanding. In fact, every definition and explanation necessarily includes the definer's or explainer's perspective! Most contemporary philosophers believe it's impossible to detach from our worldview when trying to understand things. Still, this doesn't mean we should stop listening attentively to other perspectives or seeking to be as objective and fair as possible. Nor does it assume people cannot change their view. What it does not presuppose is that we have no worldview or some allegedly neutral viewpoint—especially on important matters of life: ultimate concerns foremost. So it's no more unusual for one to have a particularly Christian approach to hermeneutics than any other approach (e.g., atheistic, pantheistic, or Islamic). Still, worldview differences should not imply all views are equally true or equally untrue. Weighing and testing claims and evidence is essential for getting to the truth. But back to the topic at hand.

Main Branches of Hermeneutics

Clearly, hermeneutics is complex. Good general explanations help, but we'll stand to benefit further from explanations describing the term's meaning and use in distinct disciplines. Let's consider how hermeneutics works in these major sub-disciplines or categories: philosophical, biblical, theological, and cultural.

Philosophical Hermeneutics

Philosophical hermeneutics represents an all-encompassing approach to understanding; it is a general or comprehensive theory of interpretation rather than a "regional" one (for instance, biblical or cultural hermeneutics). Anthony Thiselton explains some central features that make philosophical hermeneutics unique: it depends more on the reader's or hearer's receptivity to "listen with openness" as part of the process of understanding (in addition to analyzing and explaining) "texts"; it focuses more on questions that arise from within concrete situations in human life (rather than philosophical problems in abstraction); it begins from an initial and provisional understanding starting point (as opposed to beginning with doubt and the fallible human subject/individual).[11]

In sum, philosophical hermeneutics focuses on the essence of interpretation, meaning, or understanding. Our whole view of reality comprises the perceptions, beliefs, interpretations, and commitments we have. Thus, it makes sense to examine what we are believing about things (consciously or unconsciously). Critically evaluating our findings—and gaining better understanding—should lead us to revise and improve our presuppositions so that they line up better with reality. ("Reality" concerns how things really are, what actually exists, the genuine state of affairs, what is the truth or true about something, etc. In philosophy, questions about the nature of reality generally come under the category of metaphysics.)

Biblical Hermeneutics

For many Bible scholars/interpreters throughout history, *biblical hermeneutics* was virtually the same as *exegesis* (explanation of a text after detailed investigation) or following basic rules for doing exegesis responsibly. But beginning with Schleiermacher in the nineteenth century, hermeneutics transitioned into being viewed as more of an art than a science, as a broader discipline than either exegesis or interpretation as concrete procedures of explaining texts.

Biblical hermeneutics today also includes the second-order discipline of asking critically, "What exactly are we doing when we read, understand, or apply texts?"[12] Successful interpretation is the goal—that which is responsible, valid, fruitful, or appropriate. This requires drawing on various academic disciplines to answer questions connected to understanding, knowing the nature and influence of texts, biblical studies, church history and thought, and doctrine/theology.[13] In fact, many hermeneuts today recognize a threefold literary framework for arriving at the best interpretation and understanding of biblical texts:

1. "Behind the text" (author-focused) attempts to find out the intention or mind of the biblical writer/author, combined with the historical/cultural context of the writing. Just how much emphasis should be placed here is a question that stimulates extensive debate.

2. "Within the text" (text-focused) concentrates on the text itself, including literary aspects (language, genre, structure, narrative, quality, etc.), emphasizing the autonomous nature of the text (its own system of signs and meanings apart from the writer/author). Again, significant debate arises over whether this aspect undermines the authority of the author and/or the importance of the reader.

3. "In front of the text" (reader-focused) centers on the readers of the text and the meaning or understanding produced by recipients of the written (or spoken) communication. (One might wonder if there was any real communication or understanding occurring otherwise.) Still, transferring authority for the text's meaning—from either the writer/author or the text itself—to the readers raises important concerns for biblical scholars and others.

We conclude this section by briefly summing five main views of biblical hermeneutics, leaving deeper analysis to your own investigation:[14]

1. The *historical-critical/grammatical view* focuses on text analysis and background to determine the biblical author's original meaning. It involves deep analysis of grammatical elements in the text and its historical setting.

2. The *literary/postmodern view* emphasizes the biblical text's relevance to readers today. It focuses more on "within" and "in front of" than "behind" the text and the diverse ways the text may be applied by its readers nowadays.

3. The *philosophical/theological view* affirms the "hermeneutical circle" (our perspective directly impacting our reading of a text, and the text directly impacting our perspective), entailing that we should expect various interpretations since interpreters exist in different contexts—their presuppositions being based on their overall worldview.

4. The *redemptive/historical view* focuses on God's covenant of redemption in history—culminating in the person and role of Jesus Christ—as central to interpreting and understanding all of Scripture (Old and New Testaments).

5. The *canonical view* emphasizes the whole Bible's final shape ("canon"), attempting to read the canon in relation to each of its parts, and each part in light of every other part. It emphasizes a text-centered and church-related application, understanding the Bible as (a) the historical product of human agency (developed over time amidst the believing community),

(b) sacred text (under the inspiration/direction of the Holy Spirit), and (c) for calling faithful readers to salvation in Christ and maturity in faith and good works.

In sum, these five biblical hermeneutics approaches seek to understand best how Scripture ought to be viewed, studied, interpreted, and appropriated for today. It seems likely that bringing together the best insights and practices of each approach (rather than just one) makes good sense for good hermeneutics!

Theological Hermeneutics

Like biblical hermeneutics, theological hermeneutics is a regional arena within the broader frame of general hermeneutics. What makes *theological hermeneutics* unique? It's grounded in a God-centered or theologically comprehensive interpretation of the world, especially attentive to God's revelation to humankind. This revelation often is understood in a twofold sense: as a "general" revealing via creation and as a "special" unveiling via God's particular relational and redemptive interactions with humankind, as described in the Bible. Many advocates of theological hermeneutics also understand the Bible as "the Word of God"—in reference to the inspired written Old Testament Scriptures (or Hebrew Bible) and the New Testament Scriptures—and Jesus Christ as the living Word of God. Moreover, this twofold Word of God and the Spirit of God (Holy Spirit) combine to provide a full-bodied approach to knowing and understanding what is real and true. Some scholars also include additional sources for interpretation (usually understood as secondary), such as historic Christian tradition, virtual consensus among Christian communities, and/or culture.

Theological hermeneutics, then, is a faith-based approach, involving the beliefs and commitments not only of an *individual* but also of the *faith-community*—sometimes referred to as the Christian tradition/heritage or rule of faith (referring to a summary of Christian teachings/doctrines).

Cultural Hermeneutics

Cultural hermeneutics involves interpreting the signs of the times. More specifically, seeking to understand the "spirit of the age" (*Zeitgeist*): the defining attitude or mood or essence of a particular era. *Zeitgeist* also comprises the intellectual, spiritual, and moral tone we inhabit.[15] Cultural hermeneutics seeks to make sense of the world and the assorted "worlds" therein to which we each belong (like participants in different musical *genre* worlds like hip-hop, jazz, or classical). *Cultural literacy* means being able to interpret stabilizing forces and patterns/trends within the particular *Zeitgeist*.

Culture as "a way of life" and "world of meaning" works in two directions; it influences us, and we influence it. At bottom, whose interpretation and which understanding matter significantly! Ultimate authority matters most of all (be it oneself, atoms, the *Zeitgeist*, or God). A Christian worldview naturally (better, supernaturally) should involve cultural hermeneutics, seeking to discern what God is up to (God's mission/*missio Dei*) and uniting with the Holy Spirit's activity in culture—especially related to ultimate concerns.

The "Truth" about Hermeneutics

Most hermeneutics scholars agree that human interpretation and understanding is *fallible*—falling short of 100 percent accuracy. One might say "hermeneutics humbles," reminding us that we're imperfect, limited beings, even though intelligent and creative. Many suggest that doing hermeneutics well can lead to better understanding and even the truth about things (at least closer to it). Still, some believe seeking truth is ultimately meaningless (certain nihilists, for instance), but by arguing such they actually are making a universal truth claim—one that cannot be supported with logic or evidence. Most hermeneuts find value in the *pursuit* of truth itself, while others affirm truth may be perceived and/or experienced *prima facia* ("at face value"). The biggest disagreement among hermeneuts, though, concerns ultimate questions about reality—leading to differences in worldviews.

The Hermeneutical Circle or Spiral

Hermeneutics is necessarily circular to some degree. But this doesn't mean interpretation must involve illogical or fallacious reasoning; it just means that we never start from nowhere and then arrive at a perfect understanding of things. An ongoing, reciprocal interaction between texts (biblical and cultural) and our presuppositions exists. We really can't grasp a whole unless we get all its pieces, and we can't truly understand the pieces until we grasp how they work as part of the whole. Think of a puzzle.

This essential combination of (1) prior understanding (i.e., preunderstanding) and (2) whole-and-pieces understanding reveals that a hermeneutical circle (or spiral) exists—even before we make truth claims or assign particular value to things. Grasping the reality of this spiral and its implications means more skillfully navigating our "hermeneutical universe"—which can enable us to better understand and interpret the world.

Preunderstandings, Presuppositions, and Precommitments

Let's consider three important assumptions related to worldview and hermeneutics, which we'll call "the three Ps": preunderstandings, presuppositions, and precommitments.[16] *Preunderstandings* are provisional beginning points or links to a better, more well-informed understanding of things. We might think of it as a preliminary or a provisional understanding.

Presuppositions are underlying assumptions, beliefs, and theories that shape (to varying degrees) our evaluations and judgments. A presupposition is implicitly assumed to be fact or true, which then supports some evaluation or action. Some hermeneuts see presuppositions as "horizons" that limit understanding to a particular vantage point, but also may be expanded—opening up new horizons. Presuppositions powerfully shape our worldview. Sometimes they become destabilized or overturned, especially when we recognize we have been mistaken about something. Fortunately, they can be corrected. Integrity requires that we seek the truth and allow it to challenge our presuppositions.

Most people recognize that commitment includes things like allegiance, dedication, steadfastness, devotion, obligation, and promise. *Precommitments* signify strong underlying fidelity to someone or something that shapes our thinking and practice. Clearly, there's overlap between the three Ps, but let me suggest that precommitments entail greater inflexibility or solidification. You have heard it said, "She sure is set in her ways!" Even so, some slight possibility remains for moving particular worldview puzzle pieces, but most are now fixed—whether or not the whole fits together well or makes good "worldview-ish" sense.

What Difference Hermeneutics Makes in Our Daily Lives

Perhaps you've been wondering, "How can hermeneutics make a practical difference in my life?" Here are some ways we believe people benefit from understanding and applying hermeneutics wisely.

First, acquiring a basic grasp of hermeneutics leads to a better understanding of ourselves, including our assumptions about many things. We can move from merely knowing to challenging and revising certain faulty presuppositions we hold. This will help us live more consistently toward—and in light of—the truth of things.

Second, being hermeneutically informed leads us to proper humility, including recognizing our human limitations related to knowing, understanding, and living. Realizing these limits can actually benefit us. By looking beyond—rather than merely within—ourselves, we are more open to seek and know the one with limitless knowledge, understanding, and goodness. In the words of Thomas Aquinas, "And that is what we call God."

Third, understanding hermeneutics tends to increase our valuing of others' viewpoints as we recognize that multiple factors are involved in shaping each individual's perspective. Paul Ricoeur reasons that hermeneutics, well understood, can help us see "oneself as another,"[17] which reflects Jesus' directive to "love your neighbor as yourself" (Matt. 22:39). If that were all hermeneutics could do for us, perhaps that alone would be enough!

Ultimately, hermeneutics is less about method than it is about truth. Hans-Georg Gadamer appears to be right about the inseparable relationship between authority, understanding, and truth; combined, these deeply shape our moral lives. Therefore, it is important that we choose to join and belong to the most praiseworthy authorities: those providing a comprehensive, meaningful, moral, purposeful, and practical vision of reality. And that's where theology comes in.

As we argued earlier, understanding reality occurs only from within particular worldview frameworks or "grand narratives." Assessing which metanarrative is true (at least, truer than others) matters. We believe the whole Christian story—from creation to fall to redemption to consummation—represents a definitive interpretation of reality. We might say the Christian worldview is the *hermeneutical lens* through which we come to understand our place as human beings in God's world of creation and redemption. J. R. R. Tolkien (The Lord of the Rings) and C. S. Lewis (The Chronicles of Narnia) agree: the Christian story stands apart as the one true grand narrative. As such, it provides hermeneutical power for understanding and living our lives well.

> I believe in Christianity as I believe that the sun has risen, not only because I see it but because by it, I see everything else.
> —C. S. Lewis, *Is Theology Poetry?* 164–65

Questions for Reflection

1. Briefly describe one or more important aspects of each of the four main branches of hermeneutics: philosophical, biblical, theological, and cultural.
2. How might the threefold literary framework serve in interpreting and understanding biblical texts?
3. What meaningful difference can understanding or applying hermeneutics make in your own life? Give one or two examples.

For Further Reading

Gadamer, Hans-Georg. *Truth and Method*, 2nd. rev. ed., trans. Joel Weinsheimer and Donald G. Marshall. New York: Continuum, 2004.

Osborne, Grant. *The Hermeneutical Spiral: A Comprehensive Introduction to Biblical Interpretation*, 2nd ed. Grand Rapids: IVP Academic, 2006.

Porter, Stanley E., and Beth M. Stovell, eds. *Biblical Hermeneutics: Five Views*. Downers Grove, IL: IVP Academic, 2012.

Thiselton, Anthony C. *Hermeneutics: An Introduction*. Grand Rapids: Eerdmans, 2009.

Westphal, Merold. *Whose Community? Which Interpretation? Philosophical Hermeneutics for the Church*. Grand Rapids: Baker Academic, 2009.

Zimmermann, Jens. *Hermeneutics: A Very Short Introduction*. Oxford: Oxford University Press, 2015.

NOTES

1. Merold Westphal, *Whose Community? Which Interpretation? Philosophical Hermeneutics for the Church* (Grand Rapids: Baker Academic, 2009), 13.
2. Jens Zimmermann, *Hermeneutics: A Very Short Introduction* (Oxford: Oxford University Press, 2015), 3.
3. Jeff Malpas, "Hans-Georg Gadamer," *The Stanford Encyclopedia of Philosophy* (Fall 2018 edition), https://plato.stanford.edu/archives/fall2018/entries/gadamer/.
4. For instance, see Dilthey's most famous work, *The Formation of the Historical World in the Human Sciences*, in *Wilhelm Dilthey: Selected Works*, vol. 3: *The Formation of the Historical World in the Human Sciences* (Princeton: Princeton University Press, 2002).
5. "Phenomenalism," in *The Macquarie Dictionary*, ed. Susan Butler, 7th ed. (Macquarie Dictionary Publishers, 2017), https://search.credoreference.com/articles/Qm9va0FydGljb GU6NDcwNDY1MA==?aid=96349.
6. Gadamer's magnum opus is *Truth and Method*. In it, Gadamer's approach substantially broke with Schleiermacher's and Dilthey's (and Husserl's and Heidegger's at points). David Linge explains, "Unlike the essentially reconstructive hermeneutics of Schleiermacher and Dilthey, which took the language of the text as a cipher for something lying *behind* the text (e.g., the creative personality or the worldview of the author), Gadamer focuses his attention squarely on the subject matter of the text itself, that is, on what it says to successive generations of interpreters" (David E. Linge, "Editor's Introduction," in Hans-Georg Gadamer, *Philosophical Hermeneutics*, trans. and ed. David E. Linge [Berkeley: University of California Press, 1976], xx).
7. For more details, see Lauren Swayne Barthold, "Hans-Georg Gadamer," *The Internet Encyclopedia of Philosophy*, ISSN 2161–0002, www.iep.utm.edu/, 8/12/20; and Jeff Malpas, "Hans-Georg Gadamer," *Stanford Encyclopedia of History*.
8. Among the most influential of Gadamer's contemporary and later interlocutors engaging his hermeneutical thought are Donald Davidson, Gianni Vattimo, Ronald Dworkin, Robert Brandom, John McDowell, Jürgen Habermas, Jacque Derrida, Paul Ricoeur, Alasdair McIntyre, Richard Rorty, and Anthony Thiselton.

9. Anthony C. Thiselton, *Hermeneutics: An Introduction* (Grand Rapids: Eerdmans, 2009), 1.

10. Grant Osborne, *The Hermeneutical Spiral: A Comprehensive Introduction to Biblical Interpretation*, 2nd ed. (Downers Grove, IL: IVP Academic, 2006), 22.

11. Thiselton, *Hermeneutics*, 7–12.

12. Ibid., 4.

13. Ibid., 4–5.

14. See Stanley J. Porter and Beth M. Stovell, "Introduction: Trajectories in Biblical Hermeneutics," in *Biblical Hermeneutics: Five Views*, ed. Stanley E. Porter and Beth M. Stovell (Downers Grove, IL: IVP Academic, 2012), 21–23.

15. See Kevin J. Vanhoozer, Charles A. Anderson, Michael J. Sleasman, eds., *Everyday Theology: How to Read Cultural Texts and Interpret Trends* (Grand Rapids: Baker Academic, 2007), 18.

16. We're deeply indebted to Anthony Thiselton for this section focused on these three key terms. See especially his discussion in Thiselton, *Hermeneutics*, 13–17, 77–78, 155–57, and others.

17. See Paul Ricoeur, *Oneself as Another,* trans. Kathleen Blamey (Chicago: Chicago University Press, 1995).

PART 2

Logic, Reasoning, and Arguments

CHAPTER 6

What Is Logic, and What Are Arguments?

Introduction: Logic Defined

We have defined philosophy as thinking hard about things that really matter, so thinking is essential to philosophy. Since thinking is essential to philosophy, then thinking really matters; and if thinking really matters, then we must think hard about thinking. (It's ok if you need to reread that sentence again.) Thinking about thinking belongs to the branch of philosophy called *logic*. If we want to live happier, more fulfilled lives, then we need to be able to do philosophy well; we must be able to do it skillfully. Therefore, logic can't be merely thinking about thinking. Instead, logic needs to help us to think well, to think correctly, and to think more skillfully, so that we can be equipped to discover truth, gain understanding of the world, and know how to act. With all of this in mind, we now have a pretty good definition of logic: logic is the study of how to think properly.

But is there really a right way to think? What does it mean to think "properly"? If this is the first time you've heard this kind of thing, it would be easy for you to misunderstand what we mean by this. You might misunderstand this idea and conclude that logic is like a set of rules or regulations imposed on us from some source of authority describing how a person is supposed to think. If you obey the rules of thinking, you are thinking properly, and if you don't obey these rules, you are thinking improperly. And who decided what the rules are, anyway? What makes some rules of logic right and other rules wrong? Well, logic isn't really like that—it isn't really something that is imposed upon us from an outside authoritative source that we need to obey in order to think properly. Instead, the basic principles of logic are (in a sense) internal to all of us.

Every human person has a mental faculty that we call *reason*, and each of us is able to grasp the basic principles of logic by using this innate capacity. It might be helpful to think of this capacity as "common sense." The "common" part of that refers to the fact that reason is universal. Everyone has this capacity, and most students who learn the principles of logic for the first time react by saying, "Oh, yeah. That makes good sense." But if everyone already has this capacity, what is the point of creating a formal study in logic? Can't we all just use our common sense? Well, the reason we study logic is because mistakes in thinking are even more common than common sense! In later chapters, we will highlight some of the more common mistakes and show you how to avoid them. Studying logic helps us reduce our mistakes and improve our thinking skills. Ultimately, the reason we want to improve our thinking skills is because we are striving after what is perhaps the most important goal of life: truth.

LOGIC AND THE CHRISTIAN WORLDVIEW

From the perspective of the Christian worldview, each human person is made in God's image. God himself is the very foundation of rationality, and he has built that rationality into human nature. Logic reflects the order and structure of the reality that he has created. For Christians, this explains why logic is universal and why every human person has the faculty of reason.

What Is Logic All About?

In an ultimate sense, logic is aimed at truth because it is designed to equip us to discover truth. Truth has fallen on hard times, particularly since the latter part of the twentieth century. There have been some cultural movements that have denied the importance of truth, and some have even denied that there is such a thing as truth. We will return to a more in-depth discussion of truth in later chapters, but for now, it is important to point out that there is a direct connection between believing the truth and living a successful, happy life. If you believe that your job interview is at 2:00 p.m., but the truth of the matter is that the interview is at 1:00 p.m., you aren't going to have a successful interview. If you think your roommate is your uncle, but in truth, your roommate is your uncle's cat, you are going to have some uncomfortable and perplexing domestic problems. If you believe that you are an excellent communicator, but in reality, no one can figure out what you are trying to say, you are going to have a very difficult social life. We are highlighting the connection between truth and happiness here very briefly because logic, like the rest of philosophy, is ultimately aimed at truth. Logic is an essential building block in philosophy because it provides the mental tools we need in order to use our reasoning skills properly. We want to reason properly so that we can have a good grasp on the way things are in the world. Logic gives us principles and methods we can use to analyze and evaluate ideas so that we can differentiate between true and false beliefs.

The world can be a confusing place, especially if you are trying to figure out what is true and what is false. Perhaps there was a time in our past in which things weren't so confusing, when cultures were more isolated from one another, and most people were born and raised in an environment in which everyone believed pretty much the same thing. But in the age of the internet, the world seems smaller. Each of us is bombarded by a wide diversity of opinions and points of view. Take religion, for example. If you grew up in a small town where almost everyone practiced one particular religion, it may have been easy to believe what everyone else believed. But if you live in a more diverse context and your neighbor is Christian, your teacher is Jewish, your coach is Muslim, your best friend is Buddhist, and your parents are atheist, you might say to yourself, "I don't know what to believe!" You might be tempted to think that either there is no such thing as "true" belief (at least when it comes to religion) or that all of it is just a matter of opinion, and one religion can be "true" for one person but not another. Logic is an essential tool that helps us sort through all the confusion and conflicting data so that we can have confidence in what we believe. It helps us clear away the mental clutter so we can arrive at a coherent picture of the world, with our beliefs better matching the way the world really is.

To help us get to true beliefs, logic focuses on the reasonableness of our beliefs. Logic is not primarily concerned with whether an individual belief is true or false. Instead, logic examines how beliefs fit together, rationally. It focuses on thinking properly in the process of evaluating beliefs or claims about the world. When someone makes a claim that you've never heard before, logic helps you evaluate that claim in light of other things you already believe. If the new claim fits logically with beliefs that you already have, then that claim will seem reasonable to you, and you will probably accept it as true. If the claim contradicts other beliefs you have, then you are likely to reject it. Similarly, imagine you are presented with a new claim that you think is well supported by good evidence and seems reasonable and likely to be true, so you believe it. But imagine that this new belief (which seems perfectly reasonable to you) also happens to contradict some other belief you already have. Now, your common sense tells you that the new belief and the old one can't both be true. If you are interested in truth, then you will follow the logic where it leads you and abandon one belief or the other (or both). Obviously, it is not always possible to immediately solve apparent contradictions between beliefs; and sometimes we just need to postpone judgment until more evidence is available or more time is taken to think about how the apparent contradiction can be resolved. This is all a part of the process of examining our own beliefs for reasonableness.

Three Basic Principles of Logic

The ancient philosopher Aristotle was perhaps the first philosopher, certainly the most famous, to analyze logical thinking in a systematic way. Aristotle identified three basic principles of rational thought, which are to this day recognized as fundamental to logic: the law of identity, the law of noncontradiction, and the law of excluded middle. As we suggested, calling them "laws" is not meant to imply that they are imposed upon us by some external authority figure that we must obey without question. Rather, these principles simply describe the basic features of good reasoning. In fact, it is often said that Aristotle himself did not invent these principles; rather, he discovered them. So these three laws of logic are simply principles of common sense reasoning.

First, the *law of identity* says that whatever something is, it is what it is, and it is not something else. This is a very simple, easy-to-understand principle; so simple, in fact, that any explanation of it is bound to be more complicated than the principle itself! To represent the law of identity, it is sometimes written out as "A is A." This is just a formal way of pointing out the obvious: for any object A, that object is identical to itself. Here is another way to say it: all individual things exist in a particular way. Think about something like your cell phone: it has a particular size, shape, color, texture, and weight; it has a particular case on it; it has apps installed with icons arranged in a particular way on the home screen; it is your phone. It is what it is, and if it wasn't that way, then it wouldn't be that phone. This same principle applies to everything: whatever something is, that is what it is. This principle is essential to being able to understand anything about the world. Think about it: if it weren't for the law of identity, we wouldn't be able to pick out objects or ideas and differentiate them from other objects and ideas. I wouldn't know my phone from yours. For that matter, if it weren't for the law of identity, I wouldn't know the difference between my desk and the cat outside my office window. If it weren't for the law of identity, it would be impossible to have any meaningful understanding of the world around us, and we certainly wouldn't be able to have meaningful discussions with one another about the world.

Closely related to the law of identity (and just as important for understanding the world) is the *law of noncontradiction*. Like the law of identity, the principle of noncontradiction also points to the particular ways things exist (like your phone's size, shape, color, texture, and weight). Let's say your phone is grey. When I describe your phone, if it is true that "the phone is grey," then it is false that "the phone is not grey." To apply that more broadly, consider any statement at all, and its opposite (we will use the letter "S" to stand for any statement and "not-S" to stand for the opposite of the original statement "S"). The law of noncontradiction says that S and not-S cannot both be true. Said differently, for any two statements that contradict one another, the two statements cannot both be true at the same time and in the same sense. That last part is important ("at the same time and in the same sense"). If "your phone is grey" is true, then "your phone is not grey" can't possibly be true. But if you paint your phone some other color, then it was true that "your phone is grey," but now it is true that "your phone is not grey." Since those two statements are true at different times, it isn't a violation of the law of noncontradiction. Using a different illustration, sometimes people will say, "his greatest strength is also his greatest weakness." Since a weakness means "not a strength," then it seems that this phrase violates the law of noncontradiction. But usually, a statement like that just means that something that is a strength in one sense is a weakness in a completely different sense. So this is also not a violation of the law of noncontradiction.

Finally, the *law of excluded middle* follows from the same common sense that helps us understand the law of noncontradiction. The law of noncontradiction asserts that any statement, S, and its opposite, not-S, cannot both be true at the same time and in the same sense. Implied in this principle is the idea that either S or not-S must be true, and there are no other choices available. In fact, this is why this principle is called "excluded middle," because it recognizes the common-sense idea that any clearly articulated statement must be either true or false—there is no middle ground between a statement being true or false. There simply isn't anything "in the middle" between two options

IS LOGIC CULTURAL?

Because ancient Greek philosophers are famous for having studied logic in a formal way, some people have suggested that the logic they discussed is limited to that culture. It is suggested that logic is not universal but rather relative to culture. But consider the claim that "the laws of logic are not universal." The only way to meaningfully assert this claim is if you are first assuming that either the laws of logic are universal, or they are relative. You are further assuming that they cannot be both universal and relative at the same time and in the same sense. To make that claim in a meaningful way, you have to first assume that the laws of logic *are* universal. The claim that logic is relative to culture is self-defeating.

that contradict each other. For example, either "God exists" is true, or its opposite, "God does not exist," is true. There is no middle ground between those statements. Either "my phone is grey" or "my phone is not grey." There is no middle between "the earth is flat" and "the earth is not flat." Because the choices are contradictory to one another, there is no middle ground between the two options available, and one of those options must be true.[1]

These common-sense principles have stood the test of time because every rational person recognizes them as common sense. While some critics of traditional logic have attempted to refute them, the supposed refutations always turn out to be confusions or misunderstandings of what the principles mean. Without these laws, we wouldn't be able to think rationally, and we certainly wouldn't be able to talk to other people about what we believe or what is true.

Logical Arguments

Speaking of misunderstanding, perhaps no word in the study of logic is more commonly misunderstood among beginning philosophy students than the word *argument*. If your roommate came to you and said, "I just had an argument with my best friend," would you think this is good news or bad news? In everyday conversation, the word *argument* is used to refer to a heated dispute, a sharp disagreement between two people, or a shouting match. It carries the negative connotation of anger, loud voices, or being upset. With this kind of negativity surrounding the word, it might be a bit off-putting to skim through the table of contents of a philosophy book to see that "arguments" will be addressed. Fortunately, that is not the kind of argument we want to address here.

In logic, an argument is the presentation of reasons in support of a belief or claim. When a person offers an argument, that person is simply describing why they think that a particular claim is true. Arguments follow some established principles and generally follow specific patterns of structure and order. Just about every introductory philosophy textbook that addresses argumentation gives the same example to illustrate what an argument is. The example uses the name of Socrates, who was a philosopher in ancient Greece. The example goes like this:

1. All humans are mortal.
2. Socrates is a human.
3. Therefore, Socrates is mortal.

In this short example, we see the basic features of a logical argument. First, notice that the final statement offered is the main claim that is being made. The point of the argument seems to be to show that "Socrates is mortal" is a true statement. (The clue is the word *therefore*.) The term used for the main claim in any argument is *conclusion*. It is called the conclusion because that is where the line of reasoning necessarily leads us. In this example argument, "Socrates is mortal" is the conclusion of the line of reasoning. The other two statements in that example are called premises. A premise is any statement offered as a reason why we should think that the conclusion is true. If an argument has more than one premise, they will work together, being logically connected to each other and to the conclusion. In the example argument, you can see that the premises work in that way. The argument is trying to establish Socrates' mortality, so it is relevant to know that he is a human and that all humans are mortal. If those two premises are true, then the conclusion must be true. As in our example, when arguments are written out like this, the statements are usually numbered. You can see that statements (1) and (2) are the premises, and statement (3) is the conclusion. We will present additional examples and explanations of argument structure in the following chapters, but for now it will suffice to say that all logical arguments share the same basic features: they are composed of a conclusion (a claim being supported) and one or more premises (statements of evidence) that are logically connected to the conclusion and are designed to show that the conclusion is true.

Given this description, you can probably see that crafting a good argument is somewhat of a formal, systematic exercise that takes some logical skill. Nevertheless, arguments are very much a matter of common sense. They arise in everyday conversation quite often, perhaps more than you realize it. Almost no one wants a heated dispute, but in all kinds of everyday situations, people often want logical arguments. If a friend asks you to cancel your plans for Friday night and hang out with her instead, you probably will want your friend to give good reasons why you should do that. What you are asking for in that situation is an argument: you want your friend to present good, logically connected reasons why you should do as she has asked. When a preacher delivers a sermon asking the congregation to believe something, someone listening might naturally react with the question, "Why should I believe that?" This question is the demand for an argument: a systematic presentation of good reasons why we should believe what the preacher is asking us to believe. When a prosecutor claims that the accused person is guilty of the crime, the jury will want to hear clear, logically compelling reasons why they should believe this claim. In countless similar situations, we will find ourselves in circumstances in which an argument is exactly what is needed.

Why Arguments?

Hopefully, this short example and description helps you to see why arguments are such an important part of philosophy in general and logic in particular. However, we want to highlight a few reasons why everyone should be keenly interested in argumentation.

First, arguments are essential if we want to persuade others that a particular claim is true. As we stated, the primary focus of logic is on the reasonableness of our beliefs. The task of showing that a belief is true begins with laying out the logical evidence showing that the belief is reasonable. If you are taking an honest approach, you don't want people to just take your word for it or to adopt a new belief based only on your ability to give a good speech. This is especially true with the most important beliefs that we have, such as beliefs about God, morality, and the meaning of life. If you want to persuade others, you will want to appeal to their reason; you want them to adopt the new belief because they really believe it. You want them to "own it," or discover the truth of it for themselves. The best way to do that is to lay out the logical reasoning that supports that belief.

Second, logical arguments can help us evaluate our current beliefs in our quest to find truth. If we have a cherished belief that we begin to doubt, constructing an argument that shows the rational support for that belief can greatly increase our confidence. Conversely, we may discover that some belief we hold dear doesn't really have any good logical support, but if we are interested in believing the truth and not just maintaining the *status quo*, that is also a good thing. For any important belief that we have, we can engage in the practice of considering arguments for and against those beliefs. This process is far from perfect, but using arguments in this way certainly can help us get closer to truth.

Finally, arguments can also help us evaluate competing claims that we hear espoused by others. As we suggested, the world can be a confusing place, with all kinds of competing ideas coming at us from all directions. In the face of this potential confusion, the logical argument is one of the best tools we have available to sort through competing claims to see which ones have the best rational support. When we understand good logic, we are protected from being swept away by our emotions or being led astray by fancy-sounding talk. We can demand arguments from others who are making competing claims and carefully consider the evidence offered in support of those claims. Arguments help us sort through the many options in the marketplace of ideas so that we can know better what to believe.

Conclusion

In this chapter, we defined logic and explained why it is such an important part of philosophy. At the start of the chapter, we suggested that there is a tight connection between thinking properly and living a happy, fulfilled life. There is also a close connection between thinking properly and being able to discover the answers to the most important questions that we have about life. So at this point, it is important to make sure we don't lose sight of the overarching goal. When studying logic, it is essential to remember that we aren't primarily interested in following logical rules or making sure we construct arguments that follow a proper structure. Instead, we are studying logic so that we can build the everyday skill of thinking properly. Thinking properly, of course, means learning how to follow the principles of commonsense logic. In the next chapter, we will take another step toward building this skill by focusing on a particular kind of reasoning called *deductive reasoning*.

Questions for Reflection

1. In your experience, is "common sense" common?
2. Which of your most important beliefs is least reasonable?
3. How is the concept of *argument* in this chapter different from the way you have heard others use that word?

For Further Reading

Byerly, T. Ryan. *Introducing Logic and Critical Thinking: The Skills of Reasoning and the Virtues of Inquiry*. Grand Rapids: Baker Academic, 2017.

Dickinson, Travis. *Logic and the Way of Jesus: Thinking Critically and Christianly*. Nashville: B&H Academic, 2022.

Holland, Jr., Richard A., and Benjamin K. Forrest. *Good Arguments: Making Your Case in Writing and Public Speaking*. Grand Rapids: Baker Academic, 2017.

NOTES

1. While all claims must be either true or false, we will often find ourselves in the position of not knowing whether it is true or false, or (worse) not even knowing how to figure out whether it is true or false. In cases such as this, the best we might be able to do is say that the claim is possibly true. The law of the excluded middle assures us that the claim is indeed either true or false; but that does not mean that we are always in a position to say confidently whether it is true or false.

CHAPTER 7

What Is Deductive Reasoning?

Logic is the study of how to think properly. It is connected to something that all humans have: the ability to reason. This faculty gives us common sense, which we use to think about, analyze, and evaluate how beliefs fit together so we can better understand the world. The previous chapter introduced reasoning in general terms, providing an overview of the three basic principles of logic and introducing logical arguments. In this chapter, we take the next step by describing more details about what reasoning is and about the kinds of reasoning that are commonly used.

Reasoning is what we do when we are evaluating the logical connection between beliefs we already have and new information about the world that we encounter. It is an activity of the mind in which we begin with existing knowledge and then use logical arguments to make judgments and draw conclusions in our quest for truth. Two of the most common forms of reasoning are known as inductive and deductive. We will address inductive reasoning later; this chapter introduces deductive reasoning.

Deductive Reasoning

Deductive reasoning is the process of concluding what must be true, if we first assume that other relevant statements are true. Said the other way around, deductive arguments are designed to show that their conclusions must be true, if we first assume that other relevant statements are true. Perhaps the best way to explain this is with an example. Here is one we used in the previous chapter:

1. All humans are mortal.
2. Socrates is a human.
3. Therefore, Socrates is mortal.

This deductive argument first assumes that two relevant statements about the world are true: (1) all humans are mortal, and (2) Socrates is a human. The truth of these two statements shows conclusively that the third statement (3) must also be true, and this is the nature of deductive reasoning. We hope you can easily see that if it is true that all humans are mortal, and if it is true that Socrates is a human, then this leads us inescapably to the conclusion that Socrates is mortal. To employ the terminology that we introduced in the previous chapter, if we assume that the two premises of this deductive argument are true, this shows us clearly that the conclusion of the argument is also true. This is the way that deductive reasoning functions.

If we are trying to figure out what is true (and what isn't true), deductive arguments can be really helpful. After all, if we are thinking about whether Socrates is mortal, the example argument tells us that he surely is. Notice that the argument doesn't lead us to a wishy-washy conclusion like, "Therefore, Socrates might be mortal." It gives us a 100 percent guarantee that if it is true that all men are mortal, and if it is true that Socrates is a man, then Socrates is certainly mortal. No doubt about it. One of the ways to see this guarantee is to notice that the factual information presented in the conclusion is already contained—implicitly—in the premises. The conclusion, (3) Socrates is mortal, simply makes explicit (Socrates' mortality) what is already implied in the premises. All logically correct deductive arguments will share these two main features that we've discovered in this example: the truth of the premises guarantees the truth of the conclusion, and all the information in the conclusion is already contained, implicitly, in the premises.

Validity

For an argument to support its conclusion, it needs true premises. But if you were paying close attention in reading the previous paragraphs, you noticed that we sneaked in another important qualification for a deductive argument to successfully show that its conclusion is true. It isn't enough for the premises to be true. The argument also must be logically correct. By "logically correct," we mean that the argument offers premises that have the proper logical relationship to each other and to the conclusion. This proper logical relationship is seen when the truth of the premises guarantees the truth of the conclusion. The special term we use in philosophy to refer to a logically correct argument is the word *valid*. A valid deductive argument is simply one that is logically correct. To be successful in showing that its conclusion is true, a deductive argument must satisfy both conditions: the premises must be true, and the argument must be valid.

But what if the argument is not valid? What if the truth of the premises would not guarantee that the conclusion is true? We use the word *fallacious* to describe any argument that is not valid. A fallacious argument makes some kind of logical mistake, such that the premises don't have the proper logical relationship to the conclusion and thus are not able to guarantee that the conclusion is true. We use the word *fallacy* to refer to a mistake in reasoning, and an argument is fallacious if it contains one or more fallacies. A fallacious deductive argument is one in which the truth of the premises does not guarantee that the conclusion is true.

Both of the terms *valid* and *fallacy* can have entirely different uses in everyday conversation. The word *valid* is often used as a synonym for *true*, but that isn't what it means in logic. An argument is valid if there is a logical relationship between the statements, not if the statements in the argument are true. In fact, it is possible for valid deductive arguments to be composed of false statements. Here is an example of a valid argument that is made up of false premises and a false conclusion:

4. If Socrates is a cat, then Socrates is immortal.
5. Socrates is a cat.
6. Therefore, Socrates is immortal.

This argument is valid because if the premises were true, then the conclusion would also certainly be true; that is just what "valid" means. If it were true that all cats are immortal, and if it were true that Socrates is a cat, then it would certainly be true that Socrates is immortal. That is how we know that the argument is valid . . . but this has nothing to do with the fact that all the statements happen to be false. While this example is somewhat silly, you will sometimes see real arguments offered by others that are similar in that they are valid even though they have false premises and false conclusions. Here is another example of a valid deductive argument, this time one with false premises and a true conclusion:

7. If Pittsburgh is the capital city of Michigan, then it is the home of the Pittsburgh Steelers.
8. Pittsburgh is the capital city of Michigan.
9. Therefore, Pittsburgh is the home of the Pittsburgh Steelers.

In this example, the premises (7 and 8) are false; and the conclusion (9) is true. However, we can see that this argument is valid because if the premises were true, they would guarantee that the conclusion is also true. Again, whether the argument is valid is only a matter of how the statements are logically related to each other in a proper way, and not a matter of whether the statements are true or false. The premises of a valid deductive argument (no matter whether the premises are true or false) have the proper logical relationship to each other and to the conclusion of the argument, so that if the premises are true, then they would guarantee that the conclusion is true.

Similarly, in everyday conversation, the word *fallacy* is sometimes used to refer to something that is false, but that isn't what it means in logic. In logic, a *fallacy* is a mistake in reasoning. A fallacious argument—an argument that contains a fallacy—makes a logical mistake. Again, whether an argument is fallacious has nothing to do with whether any of the individual statements in the argument are true or false. Instead, it is only about how the statements are related to one another logically. Take a look at this example fallacious argument:

10. If it is raining, the sidewalk is wet.
11. The sidewalk is wet.
12. Therefore, it is raining.

Let's assume for the sake of discussion that all three of those statements are true. Nevertheless, the argument is still fallacious. We will talk more later about recognizing fallacies, but for now, you can easily see that this argument is fallacious by asking yourself this question: If (10) and (11) are true, would that *guarantee* that (12) is true? The answer, of course, is no. Even if the sidewalk is wet, this doesn't guarantee that it is raining. The sidewalk could have become wet from any number of causes, such as irrigation sprinklers, a spilled container of water, or melted snow. So even if (10) and (11) are true, they don't guarantee the truth of (12), and that is how we see that the argument is fallacious. To summarize, fallacious arguments contain some kind of mistake in reasoning and therefore don't actually support the conclusion. Only the true premises of a valid argument can support the conclusion of that argument.

The examples of valid deductive arguments we provided include one with true premises and a true conclusion, one with false premises and a false conclusion, and one with false premises and a true conclusion. However, a valid deductive argument can never have true premises and a false conclusion. Remember that if a deductive argument is valid, and if the premises are true, then the conclusion must be true. If an argument is fallacious, on the other hand, then whether the premises are true or false doesn't tell us anything about the conclusion, because the premises of a fallacious argument don't have the proper logical relationship to the conclusion.

Now that you understand the terms *valid* and *fallacious* and how they are used in logic, another important philosophical term should be understood. The term *sound* refers to an argument that is valid and has true premises. The reason we need this term is that the validity of the argument and the truth of the premises are two independent issues. An argument with true premises might be either valid or fallacious. Similarly, a valid argument might have either true premises or false premises. So we need this other special word, "sound," to describe arguments that both are valid and have true premises.

Standard Valid Deductive Forms

We know that good arguments must be valid and have true premises. But how do we know whether an argument is valid? A good deductive argument needs to be valid, but it isn't always easy to see whether the argument is valid at first glance. We might not be able to tell immediately whether the truth of the premises would guarantee the truth of the conclusion. However, some common valid forms are easily recognizable, and by learning a simple method of analyzing arguments, evaluating the validity of deductive arguments can become much easier.

To show you the simple method of analysis to determine the validity of a deductive argument, let's start with an example:

1. If Socrates is a human, then Socrates is mortal.
2. Socrates is a human.
3. Therefore, Socrates is mortal.

To start our analysis, remember that this argument's validity has nothing to do with whether its premises are true or false. Validity is about the relationship between the terms in the argument. So our first step in analysis is to get those factual statements out of the way (so to speak) by substituting each factual statement with a letter of the alphabet. Then we can focus on the logical relationship between the terms without becoming distracted by the content in the terms. This argument has only two factual statements, and those same two statements are arranged in various ways in the premises and the conclusion. The two factual statements are "Socrates is a human" and "Socrates is mortal." Let's use the letter P to stand for "Socrates is a human" and the letter Q to stand for "Socrates is mortal." It doesn't matter which letters we pick, as long as the letters we choose always stand for the same factual statement within an argument. Substituting P and Q for the factual statements, our argument looks like this:

1. If P, then Q.
2. P.
3. Therefore, Q.

Now, we just need one more step to simplify the argument by using symbols to represent the relationship between the factual terms. Notice that in the first premise, there is an "if . . . then" relationship between P and Q. This kind of statement is called a hypothetical statement. The first part of that statement (P) is called the *antecedent,* and the second (Q) is called the *consequent.* Any hypothetical statement is telling us that if the antecedent is true, then the consequent is also true. We can represent this hypothetical relationship with an arrow. We can also represent the "therefore" (designating the conclusion of the argument) by drawing a horizontal line after the premises and using the symbol ∴ to replace the word *therefore* designating the conclusion. This is how the simplified form looks compared to the original:

1. P→Q   If Socrates is a human, then Socrates is mortal.
2. P   Socrates is a human.
3. ∴ Q   Therefore, Socrates is mortal.

Now we can easily see how the terms in the argument are arranged, and it is much easier to see that it is valid. Recall our main test of validity: If the premises are true, do they guarantee the truth of the conclusion? The clear answer here is yes. If the two premises of this argument are true, the conclusion cannot possibly be false. It doesn't matter what factual content is represented by the letters P and Q, because we are just looking for validity in the argument, not the truth of the statements.

The benefit of doing the analysis this way is that any argument we see that follows the same form is also valid. Remember that the logical relationship between the statements is what determines whether the argument is valid. So for any argument we may encounter, if it follows this form, it is valid. This form is one of the most common valid forms that deductive arguments take, and there is a name for it: *modus ponens*. Often abbreviated MP, *modus ponens* means "mode of affirming." It gets its name from the fact that the second premise of the argument affirms the truth of the antecedent of the hypothetical statement in the first premise.

Another common valid form is called *modus tollens* (abbreviated MT), meaning "mode of denying." Here is its form:

1. $P \rightarrow Q$
2. $-Q$
3. $\therefore -P$

This argument form starts off just as MP, with a hypothetical statement in the first premise, but instead of the second premise affirming the truth of the antecedent, the second premise denies the truth of the consequent. The – symbol before the Q in the second premise indicates that Q is being denied. It is common to read this premise as "not Q," which is another way of saying "Q is false." Any argument that follows the MT form is valid. To help you see this, consider the following example:

1. $P \rightarrow Q$ If I studied hard all semester, then I got good grades.
2. $-Q$ I did not get good grades.
3. $\therefore -P$ Therefore, I did not study hard all semester.

In this example, P stands for "I studied hard all semester," and Q stands for "I got good grades." Premise 1 is the hypothetical statement, and premise 2 denies the truth of the consequent. If premise 1 is true, and if premise 2 is true, then the conclusion must be true. It can't possibly be false, so it is a valid argument. Any argument that follows this form, regardless of the factual content, is also valid.

Another common, valid form is known as the "hypothetical syllogism" (abbreviated HS). Here is its form and an example:

1. $P \rightarrow Q$ If I get a job, then I'm able to save money for a car.
2. $Q \rightarrow R$ If I'm able to save money for a car, then I'll be able to buy a car.
3. $\therefore P \rightarrow R$ Therefore, if I get a job, then I'll be able to buy a car.

Any argument we encounter that has three statements of fact that are arranged in this form is valid. If the premises are true, then the conclusion is guaranteed to be true.

We want to discuss two other common valid forms, but first we need another symbol. The v is a special symbol that stands for an "either / or . . . or both" relationship (sometimes called the "inclusive or" because at least one must be true, but they both could be true too). When you see something like "P v Q," that stands for "either P is true, or Q is true, or both P and Q are true." This relationship is called a *disjunct*, and a common argument form that uses this symbol is called the *disjunctive syllogism* (sometimes abbreviated DS). Here is what it looks like, along with an example:

1.	P v Q	Either the cookies have chocolate chips, or the cookies have raisins, or both.
2.	−Q	The cookies do not have raisins.
3.	∴ P	Therefore, the cookies have chocolate chips.

We hope you can see that if it is true that the cookies have either chocolate chips or raisins (first premise), and it is also true that the cookies do not have raisins (second premise), then it must be true that the cookies have chocolate chips. It is clear that it is valid. Any argument that follows this form is also valid, no matter what factual content is in the premises.

The last common valid form that we will show you is called the *constructive dilemma* (sometimes abbreviated CD). Here is what it looks like, along with an example. This time, just for variety's sake, we will use different letters of the alphabet (remember it doesn't matter what letters we pick, as long as we are consistent in how we substitute them):

1.	(A→B) and (C→D)	If I eat what is in my lunchbox, I'll eat a peanut butter sandwich; and if I go to the food court, I'll eat a chicken sandwich.
2.	A v C	Either I'll eat what is in my lunchbox, or I'll go to the food court, or both.
3.	∴ B v D	Therefore, either I'll eat a peanut butter sandwich, or I'll eat a chicken sandwich, or both.

Sometimes you'll see the CD arranged slightly differently, but the following two forms are logically equivalent:

1.	(A→B) and (C→D)	1.	A v C
2.	A v C	2.	A→B
3.	∴ B v D	3.	C→D
		4.	∴ B v D

These five common forms (MP, MT, HS, DS, and CD) are some of the most common forms of deductive arguments. It will be valuable to memorize these forms so that when you are analyzing arguments, you can more easily see whether those arguments fit one of these forms and are therefore valid.

Formal Fallacies

There are also a few common logical mistakes made in deductive arguments. It is important to become familiar with them so that when you see them in arguments, you can recognize them as fallacies. These fallacies are called *formal fallacies* because they are logical mistakes made in the form of the argument—the way in which the terms are arranged in relationship to one another. Each common fallacy has a name, and we will start by showing you the one known as "affirming the consequent." Here is what it looks like, along with an example:

1. P→Q   If it is raining, then the sidewalk is wet.
2. Q   The sidewalk is wet.
3. ∴ P   Therefore, it is raining.

Hopefully you recognize this example from earlier in the chapter. You already know that it is fallacious because even if the premises are true, that does not guarantee that the conclusion is true. To the untrained eye, this argument might look like it is MP; but it isn't. Recall that the second premise of the MP affirms the truth of the antecedent of the first premise. In this fallacious form, however, the second premise affirms the truth of the consequent from the hypothetical statement in the first premise. This is why this fallacy is called *affirming the consequent*. Any argument that follows this form is similarly fallacious and therefore cannot support its conclusion.

Another common fallacy is known as *denying the antecedent*. Here is what it looks like, along with an example:

1. P→Q   If your roommate is home, her car is in the garage.
2. –P   Your roommate is not home.
3. ∴ Q   Therefore, her car is not in the garage.

At first glance this might look like the valid MT. But notice that while the second premise of the MT denies the consequent from the first premise, this fallacious form denies the antecedent from the first premise (thus its name, "denying the antecedent"). The example we've offered will help you see why this is fallacious. Even if the first two premises of the example are true, it is still possible that her car is in the garage. Perhaps you are at the store and you see your roommate walk in, so you know she isn't at home. Nevertheless, it is possible that she got a ride from a friend and left her car parked in the garage. Yes, the conclusion could be true, but the truth of the premises in this argument do not guarantee that the conclusion is true, so we see that it is not valid.

We'll address one more common fallacious form. Here is the fallacy known as *affirming the disjunct* (or sometimes "false exclusionary"), along with an example:

1.	P v Q	Either the cookies have chocolate chips, or the cookies have raisins, or both.
2.	Q	The cookies have raisins.
3.	∴ –P	Therefore, the cookies do not have chocolate chips.

You might be tempted to think that this is perfectly valid; but it isn't. Recall that the "disjunct" relationship in the first premise is "either / or . . . or both." Since both P and Q could be true, then affirming the truth of Q in premise 2 does nothing to prove that P is false. Considering our example, just because the cookies have raisins in them doesn't mean that they don't also have chocolate chips. So, again, while it is possible that the conclusion is true, the truth of the two premises fails to guarantee the truth of the conclusion, so this form is not valid.

Conclusion

It is natural to reason deductively—it is just part of our commonsense reasoning abilities. Not only is it common but deductive reasoning is also an essential component to learning how to think properly, to communicate with others, to evaluate new ideas, to support our beliefs, and (ultimately) to discover the true answers to life's most important questions. The examples of deductive arguments that we offered here are fictitious and oversimplified, but we hope that they are close enough to real life that you are now able to recognize how deductive reasoning already fits into your life and has allowed you to think about the ways in which you have used the argument forms that we have described. Perhaps our discussion of formal fallacies has helped you see how common those are too. More important, we hope that now that you are aware of these common mistakes, you are more likely to avoid them in your own thinking.

In the next chapter, we will turn our attention to inductive reasoning, which is also both a matter of common sense and an essential component of the logical enterprise.

Questions for Reflection

1. In what ways have you used the terms *valid* and *fallacy* differently from the way they are used in this chapter?
2. Think of an argument you recently made in everyday conversation. Can you rephrase it so that it fits one of the common valid forms discussed in this chapter?
3. Can you think of anything you said recently that is an example of one of the common fallacies addressed in this chapter?

For Further Reading

Copi, Irving M., Carl Cohen, and Victor Rodych. *Introduction to Logic*, 15th ed. New York: Routledge, 2019.

Howard-Snyder, Frances, Daniel Howard-Snyder, and Ryan Wasserman. *The Power of Logic*, 6th ed. New York: McGraw-Hill, 2020.

CHAPTER 8

What Is Inductive Reasoning?

One of the things you may have noticed in our previous discussion of deductive reasoning is that it is all very cut-and-dry. Like following a math equation to the one right answer, deductive reasoning leads us down a clear path: if this is true, then that is true. But when we are thinking about real-life questions, we seldom have this kind of mathematical certainty. Instead, very often we face questions where we think, "Well, if this is true . . . then that is probably true." This is why inductive reasoning is so important, and that is what this chapter is all about. First, we will give a basic definition and compare the features of inductive arguments to the deductive arguments we discussed in the previous chapter. Then, we will discuss some more practical, ordinary ways inductive reasoning is used, including generalization, hypothesis confirmation, prediction, causation, and analogy.

Inductive Reasoning: The Basics

Inductive reasoning is the process of accumulating relevant evidence in order to conclude—based on that evidence—what is likely to be true. As such, an argument that makes use of inductive reasoning focuses on providing good, relevant evidence in support of the conclusion. For deductive arguments, if the form is valid and if the premises are true, the conclusion must be true. Here we have our first significant difference between the inductive and deductive approaches. While a sound deductive argument leads to certainty, an inductive argument can only show us what is likely to be true or probably true. Even if the premises of an inductive argument are true, this does not guarantee that the conclusion is true. A good inductive argument with true premises simply gives us good reason to accept the conclusion as true, even though there will always be room for doubt about whether the conclusion is true.

It might be tempting to think that inductive reasoning is inferior to deductive reasoning since it leaves room for doubt about the conclusion. That is not the case. In fact, inductive reasoning undergirds most ordinary informal reasoning, as well as the claims of natural science, history, psychology, political science, and a wide variety of other academic fields. Many think that inductive reasoning is superior to deductive reasoning because it helps us expand our knowledge. This leads to another significant difference between deductive and inductive reasoning. Recall that one of the main features of a deductive argument is that all the information in the conclusion of the argument is already contained, implicitly, in the premises. A deductive argument simply draws out what must be true in light of the premises, so in one sense the conclusion really doesn't tell us anything we don't already know. If we want to go beyond what we already know, inductive arguments can help. Consider this example inductive argument:

1. This cat has whiskers.
2. That cat has whiskers.
3. All cats that I have previously observed have whiskers.
4. Therefore, all cats have whiskers.

The premises of this argument present evidence that is limited to cats that I have observed, but the conclusion makes a statement about all cats, even the ones I haven't seen. Since the argument leads to a conclusion (about all cats) that is beyond current knowledge (only the cats already observed), it is giving us new information and expanding what we know. This is quite unlike deductive arguments, which have conclusions that simply draw out what is already stated in the premises.

Recall that a deductive argument is valid if the premises guarantee the truth of the conclusion. In that sense, a deductive argument is "all-or-nothing." If a deductive argument is valid, then we know that if its premises are true and the conclusion is guaranteed to be true, no new evidence can be added. But if a deductive argument is not valid, it fails to support the conclusion whether the premises are true or not. Moreover, a deductive argument's validity depends on its structure or form: the arrangement of the terms in the argument and the structural relationship between the premises and the conclusion.

All of this leads us to the third key difference between deductive and inductive arguments: inductive arguments are neither valid nor invalid in the same way deductive arguments are. Inductive arguments can indeed make mistakes in reasoning (called *informal fallacies*, which we address in chapter 9), but they do not need to conform to any structural patterns or rules. In determining whether an inductive argument is a good argument, rather than looking at the form or structure, we need to be concerned about whether the argument is strong or weak. The strength of inductive arguments is a matter of degree: they can be stronger or weaker. An inductive argument is strong if it offers good evidence, and weak if it does not. The stronger the argument, the more confidence we can have that the conclusion is true.

But what counts as "good evidence"? Few (if any) specific rules determine what makes for good evidence, but a reasonable place to start would be to focus on the amount, the type, and the relevance of the evidence. Take the argument about cats and their whiskers, for example. How can we increase our confidence in the conclusion that all cats have whiskers? One thing we can do is increase the number of cats we observe. If I've observed only a few cats, the fact that this small number of cats all have whiskers might indicate that all cats have whiskers, but I'm not very confident about it. So one obvious way to make an inductive argument stronger is simply by adding more evidence—in the case of the example, observing a larger number of cats that have whiskers makes the argument stronger. Along with the amount of evidence, the type of evidence is also important. We could observe cats of varying ages, of different breeds, or from different places in the world to rule out the possibility that only cats of a specific age, or of a particular breed, or from a certain part of the world have whiskers. It is also important to focus on relevance. If we want to know whether all cats have whiskers, it does us no good to observe other animals with whiskers (say, mice, beavers, or walruses). Since the conclusion is about cats, only evidence pertaining to cats is relevant. It also does no good to consider evidence about cats' ears or eyes, since those are also not relevant to the argument. An appropriate amount of evidence, an appropriate type of evidence, and evidence that is appropriately relevant all make for a strong inductive argument that increases our confidence in the truth of the conclusion.

Inductive Reasoning in Practice

Deduction has significant limitations because the truth of the conclusion always depends on the truth of the premises. If the audience already believes the premises, all is well and good. A valid deductive argument can show that if you believe the premises, then it is irrational to deny the conclusion. But if the audience does not already believe the premises, then the deductive argument by itself will not accomplish the goal of demonstrating that the conclusion is true. Since inductive arguments focus on accumulating good evidence in support of a conclusion, they can be quite persuasive and therefore practically useful in a wide variety of contexts. In what follows, we will highlight several common ways that inductive reasoning is used.

Generalization from Particulars

Inductive reasoning is also commonly used to draw general principles from observing particular cases. Consider the example argument about cats and whiskers. Each of the cats observed is a particular instance of a cat having whiskers. From those individual observations, a general (or in this case, universal) principle is concluded: all cats have whiskers. For a more serious real-life example, you can think of discussion forums where owners of products review and share information with one another: if every reported example of a product has a particular flaw, then it is reasonable to conclude that all examples of the product have the same flaw. On the other hand, if every reported example has excellent performance, then it is reasonable to conclude that all of them have excellent performance. Whenever we use reviews like this to decide which product to purchase, we are using inductive reasoning to draw a generalization based on specific examples of customer reviews.

It is sometimes (erroneously) said that *all* inductive arguments reason from particulars to universal generalizations, but this is not the case. Consider this inductive argument that uses universal generalizations as evidence leading to a particular case:

1. All cats are mortal.
2. All dogs are mortal.
3. All muskrats are mortal.
4. Etc.
5. Therefore, this creature (even though I have no idea what it is) is probably mortal also.

While drawing generalizations from particular observations is an important type of inductive reasoning, don't make the mistake of thinking that this is the very definition of inductive reasoning. Instead, remember the definition: inductive reasoning accumulates evidence that points to a probable or likely conclusion.

Confirming a Hypothesis

Whenever we observe an unusual or unexplained fact or event in the world, it is common to try to think of a reasonable explanation. The explanation we think of is called a *hypothesis*—like an explanatory "starting point" that comes during the early stages of observing the available evidence and the search for an explanation of the as-yet-unexplained fact. As more evidence comes in, we need to test our hypothesis to see if the conclusion is still reasonable. This kind of inductive reasoning is common in scientific research as well as a wide variety of other situations.

Consider, for example, the case of a major crime. Long before the trial takes place, an unusual fact about the world has been observed: the crime was committed! Immediately upon discovering this, the police begin to gather evidence. Pretty soon the police, and later the prosecutor, become convinced that a particular person has committed the crime. The hypothesis put forth is that this person committed the crime, in this way, and for this reason. The hypothesis is designed to give a coherent, reasonable explanation for why and how the crime was committed. In order to persuade the jury that the hypothesis is true, the prosecuting attorney gathers evidence that seems to confirm the hypothesis:

- The defendant's fingerprints were found at the crime scene.
- Witnesses place the defendant at the scene of the crime and at the approximate time the crime occurred.
- The defendant previously voiced an intent to commit the crime.
- The defendant had a strong motive to commit the crime.

Once this evidence has been used to confirm the hypothesis, it is then presented to the jury to conclude whether the hypothesis is the most reasonable explanation. Like all inductive cases, it is impossible to prove that the defendant is guilty beyond all doubt, but the standard for our legal system is beyond *reasonable* doubt. The prosecutor is responsible for gathering enough evidence to show that it isn't reasonable to doubt the guilt of the person on trial. If there is reasonable doubt, then the jury finds the defendant not guilty. Of course, what is considered "reasonable" will vary between jurors. Therefore, a good prosecutor will attempt to make the case as strong as possible by gathering as much compelling evidence as possible.

Prediction

No one really has the ability to predict the future with 100 percent certainty, but inductive reasoning is especially useful to get a good idea of what will happen in the future. This is quite common in scientific and engineering endeavors.

If you want to land a rover on Mars, you need to know a great deal about the future. No matter how well the rocket and flight control systems are designed and built, the rover will never land on Mars unless the position of the planet relative to the earth can be accurately predicted about seven months in advance. These calculations rely on repeated observations of Mars's orbit around the sun, along with how it moves throughout its orbit, Earth's orbit around the sun, and the relative position of Mars to Earth at various times of the year. These repeated observations count as good evidence in an inductive case for where Mars will be seven months after the spaceflight begins. Like any example of inductive reasoning, we are not certain about where Mars will be seven months from now; but the more evidence we have, the more confident we can be in our prediction.

Using inductive reasoning to predict the future is also quite useful in ordinary day-to-day life. You are confident that if you don't leave the house by 7:00 a.m., you will miss the 7:30 a.m. bus. Why? You are relying on repeated past observations of how long it takes you to walk to the bus stop and the times that the bus previously arrived at the bus stop in order to make an inductive case. Likewise, you could reason that since you got sick every time you previously ate at that restaurant, it is reasonable to conclude that you will get sick if you eat there again. If you just got sick one time, it is probably not reasonable to think it will happen again, but the more often and more consistently it occurs, the more confident you are in your prediction. Every time your roommate borrowed money from you in the past, she has paid you back as promised, so it is reasonable to conclude that she will pay you back this time too. In each example, we are relying on inductive reasoning that depends on a pattern of consistent observations in the past acting as evidence for the predicted conclusion.

Causation

Reasoning from causes to effects is another common type of inductive reasoning that is similar to prediction. We show interest in cause-and-effect reasoning when we ask questions like, Why is the unemployment rate high? What brought about the increase in gasoline prices? What difference will the tax cut make on the overall economy? Why aren't poverty rates declining faster? In asking these kinds of questions, either we are observing an effect and wondering about its cause, or we are considering an action and wondering what effects will come as a result. Answering these questions requires a type of inductive reasoning in which causal evidence is gathered to draw a conclusion.

In a cause-and-effect situation, one of the most important kinds of evidence is correlation. Correlation refers to the repeated observation of two associated events: every time it rains, water comes into the basement; whenever I run, I get a pain in my right ankle; whenever I put premium gas in the car, it gets better gas mileage. One or two occurrences might not get our attention (depending on the situation), but when we constantly observe the associated events, we begin to correlate one with the other. Eventually our observations will lead us to suspect a cause-and-effect relationship that explains the correlation of the associated events. Once we have established the correlation, we can add further evidence based on relevant differences or common threads. If the only relevant difference between last year's frail looking rose bushes that produced only two flowers and this year's thriving rose bushes with many flowers is the new type of fertilizer used, then we have good reason to suspect that the new fertilizer has some causal connection to the healthier bush. If we notice that perfect class attendance is the only relevant common thread among students who earned the highest final grades, we may be justified in believing that there is a causal connection between class attendance and a high final grade.

As we engage in this type of reasoning, we should avoid a couple of mistakes. One possible mistake would be to reverse the cause and effect. In doing this, we might correctly conclude that there is a cause-and-effect relationship between two events, but it might be that what we thought was the cause is actually the effect, and what we thought was the effect is actually the cause. For example, it might be easy to assume that depictions of immorality in entertainment cause a general decline in morality in society, but it might actually be that a general decline in morality in society leads to the depictions of immorality in entertainment. We also must be on the lookout for the possibility that the two correlated events don't have a cause-and-effect relationship with each other, but rather they are both effects of some common cause. If we constantly observe in various cities that an increase in church attendance and an increase in crime rates are correlated, we might be tempted to think that there is a causal connection between the two, but if we also observe growing populations in those areas, it makes more sense to conclude that the growing population is the common cause of increases in both church attendance and crime.

Analogy

Drawing inferences from analogy is another common form of inductive reasoning. An *analogy* is the comparison between two different things that are similar in some way. This comparison usually depends on our knowledge of one of the items in order to learn about the other. It is common in ordinary communication to make use of simile and metaphor as figures of speech to convey the analogy. For instance, Jesus said, "I am the bread of life. Whoever comes to me will never go hungry, and whoever believes in me will never be thirsty"

(John 6:35). In this metaphor, Jesus uses an analogy to compare himself to food and water. He is saying that just as food and water provide sustenance for life, so too is Jesus the source of true sustenance for eternal life. People understand some feature of bread and water, and Jesus uses analogy as a way to help them understand something about him.

Arguments by analogy do likewise. When an argument is based on analogy, the conclusion suggests that because two items are similar in one respect, they are also similar in another important respect. If two objects, x and y, both share characteristics A, B, and C, and if object x also has characteristic D, then it is reasonable to conclude that object y probably also has characteristic D. A famous example of an argument by analogy is William Paley's watchmaker argument for God's existence. Paley suggests that an item like a mechanical watch has design-like features that lead us to conclude that someone designed and made the watch. He then suggests that the universe also has design-like features. So he asks us to draw an inference based on the analogy: just as the design-like features of the watch lead us to conclude that there is a watchmaker, so also the design-like features of the universe lead us to conclude that there is a universe maker.[1]

Another form of analogy takes place every time you exhibit empathy toward another person. Empathy is the ability to put yourself into the shoes of another person. When you think about a situation that another person is experiencing, you can imagine what that other person must be feeling. If I observe a friend experiencing something similar to what I have experienced in the past, then I could draw on my past experience and the similarities to make a reasonable conclusion about what it would be like for me to be in the situation my friend is in. From there, the analogy is straightforward: another person is similar to me in relevant ways, so the other person is likely experiencing something like what I think I would experience if I were in that situation. Let's say my friend just injured her leg playing softball. Even if I have never had the exact injury from the exact same cause, I do know what it is like to have a similar leg injury. So it is reasonable for me to think that my friend is experiencing feelings similar to what I experienced when I injured my leg. Analogies based on similar events, circumstances, and experiences allow us to laugh with those who laugh, cry with those who cry, and celebrate with those who have good reason to celebrate.

Conclusion

In this chapter, we have defined the basics of inductive reasoning and provided several common types of inductive reasoning that are important for ordinary reasoning. In providing these examples, we hope that you not only learned what inductive reasoning is but also that you now see how often it might be useful in your day-to-day experience with commonsense reasoning. In the next chapter, we will turn to a discussion of several possible mistakes in reasoning that are quite common (and tempting) when we are engaged in inductive reasoning.

Questions for Reflection

1. Other than what we named, what do you think makes for "good" evidence for an inductive argument?
2. In making predictions about what effects your actions will bring about, what kinds of evidence can you use?
3. How has analogy helped you understand something difficult for you to understand without it?

For Further Reading

Browne, M. Neil, and Stuart M. Keeley. *Asking the Right Questions: A Guide to Critical Thinking*, 12th ed. New York: Pearson, 2018.

NOTES

1. William Paley, *Natural Theology*, Oxford World Classics (New York: Oxford University Press, 2006), 7–30. The argument is explained in the first three chapters of his book, and in the remainder, Paley goes on to offer many examples of "design-like features" in the natural world, in order to make the case that the analogy does reasonably lead to the conclusion that God exists.

CHAPTER 9

What Are Informal Fallacies?

Introduction

In chapter 6, we defined a fallacy as a mistake in reasoning. We also addressed a few of the fallacies that can occur in deductive arguments. These are called *formal fallacies* because the logical mistake is found in the form or structure of the argument. In this chapter, we want to address fallacies of a different kind. We want to address *informal fallacies*, which are mistakes in reasoning related to the content of the argument and not related to the form or structure of the argument. Since they don't pertain to deductive inferences (as formal fallacies do), informal fallacies are commonly seen in inductive arguments and in other kinds of everyday reasoning and argumentation.

Informal fallacies are very common. Everyone engages in reasoning and argumentation, but relatively few take the time to learn how to think and reason properly. So it isn't surprising that these kinds of mistakes occur frequently. The ones we mention in this chapter are some of the more common ones. We all need to be aware of these fallacies because they are tempting to commit. Remember that the person presenting an argument already believes that the conclusion (main claim) is true. Believing that the conclusion of an argument is true can create an overwhelming bias that causes us to overlook poor reasoning and logical mistakes that are offered in support of that claim. If you are not diligent in your application of logic and the principles of good reasoning, you likely would accept as valid any argument at all, no matter how bad the logic, as long as that argument seems to support your currently held beliefs. You might even think that a very bad argument is actually a very good argument just because it supports something you already believe.[1]

Before we get into the fallacies, we must make an important reminder and an important disclaimer.

- The reminder: Even if an argument contains a fallacy, the conclusion of that argument might still be true. We are not justified in saying that the conclusion of an argument is false just because the argument is fallacious (remember, "fallacious" does not mean "false").
- The disclaimer: In the following list, we give each fallacy a name, but in many respects, these names are arbitrary and are based merely on common convention. Do not take the list we offer as an official list of names. Rather, you should think of them as convenient labels for the purpose of helping you identify the mistakes in reasoning that are described. Other philosophy texts may name or categorize them differently. The important thing is for you to understand the kind of logical mistake we are talking about so that you can properly analyze the mistakes you see and avoid them in your own thinking.

Some Common Fallacies

Ad Hominem

The term *ad hominem* is Latin for "to the person." This fallacy occurs when someone attacks the character of another person instead of addressing that person's argument. When someone commits this fallacy, they are implying that a claim must be false because of some negative (but irrelevant) character trait in the person making the claim. An example of this would be saying, "The CEO of Corporation X is greedy and cares only about money, so of course he is wrong when he says that raising the minimum wage is bad for the economy." This is fallacious because whether the CEO is greedy and cares only about money is not relevant to the question of whether raising the minimum wage is good or bad for the economy. Even if the CEO is greedy and doesn't care about other people's well-being, his claim could still be true. To avoid this fallacy in your own thinking and arguments, you should resist the temptation to focus on the bad qualities people have and focus instead only on relevant information and evidence as you analyze arguments and claims.

However, not all personal attacks are fallacious. When a jury relies on the honesty of a witness in a trial, it is relevant to raise questions about that witness's honesty. It is also not fallacious to simply attack someone's character independent of any discussion of an argument or claims. It is certainly impolite to go around making character attacks, but it isn't fallacious unless the character attack is offered for the purpose of suggesting that a person's claims are false.

Ad Populum

The term *ad populum* means "to the people." This fallacy attempts to suggest that if a claim or belief is popular, it must be true: "So many people throughout history and all across the world have believed in God, so God must exist." This is fallacious reasoning because the number of people who happen to hold a belief is entirely irrelevant to whether the belief is true. This fallacy also occurs when you suggest that a belief is false because it is unpopular: "No one believes that! It can't be true." This fallacy is sometimes referred to as the bandwagon fallacy or the appeal to peer pressure.

Of course, it can be psychologically powerful to use popularity as a way to persuade someone that the popular belief is true or that the unpopular belief is false, and this gives rise to the phenomenon called "groupthink." Most people have a very strong desire to conform to their peer groups. Sometimes people may think that certain types of activities—such as academic work or science—are immune from the pressures of groupthink. This is not the case, however. Many scholars in diverse fields of study (even in the sciences) will advance claims that are popular, rather than those that have the greatest evidential support, so that they can gain esteem among their peers in the larger academic community. But truth is not subject to a popularity contest. To avoid this fallacy, each of us must prioritize truth over being accepted by others.

Appeals to Authority

Expertise is (rightly) valued. Appealing to a properly qualified authority to settle a debated point can be persuasive. In most cases, however, appealing to expert authority figures is fallacious. The stereotypical form of this fallacy is an appeal to an unqualified authority. This fallacy occurs whenever an expert in one area is cited in order to advance a claim in an unrelated topic or field of study. Professional athletes are often used in marketing materials and cited as authorities in their endorsement of shoes. Expert scientists are regularly cited to support claims in religion or ethics. Expert theologians are sometimes cited to settle biological questions. Each of these is fallacious (at least in part) because the person has no expertise in the relevant topic.

Even when the authority figure cited is an expert in the relevant topic, however, it is still usually fallacious to issue the appeal. The simple reason for this is that the expertise of a particular individual is irrelevant to the question of whether a particular claim is true or false. The proverbial "97 percent of scientists agree" is a classic example of this fallacy (with an *ad populum* thrown in for good measure). Whenever a majority of scientists reaches consensus about a particular controversial matter, it should (at the very least) point us to the possibility that the claim is true. But it should be obvious to everyone that scientists are often wrong about important scientific matters, and being unanimously wrong is not without precedent. Here are three such examples:

- It was once taken as a scientific fact that living organisms regularly generate spontaneously from nonliving matter.
- The geocentric model of the universe was once dominant among astronomers.
- Medical doctors in the past often recommended particular brands of "healthy" cigarettes and encouraged people to consume beverages containing cocaine.

Simply put, whether expert authority figures believe that a claim is true has nothing to do with whether the claim is true.

Of course, it isn't always fallacious to appeal to authority. It is quite reasonable to accept the testimony of a lawyer or legislator in questions about what the law is or a professional athlete in questions about the rules of their sport. It is not fallacious to rely on the testimony of experts when they are reporting basic facts that an expert in that field should know. But it is fallacious to rely on those same experts regarding the truth or falsity of claims—even claims within their field of study. To avoid the appeal to authority fallacy in our own thinking, it is essential that we learn to differentiate expert testimony about facts from fallacious appeals to authority, as in this example:

- Fallacious reasoning: 97 percent of climate scientists believe in human-caused global climate change; therefore, human-caused global climate change is real.
- Good reasoning: 97 percent of climate scientists affirm the accuracy of the data correlating changes in global climate with specific human activities, so the data are probably accurate.

Appeals to Emotion

Emotions are powerful and have a strong influence on our beliefs. Therefore, appeals to emotion are often used to persuade people to accept claims as true or to take certain actions. The appeal to force (sometimes called the *ad baculum* fallacy, from the Latin word for "stick") is an appeal to emotion designed to cause a person to act based on fear in response to a threat. This might occur if you suddenly begin to adopt the beliefs of your teacher if your teacher subtly lets you know that disagreement leads to a lower grade. The appeal to pity is an attempt to persuade someone to do something based on pity: imagine a TV advertisement soliciting donations based on images of sick-looking puppies or malnourished children. Fear and pity, along with love, outrage, wishful thinking, and countless others, are used as convenient tools of persuasion, urging us to adopt a viewpoint or take some action. To avoid this fallacy in our own reasoning and argumentation, it is essential to check our emotions and focus intently on relevant evidence to support our claims. We are not advocating ridding ourselves of all emotions. We believe that emotions are God-given, part of our human makeup, and serve many good purposes. At the same time, emotions can significantly interfere with logical, reasonable, and good thinking. When it comes to good reasoning, we must learn to master our emotions and keep them in their appropriate place.

Circular Reasoning

The circular reasoning fallacy is sometimes called by its Latin name, *petitio principii*, or by the term *begging the question*. This shouldn't be confused with the common term *beg the question*, which just refers to a question being raised that must be answered. The begging the question fallacy (circular reasoning) occurs whenever the truth of one or more premises offered in an argument depends on the truth of the conclusion, as in these examples:

- "We know that God must exist, because the Bible says so, because the Bible is God's Word, and God cannot lie." In order to believe that the Bible is God's Word (premise), you would already have to believe that God exists (conclusion). Rather than being an argument for God's existence, this is simply an unsupported and circular assertion that God exists.
- "We know that God does not exist because God is supposed to be a spiritual being and there is no such thing as a spiritual realm. The only kinds of things that exist are physical objects." Obviously if God does exist, then it is not true that only physical objects exist. Rather than being an argument against God's existence, this is simply an unsupported assertion.

This fallacy also occurs whenever the conclusion of the argument is logically equivalent to one or more premises. In these cases, the fallacy can be more subtle and difficult to detect:

- You can trust me because I am an honest person.
- Climbing a ladder is dangerous because you could get hurt if you fall.

- Everyone wants to buy this kind of phone because it is the most popular kind there is.
- The death penalty is immoral because killing people is wrong.

A variation of circular reasoning fallacy is called the *fallacy of the complex question*, sometimes called the *loaded question fallacy*. This fallacy occurs (as its name suggests) in the form of a question—specifically, a question that assumes the truth of some very important relevant facts that should have been proven but have simply been assumed. This fallacy is often designed to trap someone into admitting guilt or fault:

- [Police officer to driver just pulled over]: "How much have you had to drink tonight?" This question is legitimate only after it has been established that the suspect has consumed alcoholic drinks recently before driving.
- "Have you stopped lying to your best friend yet?"
- "How many tests have you cheated on?"

Circularity in our own reasoning can be difficult to avoid, for the primary reason that we already believe both the conclusion of the argument (the main claim we are making) and the supporting evidence. It takes diligence to avoid circularity by examining carefully why we believe the supporting evidence. Unless we have independent reasons for the supporting evidence, then we are in danger of being circular in our reasoning.

Confirmation Bias

Confirmation bias is a common psychological phenomenon that causes people to favor evidence supporting their beliefs and disregard evidence opposing their beliefs. While this isn't technically a fallacy, we include it in this list because confirmation bias can lead our ordinary reasoning abilities astray and cause us to believe things without proper rational support. This is what we were referring to in the introduction to this chapter: Because we already believe the claims that we make, we will tend to think that all the evidence supports our claims (or at least we will act as if all the evidence is on our side). For example, *cherry picking* is a fallacy that arises out of our confirmation bias. This fallacy occurs whenever we are attempting to make a case for a claim, and, rather than take an objective look at all the evidence, we focus only on the evidence that seems to support our claim.

SOCIAL MEDIA AND FALLACIOUS THINKING

The social media bubble changes the way we think about the world. Social media platforms are designed to learn what you like, based on what stories you click on or what items you interact with. Since these platforms operate from revenue generated from advertisements, they have a great interest in showing you things you like or that are consistent with your values. As these platforms learn things about you—your political beliefs, your religious perspective, your taste in movies—they show you what you like. You think you are viewing a picture of the real world, but actually the social media platform has created an insulated bubble populated only by your own beliefs. If you think that this bubble is a picture of the real world, you will also tend to think that your beliefs have been confirmed by the majority and that those who disagree with you are just a tiny fraction of the population, a few radicals here and there.

In today's polarized world, where people tend to gravitate toward extremes, another type of confirmation bias fallacy has become common: *kafkatrapping*. The term for this fallacy comes from Franz Kafka's 1925 novel *The Trial*.[2] In the book, the main character, Josef K., is arrested and put on trial based on charges that are never stated (to the reader or the character). The story is one in which Josef K. finds himself trapped with no way out and is eventually executed. Kafkatrapping occurs when, like Kafka's main character, a person is accused of some terrible fault (say, racism or sexism) and is trapped with no way out (other than to simply admit guilt). No matter what kind of response the accused offers, the response is taken as evidence of guilt (in the following example, the quotations are what you might say; the italicized portion is what someone committing this fallacy reads into your words):

"I'm not a racist." *Your denial of being a racist is evidence proving that you are a racist.*

"I have a long track-record of treating everyone equally, regardless of race." *You do that only so no one will suspect that you are a racist. Pointing this out now just confirms that you are a racist.*

"I think all people are equally valuable." *That is exactly what a racist would say in this situation.*

"I'm innocent!" *Of course you say that. It is what any guilty person would say!*

False Dilemma

The *false dilemma fallacy* occurs whenever a choice is presented that makes it seem as if a choice must be made between exactly two options when more options are available. In each case, the dilemma appears to be introduced for the purpose of forcing the audience to accept one option over the other.

- "We have a clear choice: we can continue to waste taxpayer money on failed drug enforcement policies, or we can finally legalize drugs and tax them so that we have a revenue source to fund important programs."
- "We can either increase funding for education, or see our children suffer and fall further behind compared to their peers in other countries."
- "You can believe in religion if you want to. I believe in science."
- "If you don't support free healthcare, you must want people to be sick."
- "If you don't agree with me on this issue, you must hate me."

In each of these examples, a dilemma is presented, and one option seems to be highlighted as the right option. In each case, however, more than those two options are available. Sometimes this fallacy is referred to as the *fallacy of black-and-white thinking*. But this is not the most helpful name for the fallacy because sometimes there is a true dilemma—sometimes there really are only two options, and we must choose exactly one of them. In such cases, it is *not* fallacious to present the dilemma. Here are two legitimate (nonfallacious) examples of dilemmas:

- God either exists or does not exist.
- If you don't support free healthcare, you must expect people to pay for it.

Genetic Fallacy

A *genetic fallacy* occurs whenever the origin of a belief is used to suggest that the belief must be true or must be false. The term comes from the word *genesis*, which refers to something's origin or beginning. It is fallacious because the origin of a belief or claim is irrelevant to whether it is true or false. Here are some examples:

- "Christianity must be false. You believe it only because you were born in a Christian society. If you were born somewhere else, you'd believe in some other religion."
- "I read about it in a *New York Times* article. It must be true."
- "The New Testament was written by Christians, so it can't be reliable."
- "You can't believe anything he says. He is a member of *that* political party."

Straw Man

The *straw man fallacy* occurs whenever a person creates a deliberately weak, distorted, or obviously false version of an opponent's argument, specifically because the weakened version is easier to defeat than the real thing. The name of the fallacy evokes an image of going to battle against a scarecrow rather than against a real person who can fight back. The aim seems to be to create an absurd version of the argument for the purpose of making the original argument look ridiculous. This can be done in various ways, such as omitting premises, exaggerating claims, quoting out of context, or even making things up that the original argument never included:

- Parent to teenager: "You need to be home by 10:00 p.m." Teenager's response: "Why do you want me to be unhappy?"
- Politician: "Continuing to increase social security spending is not sustainable. We need to find a different solution for the future that preserves a strong economy." Debate opponent: "You don't care about the welfare of seniors; all you care about is money."
- Christian: "On the basis of the arguments and evidence I have presented, it seems perfectly reasonable to believe that God exists." Atheist: "Since you don't really care about facts, you may as well believe in a flying spaghetti monster."

Red Herring

Suppose you were in a public debate, and you were working hard to deliver a nuanced but well-reasoned argument in support of your claim, and then your debate opponent responded by introducing irrelevant points to derail your presentation and focus everyone's attention on a different issue. This strategy of distraction using irrelevant information in order to change the subject of the debate is called the *red herring fallacy*. We suppose that it gets its name from a cured fish (probably a herring) that has been turned red by the curing process and emits a very strong odor. Folklore suggests that these smelly fish could be used to distract hunting dogs from pursuing their game. Unlike the straw man fallacy, which seeks to introduce distortions or falsehoods, the red herring often introduces information that is plausibly true or is worth debating. For example, a politician might present an argument making a case that abortion is immoral. The debate opponent might then say, "If you really cared about life, you'd be in favor of my proposed gun-control legislation." Even though the issue of gun control is a topic worth debating, it is fallacious to introduce it here because its only purpose is to change the subject from the issue of abortion. Presumably, people commit this fallacy as an attempt to "defeat" the argument or claim that their opponent is making, but the distraction they introduce does not actually accomplish that goal.

Conclusion: Seeking Truth, Avoiding Fallacies

Each of the fallacies we name here (and many others) have a common feature: they are an attempt to get someone to either adopt or reject a claim, but the reasoning they offer in their attempted persuasion turns out to not be good reasoning. It is still important to remember that the claims offered by those who commit such fallacies may turn out to be true claims, and they might even be well-intentioned. The key idea here is that fallacious reasoning can never settle the question of whether a claim is true or false. While committing these fallacies can be tempting, they don't help accomplish the goal of argumentation. If we are concerned about truth (and we hope you are), we must avoid such common mistakes in reasoning.

Questions for Reflection

1. What bad arguments have you been tempted to accept or advance just because they seem to support something you believe?
2. Emotions can be a very powerful tool for persuasion. In what ways have you been tempted to appeal to someone's emotions to manipulate the person to do or believe something? In what ways have you been the victim of this kind of manipulation?
3. In what ways is your thinking being affected by the social media bubble?

For Further Reading

Engel, S. Morris. *With Good Reason: An Introduction to Informal Fallacies*, 6th ed. New York: Bedford; St. Martin's, 2014.

Van Fleet, Jacob E. *Informal Logical Fallacies: A Brief Guide*. New York: University Press of America, 2011.

NOTES

1. This principle is closely related to confirmation bias, which we explain below.
2. The book was written in German by Kafka in about 1914 and published posthumously in 1925. It is available in several English translations, including Franz Kafka, *The Trial*, trans. David Wyllie (Mineola, NY: Dover, 2009).

PART 3

Epistemology

What, How, and Why We Can Know

CHAPTER 10

What Are Some Epistemic Goods?

Truth and Knowledge

Do you like good things? Of course you do! Who doesn't like good things? *Lord of the Rings, Shawshank Redemption,* and *The Mission* are good movies. Clam chowder, flounder francaise, and snow crab legs are good seafoods. Patience, forgiveness, and mercy are good moral qualities. (Okay, perhaps some of you disagree with these selections, but the point is that there are good things.) But do you know there are epistemic goods like truth and knowledge? In this chapter, we introduce them to you. Although you may be familiar with them, you may not be familiar with many of the ingredients that go into them, which make up different definitions for these epistemic concepts.

Truth

You might be familiar with Pontius Pilate's question to Jesus: "What is truth?" (John 18:38). It's a fair question—regardless of what scholars say about Pilate's intentions for asking it. Many smart philosophers define truth differently. Indeed, many of you have probably ended conversations confused because you and the other person were using two different conceptions of truth. Take, for example, the following answers given by four baseball umpires explaining what they do behind home plate.[1]

- Umpire 1: "There are balls and strikes, and I call pitches the way they are."

- Umpire 2: "There are balls and strikes, and I judge a pitch based on whether it coheres with other beliefs I have about what is a ball or strike."
- Umpire 3: "There are balls and strikes, and I determine whether a pitch is a ball or strike based on the kind of consequences I believe my call will bring about for a 'good game.'"
- Umpire 4: "There are no balls and strikes, only words I use to create a standard used to express my belief about a ball or strike."

Each umpire expresses a different take on truth. The following four theories and definitions of truth were illustrated by the umpires' answers.

The Correspondence Theory of Truth

Let's consider what Aristotle, Aquinas, and Descartes would have said in response to Pilate's question: "What is truth?"

Aristotle: "To say of what is that it is, and of what is not that it is not, is true."[2]
Aquinas: "A judgment is said to be true when it conforms to the external reality."[3]
Descartes: "[T]he word 'truth', in the strict sense, denotes the conformity of thought with its object."[4]

The common thread running through these answers is that truth is fundamentally a *relation*. That is to say, truth is a thought, statement, judgment, or belief that *corresponds* to reality. When umpire 1 says a pitch is a strike, it means the location of the pitch corresponds to a region of space making up the strike zone. Truth, on this view, is a relation between reality and whatever accurately describes that part of reality. For example, if you tell me, "There's milk in the fridge," and I look inside the fridge and see milk, then what you said corresponds to reality. Therefore, your statement is true.

The correspondence theory of truth is the traditional account, it is the commonsense account, and it is endorsed by many professional philosophers and scientists today. It is also the theory of truth we take to be true, and thus we will be using it throughout the book.

Correspondence Theory of Truth: Statement P is true if and only if P corresponds to the relevant facts about reality.

The Coherence Theory of Truth

Have you ever looked at a spider's web that has successfully trapped various kinds of insects? If yes, then you have a helpful image of the coherence theory of truth. The coherence theory of truth says a belief is true when it rationally makes sense amongst other beliefs within one's worldview. Think of one's worldview as similar to the spider's web and one's belief as similar to an object stuck in the web. A belief is true on this account when it coheres with other beliefs contained within one's worldview-web-of-beliefs. What makes a belief true is whether it's rationally supported by other beliefs taken to be true. But notice closely that the relation used in this account is not between a belief and reality but rather a belief and other beliefs within one's mind. What makes a belief true is other beliefs, not reality. When umpire 2 says a pitch is a strike, it's a strike because the umpire's belief about the pitch coheres with other beliefs about balls and strikes.

Coherence Theory of Truth: Statement P is true if and only if it is rationally supported by other beliefs taken to be true.

The Pragmatic Theory of Truth

I once knew a person who disclosed to his doctor all the different vitamins and supplements he took each day to be healthy. The doctor looked at the pills and said: "With all due respect, these pills are only giving you the most expensive urine on the block." The patient responded back with the pragmatist's creed: "No, they truly make me healthy because they work!" Notice he didn't say the pills work because it is true that they cause good health. "They work" typically refers to a perceived instrumental role truth plays toward getting some desired result.

The pragmatist theory of truth is not offering a relation between a belief and reality. Rather, it offers an explanation for how people use the term *true*. According to the pragmatic theory of truth, people use the term *true* to express that a belief or statement is instrumental toward producing good results over the long haul. That pill, promise, statement, testimony, model, explanation, and so on is true because of its usefulness toward bringing about some desired end like pleasure, peace, accurate predictions, money, popularity, acceptance, honor, and so on. When umpire 3 calls the pitch a strike, it is because the umpire believes this call will result in bringing about a "good game" people want to see.

Pragmatic Theory of Truth: A belief or statement P is true if and only if it brings about the right kind of beneficial results over the long haul.

Relativist Theories of Truth

Relativism is bigger than a theory of truth. But its variants and application to other academic disciplines (e.g., ethics, history, medicine, etc.) rest on its view of truth. A relativist view of truth rejects the claim that human minds can have cognitive contact with reality. Therefore, relativism rejects the idea that the same relation between a belief and reality (correspondence view) can be shared by all people regardless of their age, sex, ethnicity, economic class, social class, or cultural affinity. Rather, a belief or statement is true relative to what an individual or group of people believe is true. When umpire 4 calls the pitch a strike, it is because the umpire either feels like it's a strike, wants it to be a strike, is a strike based on how he defines a strike, believes it is a strike according to the story he's writing in his mind, or some combination thereof.

According to individual relativism, ten people can each believe the capital of Arizona is a term that is different from the other nine answers. And yet everyone's belief can be true! What a concept! How can this be? Because it is true . . . *relative* to them! Relativist theories of truth can, in principle, permit all beliefs to be true relative to some individual or group (cultural relativism). This is the philosophical theory of truth that undergirds familiar expressions like these: "This is my truth," "This is our truth," or "That's true for you but not for me."

Some motivation for this view of truth comes from scientism, a newfangled view of tolerance, pervasive disagreement, or some combination thereof. We'll quickly address each in turn. Some people hold to a qualified version of relativism, which is restricted to claims involving morality and religion. Because moral values and God are typically conceived as non-physical, the scope of things that can be universally true or true in the correspondence sense are limited to physical facts. Phenomenon that can be verified by the hard sciences can be true in non-relativist or correspondence ways because the working assumption is that only physical things and events can be known and resist relativistic views of truth. Because moral values and God are not physical, some assume they are—in principle—things that either can't exist (*physicalism*) or can't be known even if they do exist (*skepticism*); either way, a commitment to *scientism* (whether or not one is aware and acknowledges this commitment) can motivate a relativistic view of truth regarding matters involving non-physical entities. Despite peoples' resistance toward refraining from using moral language and moral evaluations, the truth of such statements and evaluations are taken to be relative to a belief in an individual's mind (*individual relativism*) or a consensus opinion held by a group of people (*cultural relativism*).

Some correctly value tolerance as a virtue. Indeed, it is praiseworthy to tolerate people with whom you disagree and even many of the accompanying behaviors informed by the beliefs you disagree with. (Although, of course, tolerating things like theft, rape, and murder misses the target of tolerance.) The trouble comes when one believes tolerance entails relativism, especially in the moral domain. Some think that in order to be crowned "a tolerant person," one must never disagree with another's moral belief or think some moral statement is really false. The reason this is a newfangled version of tolerance is that it's different from traditional conceptions of tolerance and, worse, it's unworkable. Tolerance always meant that even though I disagree with you, I will still treat you with respect, dignity, and fight for your right to defend a position in a civilized manner.[5] Some, however, think tolerance means never disagreeing with another or thinking no one's beliefs, especially one's moral or religious beliefs, can be false. In order to satisfy the demands of this newfangled view of tolerance, one must resist forming or having any beliefs which, of course, is virtually impossible. The reason why is simple. Merely having one belief, say, believing that-P, entails the denial of not-P. Well, of course, the likelihood of there being someone who believes not-P is going to be nonzero. So as long as there is one person who believes the contrary of what you believe, by definition, you are being intolerant. Have fun trying to be tolerant by not holding any beliefs.

Another reason for relativism on truth, especially in the moral domain, is pervasive disagreement. Many people agree statements involving the color, size, and shape of midsized objects, simple math, and logic can be known and thus be true in a universal, non-relativist sense. This is why we judge and blame people for running red lights, cheating us in our paychecks, and communicating to us in unintelligible ways by uttering contradictory or incoherent statements. But the number of people who disagree on moral matters far exceeds the number of people that disagree the traffic light is "red" and "red" means stop; and that working eight hours a day for five days equals forty hours of work; and that you can't both exist and not exist at the same time. Many people, however, do disagree on moral matters. So the inference is made from this data that some things can be known and are thus true evidenced by degrees of consensus, whereas people disagree all the time and consensus is lacking on moral beliefs. So moral statements are matters of opinion and aren't the kinds of things that can be known. Thus, they are relative to each individual, community, or culture.

It goes beyond the scope of the chapter to develop a lengthy response to this. Suffice it to say that there is surprisingly more agreement than disagreement on many moral statements than one might think, especially peoples' beliefs in the moral wrongness of stealing, raping, and murdering.[6] What's more, it just might be the case that discovering the truth in certain moral cases is difficult—perhaps, even, extremely difficult. But that's no reason to treat disagreement in the moral domain as conclusive evidence that the best view of truth is a relativistic conception of it. Much of the disagreement can be explained by disparities in the kinds of evidence people have and the differences in their worldviews, which will result in different interpretations of evidence.

The obvious problem with a relativistic view of truth, aside from its incoherency, is that it denies the existence of tools used for rational inquiry to discover truth. Indeed, it makes it impossible to defend innocent victims from crimes they didn't commit, convince people of a medical cure that can save their lives, advance the body of scientific knowledge, evaluate arguments, demonstrate the falsity of other people's beliefs, and expose outright lies.

Relativist Theory of Truth: A belief or statement P is true if and only if it is determined to be true relative to whatever invented standard is used by an individual or group.

Knowledge

Ask any ten people you meet on the street to define "knowledge" and you are likely to hear ten different definitions, including some circular ones. Trying to define the term *knowledge* to everyone's satisfaction is something philosophers have not yet achieved. Indeed, the authors of this book do not even share the same definition of knowledge. So, spoiler alert, we don't intend to give you all the necessary and jointly sufficient conditions comprising knowledge. However, we will offer some important necessary conditions. In fact, we think there are some definitions of knowledge that are considerably better than others because of the necessary conditions they list. Introducing you to these definitions will provide greater insight into what knowledge is.

Epistemology is a normative discipline. It makes evaluations that judge one state of believing as better than another. When your tooth hurts, you consult your dentist and not a three-year-old because you think the dentist's belief about what's causing the pain is better. And you think it's better because the dentist has knowledge. One important project of epistemology, then, is to explain why the dentist's belief is better by explaining the difference between people that know from people that do not know. Let us start off by considering the following two cases.

CONCEPTUAL ANALYSIS

Concepts are the building blocks of thoughts and beliefs. One important activity of philosophy is doing *conceptual analysis*. Conceptual analysis involves taking a familiar concept like "human person," "knowledge," or "goodness" and breaking it down to simpler, more manageable parts. This method of analysis aims to better understand a concept or word. Inspecting these individual parts can result in determining whether these parts are necessary and how many parts make up the concept's necessary and jointly sufficient conditions. For example, a plane shape is a necessary condition for a square, but it is not sufficient (circles are plane shapes too). A plane shape, four equal lines, and four ninety-degree angles are the necessary and jointly sufficient conditions for the concept "square."

Mechanic: Smith takes his car to his mechanic, Alex, because it's vibrating and pulling to the left. Alex explains to Smith how it's the car's worn-out ball joint causing this. Smith, then, forms the belief from Alex's testimony: "My car has a worn ball joint."

Crystal-Ball Gazing: Jones's car also vibrates and pulls to the left. He consults the internet to find out why. He writes down all the possible causes. Jones isn't sure which diagnosis is true. So he consults his trusty, old crystal ball: "Crystal ball, does my car have a bad ball joint?" After staring into the crystal ball, Jones begins imagining a worn-out ball joint appearing in the crystal ball. Jones then forms the belief from gazing into the crystal ball: "My car has a worn ball joint."

Both Smith's car and Jones's car have worn-out ball joints. It is intuitively obvious whose belief is better, right? Of course, Smith's belief is better than Jones's belief. But why?

The first definition of knowledge we introduce to you seems to adequately explain why Smith's true belief is better than Jones's true belief. This definition of knowledge is known as the *traditional account* or the *justified true belief (JTB) account*.[7] (Throughout this chapter when you see the letter P, treat it as a proposition. Propositions are abstract, like numbers, containing informational content that can be expressed in various languages. In what follows, the proposition P will express a statement. Statements can be either true or false depending on whether it accurately represents reality.)

Justified True Belief (JTB) Account

S knows P if and only if:

1. S *believes* P;
2. P is *true*; and
3. S is *justified* in believing P.

The traditional account has a lot going for it. It lists some important necessary conditions that are worth considering.

1. *Belief condition.* This seems like a necessary condition for what goes into knowledge. After all, can anyone know something they don't believe? Consider: "I know 2 + 2 = 4, but I don't believe it." This statement strikes us as incoherent. If you know P, then it sure seems like you must also believe P.[8]

2. *Truth condition.* This is another condition that seems necessary for knowledge. For example, if we said, "We know you stole your cellphone from the electronics store." But, in fact, you purchased your cellphone online. Then we don't know you committed theft because it's not true. It's intuitively obvious that in order to know P, P must be true.

3. *Justification condition.* This condition is believed to be the special ingredient explaining the difference between the mechanic and crystal ball cases. *Justification* is an umbrella term used to capture adequate grounds for a belief. Justification is the evidential basis indicating the truth of a proposition. Evidence, reasons, or arguments for a belief are examples of justification.

Because Jones's belief that P doesn't satisfy the justification condition (crystal balls are not good sources of justification), we can explain why he does not know, despite having a true belief. By contrast, we can explain why Smith does know. Smith knows because his true belief does satisfy the justification condition. Consulting a highly trained, skilled, seasoned mechanic to form a testimonial belief provides adequate grounds for thinking P is true. Smith's true belief is better than Jones's true belief because the former belief has justification, but the latter does not.

The traditional account of knowledge clearly carves out some important logical space. It makes an important distinction between a *true belief* and a *justified true belief.* Furthermore, it can explain why we intuitively believe that Smith's belief is better than Jones's belief. But is knowledge the same thing as having a justified true belief? For centuries, many philosophers answered yes to this question. But then along came philosopher Edmund Gettier, who upset the epistemic applecart, sending epistemologists scrambling in search of a better account of knowledge.

Gettier-Style Counter Examples

In 1963, it took Edmund Gettier only three pages to write what has become one of the most famous papers in contemporary philosophy.[9] In this paper he provided counterexamples to the traditional account of knowledge. Gettier showed that one can satisfy the belief, truth, and justification conditions and still not know. Since then, many different fun and interesting kinds of Gettier-style counterexamples have been constructed. Here is one that does the trick.[10]

Imagine you wake up one morning in a state of panic because you believe you overslept and will miss your doctor's appointment.[11] You look at your watch and thankfully discover it is only 6:30 a.m.—still plenty of time to get there. It turns out that the correct time of day really is 6:30 a.m., but unbeknownst to you, the watch's battery ran out of energy exactly twelve hours ago! You formed a true belief by looking at a broken watch! Question: Do you know it's 6:30 a.m.? (Think it over.) We're going to assume you share the same intuition shared by many others and answer "No! One can't get knowledge by looking at a broken clock." But according to the traditional account of knowledge, you do know. Why? You satisfy the JTB conditions. You have a true belief that enjoys justification—especially if we build into the case how reliable your watch has been over the years. So Gettier-style counterexamples show that a subject can satisfy the (JTB) conditions and still not know. Whatever knowledge is, having a justified true belief seems to fall short of it (according to most philosophers).

Is JTB Dead and Buried or Capturing Something Else?

Now, please, do not think having a justified true belief is not a good and valuable thing. It most certainly is! For starters, if your true belief about P doesn't enjoy justification, it is vulnerable to potential counterevidence that can unnecessarily elicit doubt. Doubt can cause you to no longer believe P is true. Now you've just given up and lost a true belief. But if you had some justification, you might have retained it. For example, P might be something practically important like "The directions I wrote down from the internet to my doctor's office are accurate." But during your drive you encounter some potential counterevidence, such as the directions telling you to turn right thereby causing you to travel westward. But you know the doctor's office is still much further east. This counterevidence causes you to believe the directions are wrong. You start panicking over missing your appointment. However, if you had justification, you would have been inoculated from this counterevidence. Why? Because you know the road you're on takes you to the freeway going east. After all, sometimes you have to go west to get east faster!

Some philosophers aren't impressed with the alleged weaknesses Gettier-style counterexamples reveal about JTB. They say the justification used in these cases is not good enough. Good justification requires one to have access to propositions that would indicate whether a true belief really is justified. For example, let's return to the broken clock case. There is a true proposition that if it were to be added to one's set of evidence, then one's belief would not be justified: the watch's battery is dead. So your true belief that it's 6:30 a.m. really isn't justified after all. This view has formally been developed and is known as the defeasibility theory of knowledge.[12] On this view, S knows that P exactly when all the JTB conditions are all satisfied plus an additional condition: there is no *true proposition* Q such that when added to S's set of evidence shows P is unjustified. In this case, Q would be the true belief "The clock is broken." Adding Q to one's evidence would show P really isn't justified after all.

The problem with this view of knowledge, however, is that many cases require too heavy a burden to bear. It requires amassing an amount of justification that humans are incapable of satisfying. It's Gettier-proof!—indeed, since it requires accessing all the relevant facts, it makes identifying the culprit that undermines justification look easy. What's more, having access to all the relevant facts that would undermine one's justification will make the truth condition superfluous. This is because the truth of P would already be implied or entailed by the truth of the other relevant facts one believes.[13] Since it requires knowing all the true propositions that entail or imply a culprit fact that can undermine one's justification, a subject will not make the error of forming a false belief and then adding it to one's justification. Knowledge of all these facts and what they imply or entail will already reveal whether P is true. But when we stop to think about that requirement, it seems like the kind of mind capable of knowing all those true propositions and logical relations shared between them is more superhuman than human. It may even be, perhaps, a model for God's omniscient mind. But it is something far beyond the intellectual powers and abilities of fallen, imperfect, finite humans. It paints a model of knowledge that doesn't resemble what knowledge is for human beings who seem to know lots of things in everyday situations.

In light of this, philosophers have offered different amendments to the traditional account or revised the definition of knowledge altogether. Here are some candidate definitions that have been offered in response to Gettier-style counterexamples.

Some Popular Definitions for Knowledge
No Relevant Falsehood

S knows P if and only if S's justified true belief is not inferred from any false proposition Q contained in S's set of evidence.[14]

The idea here is that, in cases of knowledge, S can't justifiably form a true belief from any false belief whatsoever. If S infers a true belief from a set of beliefs that includes at least one false belief, then S lacks knowledge. So despite having a true belief, because S's justification has been compromised—it's been tainted—S doesn't know. Consider the following set of beliefs held by Joel involving the broken clock case for illustration.

Premise-belief 1: My clock can reveal the time of day.
Premise-belief 2: My clock is a reliable source for telling time.
Premise-belief 3: My clock can be seen in the kitchen.
Premise-belief 4: My clock is working well.

Conclusion-belief: The time of day is 6:30 am.

This conclusion-belief inferred from beliefs 1–4 is not justified. According to this account, since belief-4 is false, it undercuts one's justification. Thus, it delivers the right verdict by explaining why one doesn't know despite having a true belief.[15]

Reliabilist Theories

S knows P only if S's true belief was produced by reliable belief-forming processes.[16]

The idea here is that, in cases of knowledge, S's belief will be the product of cognitive belief-forming processes that generally deliver true beliefs as opposed to belief-forming processes that generally produce false beliefs. Reliabilist accounts of knowledge don't assume perfect reliability—we're dealing with humans after all—but rather belief-forming processes that are (in general) reliable and much better than chance. It explains why S doesn't know in the broken clock case because S's perceptual faculties are not reliable—in that context and moment—at detecting a malfunctioning watch.

Proper Function Account

S knows P only if S's true belief is produced by properly functioning cognitive faculties in an appropriate environment according to a design plan aimed at getting the truth.[17]

The idea here is that in cases of knowledge, S's belief about P will be the result of *properly functioning* cognitive faculties intelligently *designed* to produce true beliefs, rather than cognitive processes not aimed at truth. These cognitive faculties are designed to get truth, but they are not 100 percent perfect at getting it. This is because the proponent of this theory is a Christian and factors in the effects of the fall, otherwise known as the noetic effects of sin.

Returning to the broken clock case, it, too, delivers the right verdict. S wouldn't know that it's 6:30 am because S's true belief wasn't produced by cognitive faculties functioning in an appropriate environment—instead they were functioning in an unlucky environment. The true belief formed is—in large measure—brought about by luck and not the result of properly functioning cognitive faculties.

Virtue Accounts

S knows P only if S's true belief is produced by intellectual abilities and/or intellectually virtuous activities.[18]

The idea here is that in cases of knowledge, S gets to the truth *because of* a credit worthy achievement—that is, S gets the truth because of S's intellectual abilities/ virtues. Intellectual abilities are things like good perception, memory, reason, intuition, and introspection. Intellectual virtues are things like intellectual-humility, autonomy, conscientiousness, courage, charitableness, perseverance, honesty, fair-mindedness, clarity, sensitivity, and love of epistemic goods.[19] This account offers the correct verdict in the broken clock case because, just like the reliabilist and proper function accounts, the subject didn't get the truth because of an intellectual ability or virtuous activity. Rather, the subject got the truth because of dumb luck!

What Is Knowledge?

It goes beyond the purpose of this chapter to defend a particular definition of knowledge. Again, the authors of this book disagree over what is the best account of knowledge. It will be up to you to explore which account you think is better than the alternatives. But here are some things many epistemologists agree upon regarding knowledge.

- Knowledge entails the truth and belief conditions.
- Knowledge is better than a mere true belief.
- Knowledge is incompatible with certain kinds of luck. If S gets the truth because of dumb luck or accident, then S doesn't know.[20]
- Acquiring knowledge is a credit-worthy achievement. One doesn't merit credit for getting the truth because of dumb luck or accident.[21]
- Knowledge is a valuable epistemic good.
- We use the term *knowledge* to refer to people and sources that possess accurate information for our practical purposes of making responsible decisions and actions.[22]

Linda Zagzebski has made an important point about accounts of knowledge and Gettier-style counterexamples: if any account of knowledge leaves too much of a gap between the truth condition and whatever else is claimed to convert true belief into knowledge, then there will be enough space for knowledge-undermining luck to rear its ugly head. This is what makes so many definitions of knowledge vulnerable to Gettier-style counterexamples.[23] In light of this, some have suggested closing the gap by introducing a "because-of relation."[24] Once this relation is included, you can see how the definitions of knowledge are more resistant to Gettier-style counterexamples and provide a more accurate evaluation as to whether S knows P and can explain why.

The No Relevant Falsehood Account can handle some Gettier-style counterexamples—specifically beliefs formed by reasoning, but it's still vulnerable to beliefs formed from perception.[25] So let us see how this "because-of relation" can improve the other definitions.

KINDS OF KNOWLEDGE

Propositional knowledge: This kind of knowledge is acquired through testimony. Books, encyclopedias, letters, journal articles, recipes, and so forth provide one with a proposition, statement, or fact, which is the object of knowledge. For example, Gary knows about Julie's place of birth, the schools she attended, and the number and names of her family members by reading a biography.

Knowledge by acquaintance: This kind of knowledge is when one's perceptual faculties are directly interacting with the object of knowledge. Persons, places, or entities perceived by a subject can be known by a subject by being directly acquainted with them. Gary knows Julie's personality traits, dispositions, facial expressions, and character traits by directly perceiving them.

Knowledge-how: This kind of knowledge is possessed by artisans, athletes, cooks, mechanics, and so forth. The object of knowledge is a specific activity needed to complete a specific task. It often gets expressed in statements such as, "Mable knows how to make a codfish stew" or "Hanson knows how to rebuild an engine" or "Bryce Harper knows how to hit a fastball."

It's important to see how one kind of knowledge doesn't entail the others. For example, one can know how to coach an athlete on how to hit a fastball through propositional knowledge but fail at doing it because of a lack of knowledge-how. Or one may have knowledge-how relative to hitting fastballs but lack the kind of propositional knowledge needed to properly instruct one on how to do it. Further, one can have a significant amount of propositional knowledge about a person but lack knowledge by acquaintance, thereby failing to have a personal relationship with that person.

Traditional Account (JTB): S knows P if and only if S believes the truth because of S's justification.

Reliabilist Theories: S knows P only if S believes the truth because S's belief was produced by reliable belief-forming processes.

Proper Function Account: S knows P only if S believes the truth because S's belief is produced by properly functioning cognitive faculties in an appropriate environment according to a design plan aimed at reliably getting the truth.

Virtue Accounts: S knows P only if S believes the truth because S's belief is produced by intellectual abilities and/or intellectually virtuous activities.

Notice how these amendments do a better job of accurately evaluating whether S knows. Did S get the truth because of "justification," "reliable belief-forming processes," "properly functioning faculties," or "intellectual abilities or virtues"? Or did S get the truth because of dumb luck or accident? We think these amendments can provide a better way of evaluating whether one knows and provide a better way of thinking about what knowledge is.

Conclusion

In this chapter, we looked at two valuable epistemic goods: truth and knowledge. After analyzing the concepts of truth and knowledge, philosophers have offered different accounts of them. In subsequent chapters, we will look at some other epistemic goods like *understanding* and *wisdom*.

Questions for Reflection

1. Do you think one's view of truth makes a difference in how one lives life? Why or why not?
2. Why is it important to know what truth is?
3. What definition of knowledge do you think best captures the common-sense view of it?
4. Do you think knowledge is something different than a justified truth belief? Why or why not?
5. Do you think a justified belief is something valuable? If so, do you think humans are morally obligated to justify their beliefs?

For Further Reading

General Level Readers

Bernecker, Sven, and Duncan Pritchard. *The Rutledge Companion to Epistemology*. New York: Routledge, 2011.

Byerly, T. Ryan. *Introducing Logic and Critical Thinking: The Skills of Reasoning and the Virtues of Inquiry*. Grand Rapids: Baker Academic, 2017.

DeWeese, Garrett J., and J. P. Moreland. *Philosophy Made Slightly Less Difficult: A Beginner's Guide to Life's Big Questions*. Downers Grove, IL: IVP Academic, 2021.

Nagel, Jennifer. *Knowledge: A Very Short Introduction*. Oxford: Oxford University Press, 2014.

Plantinga, Alvin. *Knowledge and Christian Belief.* Grand Rapids: Eerdmans, 2015.

Zagzebski, Linda. *On Epistemology.* Belmont, CA: Wadsworth, Cengage Learning, 2009.

Advanced Level Readers

Moreland, J. P., and William Lane Craig. *Philosophical Foundations for a Christian Worldview.* 2nd ed. Downers Grove, IL: IVP Academic, 2017, chapter 3.

Plantinga, Alvin. *Warranted Christian Belief.* Oxford: Oxford University Press, 2000.

Pritchard, Duncan. *What Is This Thing Called Knowledge?* New York: Routledge, 2018.

Rasmussen, Joshua. *Defending the Correspondence Theory of Truth.* Cambridge: Cambridge University Press, 2014.

Sosa, Ernest, Jaegwon Kim, Jeremy Fantl, and Matthew McGrath, eds. *Epistemology: An Anthology.* 2nd ed. Oxford: Blackwell, 2008.

NOTES

1. We borrow this helpful illustration making some modifications to it from Os Guinness, *Time for Truth: Living Free in a World of Lies, Hype, and Spin* (Grand Rapids: Baker, 2000), 12.
2. Aristotle, *Metaphysics* IV.7, 1011b25.
3. Thomas Aquinas, *De Veritate*, Q.1, A.1–3.
4. René Descartes, "Letter to Mersenne: 16 October 1639," *The Philosophical Writings of Descartes*, vol. 3 (Cambridge: Cambridge University Press 1991), 138–40.
5. Some trace a traditional view of tolerance back to Voltaire's work in *A Treatise on Toleration*. There he argued against the dangers of fanaticism which rejected hearing the reasons in support of alternative points of view and how a virtuous person (even Christian conceptions of it) requires the rejection of fanatical intolerance and violence toward people having contrary beliefs. The gift of reason invites opposing points of view to reason together and discover the truth of the matter. Tolerating disagreement is therefore just and consistent with what the virtues of compassion, gentleness, patience, and forgiveness birth in action. See Voltaire, *Treatise on Toleration and Other Essays*, trans. Joseph McCabe (New York: Prometheus, 1994).
6. See the appendix in C. S. Lewis's *Abolition of Man* (San Francisco: HarperOne, 2015).
7. The traditional account also goes by the name "The Tripartite Theory of Knowledge" or "The Justified True Belief Theory of Knowledge"—"JTB" for short. It arguably traces all the way back to Plato's writings, especially the *Theaetetus* and *Meno*.
8. We recommend thinking of a belief as a mental state—specifically, what's known as a propositional attitude of assenting to a proposition as true or thinking with a conviction that a particular proposition is true. To believe that P is to assent or have a conviction that P accurately represents the way the world is.
9. Edmund Gettier, "Is Justified True Belief Knowledge?" *Analysis* 23, no. 6 (June 1963): 121–23.
10. For the sake of simplicity, we won't use Gettier's original examples since they are less intuitive than this case. Furthermore, they require you to know some inference rules (e.g., entailment relations and the propositional logic rule of disjunction introduction) and when disjunctions

are true or false. We encourage you to read them and see how they provide cases wherein one has a justified true belief that intuitively falls short of knowledge.

11. In 1948, Russell used this case to illustrate that not all true beliefs count as knowledge. So it wasn't directly aimed at undermining the traditional account of knowledge like Gettier's 1963 paper. See Bertrand Russell, *Human Knowledge: Its Scope and Limits* (1948; repr., New York: Routledge Classics, 2009), 91, 140.

12. See Peter D. Klein, "Knowledge, Causality, and Defeasibility," in *Journal of Philosophy* 73 (1976): 792–812.

13. Linda Zagzebski, *On Epistemology* (Belmont, CA: Wadsworth, 2009), 122.

14. See D. M. Armstrong, *Belief, Truth, and Knowledge* (Cambridge: Cambridge University Press, 1973).

15. The trouble with this account may have come across in the way the broken clock case was set up. Most cases involving perception do not involve a chain of inferential reasoning. Rather, they are non-inferential, wherein a belief forms automatically. So the No Relevant Falsehood account has difficulty dealing with non-inferential beliefs that form from perception, intuition, memory, and sometimes even testimony.

16. See Alvin Goldman, "What Is Justified Belief?" in *Justification and Knowledge: New Studies in Epistemology*, ed. George S. Pappas (Boston: Reidel, 1979), 1–23.

17. See Alvin Plantinga, *Warranted Christian Belief* (Oxford: Oxford University Press, 2000), 529.

18. See Linda Zagzebski, *Virtues of the Mind: An Inquiry into the Nature of Virtue and the Ethical Foundations of Knowledge* (Cambridge: Cambridge University Press, 1996); John Greco, *Achieving Knowledge: A Virtue-Theoretic Account of Epistemic Normativity* (Cambridge: Cambridge University Press, 2010).

19. See Robert C. Roberts and W. Jay Wood, *Intellectual Virtues: An Essay in Regulative Epistemology* (Oxford: Oxford University Press, 2007); Nathan L. King, *The Excellent Mind: Intellectual Virtues for Everyday Life* (Oxford: Oxford University Press, 2021); and Linda Zagzebski, *Epistemic Authority: A Theory of Trust, Authority, and Autonomy in Belief* (Oxford: Oxford University Press, 2012).

20. This is known as the incompatibility thesis—that there are certain kinds of epistemic luck that undermine attributing one with knowledge, despite acquiring a true belief. See Mylan Engel, "Epistemic Luck," in *A Companion to Epistemology*, ed. Jonathan Dancy, Ernest Sosa, and Matthias Steup, 2nd ed. (New York: Wiley-Blackwell, 2010).

21. See Wayne Riggs, "Reliability and the Value of Knowledge," in *Philosophy and Phenomenological Research* 64 (2002), 79–96; Ernest Sosa, "The Place of Truth in Epistemology," in *Intellectual Virtue: Perspectives from Ethics and Epistemology*, ed. Michael DePaul and Linda Zagzebski (Oxford: Oxford University Press, 2003); and Greco, *Achieving Knowledge*.

22. See Edward Craig, *Knowledge and the State of Nature* (Oxford: Oxford University Press, 1990).

23. She analyzed and discovered Gettier-style counter examples use a similar pattern—a "double-luck" structure. They typically involve a subject having a justified, false belief (bad luck) that later gets neutralized by a stroke of good luck, thereby resulting in a true belief. This enables the subject to have a justified, true belief that falls short of knowledge. See Linda Zagzebski, "The Inescapability of Gettier Problems," *Philosophical Quarterly* 44, no. 174 (1994): 65–73.

24. See Greco, *Achieving Knowledge*, 44.

25. Alvin Goldman envisions a case involving a person driving through an unfamiliar county that's peppered with barn façades. The driver stops at the crossroads, looks out his window, and sees the only one true barn amid hundreds of fake ones. He then forms a true belief: "That is a barn." This perceptual belief is true and justified but falls short of knowledge and, further, since it's a belief sourced in perception, not reason. The No Relevant Falsehood account doesn't apply since this perceptual belief doesn't require making inferences from a set of statements. It's a non-inferential belief. See Alvin Goldman, "Discrimination and Perceptual Knowledge," *Journal of Philosophy* 73, no. 20 (1976): 771–91.

CHAPTER 11

Are We All Living in a Virtual World?

The Challenge of Epistemic Skepticism

S kepticism is an umbrella term capturing different ways people argue that humans lack knowledge. In this chapter, we look at a specific kind of skepticism called *external world skepticism*. This version of skepticism challenges whether humans can know things about the external world—things that exist outside one's mind. Claiming one knows that hands, chairs, trees, and buildings exist are all called into question by introducing skeptical hypotheses and arguments that suggest otherwise. Virtually all philosophers reject this kind of radical skepticism, including ourselves. But we believe it's important to interact with it because of the way it sheds new light on truth, knowledge, and understanding. Indeed, we think this version of skepticism can be a fascinating way to gain better insight into the nature of these epistemic goods.

External World Skepticism: The Virtual Reality Scenario

One way skepticism gets motivated is seizing on our limitations. We all recognize that we're not omniscient like God—humans do not believe all true statements and disbelieve all false statements. If we can't perfectly access all truths, there is reason to call into question our knowledge claims or, at least, call into question our confidence in asserting we have knowledge. Skepticism comes in many different versions. It can refer to the ways skeptics try to convince others they really don't have true beliefs or knowledge. For example, many people feel certain some belief is true, only later to discover it was false. Skepticism also comes in degrees. It can refer to how people are generally more skeptical about the truth of moral, political, and religious claims than claims in math, science, and logic. The version of skepticism we will discuss is *external world skepticism*.

Consider this scenario. There is a future time when machines become conscious. The machines wage war against humans and win. Now the machines use human beings as batteries to supply their energy needs. To do this, the machines reproduce humans inside artificial wombs. This pod of chemicals is equipped with numerous cords connected to the brain and nervous system. By directly stimulating the nervous system, the machines can cause humans to believe they're interacting with a real world. But the "world" humans interact with is a virtual one—a computational world—like a video game. Everything humans now see and interact with is a virtual reality.[1] This skeptical hypothesis[2] explains how all your perceptual beliefs about the "external world" are about 1s and 0s—not the real world. Let's consider an argument that utilizes this skeptical scenario in an attempt to conclude we lack knowledge of the external world.

RENÉ DESCARTES (1596–1650)

René Descartes gets credit for coming up with these wild and outlandish skeptical scenarios. Even though he wasn't a skeptic, he used skeptical scenarios to generate doubt to winnow away any belief that could be doubted until it was discovered what beliefs could be known with certainty. These scenarios have evolved over the years. First came Descartes' living-in-a-dream scenario, followed by having your mind manipulated by an evil demon. Then came contemporary versions, like the idea that you are only a brain-in-a-vat of chemicals manipulated by mad scientists to think you have a body. Descartes was a brilliant mathematician, scientist, and philosopher. Indeed, he is regarded by many as the "Father of Modern Philosophy," making significant contributions to epistemology, metaphysics, and science.

Argument for External World Skepticism

1. If I know this is my body, then I know I'm not living in a virtual reality.
2. I don't know that I'm not living in a virtual reality.
3. Therefore, I don't know this is my body.

Premise 1 seems true because it relies on a familiar truth—in virtue of knowing one thing (e.g., I am sitting) you can also know other things (e.g., I am not standing).[3] Knowing your body exists entails that you are not trapped in a pod of chemicals perceiving a virtual body. Real bodies are made of flesh and blood; virtual bodies are digital—made of 1s and 0s.

Why would anyone think premise 2 is true? Enter René Descartes. In *Meditation One*, Descartes lays out his reasons, which can be divided up into three steps.[4]

Defense of Premise 2

Step 1: Grant that knowledge requires evidence. Indeed, good evidence is needed to rule out alternative explanations. Good evidence is needed to close the gap between one's appearance of X and the reality of X. If one's evidence is not good enough, it can support alternative explanations that conflict with each other. You can't know, for example, the color of a widget rolling down an assembly line is red if part of your evidence includes testimony from others that a red light shines on them for purposes of quality control, exposing cracks and dust particles.[5] Good evidence enables ruling out alternative explanations that prevent one from knowing.

Step 2: Introduce a skeptical hypothesis that explains how one's perceptual evidence is consistent with being in a bad case, like virtual reality. In virtual reality, one's perceptual evidence is of 1s and 0s, not reality.[6] If we are living in the virtual reality (bad case), our evidence will appear to us the same way it would in the real world (good case). (Remember the conscious machines have the technology to create a virtual world that flawlessly interacts with your brain and nervous system.)

Step 3: Because one's evidence can't discriminate the virtual world (bad case) from the real world (good case), one can't know whether one's body is a real, flesh-and-blood body or a virtual body. The evidence you possess in the good case will appear the same way it would in the bad case. So our evidence can't rule out the virtual reality hypothesis. Therefore, we can't know things about the external world.

How One Can Respond to External World Skepticism

There are many different responses to external world skepticism.[7] But for the purposes of this chapter, we are going to focus on G. E. Moore's response, build upon it, and then show how this exploration into skepticism sheds new light on truth, knowledge, and understanding.

Moore's Common Sense Response: I Can Just *See* I'm Not in the Bad Case!

The great Cambridge philosopher G. E. Moore responded to external world skepticism by saying, I do know things about the external world (I have hands), which is why I know I am not in the bad case.[8] Moore denies premise 2 of the skeptical argument. A Moorean response will use *modus ponens* to argue against the skeptic's *modus tollens* argument.

    1. If I know this is my body, then I know I'm not living in virtual reality.
    2'. I know this is my body—I can see it!
    3'. Therefore, I know I'm not living in virtual reality.

Premise 1 relies on the idea that knowledge can be entailed by other things known, like we discussed. Premise 2' is supported by evidence from perception—"I can just see that external objects like hands, books, and chairs exist." Moore thinks this evidence is proof enough, despite not being able to satisfy the skeptic's demands and provide the kind of proof the skeptic wants.[9]

Moore's response illustrates the phrase: "One person's *modus tollens* is another's *modus ponens*." This phrase captures the fact that two different conclusions can be inferred from a conditional if-then statement. And Moore thinks his argument is just as good as the skeptic's, "unless [the skeptic] can give better reasons for asserting that I don't know that [I'm not in virtual reality], than I can give for asserting that I do know [external objects in the world exist, including my body]."[10]

Moore recognized the importance of starting off with pretheoretical, commonsense beliefs about the world before accepting certain theoretical beliefs that deny them. Indeed, Scott Soames said this methodological point is one of Moore's greatest contributions to philosophy: "Some commonsense truths are not theses to be philosophically vindicated or repudiated; they are the [common sense] data against which philosophical theories are to be tested."[11] If skeptical hypotheses or theories of knowledge can't account for common sense beliefs—especially ones we are highly confident are true—then we lack the kind of justification needed to take them seriously.

Building More onto Moore

A neo-Moorean response improves upon Moore by incorporating an account of knowledge that explains how one knows and where the skeptical argument goes wrong. It employs epistemic principles found in the great eighteenth century Scottish philosopher Thomas Reid, which G. E. Moore endorsed.[12] It also rejects a key assumption in the skeptic's reasoning: knowledge always requires evidence supporting one's belief and disclosing that evidence into an argument to vindicate or prove that one knows.[13]

Let's assume the following subjects are not suffering from any cognitive impairments, and their environment is hospitable toward getting truth. In these cases, it seems that if anyone has knowledge, then they have it.

- Joel knows he's experiencing pain in his tooth. [Introspection]
- James knows there is milk in the fridge on the basis of his mother's say-so. [Testimony]
- Braden knows the person who walked through the front door is his mom. [Perception]
- Avagrace knows she can't exist and not exist at the same time. [Intuition]
- Emmafaith knows she ate pancakes for breakfast this morning. [Memory]
- Ella knows she has $1.73 in change after adding together four quarters, six dimes, two nickels, and three pennies. [Reason]

These clear-cut cases of a subject being in a state of knowledge are good starting points for theorizing about what is knowledge.[14] Recall some of these definitions of knowledge from chapter 10:

Traditional Account: S knows a statement P only if S gets to the truth about statement P because of the justification in support of S's belief.

Proper Function Account: S knows P only if S believes the truth because S's belief is produced by properly functioning cognitive faculties in an appropriate environment according to a design plan aimed at reliably getting the truth.

Virtue Accounts: S knows P only if S believes the truth because S's belief is produced by intellectual abilities and/or intellectually virtuous activities.

S truly believes P because of justification, properly functioning cognitive faculties, or intellectual abilities—not dumb luck, accident, or coincidence. But many skeptical arguments assume that to know, one must prove it via argument. But reason is not the only game in town! Joel, James, Braden, Avagrace, and Emmafaith didn't form their beliefs from reason like Ella did. Rather, they formed their beliefs from different sources: introspection, testimony, perception, intuition, and memory, respectively. So the skeptic is just wrong in assuming that all cases of knowledge must be the result of inferential processes involving reason.

We recommend the following three principles, which explain why the skeptic's reasoning is misguided:

Epistemic Principle 1 (EP1): Not everything we know is known by proof.[15]

Perception, introspection, intuition, and memory are nonreasoning ways of forming beliefs. Humans have other intellectual powers, in addition to reason. For example, no one looks at a truck bearing down on them and then conscientiously reasons from one premise-belief to the next, ultimately arriving at a conclusion-belief: "This truck is headed straight for me!" Rather, we sometimes perceive an external object and automatically—indeed, involuntarily—form a belief with a strong conviction: "I believe I need to dodge this oncoming truck." It's the powers of perception at work within us, not the powers of reasoning. The skeptic's assumption that we must prove via arguments that external objects exist is misguided.

Epistemic Principle 2 (EP2): External objects are known by perception, not by giving an argument to prove it.[16]

There is no reason to privilege reason over other sources that bring about beliefs. Requiring all beliefs to be supported by reason alone is arbitrary, requiring a double standard to do it. Consider Thomas Reid's way of articulating this point: "Reason, says the sceptic, is the only judge of truth, and you ought to throw off every opinion and every belief that is not grounded in reason. Why, sir, should I believe the faculty of reason more than that of perception?—they came both from the same shop, and were made by the same artist; and if he pits one piece of false ware into my hands, what should hinder him from putting another?"[17] The same principle applies if the story of how we acquired our faculties is a naturalistic one wherein such faculties were selected for their conduciveness to adapt and survive. Theists and atheists alike have creation stories about their brains' origins. So whatever brought about the brain affects reason just as it would other cognitive faculties. Reason, intuition, introspection, memory, and perception are all in the same epistemic boat.

Epistemic Principle 3 (EP3): The evidence from perception, memory, intuition, and introspection is not inferior to the evidence from reason and arguments.[18]

Many different philosophical theories and arguments come to counterintuitive conclusions. Indeed, some arguments have valid forms and even premises that seem true, yet the argument's conclusions are bizarre: (1) human minds can't reliably connect with the external world; (2) torturing children for fun is not immoral; (3) human consciousness is an illusion. In cases like this, we recommend yielding to perception, intuition, and introspection, which suggests that 1, 2, and 3, respectively, are false.[19] And doing so is not inferior to appealing to reason and arguments.

How Skepticism Sheds New Light on Epistemic Goods

Truth

We think that considering the ways victims in virtual reality are deceived and manipulated is best explained by a *correspondence theory of truth*. When you look at your hand, your perceptual belief is not corresponding to the hand in the pod of chemicals, but rather, a virtual hand generated by the evil machines stimulating your brain. The coherence, pragmatic, and relativist theories of truth do an inadequate job of explaining why the subject is deceived and their beliefs false.

Knowledge

In light of the virtual reality scenario, we discover how important it is for the mind to reliably "connect to" reality; otherwise, truth can't be obtained. This is why the victim in the pod of chemicals lacks knowledge. The victim is connected to a virtual reality. Any adequate account of knowledge must account for cases involving deception.

The Neo-Moorean response points out some of the false assumptions in the skeptic's reasoning. But perhaps it still leaves one dissatisfied because one also wants to know that one's faculties *are* reliable. It's one thing to say knowledge requires one's faculties reliably connecting to reality; it is a much more desirable thing to see that from the inside they do in fact connect to reality. To be able to see exactly just how our faculties reliably hook up to reality and deliver us true beliefs is an understandable desire. Unfortunately, this desire cannot fully be satisfied this side of heaven—this is the epistemic predicament we find ourselves in. It's a predicament because we can't prove our cognitive faculties are reliable without using them to make the argument. Such attempts beg the question. This predicament can seem frustrating. But demanding a proof that borders on incoherency is not a reasonable demand to make. What's wrong with desiring or demanding a non-question-begging proof for the reliability of one's faculties? Consider these four answers.

First, the demand suffers from what William Alston, a famous Christian philosopher, diagnosed as "levels confusion."[20] This is when one assumes that to know something (first-order claim) one must also know how they know it (second-order claim). One assumes independent evidence and reasons are required to demonstrate one is, in fact, in a state of knowledge. For example, I can know that I have hands because I can see that I do, and if my faculties are reliable, then I'm in a state of knowledge. But requiring me to prove that my faculties are reliable is to go down a level—a level that pursues answers to different kinds of questions.

Second, changing the subject from explaining how I know that I have hands to requiring an additional way of seeing that I know that I know I have hands leads to an infinite regress. So why accept this demand? Perhaps questioning the demand to see if there is anything wrong with it is the way to proceed. We think there is something wrong with it: the demand can never be satisfied. For example, knowing P requires knowing that one knows P (KP only if KKP). But knowing that one knows P (KKP) will require knowing that one knows that one knows P (KKP only if KKKP). And we're off and running.[21]

Third, once we stop and reflect on the skeptic's demand that one needs to prove one's faculties are reliable without using them to make the case, we see this demand is an incoherent one.[22] It would be like your boss telling you to read him aloud the office memo without using your eyes and voice to do so. This is incoherent. What's more, you know there is something wrong with a demand if God can't satisfy it. How could God prove to the skeptic that his mind reliably gets truth without using his mind to do so? And if God can't do it, why think humans should have to satisfy this demand? It seems like there is something inherently wrong with the demand.[23]

Last, we think the additional demand of proving one's faculties are reliable in order to obtain knowledge confuses the difference between *knowledge* and *understanding*. These are two distinct epistemic goods. Perhaps this additional demand is really asking for an understanding of how and why one knows. But satisfying these conditions is what's needed for a high level and degree of understanding, not knowledge.

Understanding

There's a strong desire not only to be in a state of knowledge but also to know we are in it. We want to "see" that our cognitive faculties are reliable and that our minds do "connect" with reality. We believe these demands are really asking for an understanding of how and why one knows. But satisfying these conditions is not required for explaining what knowledge is.[24] Understanding is different and should not be confused with knowledge.

Understanding involves answering the *how* and *why* questions. For example, one can know that some event E happened. But one can be ignorant of how and why E happened. To illustrate, you may know that turning the key starts the engine. But you may lack a mental map that diagrams all the causal relations existing amongst the parts involved.[25] Seeing how all these causes work together is to have a certain level of understanding.[26]

Aristotle had an adequate account of understanding. He believed that to understand something, one must know the different causes of it. He worked with four causes—the *formal*, *material*, *efficient*, and *final* cause.[27] The formal cause is a thing's blueprint, form, shape, abstract structure, or sometimes the idea of something in the mind of a designer. The material cause is the matter, stuff, or physical makeup of a thing. The efficient cause are the necessary events, means, or processes involved in bringing something about. The final cause is the goal, purpose, or reason for bringing something about.[28]

Making a distinction between knowledge and understanding allows one to see that the demands made by skeptics for *knowledge* are usually better directed at *understanding*. Skeptics demand certain conditions for knowledge be satisfied, but such conditions are what's required for higher levels of understanding. The demand to prove one's faculties are reliable, for example, is to want an understanding of them—how they work and reliably connect to reality and produce true beliefs. This demand is reasonable; but it's a confusion to think that to be in a state of knowledge one must satisfy these demands.

Conclusion

In this chapter, we discussed external world skepticism. We motivated it by considering Descartes' three-step way of defending that we can't know things in the external world. Then we provided a response to this argument, consulting the work of some historic and contemporary philosophers. Addressing some of the problems and assumptions of this version of skepticism hopefully sheds new light on your previous views on truth, knowledge, and understanding. As a result, we hope you have gained better insight into the nature of these epistemic goods.

Questions for Reflection

1. Do you think the faculty of reason is superior to other faculties? If so, why should it be trusted more than perception, memory, introspection, and so forth?
2. Do you think the reason why many people think acquiring knowledge is so hard is because they are confusing knowledge with understanding?
3. Do you think the three epistemic principles (EP1-EP3) we listed should guide one's interactions with skepticism?
4. Why does Reid's point about the faculty of reason sitting in the same epistemic-boat as other faculties apply to both atheists and theists alike?

For Further Reading

General Readers

DeWeese, Garrett J., and J. P. Moreland. *Philosophy Made Slightly Less Difficult: A Beginner's Guide to Life's Big Questions.* Downers Grove, IL: IVP Academic, 2021.

Plantinga, Alvin. *Knowledge and Christian Belief.* Grand Rapids: Eerdmans, 2015.

Pritchard, Duncan. *Skepticism: A Very Short Introduction.* Oxford: Oxford University Press, 2019.

Zagzebski, Linda. *Epistemology.* Belmont, CA: Wadsworth, Cengage Learning, 2009.

Advanced Reader

Greco, John. *Achieving Knowledge: A Virtue-Theoretic Account of Epistemic Normativity.* Cambridge: Cambridge University Press, 2011.

———. *Putting Skeptics in Their Place: The Nature of Skeptical Arguments and Their Role in Philosophical Inquiry.* Cambridge: Cambridge University Press, 2000.

———, ed. *The Oxford Handbook of Skepticism.* Oxford: Oxford University Press, 2008.

———. "Reid's Reply to the Skeptic," in *The Cambridge Companion to Thomas Reid.* Edited by Terrance Cuneo and René Van Woudenberg. Cambridge: Cambridge University Press, 2004.

Plantinga, Alvin. *Where the Conflict Really Lies: Science, Religion, and Naturalism.* Oxford: Oxford University Press, 2011.

Wolterstorff, Nicholas. *Thomas Reid and the Story of Epistemology.* Cambridge: Cambridge University Press, 2001.

NOTES

1. This skeptical scenario is borrowed from the movie *The Matrix*. See the Wachowskis (directors), 1999, *The Matrix*, Warner Brothers production company.

2. Another famous skeptical hypothesis comes from one of the founders of analytic philosophy, Bertrand Russell (1872–1970). Russell said one can't prove that the earth and everything contained therein, including oneself, wasn't created five minutes ago. This skeptical hypothesis explains all your memory-beliefs as possible creations. The skeptical hypothesis suggests you were created five minutes ago with a lifetime of memories, and the universe was created with the appearance of age. All claims to know about events in the past can be completely separated from real past events. See Bertrand Russell, *The Analysis of Mind* (New York: Wentworth, 2019), 48.

3. In epistemology there is a principle called epistemic closure. There are different variations of the principle, but the idea behind it is roughly this: If S knows p and p entails q, then S also knows q. For example, I know that I am presently visiting New Jersey. Visiting New Jersey entails I am not in Arizona. Therefore, I know I am not in Arizona. Epistemic closure principles aim to capture the idea that if we start with knowing one thing, we can make certain logical inferences to get additional knowledge.

4. We're indebted to John Greco for simplifying Descartes' arguments into this three-step

summarization. Greco credits Barry Stroud for reconstructing it this way. See John Greco, "External World Skepticism," in *Philosophy Compass* 2, no. 4 (2007): 639–40.

5. This kind of case is borrowed from Alvin Plantinga. See Alvin Plantinga, *Warranted Christian Belief* (Oxford: Oxford University Press, 2000), 359.

6. Here's one important lesson from this skeptical scenario: both you (in the good case) and your twin (in the bad case), given the evidence, seem reasonable and rational for believing your perceptual beliefs are true. It doesn't seem like either you or your twin are blameworthy for forming perceptual beliefs and thinking they are true. But we're not focusing on rationality, reasonableness, or blameworthiness. We are focusing in on knowledge. This is called "the new evil demon problem" since it raises questions about how to think about rationality from either a first- or third-person point of view.

7. See John Greco, ed., *The Oxford Handbook of Skepticism* (Oxford: Oxford University Press, 2008).

8. See G. E. Moore, "Proof of an External World," *Proceedings of the British Academy* 25 (1939): 273–300.

9. Moore says, "I have, no doubt, conclusive reasons for asserting that I am not [in the Matrix]; I have conclusive evidence that I am [in the real world]: but that is a very different thing from being able to prove it. I could not tell you what all my evidence is; and I should require to do this at least, in order to give you a proof." Quoted from John Greco, *Achieving Knowledge: A Virtue Theoretic Account* (Cambridge: Cambridge University Press, 2008), 178.

10. G. E. Moore, "Certainty," in *Philosophical Papers (New York: Collier, 1962)*, 242.

11. Scott Soames, *The Analytic Tradition in Philosophy*, vol. 1: *The Founding Giants* (Princeton: Princeton University Press, 2014), 221.

12. We're indebted to the work John Greco has put forth in articulating this response. This is an abbreviated version of it. See John Greco, *Achieving Knowledge*, chap. 11. See also Thomas Reid, *Essays in the Intellectual Powers of Man*, in *The Works of Thomas Reid*, ed. Sir W. Hamilton (1785; Charlottesville, VA: Lincoln-Rembrandt, 1993).

13. There are roughly two main projects in epistemology: vindication and explanation. The vindicationist approach traces back to Pyrrhonian skepticism. It focuses on answering the question, "What do we know?" This project attempts to argue for an account of knowledge that vindicates human knowledge by trying to satisfy the demands of skeptics. The explanatory approach traces back to Plato's *Theatetus*. It focuses on answering the question, "What is knowledge?" The project of explanation aims to explain how knowledge is possible and how it can be acquired by human beings. Many epistemologists now recognize many of the problems generated by the Project of Vindication—especially the incoherent and unsatisfiable demands made by skeptics. See John Greco, "Epistemology," in *Columbia Companion to Twentieth-Century Philosophies*, ed. Constantin V. Bounds (New York: Columbia University Press, 2007), 172.

14. This is called a *particularist* approach in epistemology. *Particularism* takes our pre-theoretical judgments of cases to be intuitively correct insofar as, say, some subject, S, acquired knowledge or not. One's intuitive judgments, then, provide the particularist with a set of datum. The merits of the epistemological principles competing for our endorsement are evaluated on the basis of whether or not they accommodate our pre-theoretical judgments, contra *Methodism* (not to be confused with the Christian denomination). Particularism is

an epistemological project that is consistent with Plato's approach insofar as being motivated by answering the questions "What do we know?" and "How do we know?" in that order. Answers to such questions provide the kind of content needed to answer Plato's question "What is knowledge?" since it provides information about how knowledge is possible and explains the difference between cases wherein we intuitively judge that one knows versus cases wherein one intuitively doesn't know, given the details of the case. It's an approach to epistemology that contrasts with methodism, which first aims to answer the question "How do we know?" in order to answer the ancillary question "What do we know?" Notice how methodism is more at home with skepticism than Plato since it first requires some condition(s) to be met before knowledge can be acquired. In order to acquire knowledge, one must first meet the conditions spelled out in the method or principle prescribed for getting knowledge.

15. Greco *Achieving Knowledge*, 179.

16. This principle is borrowed (with slight modification) from ibid.

17. See Thomas Reid, "An Inquiry into the Human Mind and the Principles of Common Sense," in *Philosophical Works*, ed. H. M. Bracken, 2 vols. (Hildesheim: George Olms, 1983), 185. Quoted from Greco, *Achieving Knowledge*, 181.

18. This principle is borrowed (with slight modification) from Greco, *Achieving Knowledge*, 180.

19. Evidence from introspection, intuition, or perception can provide what are called "defeaters." A defeater is a belief for thinking another belief or claim is false or unjustified. The term "defeater" admits many different meanings amongst epistemologists. It was first put forth by John Pollock, whose seminal work on defeaters distinguished two kinds: *undercutting defeaters* and *rebutting defeaters*. Rebutting defeaters give you a reason or a new belief or experience for thinking your belief or a claim is false. Undercutting defeaters, however, defeat beliefs in a different way: namely, by indicating a belief's source is unreliable, thereby undercutting the belief's justification. In general, a defeater is a reason to no longer hold a belief. More exactly, a defeater is a doubt, belief, or experience that indicates one's belief is false, unreliably formed, or irresponsibly retained. Defeaters, then, can defeat a belief's justification in different ways. So, even though one sees an argument's form is valid and the premises seem true, but the conclusion seems absurd, it could be the evidence from intuition, introspection, or perception providing a defeater for the argument's conclusion. We believe intellectual responsibility still requires pointing out where the argument goes wrong. See John Pollock, *Contemporary Theories of Knowledge* (Totowa, NJ: Rowman and Littlefield, 1986), 37–39.

20. See William Alston, "Level Confusion in Epistemology," *Midwest Studies in Philosophy* 5 (1980): 135–50.

21. In addition to William Alston's paper "Levels Confusion in Epistemology," we recommend John Greco, *Putting Skeptics in Their Place: The Nature of Skeptical Arguments and Their Role in Philosophical Inquiry* (Cambridge: Cambridge University Press, 2000), 181–84. Greco does an excellent job of exposing the problems of this demand for knowledge bottoming out in circularity and being impossible to satisfy because of the regress problem.

22. This objection made by the skeptic should not be seen as pointing out the grave error of *logical circularity* but is rather something called *epistemic circularity*. The former involves fallacious reasoning, the latter does not. Epistemic circularity is when one uses the very

cognitive faculty to justify its reliability. It has been shown that it's impossible to provide a non-circular argument for the reliability of a faculty without using that very faculty to construct the argument. But since we can only use the faculties we have to form beliefs and reason from them, epistemic circularity is permissible—it's not epistemically blameworthy. See William Alston, *The Reliability of Sense Perception* (Ithaca, NY: Cornell University Press, 1993).

23. This point is attributed to Keith DeRose, which was given in a paper presented at Fordham University. More specifically, he argued that our inability to satisfy this demand is a problem (assuming it even is one) for not only humans, but for God because persons that think can only do so in virtue of the abilities they have to do it with. This reference to DeRose's point is taken from Greco, *Putting Skeptics in Their Place*, 186n29. William Alston also credits Alvin Plantinga with making the same point: namely, the inability to provide a non-question-begging response for the reliability of our faculties is not something unique to the human cognitive situation. Indeed, Alston says even "God couldn't *establish* the reliability of some belief-forming practice without using some doxastic practice to do so. And then the [regress problem] would apply." See William P. Alston. *Perceiving God: The Epistemology of Religious Experience* (London: Cornell University Press, 1991), 150n7.

24. We're indebted to Ernest Sosa and John Greco for pointing out how the skeptic's demands for a proof of the reliability of one's cognitive faculties may very well be conditions that an account of understanding must satisfy but not for an account of knowledge. See Greco, "External World Skepticism," 645–46; Ernest Sosa, "How to Resolve the Pyrrhonian Problematic: A Lesson from Descartes," *Philosophical Studies* 85 (1997): 229–49.

25. There is an ignition switch, battery, condenser, coil, starter engine, cylinders, crank shaft, air-fuel mixture, intake manifolds, intake ports, exhaust ports, combustion chambers, fuel injectors, spark plugs, pistons, intake and output valves, etc. that all work together to start the engine and keep it running. Many epistemologists take understanding to involve, among other things, grasping the causal interconnections, patterns, or structure of something. See Jonathan Kvanvig, *The Value of Knowledge and the Pursuit of Understanding* (Cambridge: Cambridge University Press, 2003); Wayne Riggs, "Understanding 'Virtue' and the Virtue of Understanding," in *Intellectual Virtue: Perspectives from Ethics and Epistemology*, ed. Michael DePaul and Linda Zagzebski (Oxford: Oxford University Press, 2003), 203–26; Lorraine Code, *Epistemic Responsibility* (Lebanon, NH: University Press of New England, 1987); Linda Zagzebski, *Virtues of the Mind: An Inquiry into the Nature of Virtue and the Ethical Foundations of Knowledge* (Cambridge: Cambridge University Press, 1996).

26. We highly recommend reading John Greco's neo-Aristotelean account of understanding to see the different kinds of understanding there are. For example, one can grasp the real physical relations existing amongst the parts of an engine (type-1 understanding). One can grasp the relation amongst the working parts of an engine by consulting a blueprint or animated diagram (type-2 understanding). One can also grasp the degree of accuracy shared between the real physical relations existing amongst the parts of an engine and the schematic blueprint or animated diagram representing it (type-3 understanding). See John Greco, "Episteme: Knowledge and Understanding," in *Virtues and Their Vices*, ed. Kevin Tempe and Craig A. Boyd (Oxford: Oxford University Press, 2014), 291.

27. See Aristotle's *Physics*, 2. 3, 194b21–22; and *Metaphysics*, 8. 4, 1044a32-b1.

28. For example, you know that an object is a chair. But why does it have that shape? Answer: the formal cause. The chair's blueprint has those specific dimensions. What is it made of? Answer: material cause. Wood is the material the chair is made from. How did the wood get shaped like that? Answer: the efficient cause. The carpenter cut, shaped, glued, and nailed pieces of wood together. Why is the chair here? Answer: final cause. The carpenter wanted to build something for students to sit on. Understanding requires seeing how these four causes fit together.

CHAPTER 12

What Is Religious Epistemology?

Epistemology is a subdiscipline of philosophy that aims to better understand concepts like truth, knowledge, and understanding, as well as concepts like belief, rationality, evidence, and justification. In this chapter, we take the tools of epistemology and apply them to God. More specifically, we employ the methods and standards used by epistemologists to determine whether one's belief in God can be justified. In chapter 10, we looked at two epistemic goods: knowledge and truth. In this chapter, we will revisit knowledge and introduce concepts like justification, evidence, rationality, and understanding as they apply to questions about belief in God.

Some Questions Religious Epistemologists Seek to Answer

Humans are naturally curious and want answers to big-ticket questions. One way to think about religious epistemology, then, is to see it as a way to think well about big-ticket questions concerning God and religious beliefs. Here are two of those questions: What is required for belief in God to be justified? And is knowledge of God possible? They're epistemic because they are about *justification* and *knowledge*. But there are many other epistemic questions. Indeed, practicing religious epistemology sometimes feels like working in a triage system of an emergency room because you're seeking answers to questions based on the urgency of your situation.

People's interest and needs in religious epistemology can have different motivations. For example, a family member or friend might demand a religious believer provide a rational defense for her recent conversion.[1] Or, perhaps, a friend wants a religious believer to provide an argument for God's existence; otherwise, he thinks religious beliefs are irrational. (I experienced many of these situations, too, as well as the ones that follow.) Or a professor might demand a Christian to prove why God permits evil before judging the student's religious beliefs as justified. Or a Christian might be thinking about why God's presence is not more obvious to others. Or a friend tells a Christian his beliefs about God are the result of early education and cultural influence. He goes on to assert that had he been born somewhere else, he would have different religious beliefs. Now the Christian is asking whether the testimony from his parents and teachers about God is true. So whether one is interested in addressing rationality, arguments, God's hiddenness, or the significance of the origins of religious beliefs,[2] religious epistemology aims to assist one to think well and better about these topics.

FAITH

There is no consensus on how Christians define the term *faith* since it's used to capture different facts about reality. Here's one way to define it. Faith is a disposition of trust—accompanied by affective states like confidence—one has toward the truth of something despite lacking conclusive evidence supporting it. (One doesn't have faith in, say, existing because the evidence for it is overwhelming.) The term *faith* also captures how Christians should—like those mentioned in Hebrews 11—confidentially trust their well-being into the care of God, whom they can be confident has their best interests in mind.

What Is Required for Reasonable Belief in God?

It's common to hear people dismiss belief in God. Some take it to be irrational, unjustified, unreasonable, or lacking sufficient evidence. But what is the argument supporting these claims? What's driving the perceived unreasonableness of belief in God? Christian philosopher Alvin Plantinga famously addressed these questions by diagnosing the kind of argument commonly used to support this objection. The argument is known as the *evidentialist objection* to belief in God.[3] It looks like this:[4]

1. One has a reasonable belief in God only if one's belief is supported by good evidence.
2. There is no good evidence for God's existence.
3. Therefore, it's not reasonable to believe in God.

This kind of argument is frequently used to attack the positive epistemic qualities we want our beliefs to enjoy. Reasonable, justified, and evidentially supported are good qualities a "rational belief" enjoys. But in 1983, Plantinga revolutionized epistemology by challenging the assumption undergirding this argument.[5]

Some epistemologists respond to this argument by attacking premise 2. Cosmological arguments, moral arguments, design arguments, and other arguments for God's existence are used to meet the demand for good evidence.[6] Indeed, this is the method used by different apologists employing evidence from history, science, morality, testimony, and so on to justify belief in God.[7] Plantinga, however, focuses on addressing the problems with premise 1. Premise 1 says that reasonable belief in God requires good evidence. But what counts as good evidence? Many believe good evidence amounts to good arguments using the right kind of premises.

Premises that were supported by beliefs that are evident to the senses, self-evident, and incorrigible were considered the gold standard for evidence—specifically, propositional evidence. These were the right kind of premises. Beliefs that are evident to the senses are when one forms the belief that "The apple is red" or "Sugar tastes sweet." Self-evident beliefs are formed after one properly understands the concepts used in a statement. For example, "An object's surface can't be entirely red and blue at the same time" or "No object can be a square-circle" or "No bachelor can be married." Incorrigible beliefs rely upon one's first-person psychological states. The evidence supporting one's seeming to see redness or one's appearance of redness on the surface of the apple can't be denied. Of course, the redness may be caused by trick lighting. But the seeming of it can't be denied. Plantinga traced this view of justification employed by evidentialism to classical foundationalism, which is a way to explain the structure of justification.[8]

But Plantinga recognized that all kinds of reasonable beliefs are not supported by arguments. For example, it's reasonable to believe that "I had eggs for breakfast," "The people in this room have minds," "I have pain in my tooth," "There is an external world," and "It's wrong to torture children for fun" without justifying them with arguments.[9] Indeed, it seems even young children and people with certain mental disabilities are not only reasonable in believing such things but can even know them. And they don't need arguments to justify their beliefs in order to be attributed with knowledge. So Plantinga evaluated the reasons for thinking that belief in God is reasonable only if one has an argument to justify it. His conclusion: there are no good reasons for thinking this because belief in God is *properly basic*. What's that? Let's consider it.

Basic Beliefs, Non-Basic Beliefs, and Properly Basic Beliefs

One of Plantinga's lasting legacies in philosophy is showing there are no good reasons for thinking a reasonable belief in God requires an argument to justify it. Plantinga famously argued that belief in God can be a properly basic belief.

A basic belief is not justified by arguments or additional beliefs. For example, the perceptual belief that "There is a bird outside my window" is not justified by an argument; rather, it's justified by the faculty of perception, which is a reliable belief-forming source. Similarly, the memorial belief that "I left my keys on the kitchen table" is justified by the reliable faculty of memory, not argument; the testimonial belief that "Our son is in the back yard playing" is justified by my wife's reliable testimony, not argument; the intuitive belief that "One can't acquire knowledge by looking at a broken clock" is justified by the reliable faculty of intuition, not argument; the introspective belief that "I have an itch in my foot" is justified by the reliable faculty of introspection, not argument. These "reliable" faculties are obviously not infallible; rather, the reliability is taken to be something far better than chance. Further, forming beliefs from these faculties is more reliable than forming beliefs from wishful thinking, emotional reasoning, consulting tarot cards, and reading tea leaves.[10]

A non-basic belief is justified by argument or appeal to additional beliefs. For example, the belief that "The car's fuel pump is failing because its gears are worn out" is justified by other beliefs and arguments, such as beliefs about the trustworthiness of the mechanics and their reasons supporting the diagnosis. But consider Smith's belief that "The Eagles will win the Superbowl." Smith formed this belief by consulting his crystal ball, not from additional beliefs or arguments. So it's a basic belief. Because Smith formed this belief by consulting a crystal ball, however, it's not a *properly* basic belief.

Properly basic beliefs are justified by reliable

EVIDENCE

Evidence indicates a belief is true. The more evidence supporting a belief, the more likely it's true. There's debate, however, on what constitutes evidence. Some take evidence to be publicly shareable, treating it as something physical that can be verified by others. Some take evidence to extend beyond this to include sensory experiences, perceptual awareness of nonphysical entities, intuitions, intellectual seemings, testimony, facts comprising a belief's etiology, dispositions of intellectual character, and memories. Mathematicians, logicians, historians, scientists, philosophers, and theologians all sift for different kinds of evidence related to their discipline. Note that if God is an immaterial, personal agent, then evidence for God's existence (e.g., having a perceptual awareness of God) will not be the kind of evidence used in the physical sciences.

sources, not unreliable ones. Perception, memory, testimony, intuition, and introspection are generally far better than chance; they are reliable sources for belief formation. Crystal ball gazing, invalid reasoning, wishful thinking, emotional reasoning, hunches, reading tea leaves, and the like are unreliable sources for belief formation. Just because a belief may be basic, it doesn't follow that it's properly basic. Properly basic beliefs are justified by reliable sources that can satisfy adequate accounts for justification or knowledge, thereby making them rational.

Plantinga argued that if Christianity is true, then belief in the Christian God can be a properly basic belief.[11] People can form beliefs about God from sources other than arguments (e.g., perception, introspection, intuition, etc.). What's more, this properly basic belief can enjoy positive epistemic qualities like being rational, reasonable, justified, and satisfy conditions for knowledge.[12] Let's consider how he arrived at these conclusions.

Plantinga's Reformed Epistemology

Properly basic beliefs are justified by reliable belief-forming sources. Plantinga reasons that if the Christian God exists, then (given God's character and purposes) God would have created humans with the powers and abilities to know him—relate with him experientially. Indeed, Plantinga says, "[God] created us in such a way that we would come to hold such true beliefs as that there is such a person as God, that he is our creator, that we owe him obedience and worship, that he is worthy of worship, that he loves us, and so on."[13]

Why does Plantinga think this? At least two reasons: First, if God is morally perfect, perfectly loving, and intends to have a personal relationship with humans, then it's reasonable to assume God would create humans with the kind of minds and agency needed to do so. God would equip us to know him, thereby designing our cognitive faculties to bring about these true beliefs. Second, Plantinga agrees with the Christian heritage and its experts like Thomas Aquinas (1225–1274) and John Calvin (1509–1564), who affirm that knowledge of God can be acquired from evidence not sourced in argument.[14] Just as perception, memory, testimony, intuition, and introspection can bring about properly basic beliefs so can the cognitive faculty Plantinga calls the "*sensus divinitatis*," which is Latin for *the sense of divinity*.[15] If all this is true, then the evidentialist objection not only fails for what makes a belief rational but also fails to account for alternative ways a belief can be justified and an instance of knowledge.

Of course, everything hinges on whether the Christian God does, in fact, exist! And Plantinga hasn't proven that God exists.[16] Rather, this work in epistemology defends the claims that belief in God can be rational, justified, and satisfy conditions for knowledge without the support of an explicit argument.[17] But one might be interested in the question "What makes one's belief in God justified?" Let's consider some epistemic approaches toward answering this kind of question.

Different Epistemic Interests and Needs Motivate Different Epistemic Approaches

We've mentioned different epistemic challenges, concerns, and questions that pique one's interest in epistemology. For example, consider the different interests and needs of Will and Jill. Will just converted to Christianity on the basis of a profound religious experience. Now he's interested in a philosophical account that explains how this evidence justifies his religious beliefs; he needs a model that explains why it's rational, reasonable, and intellectually responsible to form such beliefs. Part of Jill's conversion to Christianity involved the use of arguments to remove intellectual stumbling blocks. Now she's interested in sharing these arguments with family and friends; she needs evidence that her family and friends will find compelling—especially since her sibling is skeptical and wants more evidence.

Notice that Will's beliefs are justified in religious experience; Jill's beliefs are justified in argument. Their epistemic interests and needs are motivated for different purposes.[18] Jill wants to satisfy the skeptic's demands for more justification, whereas Will wants to explain—for his own sake—how it's possible to have justification and knowledge of God. In light of this, it's no surprise to see religious epistemologists pursue different epistemic goals.

Because of different epistemic questions, interests, and needs, it's helpful to be familiar with two separate approaches to epistemology: the *explanation approach* and the *vindication approach*.[19] The vindication approach tries to satisfy the skeptic's demands for what counts as good justification and what's required for knowledge. It takes up the project of trying to vindicate one's justification and knowledge in the face of opposition. Indeed, skeptical questions and threats are what motivate this approach. Some skeptics demand one's justification be disclosed for all to see or one's claim to knowledge be supported by a *proof.*[20]

The explanation approach is not concerned with trying to satisfy the skeptic's demands. It begins by assuming many of the skeptic's assumptions are false. It takes knowledge to be something that humans achieve quite often. Thus, the explanation approach sees the skeptic's demands as either unsatisfiable, confused, or something worse. This approach is interested, rather, in explaining what knowledge is and where skeptics' assumptions and arguments go wrong. Furthermore, it aims to provide models for understanding how it's possible for humans to get knowledge. The fruit of this work aims to explain when someone knows and doesn't know.

Justification: Internalism versus Externalism

In epistemology there are different theories for what justifies a belief. Justification is roughly that which makes a belief responsibly formed or not. Some ways of forming beliefs are more intellectually responsible than others. A justified belief, then, will satisfy certain responsibility conditions. Justification can also refer to that which indicates a belief is true or transforms a true belief into knowledge.[21] Some types of justification are harder to satisfy than others.

Given there are different epistemic interests, needs, and questions, epistemologists define *justification* differently.[22] Internalists, motivated by questions the vindicationist approach seeks to answer, take justification to be something like the standard one's belief needs to satisfy for the subject to be judged responsible or not violating any epistemic duties.[23] This version of justification typically gets defined by describing the evidence that supports one's belief from a first-person point of view. What justifies a belief is the evidence one can "internally access" by reflecting on it.[24] One can see how the evidence supports a belief, at least a significant portion of it.[25] This kind of justification will interest people like Jill. Recall that she wants to use evidence and arguments to vindicate her religious beliefs in the face of skeptical family members and friends. Internalist views of justification, then, aim at addressing many skeptical threats and challenges. This is why many apologists employ this approach.[26]

Someone like Bill, however, may satisfy his interests, needs, and questions through an externalist account of justification. Externalists believe the boundaries for what justifies a belief extend beyond what can be seen from the "inside" (one's first-person perspective). The evidence that justifies a belief need not always be internally accessible through reflection. The epistemic interest in justification, then, aims to explain how it converts a true belief into knowledge or how it's involved in reliably connecting one's mind to reality, establishing a state of knowledge. Externalists don't deny that some evidence justifying a belief is internally accessible: externalism rejects the claim that all justifying evidence can be accessed through reflection alone. Externalists believe the boundaries of justification should extend to facts that are not internally accessible. This is because the entire history of a belief's formation is epistemically relevant when determining its justification. All the facts explaining how the initial thought of "P" transformed into a belief in "P" due to all the evidence influencing it over time needs to be taken into account. From the fact that one can't internally access all the relevant evidence, it doesn't follow that there aren't important facts justifying a belief. Indeed, accounting for all these facts helps explain how knowledge is possible. This externalist approach will be of interest to people like Bill, who want to understand what knowledge is and what conditions explain the difference between knowing and not knowing. More specifically, it will assist Bill's ability to explain how knowledge of God is possible.

Divine Hiddenness: Common Ground Shared by Internalists and Externalists

One popular topic in religious epistemology is divine hiddenness. Divine hiddenness concerns questions about the absence of experiential evidence for God's existence. For example, "Why isn't God's presence more obvious?" Or if one has a perceptual awareness of God's presence, this might elicit the question: "Why doesn't God provide this kind of experiential evidence equally to others?" It goes beyond the scope of this chapter to address all the ways epistemologists have answered these questions.[27] We raise this topic because it addresses the kind of evidence most, if not all, people take as conclusive evidence for God's existence. Indeed, it's the kind of evidence God provided people throughout the Old and New Testament periods. And it's the kind of evidence that enables one to be directly acquainted with God, thereby enabling a personal relationship to ensue.[28]

Let's consider a case involving the formation of a belief in God based on religious experience. More specifically, consider Will's belief in God based on an experiential (perceptual) awareness of God's presence.[29] Some encouraging news is that many internalists and externalists now agree on these epistemic points about belief in God grounded in religious experience.

Both externalism and weak versions of internalism agree on the following:

- One need not be aware of how experiential, perceptual evidence of God's presence justifies one's belief in God.[30]
- One need not require religious beliefs to always be justified by arguments.[31]

- Beliefs formed on the basis of religious experience can be properly basic beliefs.[32]
- Sensory experience (in general) and experiential awareness of God's presence (specifically) are taken as nonpropositional evidence—evidence that brings about a belief without inferring it from premises in an argument.[33]

Many internalists and externalists agree that beliefs based on an experience of God's presence can justify a belief and need not be supported by additional beliefs and arguments (thereby being a properly basic belief). What's more, many internalists and externalists agree that justification and knowledge require a responsibility condition when forming beliefs about God.

What about the questions we started off asking? Why doesn't God provide experiential evidence more frequently and equally to all people?[34] Paul K. Moser challenges the assumption that God is obligated to provide humans with certain kinds of conclusive evidence, like audible voices from the sky or disrupting the laws of nature through miraculous events for all to see. Rather, Moser asks a prior question: What kind of evidence should we expect from a God that wants us to non-coercively enter a filial relationship with him and undergo radical moral transformation? This question is epistemically relevant because humans might be looking for evidence of God in all the wrong places.[35] Moser makes a distinction between "spectator evidence" and the evidence provided by receiving the Transformative Gift[36] through God's "divine authoritative call." Spectator evidence is the kind of evidence casual observers acquire by passively perceiving reality. This is the kind of evidence demons presumably have. According to James 2:19, having mere belief in God isn't a big deal—"Even the demons believe that—and shudder"—because it doesn't achieve God's purposes. Moser shifts the tables on skeptics' demands for spectator evidence and asks them to honestly consult their motivations in light of this question: "Am I willing to be known by God in virtue of being authoritatively challenged by God for the sake of my being transformed toward God's moral character via my being led by God in volitional fellowship?"[37] Many externalists and internalists alike can agree that one's moral and intellectual character bears on the kind of receptive attitude one will have toward receiving or repressing the kind of evidence on offer, specifically, the kind of evidence that achieves God's purposes of establishing a filial relationship resulting in the cultivation of Christ-like character. What's more, externalists and internalists can agree that the kind of evidence that brings this about is not like spectator evidence that many expect God is obligated to provide.

Conclusion

In epistemology, there are different epistemic goods we care about. Evidence, reasonableness, rationality, justification, and knowledge are valuable epistemic goods. Thinking about these relative to God and religious beliefs makes up much of religious epistemology. One epistemic good we haven't discussed is understanding. Understanding shouldn't be confused with knowledge, despite how often people mistakenly use the terms *knowledge* and *understanding* interchangeably. Chapter 10 provided some plausible definitions of knowledge. What they all share in common is that knowledge is better and more valuable than mere true belief. Getting the truth because of one's justification, intellectual ability, or properly functioning cognitive faculty is an achievement unlike getting the truth because of dumb luck or accident.

Understanding, however, is different than knowledge. Understanding involves answering "why" questions and "how" questions. Aristotle had an adequate account of understanding. He said that, in order to understand something, one must provide the four causes of it. The four causes were formal, material, efficient, and final. To take a simple example, one might ask, "Why is there a wooden chair in this classroom?" Answer: Formal cause: because the chair's blueprint has those dimensions; material cause: because wood is the material the chair is made from; efficient cause: because the carpenter cut, shaped, glued, and nailed pieces of wood together; final cause: because the carpenter wanted to build something for students to sit on. Understanding why there is a chair in this classroom, then, requires knowing how this chair depends upon these four causes. The upshot of understanding is seeing how these four causes all fit together.[38] Therefore, one can know that the object is a chair but fail to understand the how- and why-questions about the chair.

The distinction between knowledge and understanding is important to religious epistemology. Many think that to have a reasonable belief in God's existence or knowledge that God exists, one must also adequately explain why God hides and/or permits evil. But this is a false assumption for the following reasons. First, the quality or reliability of one's evidence for God's existence is not determined by whether it does additional work explaining the hiddenness of God or why God permits evil.[39] If that were true, then the evidence for my (Gary's) wife's existence must also explain her decisions and choices for acting the way she does. But after many years of marriage, I am still trying to understand why she does these things! (I'm confident she feels the same way about me, too.) But that doesn't mean my justification for believing she exists is no good or that I don't know she exists. Second, the assumption conflates knowledge with understanding: the kind of conditions needing to be satisfied in order to know are a different animal altogether from understanding why God hides and/or permits evil. As Greco states: "There is now logical space for ordinary knowledge of God without [having to provide a] philosophical or theological understanding [of why God hides and/or permits pain, suffering, and evil]."[40]

Questions for Reflection

1. What kind of questions do you think religious epistemology aims to answer? Do you think your answers reflect a vindicationist approach or an explanatory approach to epistemology?
2. When you find yourself disagreeing with someone whom you take to be a careful thinker or an expert in the matter, do you think the disagreement is evidence against the truth of your belief? If not, why isn't disagreement counterevidence? If so, how should one respond to the disagreement? Should one adjust one's level of confidence in the truth of one's belief? Should one withhold judgment until the disagreement can be explained?
3. Do you think God would provide evidence for his existence to people only through reason and argument? Do you think that belief in God can be properly basic? Why or why not?
4. How important do you think the relation is between God's character and purposes and the kind of evidence that achieves God's purposes? Can we reasonably expect God to provide evidence that is either inconsistent with God's character and/or fails to achieve God's purposes?

For Further Reading

General Readers

DePoe, John M., and Tyler Dalton McNabb, eds. *Debating Christian Religious Epistemology: An Introduction to Five Views on the Knowledge of God.* New York: Bloomsbury Academic, 2020.

Dickinson, Travis. *Wandering toward God: Finding Faith Amid Doubts and Big Questions.* Downers Grove, IL: InterVarsity Press, 2022.

Moreland, J. P. *A Simple Guide to Experience Miracles.* Grand Rapids: Zondervan, 2021.

Pickavance, Timothy. *Knowledge for the Love of God: Why Your Heart Needs Your Mind.* Grand Rapids: Eerdmans, 2022.

Plantinga, Alvin. *Knowledge and Christian Belief.* Grand Rapids: Eerdmans, 2015.

Rasmussen, Joshua. *How Reason Can Lead to God: A Philosopher's Bridge to Faith.* Downers Grove, IL: IVP Academic, 2019.

Advanced Readers

Abraham, William L., and Frederick D. Aquino, eds. *The Oxford Handbook of the Epistemology of Theology*. Oxford: Oxford University Press, 2017.

Clark, Kelly James, and Raymond J. VanArragon, eds. *Evidence and Religious Belief*. Oxford: Oxford University Press, 2011.

Howard-Snyder, Daniel, and Paul K. Moser, eds. *Divine Hiddenness: New Essays*. Cambridge: Cambridge University Press, 2001.

Moser, Paul K. *The Elusive God: Reorienting Religious Epistemology*. Cambridge: Cambridge University Press, 2008.

Plantinga, Alvin. *Warranted Christian Belief*. Oxford: Oxford University Press, 2000.

Walls, Jerry L., and Trent Dougherty, eds. *Two Dozen (or So) Arguments for God: The Plantinga Project*. Oxford: Oxford University Press, 2018.

NOTES

1. This was my own (Gary's) experience, which motivated me to study epistemology and religious epistemology.
2. There are at least two versions of this epistemic concern. The first questions the reliability of forming beliefs on the basis of testimony from parents and early education, which happens at a particular geographical place and time in history. See John Greco, "Religious Knowledge in the Context of Conflicting Testimony," *Proceedings of the American Catholic Philosophical Association* 83 (2009), 61–76; and Tomas Bogardus, "The Problem of Contingency for Religious Belief," *Faith and Philosophy* 30, no. 4 (2013), 371–92. Another version of this epistemic concern traces back to popular thinkers like Karl Marx ("opium of the masses") and Sigmund Freud ("wish-fulfillment"). Recall the genetic fallacy in ch. 9: merely describing how a belief was formed says nothing about whether the belief is true. And Freud hasn't shown that this method may be part of God's design plan for producing true beliefs. Indeed, Alvin Plantinga says, "The serious theist will think that God has created us in such a way that we come to know him and the function of that cognitive process, whatever they are, that ordinarily produce belief in God in us is to provide us with true belief. So even if she agrees with Freud that theistic belief in God arises from wish-fulfillment, she will think that this particular instance of wish-fulfillment is truth-aimed; it is God's way of getting us to see that he is in fact present and in fact cares for us." See Alvin Plantinga, *Where the Conflict Really Lies: Science, Religion, and Naturalism* (Oxford: Oxford University Press, 2011), chap. 5.
3. Alvin Plantinga traces the evidentialist objection to theses made by John Locke, David Hume, W. K. Clifford, and Bertrand Russell. The common thread running through their theses is that one is epistemically responsible only if one's confidence in the truth of the belief is proportioned to evidence supporting it. See Alvin Plantinga, "Reason and Belief in God," in *Faith and Rationality: Reason and Belief in God,* ed. Alvin Plantinga and Nicholas Wolterstorff (Notre Dame: University of Notre Dame Press, 1983), 24–25.
4. The structure of this argument was inspired by John Greco. See John Greco, "Knowledge of God," in *The Oxford Handbook of the Epistemology of Theology*, ed. William L. Abraham and Frederick D. Aquino (Oxford: Oxford University Press, 2017), 15.

5. Plantinga, "Reason and Belief in God," 16–93.

6. See chapter 18 to learn about these kinds of arguments.

7. For example, the classical method, evidential method, and cumulative case method provide various kinds of evidence for belief in God (in general) and Christianity (specifically). See William Lane Craig et al., *Five Views on Apologetics*, ed. Stanley N. Gundry and Steven B. Cowen (Grand Rapids: Zondervan, 2000).

8. Wolterstorff believes Plantinga was the first to identify and explain how classical foundationalism was supporting the evidentialist enterprise. See Nicholas Wolterstorff, "Then, Now, and Al," *Faith and Philosophy* 28, no. 3 (2011): 253–66.

9. See chapter 11, too, which addresses how this assumption is used to support external world skepticism.

10. Alvin Goldman, an important epistemologist who contributed to the development of externalist theories of justification and knowledge, said, "[C]onfused reasoning, wishful thinking, reliance on emotional attachment, mere hunch or guesswork, and hasty generalizations" are all processes or methods that share a common culprit: namely, "unreliability." See Alvin Goldman, "What Is Justified Belief?" in *Empirical Knowledge*, ed. Paul K. Moser (Totowa, NJ: Rowman and Littlefield, 1986), 179.

11. Plantinga was responding to *de jure* objections, which claim religious beliefs are somehow unreasonable, irrational, unjustified, or something worse. *De jure* objections, then, claim that even if religious beliefs turn out to be true, humans can't form or maintain them without being intellectually irresponsible. *De facto* objections aim at demonstrating religious beliefs as false or unlikely to be true. Plantinga aimed to show there's no good *de jure* objections to Christian beliefs. The best way to attack his explanations for how Christian beliefs can be reasonable, rational, and satisfy conditions for knowledge is to mount successful *de facto* objections.

12. Recall the different definition of knowledge in chapter 10. The virtue account says one knows God exists only if one acquires this true belief because of reliable intellectual abilities or virtues. The proper function account says one knows God exists only if this belief is produced by properly functioning cognitive faculties in an appropriate environment according to a design plan aimed at reliably getting the truth.

13. Alvin Plantinga, *Warranted Christian Belief* (Oxford: Oxford University Press, 2000), 188–89.

14. Ibid., 170–77.

15. This, of course, is Plantinga's view, and not all Christians agree that humans get endowed with this faculty, since perception, introspection, and testimony (especially testimony from the Holy Spirit) can do the kind of work Plantinga attributes to the *sensus divinitatis*.

16. For some of Plantinga's theistic arguments and others he inspired, see Jerry L. Walls and Trent Dougherty, eds., *Two Dozen (Or So) Arguments for God: The Plantinga Project* (Oxford: Oxford University Press, 2018).

17. See Alvin Plantinga, *Knowledge and Christian Belief* (Grand Rapids: Eerdmans Publishing, 2015), which is a more concise and accessible version of the theses developed in *Warranted Christian Belief.*

18. For additional examples of epistemic approaches developing out of different motivated interests and concerns see Trent Dougherty and Chris Tweedt, "Religious Epistemology," *Philosophy Compass* 10, no. 8 (2015), 547–59.

19. See John Greco, "Epistemology," in *Columbia Companion to Twentieth-Century Philosophies*,

ed. Constantin V. Bounds (New York: Columbia University Press, 2007), 172; and Greco, "Knowledge of God," 13.

20. Paul K. Moser reminds readers that "some skeptics demand 'proof' of God's existence, even without clarification of what they mean by the ambiguous word 'proof.' In these discussions, 'proof' is a fighting word, pure and simple." Proof is commonly taken to be a sound argument—an argument with a valid form and true premises. But adequate evidence isn't restricted to proofs. Indeed, Moser continues by saying, "Typically, proof resides in the domains of logic and mathematics. God, if real, is a personal agent, not an axiom, a theorem, or an argument; it would be a serious category mistake to suppose otherwise." See Paul K. Moser, *The Elusive God: Reorienting Religious Epistemology* (Cambridge: Cambridge University Press, 2008), 35.

21. Alvin Plantinga, an externalist, has coined the term "warrant" to capture some of the work the term "justification" does. Plantinga takes warrant ("whatever precisely it is") to be that, enough of which, can convert a true belief into knowledge. See Alvin Plantinga, *Warrant: The Current Debate* (Oxford: Oxford University Press, 1993), 3.

22. For a thorough discussion on the merits of how internalists and externalists conceive, define, and defend their accounts of justification, see Trent Dougherty, ed., *Evidentialism and Its Discontents* (Oxford: Oxford University Press, 2011).

23. Robert Audi, *Epistemology: A Contemporary Introduction to the Theory of Knowledge* (New York: Routledge, 1998), 235.

24. See John Greco, *Achieving Knowledge: A Virtue Theoretic Account of Epistemic Normativity* (Cambridge: Cambridge University Press, 2008), 48.

25. There is a distinction between access internalism and mentalism internalism. The former is stronger insofar as accessing the relevant evidence justifying a belief, whereas the latter is weaker insofar as accessing a significant portion of the relevant evidence. See ibid., 54.

26. Evidential and Classical apologetic methods primarily use an internalist version of justification. This is because what justifies a religious belief will be inducive, deductive, or abductive arguments. The "justification" is disclosable—the evidence used to justify a belief can be shared with others for their consideration in the form of a statement or premise in an argument. Reformed epistemology relies heavily upon an externalist version of justification. Since humans can form reasonable beliefs about God from sources other than arguments— like perception, testimony, answers to prayer, perceptual awareness of God's presence, the experience of new powers to love and forgive, or the *sensus divinitatis*—the conception of justification expands to include experiences, intuitions, intellectual seemings, a belief's etiology, testimony, and dispositions as evidence justifying a belief.

27. See Daniel Howard-Snyder and Paul K. Moser, eds., *Divine Hiddenness: New Essays* (Cambridge: Cambridge University Press, 2001); Veronika Weidner, *Divine Hiddenness* (Cambridge: Cambridge University Press, 2021); J. L. Shellenberg, *The Hiddenness Argument: Philosophy's New Challenge to Belief in God* (Oxford: Oxford University Press, 2015); Michael Rea, *The Hiddenness of God* (Oxford: Oxford University Press, 2018).

28. Brandon L. Richabaugh, "Eternal Life as Knowledge of God: An Epistemology of Knowledge by Acquaintance and Spiritual Formation," *Journal of Spiritual Formation and Soul Care* 6, no. 2 (2013): 204–28; Gary Osmundsen, "Sanctification as Joint Agency with the Triune God: An Aristotelian Causal Model," *Philosophia Christi* 21, no. 2 (2019): 325–54.

29. Perhaps Will has a perceptual awareness of God's presence (a) influencing his actions; (b) convicting his conscience; (c) manifesting through a beautiful scene in nature or art; (d) manifesting through the actions of another person; or (e) assisting the heart and mind to embrace a truth discovered in Scripture. There are more ways, of course, for how God can choose to reveal his presence to others.

30. Some internalists appeal to phenomenal conservativism as a weak version of internalism. See Max Baker-Hytch, "Epistemic Externalism in the Philosophy of Religion," *Philosophy Compass* (2017): 5.

31. Ibid. See also Trent Dougherty and Chris Tweedt, "Religious Epistemology," *Philosophy Compass* 10, no. 8 (2015), 547–59.

32. Ibid.

33. There is an important distinction between inferential beliefs and non-inferential beliefs. Inferential beliefs are the result of arguments. For example, one reasons from a premise-belief to another premise-belief and eventually is convinced or not that the conclusion is true based on the support of the premises. If so, then one forms a conclusion-belief based on an inferential process. Non-inferential beliefs form without making reasoned inferences. For example, one perceives a car speeding toward oneself and automatically forms the belief "This car is going to hit me." The belief is not the result of inferring a conclusion-belief from premise-beliefs—indeed, the belief most likely formed involuntarily.

34. John Greco makes an important point about the nature of testimonial evidence: namely, when a person decides to disclose personal information to another, it is inherently discriminatory. That is, persons are selective to whom they disclose valuable, personal information for the purpose of achieving certain goals. Given God is a person, it makes sense to attribute certain purposes and reasons for why God chooses to reveal God's presence to some and not others in order to achieve certain goals in peoples' lives at appropriate times. See John Greco, "Friendly Theism," in *Religious Tolerance through Humility: Thinking with Philip Quinn*, ed. James Kraft and David Basinger (Burlington, VT: Ashgate, 2008).

35. See Moser, *Elusive God*.

36. Moser defines this gift as follows: "The Transformative Gift [is by definition experienced] via conscience, a person's (a) being authoritatively convicted and forgiven by X of all that person's wrongdoing and (b) thereby being authoritatively called and led by X both into noncoerced volitional fellowship with X in perfect love and into rightful worship toward X as worthy of worship and, on that basis, transformed by X from (i) that person's previous tendencies to selfishness and despair to (ii) a new volitional center with a default position of unselfish love and forgiveness toward all people and of hope in the ultimate triumph of good over evil by X." See ibid., 134–35.

37. Ibid., 10.

38. For an excellent updated version of this Aristotelian account of understanding, see John Greco, "Episteme: Knowledge and Understanding," in *Virtues and Their Vices*, ed. Kevin Tempe and Craig A. Boyd (New York: Oxford University Press, 2014).

39. This point was first brought to Gary's attention by Paul K. Moser. See Paul K. Moser, *The Evidence for God: Religious Knowledge Reexamined* (Cambridge: Cambridge University Press, 2010), 254.

40. Greco, "Knowledge of God," 13.

PART 4

Metaphysics

Exploration into the Nature of Reality and Human Persons

CHAPTER 13

What Exists and What Doesn't?

Existence and Ultimate Reality

Christian philosopher Dallas Willard once said that genius is the ability to scrutinize the obvious.[1] Metaphysics is the subdiscipline of philosophy that showcases this ability. Metaphysicians are skilled at scrutinizing obvious things in efforts to discover many truths that often get overlooked. Let us introduce metaphysics, then, by considering some different metaphysical ways of scrutinizing a simple observation.

Simple Observation: You look across the street and see your neighbor playing fetch with her dog.

Thinking hard about this simple observation can result in the development of some profound metaphysical beliefs. For example, perceiving your neighbor, the dog, and ball might result in the belief in three distinct objects, each with their own unique parts. But is that belief true? Perhaps you're perceiving only one thing arranged in three different ways. Like one lump of clay formed into three different connected shapes. Or perhaps you perceived countless infinitesimal particles arranged in three different ways.

Monism, Pluralism, or Atomism?

Scrutinizing our simple observation has already opened three possibilities to the nature of reality. Reality consists of something. But is the fundamental nature of reality just one thing (*monism*), a bunch of independent things having parts and properties (*pluralism*), or countless tiny things not having parts (*atomism*, another version of pluralism)? The correct answer to this perennial metaphysical question will inform whether the nature of reality contains only one substance, many substances with their own properties, or countless properties bundled together in various ways, making different aggregates. Let's take a moment to clarify these significant philosophical terms.

Substance

A *substance* is a particular object that has some property, part, capacity, and/or power that is organized by its nature. A substance can also undergo change (lose one property, gain a new one) and stand in relation to other things (standing to the left of the table or is the father of James). When we talk, we typically are describing something in a substance or about a substance. You never see happiness, yellowness, or quickness just dangling about; if you see them, they will be had by something—what many philosophers call a substance. The neighbor's dog (i.e., a substance) has the properties of happiness, yellowness, and quickness. These properties depend upon a substance. The neighbor's dog also once had the property of weighing five pounds, lost it, and now weighs twenty-five pounds. The same substance underwent a change in weight.

Aggregates

Some people deny the existence of substances. Instead of substances, there are *aggregates*. Rather than seeing the neighbor's dog as a substance having a nature that organizes its properties, parts, capacities, and powers, the dog is seen as a collection of all its parts bundled together. No deeper unity or organizing principles govern and sustain the existence of the dog through time as it undergoes change. There is merely a finite set of parts (cells, organs, bones, etc.). The dog may retain some subset of the original parts, while some parts cease to exist and new parts get added. But there is no substance that continues existing—maintaining the same identity—during the adding and subtracting of parts. The "dog" just is the sum of its parts. Just as a heap of salt is nothing but the totality of its grains, so too is the dog the totality of its parts.

Back to our simple observation. When we perceived the neighbor playing fetch with her dog, did we really perceive only one substance, many substances, or no substances but, rather, mere aggregates? Philosophers have attempted to answer this question in many different ways. But for both philosophical and biblical reasons, we recommend considering the existence of many substances with God being the one necessary substance all other things depend upon for their existence.[2] By scrutinizing the obvious, we have quickly come up with three metaphysical categories: substance, property (more on this later), and aggregate.

But doesn't this assume that, when we perceive the world, our minds reliably connect to it, enabling us to perceive real physical substances with properties? This assumption is a metaphysical one that addresses the nature of mind, reality, and the mind-reality relationship. It's a question of whether knowledge is possible.

Properties

A *property* is a quality, attribute, or characteristic that is had by a substance. But the quick answer is that a substance is a particular thing that has parts, properties, and capacities. Happiness, yellowness, and quickness are properties, and there are countless others. Just consider a human person with impressive moral character. This person will have the properties associated with the fruit of the Spirit (Gal. 5): love, joy, peace, patience, kindness, goodness, faithfulness, gentleness, and self-control. An object can have the property of roundness; the banana can have the property of greenness, lose it, and gain the property of yellowness. When we speak or write, properties are commonly expressed as predicates had by the subject. Furthermore, there are essential and non-essential (i.e., accidental) properties. The former is essential to a thing's existence. If an essential property is somehow removed from a thing (e.g., the capacity for consciousness), then that thing (i.e., you) no longer exists. Whereas a thing can lose nonessential properties and still exist (e.g., hair, cells, memories, etc.). This distinction is significant insofar as thinking about what properties represent the true essence and nature of a thing and which ones are trivial, transitory, and inconsequential.

A Substance's Nature and Essence

One important feature about substances is that they are the kinds of things that have natures and essences, which aggregates lack. Sometimes the terms *nature* and *essence* get used interchangeably. But we think there is an important way to distinguish them.

The *nature* of a substance is what binds together and unifies its parts, properties, and capacities. Some essential properties may not even be actualized yet. For example, consider a twenty-week-old human being in utero. This person has the capacity for consciousness and self-awareness. Consciousness and self-awareness are real potentialities—real essential properties—even though they are not yet actualized. So a substance's nature is what's responsible for actualizing its essential properties over time. It's the nature of a substance that's guiding the process of expressing its essential properties. Moreland and Craig make the point this way:

It's the human substance's "inner nature that contains, as a primitive unity, a complicated, structural arrangement of capacities/dispositions for developing a body (and, of course, the other faculties or [properties]). . . . [A substance's nature has a principle of activity] that governs the precise, ordered sequence of changes that the substance will (normally) go through in the process of growth and development. The various physical/chemical parts and process (including DNA) are tools—instrumental causes—employed by higher-order biological activities in order to sustain the various functions grounded in [a substance's nature]."[3]

A substance's nature, then, is responsible for bringing about certain causes over time that aim toward certain goals like actualizing potentialities—especially a substance's essential properties and capacities that may or may not yet be actualized.

A nature's *essence* can be seen as a list of all its essential properties. Essential properties are those characteristics that make a thing the kind of thing it is. This is why Moreland and DeWeese say that "a thing's essence is the set of all its essential properties," which provide "the deepest, most informative answer to the question 'What kind of thing is it?'"[4] So you might think some essential properties had by humans are consciousness, capacity to reason and make decisions, capacity to know God, and so on. Nonessential properties (i.e., accidental properties) can be gained or lost, yet the substance will still exist. For example, cells, hair, pigmentation, bones, limbs, and memories are properties humans have gained or lost. Yet losing them doesn't change the essence of a human because they're nonessential properties. Humans have lost these properties and still live to tell about it. Losing humanness or consciousness yields a much different result.

Realism, Idealism, or Transcendental Idealism?

Let's consider, again, our simple observation. In general, it seems like a perception of real things in the external world. But haven't our perceptions been mistaken before? A straw in a glass appears to be bent, not straight; the sun appears to be moving, not the planet; the magician appears to be levitating, not grounded. We soon learn in life there is an important distinction between appearance and reality. Not all perceptions of the way things appear are reliable indications of the way things really are. In light of this, there is another way to scrutinize our simple observation. It involves trying to model the nature of this mind-reality relationship.

Realism

If you took the perception in our simple observation to be the way things really are in reality, then this is the *realist* view. Realism takes objects perceived in the world to really exist because the mind-reality relationship is generally reliable. Realism, then, assumes the external world really exists, and human minds can reliably hook up to it. This metaphysical relation between mind and the external world makes the acquisition of truth and knowledge possible. Thus, realism is a non-skeptical position because it takes perceptions of the external world as those that accurately capture the way things are. The mind-reality relationship is not perfect, of course; humans are not perfect, omniscient cognizers. So perceptions can be more or less accurate, corrected, or improved, especially as a result of one's worldview accumulating more true beliefs, knowledge, and understanding. But the main idea is that human cognitive faculties are directly connected to the external world, and this relationship is generally reliable for most midsized objects in hospitable environments that can be aided with the advancements of instruments and more accurate worldviews.

TIME

What is the nature of time? According to the writers that invoke time travel, the assumption is a B-theory or static view of time. This view says time is a four-dimensional, space-time block whereupon events involving change take place. When a banana changes color from green to yellow, these events actually exist and continue existing at points in the space-time block. The A-theory, or dynamic view of time, is the commonsense view. This view says only "now" exists—the past did exist, the present exists now, and the future will exist. The banana did have the property of greenness, lost it, and now has the property of yellowness. The A-theory takes statements involving change to refer to the past, present, or future. The B-theory takes statements involving change to refer to continuously existing points on the space-time block.

Idealism

Idealism conceives the mind-reality relation differently, claiming that the real building blocks of the external world are not physical things, but rather ideas. There is, of course, an external world outside one's mind.[5] It's just not made of matter or anything physical; it's made up of ideas—specifically, ideas in the mind of God. And God is constantly perceiving these ideas, thereby grounding and sustaining their existence. This is why one of the biggest defenders of idealism, Bishop Berkeley (1685–1753), said to exist is to be perceived.

We can't lay out, analyze, and assess all the arguments given in support of idealism. But the idea is not as crazy as you might think. Remember, what one person perceives through her senses can be different for another. The temperature of the room feels hot to one person, cold to another; the size of a building appears tall to one person, short to another (depending on their frame of reference); the flavor of some food tastes good to one person, bad to another; the color of an object appears green to one person, blue to another. Rather than attribute contradictory qualities to a thing, the proponent of idealism says there are just ideas about temperature, size, flavors, colors, and everything else that are relative to each person's perspective. That's why perceptions vary so much. Indeed, reality consists of only minds and ideas. There is a mind-independent world; it's just that the fundamental nature of the external world is that objects are composed of immaterial ideas. And on Berkeley's version, these ideas are created and sustained in the mind of God, who constantly perceives them, which is why he said, "To be is to be perceived."[6]

Transcendental Idealism

Immanuel Kant (1724–1804) conceived of the mind-reality relation another way. The human mind is endowed with interpretive cognitive equipment that receives information from the external world. Once received, the cognitive equipment organizes it and delivers its product to the mind's eye. This product is what is perceived—it's what mediates the external world to one's consciousness. According to Kant's *transcendental idealism*, minds don't directly perceive the external world (that's realism); rather, the external physical world (contra idealism) is mediated through ideas manufactured by one's cognitive equipment.

Notice the ideas that one's mind is directly acquainted with are not the external world. On this view, the external world can't be directly perceived because one's mind depends upon its preprogrammed categories of thought to mediate the external world to it. If this mind-reality relation is true, then a wedge exists between mind and reality. Therefore, Kant divides reality up into the noumenal realm and the phenomenal realm. The former is the external world as it is in and of itself; the latter is the world of ideas, which are the products of the mind's preprogrammed categories of thought. Humans, then, are inevitably stuck behind the veil of the phenomenal realm and can never directly access the noumenal world, which is the unmediated external world. This is why Kant didn't think humans could do metaphysics because the mind-reality relation doesn't allow one direct access to reality.

IS KANTIAN REALISM AN OPTION?

One way Kant's transcendental idealism can be tweaked into a version of realism is this. Let's grant humans are endowed with equipment that produces categories, thoughts, and ideas. But what if the products delivered to us by our cognitive equipment were designed by God to be the means by which human minds were designed to hook up to reality? Instead of seeing Kant's mediated ideas as a wedge, it might be part of the design plan God uses for us to discover truth and acquire knowledge.

DE RE VERSUS DE DICTO MODALITY

De dicto is Latin for "of what is said," concerning the statement. *De re* means "of a thing," concerning a particular thing. The statement "God will create a new heaven and a new earth" can mean two different things. To believe this statement *de dicto* is to believe, in general, that God will create a new world sometime in the future. To believe this *de re* is to believe that God will create a specific world with certain laws of physics and chemistry and countless other specific details about what the new world will be like. Now consider this statement: "Consciousness emerges from brain tissue." If we take this statement as *modality de dicto*, then the truth conditions for it are these: There is no possible world that contains consciousness without a brain giving rise to it. The scope of this statement would include all persons—God, angels, demons, humans. Taken in the *modality de re* sense, this statement is true if a particular person's consciousness could not exist in any possible world without a brain. Notice, then, how *de re modality* has to do with the way a particular thing necessarily possesses a property.

The Actual World and Possible Worlds

Another way we can scrutinize our simple observation is to ask different modal questions about it. *Modality* has to do with concepts like possibility, impossibility, actuality, necessity, and contingency. So we could ask the following questions:

- When the neighbor's dog retrieved the ball, was that a necessary event or a contingent one?
- Is it possible the neighbor's dog can fly?
- Is it possible to replace the neighbor's brain with new bits of brain matter and the neighbor still remain the same person?
- Is it possible for God to move the neighbor's mind into the dog's body?
- What if God created another person that looked just like the neighbor and shared all the neighbor's memories; is it possible the new creation is identical to the neighbor or are they still different people?

Many philosophers believe that these questions have true answers. One way they have tried to establish conditions to discover the truth of questions like these is by appealing to possible worlds. A possible world is the way the actual world could have been different. The difference between a possible world and the actual world can be trivial or significant. Trivially, one possible world might be exactly like the actual world except your cellphone is lying one inch farther to the west. Significantly, another possible world might have different laws of physics and chemistry, and living things are silicon-based instead of carbon-based. An impossible world contains at least one necessary falsehood: a world containing square-circles, a world containing a person that exists and doesn't exist at the same time and same way, or a world wherein God is morally imperfect, unloving, and evil.[7]

So what makes a statement *necessary*? To answer this, it's helpful to compare necessary things with contingent things. Something is necessary if it could not have been otherwise; contingent things don't have to be the way they are—they could have been otherwise. For example, the number 2 can't have the property of being odd; nor can the number 2 lack the property of being prime. It's impossible for the number 2 to not be even and prime. Now let's consider the statement 2 + 2 = 4. This is a necessary truth. Given the meaning of 2 and 4, and the functions of + and =, there is no possible world wherein 2 + 2 ≠ 4. Necessarily, 2 + 2 = 4. But our existence is contingent. Had our biological parents' sexual gametes not fused, we would not be here. This fusion is an event that didn't have to happen. Historical events could have unfolded differently in countless ways, thereby preventing our parents from ever meeting.

But perhaps you believe in determinism. You believe the event involving the fusion of your parent's sexual gametes had to happen because it was determined by the past and laws of nature (or some other version of determinism). Well, we can now ask: Is it possible for there to be a world that has events that are not always determined by prior events and the laws of nature? It sure seems like a real possibility. If there is a possible world wherein determinism is false, then the fact we exist is a contingent truth, not a necessary one. And determinism is not a necessary truth. There's no contradiction in the idea of a nondeterministic world. How about God? Is there a possible world wherein God doesn't exist?[8] The point here is to see how possible worlds can be used to establish conditions for determining the truth of questions or statements that have to do with how things must be or how they could be. Possible worlds aid us to see what statements must be true and couldn't possibly be false, or what statements must be false and couldn't possibly be true. What's more, possible worlds aid us to see what properties a thing possesses necessarily—what properties are essential versus what properties are nonessential (i.e., accidental).

Realism or Nominalism?

The last metaphysical topic we will introduce concerns properties. We've discussed the fruit of the Spirit as properties that people can have. James is loving;

Emmafaith is joyful; Avagrace is peaceful; Joel is patient. This age-old metaphysical challenge concerns the nature of properties. Can people or things share the exact same property? Can Joel and James both have the same property of love and courage? Or, let's return to scrutinizing our simple observation. Can the neighbor's shirt, the dog's collar, and the ball each have the same property of redness? Or are properties individually distinct from each other, despite resembling one another? These questions generate the problem known as "the one over many" problem.[9] How can many different things share the same property? And how can one kind of property show up in many different things?

We think you should at least be familiar with two broad camps that take contrary views on the nature of properties.[10] A significant part of the debate is over whether properties are *universals*. Universals are things that can show up in many different things at the same time.[11] You and I cannot be at more than one place at the same time. But universals can; they can be in more than one place at the same time. A universal's relationship to space and time is different than the things that have them. So if love is a universal (and we think it is), then the same kind of love Jesus (Matt. 5; John 14; 15) and Paul (1 Cor. 13) talk about in the New Testament can be in the heart, mind, and soul of many different people at the same time. Philosophers that take universals to be real things in the world are called *realists*. In addition to properties, realists also take various relations (e.g., mother of, father of, larger than, truth, etc.) and kinds (e.g., water, gold, humanness, canineness, marriage, etc.) to be universals. Philosophers who deny that properties, relations, or kinds are universals are called *nominalists*. One type of nominalism denies the existence of universals, and another type denies the existence of abstract objects, which are things not located in space and time (e.g., numbers, propositions, possible worlds, etc.). So nominalism is anti-realist toward universals or abstract objects (or both).

You might have noticed different conflicts in the culture over the meaning of certain terms. One of the root causes for why people disagree over the definition of certain things is whether or not universals exist. If there are certain essential properties that different kinds of things have, then there are natures to be discovered instead of invented. So if a clear liquid is not composed of H_2O molecules, then it is not water. If a hard, yellowish material lacks atoms that have seventy-nine protons in its nucleus, then it's not gold. If a person is conscious and makes choices yet lacks humanness, then it's not a human person. These molecules, atoms, and attributes are essential properties of a thing. Defining something in a way that lacks these essential properties is to misidentify it. If universals exist, then everywhere water, gold, and humans are, there will also be universal natures showing up. But if nominalism is true, then natures aren't universals, and attributing different properties and characteristics to a thing is up for grabs.[12]

Conclusion

Spending a little bit of time scrutinizing our simple observation can result in forming some commonsense metaphysical beliefs. For example, our minds seem to have access to an external world that's furnished with many independent objects—some are substances, some are aggregates—that have properties, that stand in relation to other things, and that temporally undergo change. We can conceive of possible worlds that describe the way the actual world could be different. This heuristic device aids us by establishing truth conditions for what things exist necessarily or contingently and whether certain properties (including potentialities) are had by a thing necessarily or contingently. We believe that a Christian worldview will incorporate the significance of God creating things with properties and natures after their own kinds; moreover, it includes the creation of human beings with their own natures (e.g., humanness and image of God), which implies a non-skeptical outlook about the possibility of humans acquiring truth, knowledge, understanding, and wisdom about God and creation.[13]

Questions for Reflection

1. What are some ethical implications of seeing humans as aggregates versus substances?
2. Why is it important to discover whether something has an essence or nature?
3. What are the implications (in general) and theological implications (specifically) if realism is false?
4. If nominalism is true, can historical texts, including Scripture, provide one with testimonial knowledge? Why or why not?
5. If universals exist, how would this change your current view of reality?
6. Do you think after reading this chapter that there is a case to be made that nonphysical things exist in the world?

Recommended Reading

General Readers

DeWeese, Garret J., and J. P. Moreland. *Philosophy Made Slightly Less Difficult: A Beginner's Guide to Life's Big Questions.* 2nd ed. Downers Grove, IL: IVP Academic, 2021. ch. 2.

Grossmann, Reinhardt. *The Existence of the World: An Introduction to Ontology*. London: Routledge, 1992.

Hasker, William. *Metaphysics: Constructing a Worldview*. Downers Grove, IL: InterVarsity Press, 1983.

Loux, Michael J., and Dean W. Zimmerman, eds. *The Oxford Handbook of Metaphysics*. Oxford: Oxford University Press, 2005.

Mumford, Stephen. *Metaphysics: A Very Short Introduction*. Oxford: Oxford University Press, 2012.

Advanced Readers

Kim, Jaekwon, Daniel Z. Korman, and Ernest Sosa, eds. *Metaphysics: An Anthology*. New York: Wiley-Blackwell, 2011.

Koons, Robert C., and Timothy H. Pickavance. *Metaphysics: The Fundamentals*. New York: Wiley-Blackwell, 2015.

Moreland, J. P. *Universals*. Montreal: McGill-Queen's University Press, 2001.

Sider, Theodore, John Hawthorne, and Dean W. Zimmerman, eds. *Contemporary Debates in Metaphysics*. New York: Wiley-Blackwell, 2013.

NOTES

1. Dallas Willard, *Divine Conspiracy* (San Francisco: HarperOne, 1998), 11.

2. Scripture teaches that God created everything that exists and that only God exists necessarily. See chaper 18 for the ontological argument.

3. J. P. Moreland and William Lane Craig, *Philosophical Foundations for a Christian Worldview*, 2nd ed. (Downers Grove, IL: IVP Academic, 2017), 445. This quote was used to describe a substance dualism position called Thomistic/Aristotelian dualism. We have substituted the function of the soul according to this view for the function of a substance's nature. In order to avoid the physicalism vs. dualism debate, we leave the reader to think of a substance as either physical or nonphysical, which doesn't change the function of a substance's nature.

4. Garrett DeWeese and J. P. Moreland, *Philosophy Made Slightly Less Difficult*, 2nd ed. (Downers Grove, IL: IVP Academic, 2021), 38.

5. Solipsism is the view that the external world is actually created and sustained by a person's ideas. Everything owes its existence to the act of perceiving. So if Smith is a solipsist and solipsism were true, then our existence is dependent upon Smith's mind. The reason why is because we are mere ideas in it. So if you ever encounter a real live solipsist, then it's best to make sure nothing happens to him. Don't let him take any risks that could result in death. Because if a solipsist dies, then we all die! (This is supposed to be a little bit of philosophical humor that was inspired by a joke told by Alvin Plantinga at a public lecture.)

6. Georgy Berkeley (1685–1753) said it's unintelligible to disconnect the existence of something from its being perceived. "For as to what is said of the absolute existence of unthinking things without any relation to their being perceived, that seems perfectly unintelligible. [Their existence is to be perceived], nor is it possible they should have any existence out of the minds

or thinking things which perceive them." See George Berkeley, *A Treatise Concerning the Principles of Human Knowledge*, ed. Colin Turbayne (New York: Liberal Arts Press, 1957), 24.

7. The very concept of God excludes morally defective character traits. God, as Saint Anselm said, is the greatest conceivable being. So it's not possible for a morally perfect, perfectly loving God that possesses maximally all the great-making characteristics to have imperfections, deficiencies, or moral defects.

8. See the ontological argument for God's existence in chapter 18 for a reasonable answer to that question.

9. The problem of the "one over many" traces all the way back to Plato's *Parmenides* 130a–134e.

10. For the reader who wants to explore the many other positions on the nature of properties from a Christian worldview, we recommend consulting the following texts. See J. P. Moreland, *Universals* (Montreal: McGill-Queen's University Press, 2001); James K. Dew Jr. and Paul Gould, *Philosophy: A Christian Introduction* (Grand Rapids: Baker Academic, 2019), chap. 8; and Garrett DeWeese, *Doing Philosophy as a Christian* (Downers Grove, IL: IVP Academic, 2011), chap. 5.

11. Philosophers use the words *instantiated* or *exemplified* instead of *show up*. The idea is if something is a universal, then it can be instantiated or exemplified in many different things at the same time.

12. Richard M. Weaver says, "The denial of universals carries with it the denial of everything transcending experience [and feelings]. The denial of everything transcending experience [and feelings] means inevitably [. . .] the denial of truth. With the denial of objective truth there is no escape from the relativism of 'man is the measure of all things.'" See Richard M. Weaver, *Ideas Have Consequences* (Chicago: University of Chicago Press, 2013), 3. To explore the idea of how nominalism can undermine humans' achieving knowledge, see R. Scott Smith's monograph *Exposing the Root of Constructivism: Nominalism and the Ontology of Knowledge* (Lanham, MD: Lexington Books, 2022).

13. Alvin Plantinga has this to say in support of a non-skeptical outlook on the mind-reality relation: "[If God exists, then] such a person as God, a person who has created us in his image (so that we resemble him, among other things, in having the capacity for knowledge), who loves us, who desires that we know and love him, and who is such that it is our end and good to know and love him. But if these things are so, then he would of course intend that we be able to be aware of his presence and to know something about him. And if that is so, the natural thing to think is that he created us in such a way that we would come to hold such true beliefs as that there is such a person as God, that he is our creator, that we owe him obedience and worship, that he is worthy of worship, that he loves us, and so on. And if that is so, then the natural thing to think is that the cognitive processes that do produce belief in God are aimed by their designer at producing that belief. But then the belief in question will be produced by cognitive faculties functioning properly according to a design plan successfully aimed at truth: it will therefore have warrant." See Alvin Plantinga, *Warranted Christian Belief* (Oxford: Oxford University Press, 2000), 189–90.

CHAPTER 14

What Is a Human Person?

The Mind-Body Problem

What is a human person? Answers to this inherently philosophical question will richly inform your worldview. Disciplines like chemistry, biology, psychology, anthropology, sociology, and religion certainly inform parts of the answer. But we think philosophy provides necessary information when forming an adequate answer to this question. When thinking deeply about what it means to be a human person, philosophers have often ended up thinking deeply about the mind. So this chapter follows suit, indirectly addressing facets of a human person by directly addressing five mind-body problems. The mind-body problem is, in general, trying to figure out the relationship between the mind and brain. Each of the following five mind-body problems showcases different problems between the mind-brain relation. What's more, these problems can unlock new ways of thinking about the nature of humans.

DUALISM OR PHYSICALISM?

Physicalism and dualism are contrary positions on the nature of consciousness. *Physicalism* is roughly the view that the only things that exist are physical. Physicalists believe that the mind and brain are one and the same thing—the mind is part of the physical world. *Dualism* is the view that, in addition to physical things, there is another fundamental category of nonphysical things. Substance dualists see the brain and mind as two radically different things—one physical and the other nonphysical, respectively. Property dualists see the brain as having the power to bring about nonphysical mental states. The brain has two different kinds of properties: some physical, some nonphysical.

What Does Consciousness Mean?

Philosophers take humans to be persons. Every person, however, isn't human. For example, God, angels, and demons are persons too—specifically, nonphysical persons. They are not, however, human. There are also fictional persons like Yoda, Wonder Woman, and Frodo Baggins. Human beings, however, are taken to be either embodied, nonphysical souls (i.e., dualism) or entirely physical (i.e., physicalism). What different persons have in common is rationality, and rationality entails consciousness.[1]

Consciousness is a big deal. Every morning you awaken, you begin experiencing it. The smell of bacon, the tacky sensation in your mouth, the sound of birds chirping, the thought of today's dentist appointment, the memory of how to get to the dentist's office, the belief that the directions are accurate, and your reasoned decision to get out of bed—these are all different states of consciousness. Consciousness is having subjective experiences. Most important, it is you experiencing these subjective, conscious states. Indeed, consciousness is why we enjoy living—it is why we fight to sustain it and mourn when others lose it. To be conscious is to be the kind of thing that has experiences of sensations, thoughts, beliefs, desires, memories, reasoning, and a will to make decisions and choices. To be a person, then, is—at the very least—to have the capacity for consciousness. The capacity for consciousness is an essential property of human persons.[2]

The Mystery of Consciousness:
Mental States and Brain States

Why are human beings conscious? We know consciousness is correlated with the brain. But correlation is not the same as causation nor the identity relation. After all, some persons lack brains yet are believed by some to be conscious. Take God, angels, and demons as examples. So how does the brain generate the miracle of consciousness (assuming it does)? This cerebral organ is no doubt complex—containing billions of neurons and hundreds of miles of capillaries. Indeed, it's the most complex thing we've yet to discover. Be that as it may, it's still a lump of biological tissue. Like other organs, it resembles squishy meat. Some people even eat it! So how in the world does this lump of cerebral meat give rise to consciousness?[3] If the brain doesn't give rise to consciousness, then where does it come from? It's still a mystery for experts working on it.

To better understand the mind-body problem, consider the difference between brain states and mental states. Brain states can be described physically.

Physical descriptions include a thing's shape, location, weight, and so on. Mental descriptions, however, involve describing the mental state's *content*—what the mental state is "of" or "about." Mental descriptions may also describe accompanying feelings. Mental states and physical states seem so radically different. For example, try capturing your favorite childhood memory by describing only the physical characteristics of it (e.g., the relevant neurons firing in your brain). Bye-bye, memory! Whoosh—there it goes! Your physical description of the number of neurons firing, where they're firing, and the rate at which they fire communicates nothing intelligible about the content of the memory and accompanying feelings. Experts are left asking: What is the nature of the relationship between brain states and mental states?

Five Mind-Body Problems

Mental states are radically different from brain states. These five mind-body problems exemplify that disconnect, leave experts baffled, and provide insight into the nature of humans. The fifth mind-body problem is discussed at greater length because of the light it sheds on the nature of humans.

WHAT IS PANPSYCHISM?

There is a growing trend among philosophers considering panpsychism as a model to address mind-body problems. *Panpsychism* is, roughly, the idea that consciousness is both fundamental and that every bit of matter (even particles) has some non-zero degree of consciousness. Consciousness is everywhere! It's fundamental in that it can't be reduced to something else: consciousness is a fundamental building block of reality. (Higher degrees of consciousness can emerge from more complex structures or organized systems of matter.) It's ubiquitous in that even atoms have a non-zero degree of it, a grain of sand has more, a rock still more, all the way up to worms, mice, dogs, and humans having greater and greater degrees of consciousness. So it's not just brains that have consciousness—degrees of experiences (feelings) and purposes (final causes)—but other forms of matter, too. Panpsychism is considered, by some, a third option for addressing mind-body problems—especially for materialists that share many of the same intuitions, methods (e.g., introspection), reasons, and ways of describing mental states held by dualists.

The Problem of Qualia

Mind-Body Problem 1 (MBP1): We know mental states, in part, because of the way they feel. This feeling is called a *quale* (singular) or *qualia* (plural) for multiple feelings. Philosophers use these fancy terms to capture the qualitative feelings accompanying specific subjective experiences. Here the faculty of introspection is used to directly access the phenomenology of mental states. *Phenomenology* is another fancy word used to capture the felt, qualitative texture or the what-it's-like to have a certain mental state. Qualia is a problem for neurologists and philosophers because we don't know how and why the brain generates it. We can describe the physical input (ingesting food), the neuronal events going on in the brain (the number, location, and rate of neurons firing), and the bodily outputs (satisfying smile). But experts can't explain why all these feelings go along for the ride.[4]

Insight from MBP1 on Human Nature: Notice how this problem surfaces amazing facts about human beings: humans are the kinds of things that have the capacity to experience and enjoy countless qualia. Some of it is amazing, and we want more of it. Alas, some of it is so painful and frightening that we try to avoid it at all costs. Stars, planets, worms, plants, rocks, and atoms don't seem to have this amazing capacity that makes human life so rich, enjoyable, and fulfilling.

The Problem of Intentionality

Mind-Body Problem 2 (MBP2): Humans have the amazing capacity to think *about* things. We even have thoughts about our thoughts. Our thoughts are sometimes directed at people and places outside our mind. For example, the thought of your parent is about a specific person; your memory of graduating is about a specific event; your desire for cheesecake is about a certain food across the room. Philosophers call mental content *intentionality*, which is all about *aboutness*. It's a mind-body problem because we don't know how neurons can even be about anything. What's that even mean? How can mere physical neurons be about something, much less direct themselves outwards toward other things? Intentionality leaves experts puzzled. Yet it seems intuitive that our thoughts, beliefs, reasons, desires, and sensations are about things even if we can't discern the content of them by investigating neurons. Describing the physical characteristics of neurons doesn't explain how or why mental states have intentionality.

Insight from MBP2 on Human Nature: This mind-body problem sheds light on a fascinating capacity of human persons: human minds produce thoughts, memories, beliefs, reasons, and desires that are about all kinds of wonderful, stimulating, meaningful content. This capacity makes possible humans' ability to create languages and intelligibly communicate with other people.

The Binding Problem

Mind-Body Problem 3 (MBP3): We often experience multiple mental states at once. For example, a baseball player steps into the batter's box. He experiences (1) a perception of where the infielders are positioned, (2) the belief that "My goal is to bunt," (3) a sensation of anxiousness about failing, and (4) a perception of the pitcher beginning his windup—all at once in a unified way.[5] Investigations into the brain only reveal different regions having neurons correlated with different mental states.[6] There are coordinated functions shared between different parts and systems of the brain. But what binds all these mental states together, enabling us to experience them all at once? What's more, what is the thing that has this unified experience? Even postulating a specific part of the brain binding these mental states together leaves us asking: Is that physical part of the brain identical to me? Experts can't agree, much less explain how the brain binds together all these mental states and causes a unified center of consciousness experiencing them.

Insight from MBP3 on Human Nature: This problem sheds light on the fact that human beings are the kinds of things that have a unified center of consciousness that can experience multiple mental states at once.

The Problem of Free Will

Mind-Body Problem 4 (MBP4): Everyday people make moral evaluations. It's likely you already praised or blamed someone today. Perhaps you blamed someone for driving recklessly or cutting in line. Perhaps you praised someone for performing a kind, generous act. Moral evaluations make sense only because we take people to be responsible for their actions. But if all the physical things in the universe, including humans, are determined by the past and laws of nature, then how are human persons free? Neuronal events, like other physical events, are determined by prior physical events governed by the laws of nature. So how can free will fit into that scientific, physicalist view of the world?[7]

Insight from MBP4 on Human Nature: This problem sheds light on the fact that human beings intuitively are the kind of things that have agency. Humans have the power and capacity to deliberate and make decisions to act for reasons. Humans have the kind of free will that makes moral responsibility and love relationships possible.

The Problem of Personal Identity

We introduce this fifth problem last because we want to spend more time mining it for insights on human nature. Let's start with a fun thought experiment. There's a famous ship in philosophy called *The Ship of Theseus*. It traces back to Plutarch's (AD 46–119) work titled *Parallel Lives*. Theseus was a mythical king that went on many adventures, greatly influencing Athenian culture. In honor of Theseus, the Athenians preserved the ship he traveled on. Preserving Theseus's ship involved, among other things, swapping rotting planks with new ones.

Let's consider the following scenario. The ship is comprised of 365 planks. Starting January 1, every day one of the ship's planks gets replaced with a new one. By New Year's Eve, the ship will have an entirely new set of planks. Here is our question: What day of the year did the *Ship of Theseus* become a new ship? Was it July 2, a day over the halfway point, when the ship had 183 new planks and 182 original planks? Or is it not a new ship until all the planks are replaced? Perhaps it is a new ship January 2, when only one plank has been replaced? Here's a wrinkle to the original question. After the year ends, suppose the original 365 planks are used to build another ship. Which of the two ships is *The Ship of Theseus*?

Mind-Body Problem 5 (MBP5): It's one thing to ask, what makes *The Ship of Theseus* the same ship across time after planks are replaced? But what makes a human the same person across time? Presumably, the picture of you blowing out candles at your ten-year-old birthday party is a picture of you. But what makes you the same person now as the person blowing out the candles then? Physically, we are daily replacing cells with new ones that comprise our physical makeup.[8] Indeed, roughly every nine years we virtually have a new set of cells. So what makes you the same person over time while parts continue getting replaced? Stated more formally:

> *Personal Identity Question*: If a person x exists at one time and a person y exists at another time, under what possible circumstances is it the case that x is [identical to] y?[9]

This question seeks to understand what it means to say Past-You, Present-You, and Future-You are the same person across time. Intuitively, we take this to be the case. This is why virtually everyone says the person in the picture taken years ago is them. It's also why we are concerned about future events because we think we will be the ones experiencing them. There have been different views offered. Let's consider some of them.

Personal Identity: Memory View

John Locke (1632–1704) is known for developing the memory view for personal identity. Past-, Present-, and Future-You are identical with each other, exactly when an experience had by one is connected to the others through shared memories. Psychological consistency—maintained by the "glue" of memories—is what makes you the same person over time. For example, a child, middle-aged person, and elderly person are the same person over time because they all share the same memories. You go where your memories go.

Objection to Memory View

Thomas Reid (1710–1796) famously provided the following objection. First, identity relations have properties. For example, one property is *transitivity*.[10] This means that if A = B, and B = C, then A = C. But this feature doesn't always apply to the memory view. Reid gives the following counterexample. Consider a child once flogged at school. This child later becomes a brave soldier capturing the enemy's flag. This soldier later becomes a general. What happens if the retired general remembers capturing the enemy's flag but doesn't remember being flogged as a child? On the memory view, the retired general is identical to the brave soldier but not identical to the child.[11] But since identity is transitive, the memory view is false because it can't account for the retired general being the same person as the child. The intuition, of course, is that they are the same person. The memory view, however, can't account for it.[12]

Personal Identity: Body View

The body view says Past-, Present-, and Future-You are identical with each other exactly when they have the same body. Instead of memories grounding identity, this view says it's the body. You go where your body goes. A person's body may undergo physical change over time so long as the change is gradual. Sudden changes to the body resulting in radical alterations can sometimes break the physical continuity needed to retain personal identity.

Objection to Body View

One famous objection to the body view, though intended to make a different point, comes from John Locke.[13] Locke asks us to consider a case involving the possibility of two souls (nonphysical substance) swapping bodies.[14] If it's possible the soul of "the prince" enters the body of "the cobbler" and vice versa, then "the prince" would continue living in the body of "the cobbler" and vice versa. The kind of evidence needed for who is really "the prince" seems to be things like the prince's personality traits and memories. If persons are identical to their bodies, this would be an impossibility. But this scenario does seem possible for some people.

Personal Identity: Brain View

Because of advancements in neuroscience, many think humans are identical to their brains. Since mental states are correlated with brain states, some take an additional step and infer the mind just is the brain. We all know of people who have sustained brain damage, thereby causing mental and psychological alterations. Damage to the brain is damage to the person, so the reasoning goes.

Indeed, if the brain is the storehouse for consciousness, personality traits, and memories,[15] then you go where your brain goes. Past-, Present-, and Future-You are identical with each other because they share the same brain.

Objection to Brain View

One objection to this view traces back to Gottfried Wilhelm Leibniz (1646–1716).[16] Leibniz questioned whether the brain is even the kind of thing that can be conscious. The idea is that thought and perception cannot be explained by mere movements of physical objects. To get a handle on this, consider what it would be like traveling about the watery environment of someone's brain. (Imagine you and a personalized submarine reduced to a microscopic size and injected into a human body via syringe.)[17] At no point will you see consciousness. Merely observing an arrangement of neuronal events tells you nothing about consciousness nor the person who has consciousness. If this is right, then neither consciousness nor the person is identical to the brain.

Another objection to the brain view meriting consideration is this. Imagine a person is suffering from a brain disease that is destroying brain tissue. The disease will start out from the left hemisphere and move across to the right hemisphere. A team of neuroscientists will combat the disease by following the path of destroyed brain tissue left by the disease—replacing the dead tissue with new brain tissue. The patient will be under local anesthesia (enabling the patient to remain conscious throughout the operation). Note that it's common for brain operations to use local anesthesia and not general anesthesia (i.e., "go under"), especially since the brain lacks pain sensors. Let's say the rate at which the disease spreads throughout the entire brain is ten hours. So every hour, the team of neurosurgeons replaces roughly 10 percent of the patient's brain to keep pace with the disease. The point of this thought experiment is this. It seems logically possible that the patient can remain conscious throughout the duration of the ten-hour operation. It seems logically possible that the patient maintains consciousness—thinking, talking, perceiving, and so forth—throughout the operation and by the end have a completely new brain. If that's logically possible, then humans can't be identical to their brains.[18]

Personal Identity: Soul View

Joseph Butler (1692–1752) and Thomas Reid (1710–1769) are notable philosophers who defended the soul view.[19] The soul view is also known as *substance dualism* or *mind-body dualism*. The main idea is that the soul is an immaterial substance (not composed of physical parts). The soul is taken as the metaphysical storehouse, seat, or ground for countless powers, potentialities, capacities, functions, and abilities that we all know and love. For example, the soul has the potential to learn new skills, the capacity for consciousness, the ability to think and form beliefs, the powers to animate the body, and the executive function to make decisions. This view says Past-, Present-, and Future-You are identical because they have the same soul. Your soul is what endures through time even though your body and brain undergo physical change. The soul contains one's memories (or the mind does, which is a capacity of the soul). You are a soul that has a body. The body is needed to express many of the soul's powers and capacities. One can exist apart from the body, but this mode of existence is incomplete. The reason is that many Christians believe God created human souls to be embodied.[20] Thus, disembodied souls are incomplete because they were created for bodies. According to the soul view, then, you go where your soul goes.

Objection to Soul View

It's not uncommon to hear people dismiss this view by mocking it.[21] A challenging objection to the soul view, however, is the *interaction problem*. Elisabeth of Bohemia (1618–1680) famously challenged her friend René Descartes' argument for dualism.[22] She pointed out that nonphysical things can't bring about causes in physical things. For example, one can't use the multiplication table to hammer a nail. So how is it possible for an immaterial soul to animate the body?

Attempts to address this objection have been offered. One may try to first soften another up to the idea of non-physical causation. This can happen by first suggesting the possibility that an immaterial being like God can cause events in the hard, heavy, physical world—a non-physical cause bringing about a physical event. Many think that's possible. After all, there is the doctrine of *creatio ex nihilo*—God creating things (like the universe) out of nothing. The idea is neither contradictory nor incoherent. Sometimes conceivability is a test for possibility. So not all causes must be physical. Indeed, many arguments from evil against the existence of God assume a non-physical substance (i.e., God) should be interacting with the physical world (natural evil) and human bodies (moral evil) to prevent pain, suffering, and evil. The very accusation, then, assumes it's possible for a non-physical person to interact with physical things and cause events in the physical world.

Consider cases involving knowledge of past and future events. Take, for example, my memories of my children's births. These events are in the past and no longer exist, but I can still recall them. Each time I choose to delight in these memories, the past physical event need not exist to cause the memory.[23] But my knowledge is about this past event. While my brain is necessary for these memories, it's not the same as the physical events I'm remembering. This is true not only for memorial knowledge but also for knowledge of things that haven't happened yet. Future events don't exist, so they can't be directly causing our knowledge of them.

Let's now consider this. We experience ourselves directly moving parts of our body. The faculty of introspection delivers us evidence that justifies our belief that we sometimes act as a first, un-caused cause or unmoved mover. Sometimes we are the originating sources of an action and not some previous event in the physical chain. This would violate the laws of nature. The best available explanation to account for this, then, is that the cause is brought about by a non-physical substance or soul—something that is not controlled, governed, or determined by past physical events and the laws of nature. But from the fact that we have evidence that justifies free will or even that we know we sometimes act freely, it doesn't follow that we understand exactly how the soul injects power into the body to animate it. Similar to this point: we don't understand exactly how the mind has and utilizes the faculty of memory and how a past—no longer existing—historical event can cause an instance of memorial knowledge, or how a mind can know about a non-existing future event without that future event causing it. But we know that memorial knowledge and knowledge of future events are possible. This, then, is an epistemic response: Knowledge of some fact is not the same as answering the how and why questions related to that fact. One can know that something is true (in this case, my soul best explains how I can act as an uncaused, first-cause) without having to fully understand how exactly the soul interacts with the body to animate it.

Admittedly, this kind of response, in addition to others, has not satisfied everyone. This is why the mind-body problem is ongoing.

Insight from MBP5 on Human Nature: This problem sheds light on the fact that human beings seem to be identical to their souls, which share a rich, interactive relationship to the body and brain.

Some Christians, and many philosophers, deny the existence of an immaterial substance we're calling a soul. But we believe the soul is the best answer to personal identity for the following reasons. First, because it is a nonphysical, simple substance (not composed of parts), it is immune to counterexamples involving the removal or replacement of parts from the brain or body, as well as memories conceived as parts in the brain. The fact that our cells (and the atoms of those cells) are constantly getting replaced makes it hard to explain how we are the same people across time. Virtually all of us share a strong intuition, however, that we are the same person now that we were in the past and will be in the future. This is why Moreland says, "Fear of some painful event in the future or fear of blame and punishment for some deed done in the past appear to make sense only if we implicitly assume that it is I myself who will experience the pain or who was the doer of the past deed. If I do not remain the same through time, it is hard to make sense of [cases involving] fear and punishment."[24] The same goes for other people: Does justice require all serial murderers be released from prison because they are no longer the same physical stuff of the murderer's body and brain ten years ago? Of course not! There is an objective fact for why you and I are the same person across time, and the soul seems to be the best available explanation for this. "You go where your soul goes" seems more plausible than going where the body, brain, or memories go.[25]

Second, we think introspection delivers conclusive evidence that we maintain strict identity across time despite our parts constantly undergoing change, replacement, and/or removal. Indeed, some of this evidence comes to you from the fact that you take yourself to be the same person reading this sentence (Person-1) as the person who started reading this chapter (Person-2). Person 1 is identical to Person 2, despite atoms and cells undergoing change and replacement.

Third, the soul view is the commonsense view and thus enjoys default justification until sufficient counterevidence suggests otherwise. The late Jaegwon Kim, one of the leading experts in the philosophy of mind, said, "We commonly think that we, as persons, have a mental and bodily dimension. . . . Something like this dualism of personhood, I believe, is common lore shared across most cultures and religious traditions."[26] People throughout history, across varying cultures, take themselves to be a unified, indivisible center of consciousness that has a body but is not identical to it. Humans throughout history have taken themselves to be a unified subject of experience that has sensations, thoughts, beliefs, desires, and a will muscle we flex to make decisions.

Fourth, we pretheoretically think of persons as all-or-nothing kinds of things. Unlike physical objects, persons don't come in degrees—a person without legs or a person with 50 percent of brain mass or a person who has only 50 percent of their memories is not half a person.

Last, we believe the most plausible view will be able to better account for all five mind-body problems. These five mind-body problems appeal to specific data. The soul view seems better equipped to account for the data of subjective, nonphysical characteristics of qualia, intentionality, the unity of consciousness, same identity over time, and that which has the power and capacity for free will. Physicalist views seem inadequate to account for this data, and some even eliminate them because they can't account for them.[27] We believe the soul view does this better than alternative ones. Biological tissue doesn't seem to be the right kind of thing that can have or bring about thoughts, beliefs, desires, sensations, a will to make choices, and all the relevant qualia going along for the ride.

Philosophy of Mind and Philosophical Anthropology

So what is a human person? From philosophy of mind we can say, perhaps, something like this: A human person is an embodied soul that has:

1. a *mind*—a component of the soul having a center of consciousness, which has the powers and capacities for rational thought, language, deliberation, and storing memories, including all the rich intentionality and qualia contained therein;
2. *agency/will*—the power and ability to act for reasons, including entering loving relationships with other persons and fulfilling moral obligations;
3. a rich, interactive *relation to a physical body and brain*—a physical mode of the soul that enables countless powers and capacities to actualize and express themselves in this embodied mode of existence.

And if we include biblical anthropology, we can include this as well:[28]

4. a *heart/spirit*—an inner core component of the soul that organizes cognitive, conative (esp. motivations), and affective states; moreover, the heart/spirit empowers and enables human persons to be aware, responsive, and morally accountable in their awareness (i.e., conscience), interactions, and relationships with other persons (esp. God).

Conclusion

Believing in the existence of the soul has been held by virtually all cultures throughout history. It's the most intuitive, common-sense view. The soul can explain much more about consciousness and human agency than any mechanistic, physicalist description and model can offer. It seems to be a view that can account for the data constituting the five mind-body problems in a more consistent, coherent, and systematic way than the alternatives. But for the Christian, in addition to philosophical explorations, many passages of Scripture seem to point to humans having an immaterial component called the soul.

Questions for Reflection

1. Do you think consciousness is something that can be fully explained by science and mechanistic explanations? Why?
2. If consciousness is fundamental and not reducible to something else, what is the best available explanation for its existence? Does it depend upon something else, or has it always existed?
3. What other parts, capacities, or powers can philosophy discover about human persons? Which ones does biblical anthropology address that philosophy can't?
4. How has this chapter assisted you in thinking better about personal identity and what makes you the same person over time?
5. What ways does philosophical anthropology address and inform ethical and bioethical questions?

For Further Reading

General Level Readers

Farris, Joshua R. *An Introduction to Theological Anthropology: Humans, Both Creaturely and Divine*. Grand Rapids: Baker Academic, 2020.

Green, Joel B., and Stuart L. Palmer, eds. *In Search of the Soul: Four Views of the Mind-Body Problem*. Downers Grove, IL: InterVarsity Press, 2005.

Kim, Jaegwon. *Philosophy of Mind*, 2nd edition. Cambridge, MA: Westview, 2006.

Lowe, E. J. *An Introduction to the Philosophy of Mind*. Cambridge: Cambridge University Press, 2000.

Moreland, J. P. *The Soul: How We Know It's Real and Why It Matters*. Chicago: Moody, 2014.

Rasmussen, Joshua. *Who Are You, Really? A Philosopher's Inquiry into the Nature and Origin of Persons*. Downers Grove, IL: IVP Academic, 2023.

Advanced Level Readers

Loose, Jonathan J., Angus J. L. Menuge, and J. P. Moreland, eds. *The Blackwell Companion to Substance Dualism*. Oxford: Wiley-Blackwell, 2018.

Moreland, J. P., and Brandon Rickabaugh. *The Substance of Consciousness: A Comprehensive Defense of Contemporary Substance Dualism*. Hoboken, NJ: Wiley, 2023.

O'Conner, Timothy, and David Robb, eds. *Philosophy of Mind: Contemporary Readings*. New York: Routledge, 2003.

Swinburne, Richard. *Mind, Brain, and Free Will*. Oxford: Oxford University Press, 2013.

NOTES

1. Rationality is a unique property separating human persons from other conscious animals like birds, mice, and cows. Boethiuis (480–524 AD) defined a person as "an individual substance

of a rational nature." This definition captured an essential property believed to distinguish persons from other kinds of animals. See Boethius, *The Theological Tractates and the Consolation of Philosophy*, trans. H. F. Stewart, E. K. Rand, and S. J. Tester (Cambridge, MA: Harvard University Press, 1973), 85.

2. We emphasize the capacity for consciousness rather than consciousness itself, since sleeping or experiencing the effects of anesthesia would eliminate personhood, which seems like a false implication.

3. Colin McGinn does an excellent job defamiliarizing consciousness by appealing to a science fiction story written by Terry Bison. Bison uses a dialogue between two aliens discussing the source of human consciousness. After probing and analyzing a human body and brain, the alien researcher learns consciousness is caused by the brain. Sharing this information with an alien colleague is met with incredulity. "'That's ridiculous. How can meat make [complex machines]? You're asking me to believe in sentient meat?' [. . .] 'Yes, thinking meat! Conscious meat! Loving meat. Dreaming meat. The meat is the whole deal! Are you getting the picture?'" See Colin McGinn, *The Mysterious Flame: Conscious Minds in a Material World* (New York: Basic Books, 1999), 6–8.

4. Two related questions the problem of qualia generates are these: Why do these specific neuronal events generate this specific kind of qualia? Do other people have the same qualia when the same pattern of neurons fire?

5. This problem is viewed by some as providing strong reasons in favor of substance dualism. See J. P. Moreland, "Substance Dualism and the Unity of Consciousness" in *The Blackwell Companion to Substance Dualism*, ed. Jonathan J. Loose, Angus J. L. Menuge, and J. P. Moreland (Oxford: Wiley-Blackwell, 2018), 184–207.

6. Neuroscience has made tremendous progress identifying what regions of the brain are correlated with certain mental activity. For example, whenever a mental state of type M1 is present (say, emotion of empathy), a neural event of type N1 is present (say, mirror neurons firing). As important and fascinating as these discoveries are, it is important not to confuse correlations with identity statements and causal relations. A correlation is a relation between two or more things based on a co-occurrence. A and B may show up at the same time. But from the fact that there exists a correlation between neuronal events and mental events, it doesn't entail that neuronal events are identical to mental events. That is a further question which many experts disagree about. Recall from chapter 6 the law of identity. It says if A is identical to B, then all properties true of A must also be true of B and vice versa. A and B may stand in a relation of correlation, but if there are properties true of A that are not true of B, then they are not the same thing. Nor does correlation mean causation. Just because A and B are correlated, it doesn't mean A causes B or vice versa (e.g., a rooster crowing doesn't cause the sun to rise even though the two events are correlated).

7. We will discuss this problem in more detail in chapter 15.

8. It's true that some neuronal cells remain, but their proteins, molecules, and atoms still get replaced. Moreover, we can grow new neuronal cells (adult neurogenesis) in different regions of the brain (e.g., hippocampus). See Embla Steiner, Mathew Tata, and Jonas Frisén, "A Fresh Look at Adult Neurogenesis," *Nature Medicine* 5 (April 2019): 542–46.

9. Eric T. Olson, "Personal Identity," *The Stanford Encyclopedia of Philosophy* (Spring 2021 edition), ed. Edward N. Zalta, https://plato.stanford.edu/archives/spr2021/entries/identity-personal/.

10. Identity has three characteristics: it's transitive, reflexive, and symmetrical. Regarding transitivity, if X = Y and Y = Z, then X = Z. Regarding reflexivity, if some relation R is reflexive, then for all X, X stands in R to itself. For example, I can be 'the same size' as myself; I can't be 'larger than' myself at the same time and in the same relation. Identity is symmetrical because for any X and Y, if X = Y, then Y = X. For example, if Harry Potter = Lily Evans's son, then Lily Evans's son = Harry Potter.

11. See Thomas Reid, *Essays on the Intellectual Powers of Man*, ed. Derek R. Brookes (1785; University Park: Pennsylvania State University Press, 2002), 276.

12. Memories seem neither necessary nor sufficient for personal identity. Memories are not necessary for the simple reason that many people suffer from amnesia. A loved one suffering from amnesia doesn't cease to exist and become a new person. (Just imagine a future cure for them. After receiving the cure, they don't begin existing again after ceasing from existing. They always did exist; now, after the cure, their mode of existence is back to normal.) They're not sufficient because even if all of Smith's memories were somehow duplicated and injected into Jones's mind, Smith would not be identical to Jones. Jones would possess apparent, foreign, false memories involving someone else.

13. Locke wanted to argue that the soul doesn't provide the kind of explanatory work the memory-view provides. For even though the prince's body has the cobbler's soul and vice-versa, what would we say if they swapped memories? It seems as though the cobbler's body, inhabited by the prince's soul but possessing the cobbler's memories, would be evidence that the cobbler goes where his memories go rather than the soul.

14. See John Locke, *An Essay Concerning Human Understanding*, ed. Roger Woolhouse (1689; London: Penguin, 1997), 306–7.

15. For example, consider the company Nectome. It's a startup company that aims to develop the technology needed for "memory extraction" so that memories can later be downloaded into a computer. This is one theoretical way of "beating" death by having your memories "survive." See https://nectome.com.

16. See Nicholas Rescher, *G. W. Leibniz's Monadology: An Edition for Students* (Pittsburgh: University of Pittsburgh Press, 1991), 83–85. Leibniz had impressive raw intellectual powers; he made considerable contributions to the fields of philosophy, math, physics, theology, and law, among others.

17. This idea was inspired by the 1987 movie *Innerspace* starring Dennis Quad, Martin Short, and Meg Ryan.

18. This thought experiment was inspired by Richard Swinburne. See Richard Swinburne, *Mind, Brain, and Free Will* (Oxford: Oxford University Press, 2013), 155–57.

19. See Thomas Reid, *Essays on the Intellectual Powers of Man*, 264. Two of the strongest defenses for substance dualism are the following books: Loose, Menuge, and Moreland, *Blackwell Companion to Substance Dualism*; and J. P. Moreland and Brandon Rickabaugh, *The Substance of Consciousness: A Comprehensive Defense of Contemporary Substance Dualism* (Hoboken, NJ: Wiley, 2023). Contemporary defenders of different versions of dualism are Richard Swinburne, E. J. Lowe, J. P. Moreland, William Hasker, Brandon Rickabaugh, Robert Koons, Alvin Plantinga, Uwe Meixner, Alexander Pruss, Stewart Goetz, Todd Buras, Charles Taliaferro, C. Stephen Evans, Dean Zimmerman, and Joshua Rasmussen. Historically, dualism has been defended by Plato, Aristotle, Augustine, Thomas Aquinas, René Descartes, Gottfried Wilhelm Von Leibniz, and Thomas Reid.

20. Plato thought just the opposite: a more complete mode of existence is when the soul breaks free from the shackles of the body, which hinders the ability to think, reason, contemplate, and attain the truth.

21. Philosopher Gilbert Ryle dismisses the soul view by calling it "absurd," "a myth," and "the dogma of the Ghost in the machine." See Gilbert Ryle, *The Concept of Mind* (Chicago: New University of Chicago Press, 2000), 15–16.

22. See Princess Elizabeth of Bohemia in *The Correspondence between Princess Elisabeth of Bohemia and René Descartes*, ed. and trans. Lisa Shapiro (Chicago: University of Chicago Press, 2007), 41.

23. I borrow this point from William G. Lycan, "Giving Dualism Its Due," *Australasian Journal of Philosophy* (2009): 555.

24. J. P. Moreland, *The Soul: How We Know It's Real and Why It Matters* (Chicago: Moody),135.

25. One area this chapter hasn't explored is the relevance of near-death experiences (NDEs). There are too many medical cases at this point to ignore the hypothesis of the soul in order to explain some of them. Cases involving subjects meeting brain death or death by neurological criteria yet still maintaining consciousness and testifying about it after being revived continue to grow. Cases wherein one acquires new knowledge (e.g., blind person seeing color or a person seeing objects in locations that are out of the body's scope of vision) are much harder to dismiss as mere delusions. See J. P. Moreland, *A Simple Guide to Experience Miracles: Instruction and Inspiration for Living Supernaturally in Christ* (Grand Rapids: Zondervan, 2021); Paul Badham, "Religious and Near-Death Experience in Relation to Believe in a Future Life," *Mortality* 2, no. 1 (1997): 7–21; Jeffery Long, *Evidence of the Afterlife: The Science of Near-Death Experiences* (New York: HarperOne, 2010); and P. M. H Atwater, *The Big Book of Near-Death Experiences: The Ultimate Guide to What Happens When We Die* (Charlottesville, VA: Hampton Roads, 2007).

26. See Jaegwon Kim, "Lonely Souls: Causality and Substance Dualism," in *Soul, Body and Survival*, ed. Kevin Corcoran (Ithaca, NY: Cornell University Press, 2001), 30; quoted from Moreland, *The Soul*, 9.

27. For example, see Daniel C. Dennett, *Consciousness Explained* (Boston: Little Brown and Company, 1991); Jaegwon Kim, *Physicalism, or Something Near Enough* (Princeton: Princeton University Press, 2005). To be fair, consciousness isn't denied full stop, but specifically phenomenal consciousness—that is, the qualia (subjective experiences) accompanying mental states.

28. See, e.g., Matt. 10:28; 22:23–33; 26:41; Mark 7:18–23; 12:18–27; 14:38; Luke 12:4–5; 20:27–40; 23:46. For a more thorough treatment of a dualist biblical anthropology, see Moreland, *The Soul*, chap. 2.

CHAPTER 15

Am I Doing What I
Choose to Do?

Free Will and Determinism

Free will is a concept that elicits many different meanings. In this chapter, we are interested in the kind of free will that helps us understand more deeply what a "person" is. More specifically, human persons are the kind of things that have consciousness. Consciousness enables one to reason, choose, and make decisions for reasons. Human persons can be the proper objects of moral evaluations because they are morally responsible for some of their actions. And human persons can freely enter into loving relationships. Free will provides persons the kind of agency needed to make all that possible. After looking at how these important things presuppose free will, we look at how determinism can undermine free will. But determinism is another concept that elicits many different meanings. So this chapter aims to clarify what free will is, what determinism is, and whether free will and determinism can coexist.

What Is Free Will?

Virtually everyone has an idea of what it means to have free will. Most people take free will to mean *the ability to make a choice from a set of alternatives that is under one's control.* An action chosen for certain reasons believed to achieve a specific goal requires free will. But an action caused by random, chaotic events (e.g., a neurological tick) undermines free will. What's more, actions that are coerced, forced, compelled, constrained, or determined intuitively undermine free will to one degree or another. The reason is that the control principle gets violated.[1] This principle says we are morally assessable for only those factors that are under our control. If I spill a drink on your shirt because someone ran into me, then I am not morally responsible for staining your shirt. I wasn't in control of the cause. The cause was the person who rudely ran into me, which then caused the liquid to move from my cup to your shirt.

What Is Determinism?

Determinism says every event has a prior cause that guarantees the subsequent event must happen. It is the idea that every event in the universe (including your decisions and actions) is fixed by prior events, states, or objects that are governing them to only one possible outcome. Different versions of determinism pop up whenever the "prior event, state, or object" gets described in more detail. Biological genes (nature), environmental inputs (nurture), the laws of logic, and God have all been used to generate different versions of determinism. Pierre-Simone Laplace (1749–1827) once said, "If a supremely intelligent observer knew the exact location and velocity of every particle in the universe and all the laws of physics, he could predict with certainty every future state of the universe."[2] This quote captures facets of two different versions of determinism that we will explore: causal physical determinism and theological determinism. Some believe determinism undermines free will, and others don't. Let's look at both.

Causal Physical Determinism

This first argument aims to show that free will doesn't exist if determinism is true.[3] It's called the *consequence argument* because if determinism is true, then everything is the consequence of the past and the laws of nature, and free will doesn't exist. The way philosophers express this is to say that free will and determinism are not compatible. Those who are convinced this argument is sound are called *incompatibilists*. They believe determinism and free will are in deep conflict. Those that deny this are called *compatibilists*.

Consequence Argument

1. There is nothing we can do to change past physical events and the laws of nature. (Past events and the laws of nature are outside our control.)
2. If determinism is true, our present actions are necessary consequences of past physical events and the laws of nature. (It must be the case that,

given past physical events and the laws of nature, our present actions occur—we cannot do anything other than what we in fact did.)

Therefore,

3. The actions we perform are not caused by us but rather by past physical events and the laws of nature. [From 1 and 2]

Therefore,

4. There is nothing we can do to change what actions we perform. [From 2 and 3]

It's both past events and the laws of nature animating our bodies. But since we have no control over these things, there are no true alternatives. Whatever action we perform, we could not have done otherwise since we have no control over what's causing our actions. For many, the picture causal physical determinism paints depicts humans as mere parts of an engine. Think of a piston inside of an engine moving up and down a cylinder. Does it have control over what it does? Can it do something other than what it does? Are the pistons moving in accordance with reason? No, no, and no.

What the consequence argument shows is that if determinism is true, then a necessary ingredient for any conception of freedom worth its salt is the principle of alternative possibilities (PAP). This necessary condition for free will has been challenged by Frankfurtian counterexamples. Here's an example: Mad scientists have implanted a chip into the brain of assassin Jones. This new technology ensures Assassin Jones never backs down from completing an assassination. Were assassin Jones ever to back down by deciding to abort the mission, the mad scientists would see in real-time the beliefs and reasons informing assassin Jones's decision on their monitors. One day, assassin Jones is assigned to assassinate his friend, Smith. The mad scientists, however, are not worried that assassin Jones will back down because they can activate the brain-chip to produce the right belief-desire states that will causally determine him to kill his friend. As it turns out, assassin Jones goes through with the assassination and the mad scientists never had to use the brain-chip. This thought experiment is supposed to show that even though assassin Jones could not have done otherwise— therefore, violating PAP—nevertheless, he is still responsible for murdering his friend.[4]

Incompatibilism versus Compatibilism

In light of the consequence argument, there is a position called *incompatibilism*. Again, incompatibilists say that if causal physical determinism is true, then humans are not genuinely free—humans lack free will. Compatibilists believe free will and determinism not only are compatible but that free will requires determinism. Many compatibilists think that if determinism is false, then we are left with *indeterminism*. The problem with indeterminism is that human actions are taken to be the result of random, chaotic, or chancy events. And we have no control over those kinds of events. Physical events like beliefs, desires, character traits, or some combination thereof are needed to determine what action is performed.

There are roughly two kinds of incompatibilists. One kind is called *libertarianism* (not to be confused with a particular political philosophy). Libertarians do not think free will is compatible with determinism. The other kind of incompatibilism is called *eliminativism* or hard incompatibilism. Eliminativists roughly agree with the reasoning for why libertarians reject the alleged compatibility between free will and determinism. The major difference is that eliminativists think causal physical determinism is true and only event-event causation exists, which eliminates the possibility for free will. Eliminativists or hard incompatibilists deny free will exists.

Incompatibilists agree that beliefs, desires, and character traits play a role in actions brought about by free will. But they reject that these things can provide a coherent understanding of free will within a deterministic framework. Many incompatibilists—specifically, libertarians—do not believe in determinism full stop. That is to say, many libertarians believe that every event must have a cause, but not every cause must be a physical event, specifically one determined by past physical events governed by the laws of nature. Sometimes the cause is a person—an agent—with causal powers that can act as an uncaused, first cause or unmoved, first mover.[5]

Many libertarians thereby believe that, in addition to event-event causation, there also exists agent-causation.

- *Event-Event Causation:* Any event E is the result of prior physical events or physical states connected to E. These prior physical states are sufficient to bring about E. A full description of the relevant prior physical states will explain how E (a subsequent physical event) occurred.
- *Agent-Causation:* Event E is caused by a person exercising causal powers to bring about E as an *originating source*. Event E is not caused by some prior physical state within a person; rather, the person—the agent—acts as an uncaused first cause, bringing about event E. Event E is brought about by

an agent exercising causal powers. This causal power involves the ability to choose from a limited set of alternatives and bring about an entirely new sequence of events.[6]

Influencing versus Determining

At this point we think it's important to consider an important distinction that often gets overlooked. In discussions involving the relationship between free will and determinism, many people appeal to factors involving nature or nurture (or both). The thought is that things like biological genes, IQ, economic systems, societal structures, cultural norms and values, systems of law, and so on are the prior events, states, or objects that determine human decisions and actions. These prior causal objects guarantee how a person's life will unfold. Call it psychological determinism, biological determinism, structural determinism, or what have you. But why think a thing like that? There are other—perhaps, more plausible—ways to account for human actions.

For starters, one's genes, IQ, beliefs, desires, emotions, thoughts, character traits, health, parents, time and place of birth, surrounding cultural norms, values, and systems of law and governance, among others, are certainly going to influence one's daily decisions and actions. But to say that they determine one's decisions and actions is quite another. Indeed, to say they determine one's actions requires a herculean effort to produce such a convincing argument. To this day, no such argument exists. Causal physical determinism also flies in the face of common sense, as we'll see.

An alternative way to interpret the role nature and nurture play on free will is that of *degreed influence*. One can happily agree that any number of variables attributed to the categories of nature and nurture will certainly influence an agent's thoughts and actions, both in kind and in degree. For example, merely pointing to the way the furniture in your house is situated will influence the set of routes you can take from the couch to the refrigerator. Most will choose the shortest route that requires the least amount of effort. So you get up from the couch, avoid hitting the kitchen table, and head straight to the fridge for a cold beverage. But you could—if you decide to—stand on the couch, leap to the ottoman, leap to the kitchen table, and jump off to the fridge. The way the furniture is situated only influences what path you take; it doesn't determine the path you choose.

The same goes for things like desires, emotions, beliefs, thoughts, and character traits. They will most certainly influence the decision one makes. But they don't always have to determine what action an agent performs. The reason why is because the agent can sometimes bring about certain thoughts and/or actions as an originating source or uncaused first cause. The alleged determining variables only influence the range of recognizable alternatives. Many incompatibilists (viz., libertarians) thus reject that physical event-event causation is the only kind of causation. Many libertarians believe that events have causes, but not all causes are restricted to prior physical events because the agent can sometimes act as uncaused first cause.

The Key Question to the Debate over Free Will and Determinism

We believe it doesn't matter very much which kind of determinism might undermine free will. Causal physical determinism, biological determinism, structural determinism, logical determinism, and theological determinism all offer different kinds of prior events, states, or objects that are taken to causally determine human actions. The key question is this: Can humans sometimes act as an uncaused first cause—are they the ultimate, originating source of their decisions and actions? Asked differently: Do humans have the causal powers associated with agent-causation—can humans act as first causes, bringing about an entirely new sequence of events? If the answer to these questions is yes, then ways of conceiving determinism are false. Now there are only challenging intellectual puzzles to solve.

Divine Determinism and Free Will

One puzzle philosophers and theologians have wrestled with is theological determinism. Theological determinism can come in many different versions. What they all have in common are certain ideas about God's relation to creation, including humans. For some, certain theological doctrines undermine free will or generate challenging puzzles for how free will might be compatible with them.

The first doctrine is *divine predestination*. When God predestines certain events to happen, God's agency—God's activity—directly causes the event. God's activity brings about the event. Predestination, then, is commonly interpreted as a causal notion. To say God predestines us to be adopted sons through Jesus Christ according to the purpose of his will (Eph. 1:5) is to say God somehow causes this event to happen. So if God predestines things to happen, does that eliminate human freedom? If God predestines you to do action A, doesn't that eliminate your ability to freely choose to do action A?

The second doctrine is *divine foreknowledge.* Traditional theology holds that God is omniscient. God knows all true statements and doesn't believe any false statements. Some statements are about the future. So God knows what happens in the future. But if God knows you will wake up tomorrow and go for a run, are you free to run? Does God's knowledge of how you will act eliminate genuine freedom? These questions have generated concerns over whether divine foreknowledge presupposes a type of theological determinism that undermines freedom. The crucial question, of course, is: How does God know the future?[7]

The third doctrine is *divine sovereignty.* The sovereignty of God typically refers to how God alone possesses ultimate authority, power, and control over all things. Both heaven and the universe (and everything contained therein) are ultimately under God's power, authority, and control. The sovereignty of God, then, captures the idea that God is in control over all things and has the authority to bring about events that achieve his purposes, goals, and aims. But if God is in control over bringing about all things in heaven and earth, then does that eliminate your ability to choose between genuine alternatives? How does God's sovereignty not undermine free will? This is how divine sovereignty can generate theological determinism.

The fourth doctrine is *divine providence.* God's providence captures the idea that God sustains the existence of all things (general providence). If it weren't for God's providence, the natural order of the universe—the cosmological constants and laws governing it—would cease, and everything would devolve into chaotic disorder. Divine providence also captures the idea of God actively sustaining and caring for all of creation. This includes bringing about what's good for humans (special providence). When God brings about some specific goal through natural events or supernatural ones (i.e., miracles), it is sometimes referred to as God's "providential hand at work." But if God is providentially working out all things for his purposes, goals, and aims, is free will undermined? This is how divine providence can generate theological determinism.

Again, notice the similarities between causal physical determinism and divine determinism: both work within the idea that every event is caused—determined—by some prior state, event, or object. Causal physical determinism appeals to more prior physical states as the determining cause. Divine determinism appeals to a prior person as the determining cause—specifically, God's intentional actions. It is not the purpose of this chapter to offer attempted solutions to these philosophical and theological puzzles. Nor are we going to endorse and defend our preferred models used within certain theological traditions. However, it is important to see where people of good will disagree with each other.

And it goes back to that important question about agent-causation: Did God create humans with the powers and capacities for agent-causation? If yes, then it's not that the theological doctrines are false—far from it! The challenge becomes how to best understand divine predestination, foreknowledge, sovereignty, and providence in light of God creating humans with agent-causation.

It's important to know that theists (in general) and Christian theists (in particular) are divided over these issues. There is no consensus on these topics. One reason for this are the challenges facing each position. (There are trade-offs for every philosophical and theological position.) Here is one significant challenge facing both camps. For libertarians, they must resolve the tension between divine foreknowledge and libertarian freedom, which motivates at least two difficult questions: (1) How can God know what a person will freely do in the future when that event hasn't happened yet? (2) If God knows the truth about future statements, what makes them true since, again, that event hasn't happened yet?

The Free Will defense by Alvin Plantinga (*God, Freedom, and Evil*, 1974) is a response to an argument made famous by J. L. Mackie ("Evil and Omnipotence" in the journal *Mind*, 1955). Mackie argued that the existence of evil and God is like a square-circle—logically incompatible; they can't both co-exist. More specifically, the idea is that, since God is all-knowing (omniscient), all-powerful (omnipotent), and all-loving / morally-perfect / perfectly-loving (omnibenevolent), then God is smart enough to know how to prevent evil, powerful enough to do it, and loving enough to want to do it. Yet evil still abounds. So God must not exist. Plantinga's free will defense demonstrated that God's attributes are not logically incompatible with evil. God can't create humans with free will while at the same time never allowing them to use their free will in evil ways. Humans either have free will or they don't. And creating a world with free will (other things being equal) is so much more valuable than a world without it. Furthermore, God may have morally sufficient reasons that are beyond our ability to fully understand for permitting humans to use their free will to commit evil acts. It's a defense (shows God and evil are not logically contradictory), not a theodicy (providing justificatory reasons for why God permits evil). The logical problem of evil assumes God can do logically impossible things and that God can't possibly have a morally sufficient reason for permitting humans to use free will inappropriately and disobediently, which are implausible assumptions. Another related problem that some contemporary philosophers work on today is the evidential or probabilistic problem of evil. This problem doesn't argue that God and evil can't co-exist, but rather, the amount and kind of evil that exists makes God's existence unlikely.

For compatibilists, they have the problem of evil. Compatibilists can't use the Free Will defense. Alvin Plantinga famously argued that God is not the author of evil; humans are responsible for evil actions because of misusing their free will.[8] But if compatibilism is true, then God is causally responsible for humans performing evil acts.

We conclude this section by offering you some relevant distinctions for your consideration that often get overlooked or conflated.

- God actively causing a person to do A versus God using that person's free decision to do A to achieve God's intentions, purposes, and aims
- God as the direct cause of bringing about A versus God using humans' free will as intermediary causes to bring about A
- God directly causing a person to do action A versus God permitting a person to do action A
- God bringing about A by either directly causing a person to do A or choosing to create a world wherein God knows that a person will freely do A

The Big Picture: Why Free Will Matters

In chapter 11, we considered an argument for external world skepticism. Recall that this argument concluded that humans don't know anything about the external world because we can't prove we're not living in a virtual world. This would be a disaster. We could not know that our beliefs about the people and things we are interacting with are true, including our very own bodies we're perceiving. But now consider the implications if we really were living in a virtual world, setting aside whether we can prove we are not in a virtual world. The people we loved, invested in, and sacrificed for are not real. The lives we created for ourselves take place in a world of deception. We would be the butt of one of the cruelest jokes—indeed, victims of one of the most elaborate hoaxes of all time.

But here's the real kicker: if humans lack free will, our situation is far worse than being trapped in a virtual world! The reason is this. In a virtual world, at least you still have free will. Mental equilibrium and integrity are still intact. You can still freely choose what to think, how to reason, how to act, where to move, whom to interact with, and so on. Even though the people and places you're interacting with are not real, you still have your agency. Your environment is fake, but your mental life and agency are not. But if we lack free will, then the scope of deception is breathtaking. We are like robots or something worse.

Despite experiencing free will, it's all an illusion! An illusion! Living in this scenario would be one of the cruelest jokes. The world we believed in and the kind of things we take ourselves to be no longer exists . . . madness would ensue.

The good news, however, is that, just as common sense was used to combat this skeptical scenario, we think common sense can justify the existence of free will. The following examples seem to provide adequate evidence for free will from the faculty of introspection. It's free will that makes the existence of reason, moral responsibility, moral evaluations, and loving relationships possible. Any argument leveled against free will needs to provide stronger evidence than the evidence we daily get from introspection. We believe exploring this kind of evidence will assist you in better understanding free will.

The Qualia of Free Will

Qualia is a fancy word philosophers use to describe the feeling of what-it's-like to experience something. There's a what-it's-like to taste ice cream, smell perfume, touch something cold, see something beautiful, and hear something melodious. Free will is accompanied by qualia. There are many qualia of free will often overlooked. We know what-it's-like to freely make a choice. You go to a buffet and freely choose to put some foods on your plate and refrain from choosing others. This quale is very different from what-it's-like to be coerced, forced, or compelled. Every day we experience what-it's-like to make decisions. Indeed, it seems self-evident that you can—right now—decide to continue reading or stop reading. Whichever you decide (we hope it's the former), there is evidence for it from introspection: there's a what-it's-like to decide to continue reading. This evidence justifies the commonsense belief that free will exists.

The *Action* of Reasoning

Consider the act of reasoning. It's a commonsense belief that humans can reason. More specifically, humans seem to have control over their mind's ability to reason. Indeed, what we think about, focus our attention on, and form reasoned beliefs about seems like a power and ability humans possess. Consider deliberation. We deliberate over which car repair needs to be factored into next month's budget. We consider the mechanic's recommendations, the cost of each one, and then reason which repair to pay for first. The qualia accompanying deliberation is rich and multifaceted. There's a what-it's-like to have direct control over sifting for evidence, weighing it, formulating it into reasons, and assessing the reasons justifying our belief. This is the hallmark of rationality.

Notice, however, that we don't have direct control over the liver, kidneys, digestive system, and immune system. Nor do we have direct control over the sensations, thoughts, or memories our nervous system sometimes generates within us. The act of reasoning, however, is different. We can decide to read an argument, see whether the argument's form is valid, accept whether the premises are more likely to be true than their denial, and observe whether the premises adequately support the conclusion. If the premises support the conclusion, we can control the act of accepting the conclusion as likely to be true. Accepting the argument's conclusion as true explains why one performs action A over action B. If that's right, then one has direct control over choosing to act for a purposeful reason. Introspection delivers evidence of having direct control over the act of reasoning. There's a what-it's-like to deliberate, accept, and choose, which all presuppose free will.[10]

Moral Responsibility and Moral Evaluations

We make moral evaluations every day and believe the judgments are true. Without free will, however, it seems impossible to make sense of this. For example, notice how our moral evaluations of human actions differ from how we evaluate animal actions. No one calls 911 to report a theft when a hawk takes a salmon from a bear. We do call 911 to report a carjacking. What's more, we praise or blame humans for their actions, believing some should be rewarded and others punished. This all seems rational to us because of the kind of agency we believe humans have, which animals and inanimate objects lack. Concepts like praise, blame, punishment, and reward presuppose free will, which makes moral responsibility possible and moral evaluations rational.

Moral evaluations presuppose that one could have acted differently. To say one should or ought to have acted differently presupposes that one could have acted differently. This is why Immanuel Kant famously said, "Ought implies can." The very idea of thinking a person ought to act one way (e.g., treat this person the way you'd want to be treated) versus another (e.g., murder an innocent victim) assumes some human actions aren't determined. Humans have the ability to do otherwise and the power to choose from a set of alternatives. Why should we feel guilty for breaking our promises? We feel guilty because we know we could

Consider these thoughts about the relation between free will and determinism. E. J. Lowe (1950–2014): "If what [determinists] say is true, then the movements of their minds that have led them to say it are simply consequences of certain causal laws governing these movements. Hence, these movements of their minds may at most replicate valid reasoning but do not and cannot constitute it. Consequently, their belief in the conclusion—that we have no rational free will—is not a rationally held belief." Epicurus (341–270 BC) saw this problem over two-thousand years ago: "The man who says that all things come to pass by [determinism] cannot criticize one who denies that all things come to pass by [determinism]: for he admits that this too happens [as a result of determinism]."[9]

have been more responsible and fulfilled our promises. Whether we are morally evaluating other's actions or our own, moral evaluations presuppose free will.

Entering into Loving Relationships

Without going into a comprehensive treatise on what love is, many—if not most of you—will agree that love is something like providing another person—for their own sake—that which promotes his/her health, happiness, well-being, and flourishing. If I love my wife, then I will act in ways that foster these goods for her because of who and what she is. If someone is doing actions that promote your good, that person is loving you. Loving another can be a one-way street. But a loving relationship is a two-way street requiring some level of mutual reciprocation toward fostering these goods for each other.

Well, then, the very idea of love relations presupposes free will. Because loving another requires a decision made by a person to will the good of another. And this decision can't be brought about by past physical events, governed by the laws of nature, determining one to do so. The reason why is because the motivation and agency needed for love is undermined. Indeed, the idea of forced love, coerced love, or compulsory love seem nonsensical, even contradictory. Indeed, loving relationships involve acts of yielding and cooperating with another's will. It's unreasonable to say one can be loved by a rock, plant, or computer. Since they lack the capacity for free will, they can neither make the decisions nor perform the actions needed to will one's good. Loving another and being loved by another presuppose free will.

Conclusion

The purpose of this chapter is to introduce you to the topic of free will and discuss some important topics that fall out from it. The challenges presented by the theological doctrines we listed and whether they undermine free will is a case in point. Rather than trying to present all the different positions and answers that have been offered, our aim is to present the topic and provide the kind of framework and parameters to assist you in studying these topics further. In addition to framing this debate and providing some positions and arguments, we hope you see how this chapter offers tools and distinctions to better assist you in thinking about free will because the beliefs you form about the powers and parameters of your agency will determine the kind of goals, expectations, and responsibility you afford to yourself and others. These beliefs, then, will inform how you think about human potential, development, character, relationships, morality, moral evaluations, law, justice, and many other significant topics.

Questions for Reflection

1. Do you think the consequence argument is sound? Why or why not?
2. What do you think about the difference between that which determines you to act versus that which only influences what choice you will make? What are some implications of not keeping these two things distinct from each other?
3. How many ways do you think God could possibly know the future? How will each of those ways God could know the future contribute to interpreting divine predestination, sovereignty, and providence?
4. Can things like moral praise and blame, and punishment and reward, be understood independently of understanding free will? Why or why not?
5. Do you think the faculty of introspection provides strong evidence for free will? Why or why not?

For Further Reading

Basinger, David, and Randall Basinger, eds. *Predestination and Free Will: Four Views of Divine Sovereignty and Human Freedom.* Downers Grove, IL: IVP Academic, 1986.

Beilby, James K., and Paul R. Eddy, eds. *Divine Foreknowledge: Four Views.* Downers Grove, IL: IVP Academic, 2001.

Capes, Justin A. *Moral Responsibility and the Flicker of Freedom.* Oxford: Oxford University Press, 2023.

Fischer, John Martin, Robert Kane, Derk Pereboom, and Manuel Vargas. *Four Views on Free Will.* New York: Wiley-Blackwell, 2007.

Gundry, Stanely N., and Dennis W. Jowers, eds. *Four Views on Divine Providence.* Grand Rapids: Zondervan, 2007.

Kane, Robert, ed. *The Oxford Handbook of Free Will*, 2nd ed. Oxford: Oxford University Press, 2011.

Moreland, J. P., and William Lane Craig. *Philosophical Foundations for a Christian Worldview*, 2nd ed. Downers Grove, IL: IVP Academic, 2017.

Timpe, Kevin. *Free Will: Sourcehood and its Alternatives*, 2nd ed. London: Bloomsbury Academic, 2013.

NOTES

1. Stated more formally, the Control Principle says we are morally assessable only to the extent that what we are assessed for depends on factors under our control. See Dana K. Nelkin, "Moral Luck," *The Stanford Encyclopedia of Philosophy* (Spring 2023 edition), ed. Edward N. Zalta and Uri Nodelman, https://plato.stanford.edu/archives/spr2023/entries/moral-luck/.

2. This philosophical position is what makes the Hollywood movie *Minority Report* a coherent idea in order for the plot to pass simple plausibility tests.

3. This argument is adopted with slight modifications from Robert Kane, "Incompatibilism," in *Contemporary Debates in Metaphysics* (New York: Blackwell, 2008), 287. The argument originally appears in Peter van Inwagen, *An Essay on Free Will* (Oxford: Oxford University Press, 1983), 56.

4. See Harry Frankfurt, "Alternative Possibilities and Moral Responsibility," *Journal of Philosophy* 66 (1969): 829–39. As clever as this thought experiment is, no libertarian should accept it. The reason why is that it begs an important question: the Frankfurtian counterexample assumes that event-event causation is the only game in town, which is what makes it possible for the mad scientists to know what assassin Jones will do by observing his brain-states. But a libertarian (an incompatibilist who believes in agent causation and is not to be confused with the libertarian political party) will reject the assumption that such brain-states are the prior causes guaranteeing a subsequent action will occur. Rather, the varying beliefs, desires, thoughts, reasons, etc. are merely influencing the number of options and ultimate decision that assassin Jones will make, because it is assassin Jones—as an agent acting as an originating, uncaused first cause—that is the cause of his action, not his prior brain-states. So the libertarian will not grant the kind of event-event causation needed for this Frankfurtian counterexample to work. There is agent-causation. What's more, if agent-causation exists, then the mad scientists could not know what assassin Jones will do because all they have access to are prior events that influence, but don't ultimately cause, the action assassin Jones performs. For a more thorough discussion of why Frankfurtian counterexamples do not seem to undermine the principle alternative possibilities (PAP), see Justin A. Capes, *Moral Responsibility and the Flicker of Freedom* (Oxford: Oxford University Press, 2023).

5. Aristotle famously said that "a staff moves a stone, and is moved by a hand, which is moved by a man" (*Physics*, book VII, chap. 5, 256a, 6–8) to illustrate the power agents had to bring about action as an uncaused, first cause—the starting point of an action as opposed to some event running through the agent.

6. The set of alternatives will naturally be limited, given an agent's circumstances, environment, beliefs, knowledge, understanding, wisdom, emotions, and character traits constraining the number of available alternatives. But even though said factors influence and constrain the available alternatives to choose from, they are not sufficient to determine what an agent will in fact choose because an agent can sometimes act as an uncaused, first cause.

7. As Craig and Moreland point out, "It is true, given that determinism is the case [for compatibilists], that only one future course of events can happen. But it does not follow that this future course of events will occur irrespective of [human] deliberations and choices." See J. P. Moreland and William Lane Craig, *Philosophical Foundations for a Christian Worldview*, 2nd ed. (Downers Grove, IL: IVP Academic, 2017), 312. See also James K. Beilby and Paul R. Eddy, eds., *Divine Foreknowledge: Four Views* (Downers Grove, IL: InterVarsity Press, 2001); William Lane Craig, *The Only Wise God: The Compatibility of Divine Foreknowledge and Human Freedom* (Eugene, OR: Wipf and Stock, 2000).

8. See Alvin Plantinga, *God, Freedom, and Evil* (New York: Harper and Row, 1974).

9. See E. J. Lowe, "Substance Causation, Powers, and Human Otology," in *Mental Causation*

and Ontology, ed. S. C. Gibb, E. J. Lowe, and R. D. Ingthorsson (New York: Oxford University Press, 2013), 171. See Epicurus, *The Extant Remains*, ed. Cyril Bailey (Oxford: Clarendon, 1926), 112–13, fragment XL.

10. For further reading on the topic of how the existence of reason requires free will and thus undermines causal physical determinism's effect on human agency, see C. S. Lewis, *Miracles: A Preliminary Study*, rev. ed. (1947; New York: Harper Collins, 1996), chap. 3; Victor Reppert, *C. S. Lewis's Dangerous Idea: In Defense of the Argument from Reason* (Downers Grove, IL: InterVarsity Press, 2003); and James Beilby, ed., *Naturalism Defeated? Essays on Plantinga's Evolutionary Argument against Naturalism* (Ithaca, NY: Cornell University Press, 2002).

PART 5

Philosophy and Science

Complementary and Conflicting

CHAPTER 16

What Is Science and How Does It Work?

Its Definition, Explanation, and Interaction with Faith

The picture of science that we have from elementary school and high school is familiar to all of us. We state a hypothesis about what we think will occur when we perform a certain experiment. Then we perform the experiment, collecting data. Finally, we analyze the data, crunching the numbers, and compare the results with the original hypothesis. Then we state our conclusion about what is actually the case—whether our hypothesis was correct or incorrect. And, voila! We have come to know how the natural world works by employing the scientific method.

Is this how science really works? Is this the method that science employs all the time and in every case? What is "science" really, and what does it attempt to explain? The philosophy of science digs deeply and probes into these foundational questions of the nature of science. As we consider these questions, we will see that the answers to them are somewhat difficult to nail down, contrary to what most of us have learned or been told. The definition of science, the explanations we often give in science, and even how science interacts with faith (or theology) are more complex than what first meets the eye.

What Is Science?

Everyone talks about "science" as if we all know what it is. Interestingly, however, there really are no necessary or sufficient conditions by which to define science.

What exactly does this mean? A *necessary condition* for the definition of science means that there is something that must (necessarily) be included in the definition of science in order for a particular study or activity to be identified as science. On the other hand, a *sufficient condition* is one that adequately defines the term *science* in order to identify a particular study or activity as science. We will see how this plays out specifically in the following. The important thing to note here is that there are no necessary or sufficient conditions to claim a particular study or activity as science. As unbelievable as this may seem, this difficulty is well known among philosophers, so much so that it is known as the *demarcation problem*. Philosophers J. P. Moreland and William Craig state it aptly: "No one has ever been able to draw such a line of demarcation [between science and non-science] and such a thing does not exist."[1] To see why, let's take a look at four popular proposals and why they fail to provide necessary or sufficient conditions.

Science Is What Can Be *Tested*

Probably one of the most popular ways science is defined is by *testability*. It is often said that science is anything that can be tested in a lab. To discern whether this is a good definition, we must ask first if testability is a necessary condition for an activity to be considered science. At first glance, it may seem so. After all, much of science takes place in a lab. Upon deeper consideration, however, we can find examples of what we consider to be science that cannot be tested. What about the Big Bang theory? Can this be tested in the laboratory? Obviously not. It was a one-time event. But we consider the Big Bang theory as a part of the scientific endeavor. As such, testability cannot be a necessary condition for science. Otherwise, we would have to exclude studies like the Big Bang as unscientific.

Maybe, on the other hand, testability is a sufficient condition for the definition of science. This would mean that any activity or study that includes testing in a lab ought to be considered science. But is this true? To discern this, we can simply ask, "Are there any activities that include testing in a laboratory that we would not consider to be science?" The answer is obviously, "Yes!" Alchemy, for example, can be practiced in the lab through various tests, but no one would consider it science today. The predictions and methods of witchcraft could be practiced in the lab, but most would not consider it to be science either. Therefore, testability is not a sufficient condition when defining science. There are just too many activities that are testable but certainly ought not be considered science. In summary, testability is neither a necessary nor a sufficient condition for science.

Science Is What Can Be Demonstrated with *Certainty*

Another popular way science has been defined is as what can be demonstrated with *certainty* or proven. This understanding goes back to the time of Aristotle and continues to be popular today. In some ways, certainty appears to be a good necessary marker for science. There are many scientific theories, such as heliocentrism or the laws of thermodynamics, that seem to have been proven.

Upon further investigation, however, certainty or provability cannot be a necessary or sufficient condition for science. (For a helpful discussion in connection with inductive reasoning, see chapter 8.) To see why, think of contemporary physics. It deals with some very strange ideas in the study known as quantum mechanics. In this field, there are quite a few interpretations of subatomic events. The result is that there is no certainty about what is occurring at the subatomic level. Thus, if certainty is to be a necessary condition for science, we would have to conclude that quantum mechanics is not science. But it is highly unlikely that anyone would consider this to be the case. Moreover, the history of science is littered with examples of theories being modified, changed, or even entirely scrapped. Geocentrism (the idea that the earth is the center of the universe), for example, was once thought to be certain and proven by the Ptolemaic model of astronomy. Much later, however, Copernicus showed otherwise. Was the Ptolemaic model not science, then, because it was thought to have been proven, but in fact it was not? Most would not say so. Geocentrism was science; it was just incorrect and later changed.

Should we consider certainty to be a sufficient condition? Again, we can answer this question by asking ourselves whether any study or activity exists that provides certainty but we would not consider it science. Interestingly, there are some activities that meet such a standard. Magic, for example, provides certainty in outcomes. A good magician will always pull a rabbit out of his hat. But should magic be considered science? Most would not think so, and for good reasons.

Science Is What Is Accomplished by the *Scientific Method*

A third way in which science has been defined is as anything that is studied via the scientific method. This method is often thought of in terms of *induction*: the gathering of data and then coming to a general conclusion. This understanding of the scientific method has been popular since the time of the modern scientist Francis Bacon (1561–1626; see sidebar).

Although much of science has been and is accomplished by induction, not all scientists agree that this method is the only way (or even the main way) science is accomplished. Another way the scientific method has been understood is as *abduction*. This is when scientists infer the best available explanation to an inquiry. The first to introduce this idea was the philosopher and scientist

FRANCIS BACON (1561–1626)

Francis Bacon was an Englishman who is often viewed as a transitional figure from the Renaissance to the Modern period. His popular work, the *Novum Organum*, is known for laying out the new inductive approach to science. Traditionally, since the time of Aristotle, science generally was approached in a deductive manner: it began with accepted or established axioms and then deduced further conclusions. Bacon challenged this idea, arguing for scrapping all that was known in science in favor of collecting data through experimentation. This inductive method was foundational for contemporary science.

Charles Peirce (1839–1914). Another and more popular contemporary way to speak about the scientific method is to say that science must approach its discipline by *methodological naturalism*, which assumes that the worldview of naturalism is true (at least for the sake of experimentation) when doing science.

As we can see, defining science as "whatever follows the scientific method" is problematic just for the fact that there is no consensus on what comprises the scientific method itself! But even if agreement were possible, using this as a necessary or even sufficient condition for the definition of science would fail. Whether it exclusively uses induction, abduction, methodological naturalism, or something else, many examples can be given to show that these are not necessary or sufficient to be deemed science. As a quick example, think of induction: science does not always, and perhaps very rarely, approach its study by merely collecting data points. A perfect example would be Albert Einstein's inquiry that led to his theory of General Relativity. His study began by using two primary thought experiments: (1) what would it be like to travel alongside a beam of light? and (2) what would it be like to travel in an elevator in space? Such questions are not close to induction. They are not even close to anything empirical: they are merely thought experiments! Nevertheless, they were the seedbed to Einstein's theory, which has become the bedrock of modern physics. Surely, then, induction is not a necessary condition for an activity to be considered science. Otherwise, Einstein was not practicing science!

Science Is What Can Be *Falsified*

We would be remiss if we did not mention one very significant way science has been defined: as that which can be falsified. *Falsificationism*, as it is known and stated by its proponent Karl Popper (1902–1994), says that "statements or systems of statements, in order to be ranked as scientific, must be capable of conflicting with possible, or conceivable, observations."[2] If a statement cannot be falsified, then it is not scientific.

Again, like all the other attempts, falsificationism fails to be a necessary or sufficient condition of science. First, it is not a necessary condition because not all scientific inquiries, hypotheses, or theories can be falsified. At present, it is not conceivable, for example, to falsify the multiverse hypothesis.[3] But many clearly see this as an aspect of science.

Second, we can think of many activities that would involve falsification but would not be considered science. Astrology, for example, can be falsified, but we would not consider such practice to be science. Moreover, it should be noted that falsificationism fails to recognize that the history of science has numerous examples of theories that were considered to be unfalsifiable, such as geocentrism or Newtonian physics, but over time they have become falsifiable.

Since there are no necessary or sufficient conditions for defining science, then are we left to say that there is no such thing as science? Philosopher J. P. Moreland asks, "Does [this] mean that we can never recognize a case of science or nonscience when we see it?" He answers, "No, it doesn't." It is probably best to provide just a general idea of what science attempts to do and then be cautious about claiming some activities as "unscientific." Moreland does just this when he states, "In a *general way*, science is a discipline that in *some sense* and *usually* appeals to natural explanation, empirical tests, and so forth."[4]

What Is Science Explaining?

Just as defining science is difficult, so, too, is discerning what science specifically attempts to explain. The question here is ultimately whether scientific theories explain, or give a picture of, the actual world or whether they are merely helpful or useful for some other purpose. The view that states scientific theories explain and reflect the actual world is known as *scientific realism*. In contrast, the view that says science does not explain or reflect the actual world is termed *antirealism*. In the following paragraphs, we will briefly lay out these two opposing views.

Scientific Realism

As already stated, scientific realism says that scientific theories reflect how the real world actually operates. Thus, when Isaac Newton formulated his second law (Force = mass x acceleration), it was understood that this law explains that the real world is such that when an object's mass is multiplied by its acceleration, the result is an actual, particular force. The second law directly explains how force is related to an object's mass and acceleration.

There are some various approaches to scientific realism, but philosophers Moreland and Craig provide some helpful "core tenets" that all realist approaches have in common.

- All theories are understood to be true or at least approximately true.
- Terms used in theories refer to something in the real world.
- There are good reasons to think that one scientific theory is more probably true or approximately true than another (i.e., relativism in science is false, not all theories or explanations can be true).
- Scientific theories exhibit certain characteristics (often called "epistemic virtues"), like clarity, simplicity, or successful prediction, when they are true or approximately true.
- The objective of scientific investigation is to discern how the world actually works, and, as time goes forward, we get a clearer picture of the world as theories are refined or jettisoned for better theories.[5]

An obviously positive feature of this approach is that it enables us to claim an understanding of the actual world while avoiding a willy-nilly universe that does not operate in any consistent or orderly manner. It provides a rational and stable foundation in which to practice science. If antirealism were true, it could be argued that the universe is chaotic and devoid of many features of the world we take for granted, like cause and effect. And if features such as these are actually not real, then the entire scientific enterprise seems to be in question. Moreover, not much of an explanation could be given as to why the universe at least appears to be orderly when, if antirealism is true, everyone's perception of it would be different (i.e., relative). If relativism is true, then why is virtually everyone's perception of the universe similar?

Of course, the main objection to the realist position is that scientific theories are modified or changed. One example of this would be the long-held scientific belief in geocentrism. The perfect illustration of this is the Ptolemaic mathematical and observational model of the planets. The model's wonderful explanation and very good predictability of planetary motion solidified it as the reigning model in astronomy for thousands of years. As we all know, however, it was fundamentally incorrect. The earth is not the center of the universe; the sun is. Hence, some have preferred the antirealist view of science.

Antirealism

Antirealism entails a family of viewpoints. Here we will look at the popular view known as *instrumentalism*. It is named for its belief that scientific theories merely serve as instruments, or useful tools, to predict and explain what we humans seem to observe or think is occurring in the world around us. Theories do not reflect the real world. There is nothing objectively true about scientific theories. In a real sense, theories describe something about the scientist, not the world.

What exactly do instrumentalists believe science is useful for? There are a variety of answers to this question. Some believe scientific theories are merely helpful ways to describe what we human observers perceive and then try to predict what we may perceive in the future. Others think that theories are helpful in merely solving problems we observe. For example, we observe that the planets move across the night sky, so science tries to solve the problem of why we observe this. Science has nothing to do with explaining whether or how planets actually move across the night sky. This is irrelevant according to this view. Still others think that science is useful in other ways. The underlying point for all these views is that theories are just useful tools and explain more about the observer's perception than the world itself.

Probably the most positive feature of this view is its highlight of perception, or bias, in the observer. It is true that scientists do not live in a vacuum apart from past ideas, influences, and other factors that may cloud one's perception. Bias is intrinsic to every person. It can be tempting to think that science is somehow exempt from the influences of one's worldview, but this is clearly not the case (especially as we will see in the next chapter on Scientism).

On the other hand, some are quick to point out that one's perception does not have to mean that scientific explanations can never be true or approximately true. If it did, then how do we explain scientific consensus on numerous theories, like heliocentrism, thermodynamics, and General Relativity? Furthermore, how would we explain the refining and refutation of scientific theories if a scientist's perception clouds his theories to the point of making it impossible to know how the world works? Refining and refuting theories and coming to a consensus implies that we, in fact, know something about the universe and can discern whether scientific theories are true.

From a Christian perspective, it seems best to affirm scientific realism to some degree. The Christian doctrine of creation teaches us that there is an objective world that God created and which can be studied and understood (cf. Ps. 19:1–2, 111:2; Rom. 1:18–23). Also, a Christian worldview of truth as objective and corresponding to reality supports the idea that scientific theories can be true or approximately true. Therefore, Christians ought to understand scientific theories as referring to how the world actually works, or at least as approximately true, and can be modified as we learn more. Still, we should be humble and cautious when doing science. The Christian doctrines of sin and creation point to human situatedness, finitude, and sinful nature, which can distort the scientific enterprise. As such, we should always be open for correction to our theories. Although humanity is frail, the scientific theories it puts forth are saying something about the real world.

Do Science and Faith Go Together?

When discussing the philosophy of science from a Christian perspective, one question often raised is the relationship between faith (or theology and the Bible) and science. It is popular to view the two as opposed to each other. A title to a popular atheist's book reveals this: *Faith versus Fact: Why Science and Religion Are Incompatible.*[6] In fact, some would say they are at war with each other. Richard Dawkins, a well-known atheist, posits that religion (fundamentalism in particular) is actually evil, because it subverts science.[7] Interestingly, even some Christians believe science is at war with faith.[8]

Are science and theology at war with each other, or are they compatible? What exactly is the relationship between science and faith? In answer to this question, there are four primary positions: conflict, independence, dialogue, and integration.[9]

Conflict

The *conflict view* of science and faith states that the two are always in conflict or at war. This view is often referred to as the *warfare thesis.* The idea is that faith and science make claims that cannot cohere, or go together, and they are always competing for the correct view upon a particular topic. One example would be origins. The conflict view says that faith wars with the contemporary scientific view of evolution. Faith says God is the origin of the physical universe; science says that merely nature and physical laws are the origin. Another example would be the age of the earth. The conflict view says that Christianity teaches that the earth may be somewhere around 10,000 years old, whereas contemporary science estimates it to be 4.5 billion years old. Since these claims are in obvious opposition, it is argued that science and faith are in conflict.

It should be noted that this view is relatively recent. The warfare thesis was primarily made popular with the publication of John Draper's *History of the Conflict between Religion and Science* in 1874.[10] This was followed by Andrew White's work *A History of the Warfare of Science with Theology in Christendom* in 1896.[11] This conflict view has been shown to be historically inaccurate. In fact, the opposite is true: science has been viewed throughout history as complementary and helpful to faith. Many of the early scientists who laid the foundations for today's science were Christians (or theists of some sort). Nicholas Copernicus (1473–1543), himself a Christian, believed the study of astronomy led one to contemplate God himself. Later, Isaac Newton (1642–1727) commented about the cosmos: "This most beautiful system of the sun, planets and comets, could proceed only from the counsel and domination of an intelligent and powerful

Being."[12] Over 2,000 years earlier, the Psalmist of the Old Testament proclaimed the same: "Great are the works of the LORD, they are pondered by all who delight in them" (Ps. 111:2).

Even today, Christians and other theists do not view science and faith as at odds. One popular example would be Hugh Ross. As a Christian and astrophysicist, he thinks the scientific consensus view of the age of the earth can be reconciled with a faithful interpretation of Scripture. Francis Collins, geneticist and former Director of the National Human Genome Research Institute, finds evolution to be compatible with faith. Rather than being an enemy of science, then, it seems that faith supports it and encourages its study.

> ## GALILEO GALILEI (1564–1642)
> It is sometimes argued that Galileo is an example of the war between science and faith. In 1633, he stood trial before the Inquisition on the account of teaching the heresy of heliocentrism. This event, however, is much more complex. Numerous political events and Galileo's disposition are probably more to blame for his trial than his belief in heliocentrism. Although he was found guilty, he was never executed but put under house arrest.

Independence

The *independence view* states that both science and faith have their own domain of study, and the two never overlap or have anything to do with each other. (See Fig. 16.1.) This is different from the conflict view in that science and faith are viewed to be investigating and claiming entirely different things. Thus, there is no war between the two. The late Harvard paleontologist Stephen Jay Gould (1941–2002) is representative of this view. He termed his model "nonoverlapping magisteria," or NOMA.

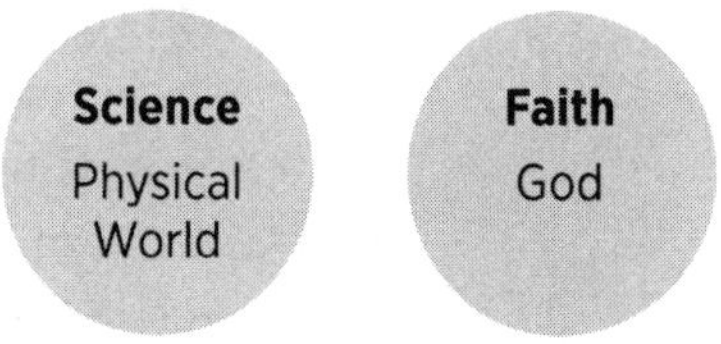

Science Physical World   **Faith** God

FIG. 16.1

Although this view seems plausible in some areas, one observation often made is that science and faith sometimes seem to overlap. They often investigate and make claims about similar subjects: for example, origins. Both science and faith claim something about the origin of the universe and human life. Both science and faith make claims about human psychology and nature. It seems that viewing science and faith as consisting entirely of two different domains may be too "neat."

Dialogue

Another view of science and faith is the *dialogue model*, which states that the two disciplines can and ought to be in conversation with each other. It is recognized that there are separate elements found in each discipline that can help the other to gain a more robust understanding of the world. For example, faith provides understanding of ethics that can help the scientific endeavor, especially in the area of medicine and life and death issues (bioethics). On the other hand, science can help faith understand aspects of the human body that can benefit health, which cannot be understood partially or exclusively from a faith perspective (neuroscience). One of the most positive features of this view is that it recognizes the legitimacy of each discipline and the different benefits that each discipline can bring to the table to aid one another. One negative, however, is that it does not provide a way to adjudicate between competing claims of science and faith. Does science provide a better explanation of human consciousness or does faith? This is one pressing issue that would need to be addressed more fully. (See, e.g., chapter 14 on the philosophy of mind.)

Integration

The final view to be discussed here is the *integration view*. Although this view has various approaches, in general it states that science and faith ought to accomplish investigation of their topics in the same or similar manner. An important point for this view is that it is not always clear where science ends and theology begins, or vice versa. The idea that each has its own domain and methods exclusive from the other needs to be abandoned. Science and faith can, must, and often do interact with each other at many different levels.

A positive of this view is that it acknowledges that cases may exist in which science helps Christians interpret the Bible. One example was during the controversy of Copernicus's heliocentric model, that is, that the planets orbit the sun. Until the time of Copernicus, theologians had interpreted numerous biblical texts as affirming the reigning geocentric (the earth as the center) scientific paradigm. But, as we know, Copernicus showed otherwise, and it was this science that led Christians to re-evaluate their interpretation of Scripture that supported geocentrism. Eventually, it led Christians to reinterpret those passages.

One negative, however, is that this view does not always make it easy to discern when science ought to take precedence over a traditional biblical interpretation. This problem is seen especially in the topic of the age of the earth. Those who think science has shown the earth to be approximately 4.3 billion years old (known as Old Earth Creationists) believe that science has helped make a better interpretation of the days described in Genesis 1. Those who believe that the more traditional interpretation of the days of Genesis 1, however, claim that science ought to be jettisoned here in favor of the historical consensus position. It needs to be pointed out that, although there is some difficulty and ambiguity here, all Christians are attempting to figure out how to engage both science and faith. Both are beneficial to understanding the world around us, and they ought to be integrated in some way.

Summary

After considering the philosophy of science, we can better appreciate the complexity of science. It is not as easy as it is often portrayed to be, especially when we attempt to demarcate it from other activities, or non-science. Science seems to escape a precise definition, having neither necessary nor sufficient conditions. Moreover, specifically what science attempts to explain can often be foggy: is it explaining actual realities of the world, or are its theories just symbols of things that help us explain phenomenon we humans perceive? Then, when we step in the direction of faith, science becomes even more elusive in some ways. Exactly how should science and faith relate? From a Christian perspective, science and faith ought to be at least partners in dialogue, and it seems best to integrate them in some way. After all, the Christian faith teaches that God created the world, and we ought to study it using the human faculties the Creator has given us all. The difficulty always will seem to be discerning their boundaries in any definite way.

Questions for Reflection

1. Why is defining science so difficult, and in what ways could you illustrate this?
2. If scientific theories are continually changing or being modified over time, how do we know that the theories are, in fact, true? How should we understand the term *true* when referring to theories?
3. Which view of science and faith makes the most sense and why?
4. Does the war thesis accurately describe the relationship between science and faith? Why or why not?

For Further Reading

Hardin, Jeff, Ronald L. Numbers, and Ronald A. Binzley, eds. *The Warfare between Science and Religion: The Idea That Wouldn't Die*. Baltimore: Johns Hopkins University Press, 2018.

Hendrix, Scott E. *Gods, Philosophers, and Scientists: Religion and Science in the West*. Mechanicsburg, PA: Oxford Southern, 2019.

Lindberg, David C., and Ronald L. Numbers, eds. *When Science and Christianity Meet*. Chicago: University of Chicago Press, 2003.

Moreland, J. P. *Christianity and the Nature of Science: A Philosophical Investigation*. Grand Rapids: Baker Books, 1989.

Rosenberg, Alex, and Lee McIntyre. *Philosophy of Science: A Contemporary Introduction*. Routledge Contemporary Introductions to Philosophy. 4th edition. New York: Routledge, 2020.

NOTES

1. J. P. Moreland and William Lane Craig, *Philosophical Foundations for a Christian Worldview*, 2nd ed. (Downers Grove, IL: IVP Academic, 2017), 382.
2. Karl Popper, "Science: Conjectures and Refutations," in *Philosophy of Science: An Historical Anthology*, ed. Timothy McGrew, Marc Alspector-Kelly, and Fritz Allhoff (Malden, MA: Wiley-Blackwell, 2009), 475.
3. Physicist Alexander Vilenkin says, "The problem is, however, that there is not one iota of evidence to support this hypothesis. Even worse, it does not seem possible to *ever* confirm or disprove it. . . . The evidence for the multiverse is, of course, indirect, as it will always be. This is a circumstantial case, where we are not going to hear eyewitness accounts or see the murder weapon." Alexander Vilenkin, *Many Worlds in One: The Search for Other Universes* (New York: Hill and Wang, 2006), 134, 151.
4. J. P. Moreland, *Christianity and the Nature of Science: A Philosophical Investigation* (Grand Rapids: Baker Books, 1989), 42, emphasis in original.
5. Moreland and Craig, *Philosophical Foundations*, 354.
6. Jerry Coyne, *Faith versus Fact: Why Science and Religion Are Incompatible* (New York: Viking, 2015).
7. See chapter 8 in Richard Dawkins, *The God Delusion* (Boston: Mariner Books, 2008).
8. See, for example, Henry Morris, *The Long War against God: The History and Impact of the Creation/Evolution Conflict* (Green Forest, AR: Master Books, 2000).
9. These subdivisions are borrowed from Alister McGrath, *Science and Religion: A New Introduction*, 2nd ed. (Malden, MA: Wiley-Blackwell, 2010).
10. John William Draper, *History of the Conflict between Religion and Science* (New York: D. Appleton and Co., 1874).
11. Andrew Dickson White, *A History of the Warfare of Science with Theology in Christendom* (New York: D. Appleton and Co., 1896).
12. Isaac Newton, *Mathematical Principles of Natural Philosophy*, ed. Robert Maynard Hutchins, trans. Andrew Motte, Great Books of the Western World, vol. 34 (Chicago: University of Chicago Press, 1952), 369.

CHAPTER 17

What Is Scientism?

In the previous chapter, we discussed the subject of the philosophy of science. This should not be confused with the topic of this chapter: scientism. Scientism is actually a type of epistemology, or theory of knowledge, and so it will be encountered in various places throughout the text, especially in the section on epistemology. For our purposes, however, scientism is best discussed more thoroughly here as a kind of addendum to the previous chapter because it is popular to define science as the be-all and end-all of learning. *Scientism*, then, is exactly this: it is the belief that science (in particular, the "hard" sciences, like physics, chemistry, and biology) is the best, or only, valuable and authoritative means by which humans can gain knowledge.

There are two versions of this view. We will begin our discussion with these two types and then discuss the various problems with scientism. We will conclude by showing that science is just one way to gain knowledge of the world, and that it, in fact, must assume certain knowledge of the world in order to be practiced. Ultimately, we will see that scientism is an impoverished, self-refuting, materialistic view of everything, and therefore, we ought to be open to other avenues to obtain knowledge of our universe and the things in the universe and not give pride of place to science.

A Materialistic View of Everything

As already mentioned, scientism states that science is the best or exclusive means by which knowledge can be obtained. But there is something more fundamental to this view. At its most basic level, scientism is intrinsically a materialist view of everything. *Materialism* is the belief that all that exists is physical "stuff," or material: there is nothing immaterial or spiritual (like God, angels, or human souls). This assumption grounds scientism itself. Because nothing exists beyond the physical universe, there is only one way to know things: through some kind of empirical investigation. In the previous chapter, we saw that this was a popular definition of science. As such, we can see how materialism undergirds scientism.

There are two views of scientism: a strong version and a weak version. Although there is some difference between the two, it is subtle, and both versions assume the same materialist view of everything.

Strong Scientism

To borrow the definition from philosopher J. P. Moreland, *strong scientism* states that "something is true, rationally justified, or known if and only if it is a scientific claim that has been successfully tested and that is being used according to appropriate scientific methodology."[1] It is the belief that science alone can provide knowledge of the universe and all reality (defined materialistically).

Weak Scientism

Weak scientism states that science is the most authoritative and best way to gain knowledge of the universe and all reality; it is not the only way. Other means to knowledge may be possible (like through the "soft" sciences of psychology or sociology), but (hard) science is the only certain means to knowledge. If some other discipline happens to stumble upon the truth, we still need physics or biology to verify it. In the end, and practically speaking, there is not much difference between strong and weak scientism. Both views still understand the world materialistically and believe that science is the primary way to obtain knowledge.

Self-Refuting and Impoverished View of Everything

Scientism, whether the strong or weak version, might seem sound and helpful at first blush. It fails, however, in multiple ways. First, strong scientism fails by being *self-refuting*: it contradicts itself by having the inability to support itself by its own claims. To see this clearly, consider the following statement as encapsulating strong scientism:

Science is the only valuable way to obtain knowledge.

Is this statement true or false? If it is true, then the statement itself must be false because the statement is not a statement of science; it is a statement about science. Specifically, it is a philosophical statement about the nature of science. As such, scientism defeats itself by not having the ability to pass its own test to be categorized as science. Therefore, strong scientism must be false.

Weak scientism, although not as dogmatic and self-refuting, fails as well. First, it has been recognized by many philosophers that some non-scientific statements can be known with a greater degree of confidence and, perhaps, even more certainty than some scientific statements. For example, we can be more confident knowing (even certain) that "enslaving human persons is evil" or "torturing people for fun is evil" than statements about quantum mechanics. Even mathematical statements can be known with certainty, unlike some scientific ones. It's self-evident (or obviously true) that $1 + 1 = 2$ is true but not so for Newton's First Law of Motion ("an object at rest remains at rest unless acted upon by an outside force"). To grasp that non-scientific statements can be known with a high degree of confidence (even certainty), unlike some scientific ones, consider a future time when humanity's understanding of quantum physics or Newton's First Law could be revised or even rejected. It is, however, quite difficult to envision a future in which humans revise the idea that $1 + 1 = 2$ or that enslaving African Americans is evil.

Another problem with scientism, both weak and strong forms, is pointed out from a Christian theological perspective. If scientism is true, then Christian theological claims cannot be viewed as knowledge claims. In effect, it makes theology impossible. If strong scientism is true, then Christian claims are, at best, pure speculation. At worst, they are irrational opinions based upon something like subjective feelings that have nothing to do with reality. On the other hand, if weak scientism is true, then theological statements must always be brought before science to be judged for validity. In this case, Christians must stand idly by, waiting for science to speak so their theological beliefs can conform to accepted scientific hypotheses and theories or be rejected based upon current scientific beliefs.

Such a view of Christian beliefs flies in the face of what the Christian worldview claims about its theological statements. Christianity affirms that its statements of belief are, in fact, true. Christians do not merely believe that Jesus is the God-man who died on a Roman cross and was raised from the dead on the third day. They claim to know this is true. Indeed, many have claimed to have encountered God and/or witnessed God testifying about the risen Jesus (cf. 1 Cor. 2:4–5, 9–10; 12:3; 15:3–8). The apostle John wrote, "We *know* that we have come to *know* him if we keep his [God's] commands" (1 John 2:3; emphasis added).

Jesus himself stated, "If you hold to my teaching, you are really my disciples. Then you will *know* the truth, and the truth will set you free" (John 8:31b–32; emphasis added). Christian beliefs are knowledge claims, just like claims of science.

The foundational problem that the Christian worldview has with scientism is its assumption of materialism. This belief is contrary to the Christian doctrine of creation. Christian theology teaches that there is more to reality than just the physical universe. There exists an immaterial, non-physical realm—one of God, angels, demons, and even the human soul. "For in him all things were created: things in heaven and on earth," wrote the apostle Paul, "visible and *invisible*, whether thrones or powers or rulers or authorities; all things have been created through him and for him" (Col. 1:16; emphasis added). Thus, any approach to the study of the world that rejects the spiritual (immaterial) world out of hand is not acceptable for the Christian worldview.

We should note that scientism's acceptance of materialism creates an unnecessary split in reality: one of knowledge (to be ascertained only by science) and one of faith (to be believed apart from science or any evidence whatsoever). This split in reality was described and criticized by the popular Christian thinker Francis Schaeffer (1912–1984) as the *two-realm theory of truth*.[2] This theory incorrectly states that the world should be understood in terms of an "upper story" and "lower story," where the upper story is the non-rational, noncognitive, subjective truth, and the lower story is the rational, verifiable objective truth of reality as understood through science. (See Fig. 17.1.) The upper story is made up of personal beliefs and values. It has nothing to do with knowledge. The lower story is made up of objective scientific statements and has everything to do with knowledge.

Upper Story
no knowledge, non-rational, subjective, religion, morality

Lower Story
knowledge, rational, objective, science, reality

Two-Realm Theory of Truth

FIG. 17.1

This two-realm theory of truth, as Schaeffer pointed out, creates a false and unnecessary division in human learning and understanding of knowledge and truth. Why should we accept the idea that materialism is true and that science is the best way to obtain knowledge? Some would answer that it is because science is capable of proving or demonstrating what is true with certainty, and faith/religion is just mere opinion and thus cannot be proven to be true. This reply, however, begs the question; it assumes that science is the only means to prove that a statement is true.

It also assumes a particular definition of *proof*. What does it mean to prove something? Perhaps one might say it is to show beyond doubt that a statement is true via disclosing physical evidence or lab experiment. Such a proposal, however, takes us back to the problem of defining science as discussed in the previous chapter. There are many activities that we consider to be science but cannot be demonstrated or performed in a lab. Furthermore, it overlooks how epistemology (in general) and lessons from skepticism (specifically) teach us that claims outside of logic, math, and geometry can't be proven in a way eliciting certainty that the conclusion is true. Also, as noted previously, certainty of scientific theories is just not possible. History demonstrates that they are revised, amended, or even rejected.

The Christian perspective is that the division between the upper story and lower story ought to be eliminated. It is much more desirable to approach learning more holistically. Let us as humans consider any and all factors that may exist to gain knowledge of the universe and all that is in it. To jettison what faith or religion may say just because it is faith or religion is arbitrary, superficial, and assumes scientism. It could also leave the impression that there is something (perhaps supernatural) that we do not want to be true, and so, to avoid it, we eliminate it as a possible explanation. This does not appear to be an honest or the best way to approach a study of the world. In fact, it seems like it would be a way to destroy science because it hand-ties humanity by limiting what can and cannot be studied or explained. Scientism turns out to be an impoverished view of everything.

MAX PLANCK ON THE EXTERNAL WORLD

Max Planck (1858–1947) was a contemporary of Albert Einstein and one of the leading physicists in the study of quantum mechanics in the early twentieth century. He received the Nobel Prize in Physics for discovering energy quanta. He believed that science itself could not prove the existence of the external world. He once stated, "As Einstein has said, you could not be a scientist if you did not know that the external world existed in reality. But that knowledge is not gained by any process of reasoning. It is a direct perception and therefore in its nature akin to what we call Faith. It is a metaphysical belief."

Scientism Destroys Science

Scientism is not only self-refuting and an impoverished view of the world. Ironically, it turns out to undermine, and even destroy, the very thing it claims to support: science. The reason why is because science cannot be practiced without assuming metaphysical realities that science itself cannot prove exist without begging the question. In this final section, we will take a look at some examples of this.

First, the practice of science relies upon the fact that an external world exists. But science assumes that the external world exists. It cannot prove it exists without assuming it exists, thus committing the informal fallacy of begging the question. (You might think the idea of calling into question the existence of the external world is a silly idea, but recall the discussion we had on skepticism in chapter 11.)

Think about it this way: if science wants to prove that the external world exists, it must assume that instruments and other objects (outside the scientist trying to prove it) exist to discern whether the external world exists. Such instruments and objects, however, are things that make up the external world. Thus, science cannot prove the world's existence without using instruments and objects that make up the external world. This is a classic case of begging the question. Science must yield to philosophy in order to argue for the existence of the external world. Therefore, if scientism were true, there would be no basis to study one of the primary things science intends to study: the external world.

A second assumption science must make and cannot prove is the general reliability of the human senses and cognitive faculties. To study the world around us, we assume that our senses of smell, taste, sight, touch, and hearing are generally reliable. But why do we assume this? It is not because science itself has proven the senses to be reliable. And, again, it cannot prove them to be reliable without begging the question. If scientism is true, then it must assume that our senses are reliable in order to prove that the senses are reliable because there is no other way to show that they are. It would also have to assume that human cognitive faculties are generally reliable at discovering truth. Science cannot prove that they are reliable without assuming the reliability of the very thing (human cognition) it is attempting to prove is reliable.

There are numerous other assumptions that also must be made for science to be practiced, things like the Laws of Logic, the phenomenon of cause and effect, uniformity of nature, adequacy of language, human consciousness, and the existence of numbers in some way. If scientism were true, then none of these could be accepted without proving them, and in order to prove them, we must use them to prove them, which amounts to begging the question (again, recall chapter 11).

Interestingly, one of the most unrecognized, yet very important, assumptions science must make is the existence of values, like integrity. We rely upon scientists to be honest and have integrity with their studies, experiments, and conclusions. This is a necessary value that must be upheld in the scientific discipline. But if scientism were true, there is no foundation to believe in values. Virtues cannot be proven by science. If someone were to attempt to do so, it would have to be assumed to exist just like all the other aforementioned assumptions and thus beg the question once again. Scientism, therefore, makes science itself impossible. It truly is a self-refuting, impoverished view of everything, including science.

Summary

We have briefly looked at a view of science known as scientism, and we have found it to be incompatible with the Christian worldview. Whether it is strong or weak scientism, it assumes that materialism is true, which runs contrary to the Christian doctrine of creation. It also places the Christian in the odd place of waiting for science to inform the Christian faith about what it can take to be true or false about reality. Scientism is also very limited in its explanations because it rejects outright the idea that such knowledge can be obtained by any means other than science. Effectively, however, scientism destroys the basis and justification for practicing science. It is self-refuting and cannot account for the assumptions science must make in order to be practiced, like the existence of the external world. As such, the Christian worldview advocates for jettisoning scientism. The Christian approach to discovery ought to allow for multiple means of obtaining knowledge of the world rather than setting up a superficial split reality or two-realm theory of truth. A holistic approach to learning is to be preferred.

Questions for Reflection

1. Why might a scientist believe in scientism?
2. In what ways is scientism self-defeating? Can you think of more ways than what are discussed in this chapter?
3. How many assumptions can you list that science must make to do science?
4. Does the two-realm theory of truth describe how you view reality? Why or why not? Is this a good theory to accept?

For Further Reading

Moreland, J. P. *Scientism and Secularism: Learning to Respond to a Dangerous Ideology.* Wheaton, IL: Crossway, 2018.

Riddler, Jeroen de, Rik Peels, and René van Woudenberg. *Scientism: Prospects and Problems.* New York: Oxford University Press, 2018.

Stenmark, Mikael. *Scientism: Science, Ethics and Religion*. New York: Routledge, 2001.

Williams, Richard N., and Daniel N. Robinson, eds. *Scientism: The New Orthodoxy*. New York: Bloomsbury Academic: 2016.

NOTES

1. J. P. Moreland, *Scientism and Secularism: Learning to Respond to a Dangerous Ideology* (Wheaton, IL: Crossway, 2018), 29.
2. For a brief discussion of this, see the introduction to Nancy Pearcey, *Total Truth: Liberating Christianity from Its Cultural Captivity* (Wheaton, IL: Crossway, 2004). For a thorough discussion, see Francis Schaeffer, *A Christian View of Philosophy and Culture, The Complete Works of Francis Schaeffer*, vol. 1 (Wheaton, IL: Crossway, 1985).

PART 6

Philosophy of Religion and Philosophical Theology

The Relation between Philosophy and Faith

CHAPTER 18

What Is Philosophy of Religion?

Studying Faiths, Beliefs, and Their Claims

The philosophy of religion historically has been a broad area of study. It often has overlapped or not clearly been differentiated from philosophical theology, which is the topic of the next chapter. In general, the philosophy of religion has studied the questions of religious beliefs and claims. Specifically, it has dealt with the nature of religion, arguments for God's existence, the nature of God, the nature and problem of evil, miracles, religious pluralism, life after death, and numerous other subjects that lie within the scope of religious belief.

For the purpose of this text, philosophy of religion will be differentiated from philosophical theology in the following way. Philosophy of religion will cover the more theoretical topics of religious beliefs, such as the nature of religious claims and their relationship to the concept of worldview, the relationship of faith and reason, the existence and nature of God, the nature of evil, religious pluralism, and life after death. Due to space considerations, we will cover only the relationship between faith and reason, the existence of God, and the problem of evil. Philosophical theology will deal specifically with Christian theological doctrines, including the Trinity, incarnation, atonement, and resurrection. Thus, it can be said that the *philosophy of religion* deals with theoretical religious beliefs while philosophical theology deals more with explaining Christian beliefs philosophically.

A Misunderstanding

Before broaching a discussion on the philosophy of religion, a misunderstanding needs to be addressed. In our present skeptical and relativistic culture, the philosophy of religion is often understood to be a topic that has nothing to do with reality and facts but is merely an enterprise about subjective opinions. Philosophically speaking, it is popular to think that religious beliefs and claims have no truth value.

Let's pause for a moment to think about this. How do philosophers of religion think about this topic? To discern whether religious beliefs and claims have truth value, imagine the following exercise. Picture a table with two columns. (See Table 18.1.) In the left column are the following statements:

$1 + 1 = 2$

Abraham Lincoln was the sixteenth president of the United States.

The earth revolves around the sun.

Are these statements "facts" or mere "opinion"? Many people in our culture would say they are facts.

Now, in the right column, are these statements:

Jesus is God's Son who takes away the sins of the world.

Muhammad is Allah's prophet.

Murder is morally wrong.

Are these "facts" (or false) or mere "opinion?" Many would respond by saying they are merely opinion.

This exercise illustrates a common misunderstanding of the philosopher's task in regard to religion and whether religious claims have true value. The western culture has made a wall between the statements on the left (which are statements of science, history, and math) and statements on the right (which are comprised of religion and morality).

This approach entirely misunderstands the philosophy of religion, especially from a Christian worldview. The philosophy of religion does not relegate statements of religion and morality to a column labeled "opinion," set off

So-Called FACTS	So-Called OPINION
1 + 1 = 2	Jesus is God's Son who takes away the sins of the world.
Abraham Lincoln was the sixteenth president of the United States.	Muhammad is Allah's prophet.
The earth revolves around the sun.	Murder is morally wrong.

TABLE 18.1

from the real world of facts. Rather, it attempts to evaluate religious and moral statements like any other statement: as either true (i.e., factual) or false. Recall chapter 6 on logic and critical thinking: *every statement has a truth value.* This is the same for statements of history, science, and math, as well as religion and morality. Either the statement "murder is morally wrong" is true, or it is false. Either murder is truly morally wrong, or it is not. (How we know which statements are true or false, although interesting and important, is irrelevant here. The point for now is that, metaphysically speaking, such statements must be true or false.)

This point is important to grasp. As a beginning philosophy student, you want to ensure that you understand that philosophy of religion is not just about mere opinions. It is attempting to obtain the truth value of religious and moral claims. They are not mere opinions. For some, this may be a difficult concept to grasp. It may challenge one's present modern or skeptical worldview. Nevertheless, this is how the Christian worldview approaches questions pertaining to religion.

The Relationship of Faith and Reason

One primary topic that philosophy of religion deals with is the relationship between faith and reason. This is more of a theoretical than practical question (like how to deal with the problem of evil). The question of how faith relates to reason is, however, very important. For one, it helps us understand whether one's religious beliefs are entirely based upon faith (however defined) and/or human reasoning. For another, it helps us understand what role reason plays in explaining religious beliefs. There are several answers to these types of questions. We will focus upon just four here: one from the history of philosophy and three from a Christian perspective.

In the History of Philosophy

How did the early philosophers, like Plato and Aristotle, view the relationship between faith and reason? In contrast to today's popular notion that faith has nothing to do with reason, both Plato and Aristotle thought differently. Plato, in his work *Phaedo*, strongly implied that truth is obtained only by reason.[1] This includes what we would consider religious truth. This was evidenced by his use of reason to conclude his teaching of the Forms, especially the concept that God (what he called the "Demiurge") fashioned the physical world after the pattern of the Forms. Also, Plato's understanding of the afterworld (or immortality of the soul) was concluded entirely from reason.

Likewise, Aristotle based what we would understand as religious beliefs on mere reason. One of his most popular philosophically religious concepts is that of the Unmoved Mover, or God. To recall from chapter 3, Aristotle reasoned that if all the universe is in motion (or has been actualized), then there must be an initial (or First) cause of all motion or actualization, which is itself unmoved by anything outside itself. This Unmoved Mover is not like the Creator God of Christianity who is personal and can have relationships with people; he simply formed or actualized the world. The name Unmoved Mover leaves the impression that there was only one Mover, but it is difficult to discern if Aristotle believed in one or many Movers.

Aristotle also reasoned that God, or gods, must exist based on reasoning from design (or teleology). In what would eventually develop into teleological arguments for God's existence, Aristotle reasoned that, by observing the natural world (like the stars, planets, and the moon), one could readily recognize these as the works of God (or gods). He also reasoned from "degrees of perfection" to conclude that God must exist. If there is a "better," there must be a "best."[2] Aristotle, like Plato, used reason to conclude that God exists and other religious beliefs. Reason and faith were viewed as friends. More specifically, reason discerned religious truth. Reason related to faith magisterially—reason was faith's authority.

In the Christian Worldview

Faith and reason have had somewhat of a love-hate relationship within the Christian worldview. Some have viewed faith and reason as complementary, and others have viewed them to be at odds. We begin with the perspective that views them to be more enemies than friends, or the Reformed view.

The *Reformed view* is called this because its development has roots in the Protestant Reformation. Reformers such as Martin Luther (1483–1546) and John Calvin (1509–1564) state what at times could be understood as an antagonistic view of reason. Both Luther and Calvin believed that mere human reason could in no way conclude with any certainty that God exists because it was so distorted by sin, which is often referred to as the noetic effects of sin ("noetic" comes from the Greek word *nous*, meaning "mind"). In fact, Luther is well known for stating that human reason was "the devil's whore." He especially believed that the manner in which medieval theologians used the philosophy of Aristotle to expand upon theological teachings was illegitimate. He referred to Aristotle as "the stinking philosopher."

Although it is now recognized that Luther's view of the relationship between faith and reason was more complex than merely antagonistic, much of his rhetoric and criticism of reason influenced the views of some theologians who succeeded him. One good example is the twentieth-century Dutch theologian Cornelius Van Til, who once commented, "Without the light of Christianity it is as little possible for man to have the correct view about himself and the world as it is to have the true view about God. On account of the fact of sin man is blind with respect to the truth wherever the truth appears."[3] Self-autonomous human reason just has no place in faith.

This view of faith and reason is often summarized by Tertullian (c. 155), a second-century Christian. He once asked, "What has Athens to do with Jerusalem? What concord is there between the Academy and the Church?" The idea here is that Greek philosophy had nothing to do with the Christianity that began in the city of Jerusalem, and so Greek philosophical reasoning has no place in Christianity. (Whether Tertullian actually held this view has been debated among historians and philosophers).

Some Christians, on the other hand, view faith and reason not necessarily as enemies, but neither are they intimate friends. Reason is to be suspended in light of faith. Faith is based upon experience, not reason, and so reason is not very helpful in matters of faith. This view is often referred to as *fideism* ("fideism" comes from the Greek word *fide*, meaning "faith"). One who held this view was the Danish theologian and philosopher SØren Kierkegaard (1813–1855). He held that Christian teaching must be believed in faith apart from reason. Reason cannot make sense of Christian doctrine, and, in fact, it must be believed contrary to reason and even when it is thought absurd to do so.

Finally, some have viewed faith and reason as friends. This view believes that, although the noetic effects of sin are real, humans still can reason about certain things concerning God. For example, philosophical reasoning can show that God exists and what he is generally like, that he is the creator and is all powerful. This view is probably best exemplified by the great medieval Catholic theologian and philosopher Thomas Aquinas (1225–1274). In his most popular work, *Summa*

Theologica, he discusses his famous *Five Ways*, or five arguments in which reason can show that God exists. He also explains that reason shows that God must be the creator, all powerful, simple, and several other characteristics. He argues clearly, however, that reason is limited. If a person wants to know who God is more fully, he must rely upon faith, or *special revelation*—information revealed to humans by God through the Christian Scriptures, the Bible.

Other examples of this view include the theologians and philosophers like Justin Martyr (c. 100–165), Aurelius Augustine (354–430), and the modern theologian B. B. Warfield (1851–1921). More recently, the philosophers William Lane Craig, J. P. Moreland, and Norman Geisler (1932–2019) have defended such a view of faith and reason. They have provided and defended numerous philosophical arguments for the existence of God, including the *kalam* cosmological argument to be presented briefly in the following.

Before moving forward, an important point must be made. Although these three views disagree about the relationship between faith and reason, they all believe in the legitimacy of using reason within theology, or explaining Christian doctrine by using human reason. This idea is typically stated in the medieval phrase "reason is the handmaid of theology." Theology is superior to human reason, but reason (especially reason within the bounds of faith) can be used to help explain the teachings of the Christian faith.

The Existence of God

Does God exist? This is another important question in the philosophy of religion. What may come as a surprise is that numerous philosophical arguments have been developed over thousands of years to show that God exists. In fact, there are so many that it is impossible to cover every one of them here. We will be looking at just four types of arguments for God's existence, briefly laying them out in syllogistic form: the ontological, cosmological, teleological, and moral arguments. We will also look at religious experience as a reason for belief in God. Finally, we will present a naturalistic explanation for why many believe in God and respond to it from a Christian worldview perspective.

Ontological Arguments

The term *ontological* is taken from the Greek *ontos*, meaning "being." From this, we can see that such arguments are concerned with arguing for the being or existence of God by using human reason alone. These are probably the most difficult arguments to grasp because they are abstract and often argue from the conception of God in the mind to the reality of his existence.

One of the most popular ontological arguments was posited by Anselm of Canterbury (1033–1109). In his work, *Proslogion*, he begins by asking what we conceive of in the mind when we think of the term *God*. Anselm replies that God is "that-which-nothing-greater-can-be-conceived." What this amounts to is that God is that which is omnipotent, omniscient, and omnibenevolent, among other great-making characteristics. God is the greatest conceivable Being anyone could ever conceive.

Following this reasoning, Anselm continues by asking whether is it greater for "that-which-nothing-greater-can-be-conceived" to exist only in the mind or to exist in the real world? The answer seems obvious: to exist in the real word is greater. The conclusion, then, is that God (the greatest conceivable Being) must exist because existence is greater than non-existence.

This argument may seem like a sleight of hand. Others, however, find it persuasive. At the very least, it is intriguing. Philosophers have debated its validity since its inception. It has had its harsh critics (like Immanuel Kant) and enthusiastic embracers. Still others have attempted to tweak it a bit, namely Alvin Plantinga (for his argument, see the sidebar).

PLANTINGA'S ONTOLOGICAL ARGUMENT

One contemporary ontological argument has been given by the philosopher Alvin Plantinga. It takes the following syllogistic form.

1. It is possible that there is a being that has maximal greatness.
2. So there is a possible being that in some world W has maximal greatness.
3. A Being has maximal greatness in a given world only if it has maximal excellence in every world.
4. A being has maximal excellence in a given world only if it has omniscience, omnipotence, and moral perfection in that world.

Therefore, it follows that there actually exists a being that is omnipotent, omniscient, and morally perfect: God.

Cosmological Arguments

The term *cosmological* comes from the Greek term *kosmos*, meaning world. These types of arguments begin with some feature of the world's/universe's existence and then conclude that God must exist. (Aristotle's Unmoved Mover belongs in this category.) There are numerous cosmological arguments. We will focus upon the *kalam* argument which has been popularized by the contemporary philosopher William Lane Craig.

The kalam argument was first developed by the Islamic theologian Al-Ghazali in the sixteenth century. William Craig's formulation of it is as follows:

1. Everything that begins to exist has a cause.
2. The universe began to exist.
3. Therefore, the universe has a cause.

This cause we call God.

Like all syllogisms, if the premises are true, then the conclusion must follow. But are 1 and 2 true? The first premise is not controversial at all. Craig argues that if it were false, it would be worse than believing in magic. With magic, we at least have a magician and a hat. You would have nothing if 1 were false.

Craig then spends most of his discussion on showing why premise 2 is true. Historically, Craig contends, the universe has been understood to be infinite with no beginning. Relying upon the most recent physics, however, like the classical Big Bang theory, Craig maintains there is now an overwhelming abundance of evidence to support that the universe began to exist. He also relies upon mathematical and philosophical arguments to demonstrate the beginning of the universe and the impossibility of an infinite one.

Craig concludes that the universe has a cause for its existence. But to arrive at the concept of God, he teases out what the cause of the universe must be like, considering that everything in the universe (including space, time, matter, and energy) had to come into being. The cause, contends Craig, must be timeless, changeless, immaterial, personal, and very powerful, which sounds a lot like God.

Teleological Arguments

The term *teleological* is from the Greek *telos*, meaning "goal." These types of arguments deal with some feature of the universe that appears to be designed to conclude that a Designer (God) must exist. Because of this, these types of arguments are often referred to as *design arguments*.

One teleological argument that has become prominent in contemporary times is the *fine-tuning argument*. It is as follows:

1. The fine-tuning of the universe is due either to necessity, chance, or design.
2. The fine-tuning of the universe is not due to necessity or chance.
3. Therefore, the fine-tuning of the universe is due to design.
4. The fine-tuning of the universe due to design implies a Designer: God.

To understand this argument, the concept of fine-tuning must first be understood. Fine-tuning refers to the features of the universe, specifically physical constants, that allow for life of any kind to exist in the universe. If any one of these physical constants were different by a very small number, then life of any kind would be impossible. Some examples are the expansion rate of the universe, the nuclear force that binds protons and neutrons, and the force of gravity, among many others.[4]

How did the world get finely-tuned? The first premise lays out all the possibilities: necessity, change, or design. Necessity can be eliminated as a possibility rather quickly. The overwhelming majority of scientists and philosophers agree that the physical constants of the universe could have been otherwise. The physical constants do not have to be the way they are; life does not have to exist. The constants could have been different and the universe just not have life.

What about chance? Could the physical constants just happen to be the way they are? Many naturalists and atheists believe so. Evolution, they say, is an impersonal driving force, and it just so happens that the constants turned out the way they did, allowing for the possibility of life. The well-known biologist Francis Crick is noted for saying that "biologists must constantly keep in mind that what they see was not designed, but rather evolved."[5] Although the biological organisms may look designed, scientists have to remind themselves constantly that they are not. This represents well the naturalistic view of not only biological organisms but the physical constants of the universe. The constants give the illusion or appearance of design, but it was all by chance.

In response, many Christian philosophers and scientists point out that the probability of all the constants being so precise to allow for life is so astronomically low that it is unreasonable to conclude that it was by chance. For example, the physicist Roger Penrose has calculated the odds of the universe's initial low entropy conditions coming into existence by chance to be 1 in $10^{10^{123}}$. Just this constant alone has the probability of practically zero. Therefore, it's much more reasonable, it is argued, to believe that the fine-tuning is due to design, not chance. Scientist Robin Collins illustrates that the probability of the constants being what they are by chance is like trying to hit an inch-wide target on a dart board the size of the galaxy.[6] Not very good odds!

The conclusion, therefore, is that the fine-tuning for life is due to design. And if this is the case, there must be a Designer, or God.

Moral Arguments

In general, moral arguments for the existence of God begin by observing the existence of objective moral values and duties. Where did these standards of morally right and wrong come from? The answer to this question is what the moral argument focuses upon to show the necessity of the existence of God. If there is a moral law, then there must be a moral Lawgiver, or God.

The argument is typically laid out in a similar fashion as follows:

1. If God does not exist, then objective moral values and duties do not exist.
2. Moral objective values and duties exist.
3. Therefore, God exists.

This is a typical modus tollens syllogistic form, and it is therefore a valid argument. The question is: are the two premises true? Interestingly, premise one is the least controversial. Most philosophers, including atheists and naturalists, agree that if God does not exist, then there are no objective moral values and duties, or no actual, morally right and wrong actions. The reason why is because if God does not exist—a Being outside the human experience—then there is no standard by which to measure human moral actions. By consequence, moral right and wrong are based upon human standards which vary among people and change with time, the very opposite of what it means to be objective. Premise one, therefore, is true.

What about premise two? This is the controversial claim, especially in cultures (like twenty-first century America) where relativism and subjectivism are popular. Many disbelieve that any action is objectively right or wrong. At least this is what many claim. Upon further investigation, however, this seems to betray what most humans take to be the case. For example, is torturing people for fun objectively morally right or wrong? What about rape or the killing of innocent children? Most people take such actions to be objectively (not subjectively) morally evil. If this is the case, then premise two is true, and the conclusion that God exists necessarily follows.

Religious Experience

Another popular way in which some have demonstrated the existence of God is by religious experience. This approach emphasizes one's faith (and sometimes of the faith community) over and against philosophical arguments to affirm God's existence.

One of the most popular figures who illustrated this approach was SØren Kierkegaard (1813–1855). Although he did not promote an irrational faith devoid of any reasons, he certainly thought that rational thinking and philosophical argumentation could be a hindrance to belief in God. What one needed most important was an experience of God. For Kierkegaard, faith was not merely a cognitive exercise; it was mostly about a relational experience of God himself. This, and not a philosophical "proof," affirmed the existence of God.

The great Protestant Reformer, John Calvin, could also be viewed as emphasizing religious experience over philosophical argumentation. His perspective, however, was somewhat different than Kierkegaard's. Calvin believed that everyone has a sense of God, or what is referred to as the *sensus divinitatis* (from the Latin, meaning "sense of the Divine"). This sense of God is innate in every person, and so it is irrelevant to provide philosophical arguments for God's existence. Partly relying upon Romans 1:19–23, Calvin argued that humanity knows God exists by virtue of observing the natural world. The only obstacle to this knowledge is that it ends up being suppressed by humanity's sinful reasoning, which results in humans worshiping idols and false gods.

It is not just the great theologians of the past who have testified to having an experience of God. People claiming to have encountered God has been the norm throughout history. Moreover, the overwhelming majority of humanity say they believe in God (or gods) and experience him. Philosopher Harold Netland comments, "The widespread occurrence of theistic experiences across time and cultures, along with the distinctive nature of these experiences, can be regarded as phenomena demanding some explanation."[7] The conclusion by many is that the best explanation for these claims is that God must, indeed, exist.

Is such an idea persuasive? For some it is and others it is not, for various reasons. It does, however, provide additional weight to the philosophical arguments for God's existence. Religious experience is certainly subjective rather than objective. But subjective experience, although difficult to evaluate, is an important and significant part of being human. It cannot be easily dismissed.

Naturalistic Explanations

We would be remiss if we did not consider the naturalistic explanation for belief in God. It would be better to understand this explanation as an objection to belief in God rather than confirmation that God exists. For naturalists, only the natural physical world exists, and anything beyond it does not. As such, anything "spiritual" can be explained as a property of something physical, or at least be reduced to something physical. Because of this, naturalists explain the belief in God's existence naturally. God does not exist, and the belief in God can be explained as a sort of malady that has befallen humanity.

There are two popular ways in which naturalists explain belief in God. One was developed by Karl Marx (1818–1883), the co-author of *The Communist Manifesto*. In Marx's view, people believe in God to escape the economic trials and tribulations of this world. He called religion "the opiate of the masses." It is a salve to ameliorate the psychological sufferings induced upon the working poor (what he called the proletariat) brought upon by the wealthy owners of industry (what he called the bourgeoisie). Thus, for Marx, God did not exist. It was a fictitious human invention, even an illusion.

A second naturalistic explanation for belief in God comes from the famous psychologist Sigmund Freud (1856–1939). Similar to Marx, Freud thought belief in God is produced by the human psyche to deal with the horrible nature of reality. The difference, however, is that this belief is due to wish-fulfillment, a desire to be protected by a father figure, one more powerful and caring than a biological father. Therefore, for Freud, God did not exist.

How would a theist possibly respond to Marx and Freud? The biggest problem with both Freud's and Marx's assessment of belief in God is that explaining the origin of a belief says nothing whatsoever as to whether a belief is true or false. Thus, both patterns of reasoning commit the genetic fallacy. (See chapter 9.)

The Problem of Evil

The final topic to be discussed in this chapter is the problem of evil. We have all faced or will face sometime in life the death of a loved one, perhaps dying prematurely or by some horrific disease. We may have come across a news story about a child who succumbed to cancer and died at the age of two. Why do things like this happen? As the oft-asked question goes, "Why do bad things happen to good people?" A question that often follows is, "Where was God in all this? If God exists, doesn't he care? Why didn't he heal my loved one?" This is the problem of evil.

No matter what religious or philosophical worldview one holds, the problem of evil must be dealt with. From a theistic worldview, this can be difficult. The eighteenth-century skeptic philosopher David Hume once intimated, "Is [God] willing to prevent evil, but not able? Then he is impotent. Is he able, but not willing? Then he is malevolent. Is he both able and willing? Whence then is evil?" If God exists, then he is either incapable of eliminating evil or he is not very loving. Either way, the existence of evil presents a problem for the existence of God.

The problem of evil is often presented in a two-fold way: the logical (or deductive) form and the evidential (or inductive) form. The logical problem states that it is logically contradictory for both statements to be true, that (1) God exists and (2) evil exists. As already noted, Hume effectively presented the problem for both to be true: God is either not really the God we take him to be (omnipotent and omnibenevolent), or he just does not exist if evil exists. Neither is a good option, but many take the latter.

How does a theist respond to the logical problem of evil? In this case, the response is philosophically straight-forward: there is no logical contradiction between the two statements. For a contradiction to hold, the two statements must be contrary, or opposite, to each other. The contrary to (1) God exists is not (2) evil exists, but (3) God does not exist. Since (2) does not contradict (1), then the logical problem of evil disappears. This is recognized by not only theists but also atheists. The atheist and philosopher William Rowe has stated, "Some philosophers have contended that the existence of evil is logically inconsistent with the existence of the theistic God. No one, I think, has succeeded in establishing such an extravagant claim."[8]

But what about the evidential problem of evil? According to this objection, the evil that takes place in the world is more than just evil. It is gratuitously evil. By the time we add up all the abuse of children and women, wars, torture, extremism, terrorism, and numerous other evils, the problem is not that there is just some evil here and a little there. There is an overabundance of it. Given this overabundance, it seems highly improbable that God exists. Surely no good, powerful God would allow all this evil?

Some answers have been proffered by several theistic philosophers. The primary rebuttal is that the evidential problem has the underlying assumption that God has no good reason to allow evil. Why should this assumption be accepted? Is any human in a good position to make such a judgement? It does not seem so, considering no human is omniscient or omnipotent. No human is God and cannot know the mind of God.

Theist and philosopher Paul Copan makes an additional observation.[9] A distinction should be made between gratuitous evil and inscrutable evil. "Gratuitous" implies that the evil in question is unnecessary and unjustified. "Inscrutable," on the other hand, is evil whose justification is unknown. As such, the evil we may describe as gratuitous is better categorized as inscrutable. Just because the reason for God allowing evil may be unknown, it does not logically follow that it is unjustified. Perhaps God has morally sufficient good reasons to allow evil. One reason, for example, may be what C. S. Lewis once exclaimed: Pain is "God's megaphone to rouse a deaf world."[10]

Ultimately, the theist responds by explaining that the problem of evil should be laid at the feet of humanity. God gave humans free will, and they used it to rebel against their loving Creator. This is known as the *free will defense*. Theists defend the co-existence of God and evil based upon the fact that God gave Adam and Eve in the Garden of Eden a choice: to obey or disobey him. They chose to rebel. From this time forward, humanity has chosen against God, to use its free will to live life its own way. As a result, evil exists. Rather than humanity asking, "Why does God allow bad things to happen?" perhaps God is legitimately asking us something similar: "Why are you humans using your free will to commit evil?"

Summary

As we conclude this chapter, recall that the philosophy of religion is a broad study which includes numerous subjects that pertain to religion. We have touched upon only a few of these subjects. Two primary ideas should be taken away from this short introduction: (1) the philosophy of religion is concerned with truth values of religious statements, just like statements about math and science, and (2) faith has a relationship to reason, although differing views exist about this relationship. Also, remember that numerous arguments have been developed to show that God exists. Finally, the problem of evil is a real-life experience for everyone, and the philosophy of religion is concerned with such matters. In the following chapter, we will take a look at how philosophical reasoning is implemented in Christianity to explain its core doctrines.

Questions for Reflection

1. Why do you think some people view faith as opposing reason? Do you think they are enemies, or are they compatible?
2. Is belief in God contrary to human reason?
3. If God exists, why does evil exist?
4. What is the most persuasive argument for God's existence? Why?

For Further Reading

Copan, Paul. *Loving Wisdom: A Guide to Philosophy and Christian Faith*. 2nd ed. Grand Rapids, MI: Eerdmans, 2020.

Copan, Paul, and Chad Meister, eds. *Philosophy of Religion: Classic and Contemporary Issues*. Malden, MA: Blackwell, 2008.

Craig, William Lane, ed. *Philosophy of Religion: A Reader and Guide*. New Brunswick, NJ: Rutgers University Press, 2002.

Meister, Chad. *Introducing Philosophy of Religion*. New York: Routledge, 2009.

NOTES

1. See Copleston's commentary in Frederick Copleston, *A History of Philosophy*, vol. 1: *Greece and Rome from the Pre-Socratics to Plotinus* (New York: Image, 1993), 171–72.
2. If Aristotle's arguments for God seem familiar, there is a reason for this. Thomas Aquinas

relied heavily upon Aristotle for some of his arguments for the existence of God in his famous work *Summa Theologica*.

3. Cornelius Van Til, *The Defense of the Faith*, 3rd ed. (Philadelphia: Presbyterian and Reformed, 1967), 73.

4. For more fine-tuning parameters and explanation, see Jay W. Richards, "List of Fine-Tuning Parameters," *Research*, Center for Science and Culture, 283–90, www.discovery.org/m /securepdfs/2018/12/List-of-Fine-Tuning-Parameters-Jay-Richards.pdf.

5. Francis Crick, *What Mad Pursuit: A Personal View of Scientific Discovery* (New York: Basic Books, 1988), 138, quoted in Stephen C. Meyer, *Return of the God Hypothesis: Three Scientific Discoveries That Reveal the Mind behind the Universe* (New York: HarperOne, 2021), 165.

6. See Robin Collins, "A Scientific Argument for the Existence of God: The Fine-Tuning Design Argument," in *Reason for the Hope Within*, ed. Michael J. Murray (Grand Rapids: Eerdmans, 1999), 47–75.

7. Harold A. Netland, *Religious Experience and the Knowledge of God: The Evidential Force of Divine Encounters* (Grand Rapids: Baker Academic, 2022), 9.

8. William Rowe, "The Problem of Evil and Some Varieties of Atheism," *American Philosophical Quarterly* (1979): 49n, quoted in Paul Copan, *Loving Wisdom: A Guide to Philosophy and Christian Faith* (Grand Rapids, MI: Eerdmans, 2020), 217.

9. See Copan, *Loving Wisdom*, 222–24.

10. C. S. Lewis, *The Problem of Pain* (New York: HarperCollins, 2001), 91.

CHAPTER 19

What Is Philosophical Theology?

Beginning with God

What is philosophical theology? Why does it matter? We hope this chapter will help you understand what it is and why it's important. To that end, we will (a) introduce and provide an overview philosophical theology, (b) explain essential concepts and terms related to it, (c) discuss different assumptions and approaches to the relationship between philosophy and theology, and (d) examine some key theological doctrines using a Christian philosophical theology approach.

Philosophical theology has existed for as long as people have been thinking about important questions—especially about God and the spiritual dimension of life. Ancient Greek philosopher Aristotle (384–22 BC) minimally engages in philosophical theology, while Thomas Aquinas (1224–74) does so maximally, earning the title "philosophical theologian." Aquinas is a Christian theologian and an Aristotelian philosopher who strongly affirms Christian faith while also employing the philosophical methods of "the Philosopher" (Thomas's term for Aristotle, whom he considered the greatest philosopher). Even so, Aquinas doesn't always agree with the Philosopher—especially about ultimate reality and highest priorities in life. Aristotle mainly employs philosophical theology in trying to discover underlying principles for how the world operates. Reason, for Aristotle, sufficiently demonstrates that a greatest being exists. While Aquinas appreciates Aristotle's use of "natural revelation," his strong theological beliefs open more space for the doctrine of God and other important Christian doctrines.[1]

The Focus of Philosophical Theology and Christian Philosophical Theology

The approaches of Aristotle and Aquinas represent the similarities and differences that exist between general, and specifically Christian, approaches to philosophical theology. Looking more closely at the distinctives, we see that *philosophical theology* is often associated with philosophy of religion, which usually focuses on broad theological questions (such as the existence and nature of God, the problem of evil, and the afterlife). *Christian philosophical theology*, though, ordinarily focuses on specific Christian doctrines—like the Trinity, incarnation, atonement, and resurrection—utilizing the tools of philosophy to better understand theological concepts and claims. Most Christian philosophical theology thinkers are "philosophical theologians." They value interrelating (to varying degrees) the disciplines of philosophy and theology—especially when seeking answers to questions about God, Christ, humanity, salvation, truth, knowledge, morality, purpose, and the like. While both theists and non-theists can do philosophical theology work, most often it's done by theists, and most who employ Christian philosophical theology are Christian theists.

The Question of Integration

Nonetheless, there are some differences even among believing scholars about how—and how much—philosophy and theology should be integrated. Christian intellectual history shows us that leading thinkers have grappled with this challenging issue of integration. For instance, early Christian thinker Tertullian (c. 155–c. 230) questions philosophy's worth altogether—wondering whether it should have any affect on Christian doctrines—because of philosophy's ability to produce heresy. In contrast, his older contemporary Justin Martyr (c. 100–c. 165) deeply appreciates the way philosophy can assist and benefit theology. Justin even claims some ancient Greek philosophers (like Socrates and Plato) were "Christians *before* Christ"! That's because they willingly sought the Truth, being illuminated—if only dimly—by the *Logos* (the Word of God). Justin was a philosopher before converting to the Christian faith; after conversion, he claimed Christianity alone is "the true philosophy." Rather than an extensive historical treatment here, we'll modestly consider the meanings and relationship of our

DEFINITION OF CHRISTIAN PHILOSOPHICAL THEOLOGY
Christian philosophical theology entails thinking deeply about key Christian doctrines, skillfully using philosophy's tools to better grasp theological concepts and truths. Philosophy—properly used—helps us better understand theology.

two key terms, philosophy and theology, before turning to consider philosophical theology approaches to four core doctrines of the Christian faith.

Essential Terms and Their Relations: Philosophy, Theology, Worldview

The term *philosophical theology* obviously combines two words: philosophy and theology. Etymologically, *philosophy* may be defined as "the love (or pursuit) of wisdom," and *theology* as "the study of God." You probably noticed the word *philosophical* being used to modify (or qualify) the word *theology*. With primary focus on the subject/noun (theology), philosophy normally concentrates on concepts, reasoning, and arguments within the theological terrain.

Perhaps at this point, it has become clear that philosophical theology encompasses "the process of doing theology with the aid and support of philosophical reflection, language, and methods."[2] More simply, it is the use of philosophy for theological purposes.

Before moving into theological territory, we first need to consider how one's worldview can affect one's use of philosophy for illuminating theology. As you might recall from previous chapters, when we think deeply about life's big questions—like those involving ultimate reality—we're already bringing our basic assumptions to the table.[3] When it comes to philosophical theology, the same reality applies. One either begins with belief in a personal God (theism) or with nonbelief in such a God (atheism or pantheism).[4] We (authors) share theistic worldview assumptions (e.g., "God exists"). More particularly, we hold to Christian theism since, for example, we endorse the ancient Christian confession, "Jesus is Lord" (Rom. 10:9). This reflects a Christian philosophical theology approach. For our purposes, then, we'll be employing this approach to explain and evaluate four core theological convictions or doctrines of the Christian faith: the Trinity (i.e., the triune God: Father, Son, and Spirit), the incarnation, the atonement, and the resurrection (of Jesus Christ).

Philosophical Theology Approaches to Four Core Christian Doctrines

Assumptions and Commitments

We begin this section with some stated assumptions. First, we expect there to be differing beliefs and responses to the theological topics we're exploring—and for distinct reasons, such as the plurality of world-views among our readers. We recognize that Christian theists, non-Christian theists, and non-theists aren't likely to share much common ground about the truth-value of particular Christian doctrines (i.e., the truth or falsehood of doctrinal propositions or claims).[5] Second, there are more than intellectual differences involved—competing

> The Christian faith's very existence entirely depends on Christ's resurrection (1 Cor. 15:14). Remove it and Christianity dies; reiterate it and Christianity thrives.

moral values impact everyone's assessments differently. Third, each person must decide on who or what carries ultimate authority for determining the nature of reality and truth, including religious doctrines. Candidates for ultimate authority include divine revelation (e.g., the Bible, the triune God, Jesus Christ, the Spirit's illumination, personal spiritual testimony, individual and/or Christian community experiences of God), logic/reason, science, family, friends, social media, experience, intuition, and so on. We authors are committed to divine revelation as revealed in Scripture as our ultimate source of authority, while we also recognize the value of penultimate sources of authority (especially early Christian creeds, Christian tradition/community, reason, conscience, testimony, and individual/Christian community experiences of God).

Goals and Method

Our two goals for this section include (1) explaining some significant differences between philosophical theology positions on theological doctrines, and (2) presenting doctrines from a specifically Christian philosophical theology perspective. For us to do both, we'll consider the first doctrine to be discussed—the resurrection—according to our first goal. To do this, we will compare five distinct types of philosophical theology approaches, using a simple conceptual five-point Likert scale. (We are employing the Likert scale as a heuristic device [i.e., a practical, sufficient model for reaching an immediate approximation goal] rather than for mathematical precision or proof.) In the process, we'll notice that two to three of these positions, depending on certain variables, likely indicate a distinctly Christian philosophical theology approach. For the other three doctrines to be discussed—the Trinity, the incarnation, and the atonement—we'll focus on accomplishing our second goal: utilizing a Christian philosophical theology approach. Through use of the Likert scale, we'll first consider how each type/position views the integration of philosophy and theology generally and then specifically, as it concerns the doctrine of the resurrection of Christ.

Position 1 on the Scale views philosophy as entirely controlling theology. From this position, one might hear, "Theology is irrational, so ignore it," or "Don't bring God or the Bible into the picture because we know miracles don't happen." Conversely, position 5 (opposite end of the scale) reverses control—theology entirely controls philosophy. On this view, statements such as "Philosophy is the enemy of theology" or "The Bible unites, philosophy divides" likely dominate. We authors agree that positions 1 and 5 are unconvincing and extreme and so should be avoided. We favor the more integrative approaches of positions 2, 3, and 4. To differing degrees, each of these strategies values philosophy-theology integration.

However, for someone who prefers not to bring God or the Bible into the picture (which would align with position 1), it might be more fruitful to study philosophy of religion rather than philosophical theology. Philosophy of religion is a wider-ranging discipline that examines many religious beliefs that do not necessarily include a personal, relational Being: for example, pantheism (wherein all is divine, humans as well as other sentient beings) or *a*theism (at least atheism that includes active dedication or even devotion, as evidenced within the so-called "New Atheism" movement).[6] Conversely, for Christians who only want to know "what the Bible has to say" (position 5), a simple devotional level approach may be preferred. However, without understanding even basic theology or philosophy, an anti-intellectualism may prevail—rarely leading to sound Scripture interpretation or genuine intellectual (or even spiritual) formation.

Philosophical Theology Approaches to Resurrection

Applied to the doctrine of the resurrection of Jesus Christ, position 1 dismisses it altogether, concluding something like "the so-called resurrection isn't part of reality as modern people know, even if first-century Christians believed it; perhaps they even made it up for their own purposes." Conversely, position 5 likely claims the resurrection as an "undeniable fact" since the New Testament states it happened as a clear-cut historical event. "One simply either accepts or rejects it, period; there's no need to 'theologize' or 'philosophize' about it."

Unfortunately, positions 1 and 5 miss crucial considerations that we'll discuss shortly. Both one-sided approaches diminish the potential for deepening our understanding about important theological assertions using philosophical language and thinking.

Considering the middle-position approaches, beginning with position 2, may prove more fruitful. While position 2 sees a preeminent place for philosophy, it also attributes some value—even if limited—to the theological realm and doctrinal claims. As long as no evident conflict arises between philosophy and theology, all may go well. But once a controversial claim surfaces—like the resurrection of Jesus—philosophical concerns typically overrule theological ones. So with the resurrection, position 2 thinkers likely opt for some alternative explanation to New Testament claims about Jesus bodily rising from the tomb. Therefore, we'd probably hear something like, "We know things like that don't happen in the 'real' world." Perhaps some type of "spiritual" resurrection gets proposed: a sort of reawakening in the hearts and lives of Jesus' followers occurring after his crucifixion as they recall his teachings. Others may draw parallels between the deaths of Socrates and Jesus: both being condemned unjustly for what the authorities viewed as seditious or irreverent behavior. In any case, "the supernatural problem" has been removed and a resurrection "revision" declared. Now let's move back and consider position 4 on the Scale: the reverse of position 2.

Position 4 likely will engage seriously with theological claims and doctrines, while also considering potential philosophical insights as helpful, albeit secondary. And like counterpart position 2, if there's no conflict between the disciplines (theology and philosophy), harmony can prevail. But when disputed claims appear—as with the resurrection—theological matters ultimately outweigh philosophical problems. So as you might imagine, many Christian thinkers practicing Christian philosophical theology stand at (or near) position 4, affirming that Jesus really did resurrect, and philosophical terms or categories may be helpful in understanding or clarifying certain details (for instance, ideas or evidence associated with resurrections contrasted with reincarnations).

At position 3 on the Scale, philosophy and theology are theoretically equal partners when considering doctrinal claims. So as to the resurrection, equal weight supposedly is granted to each arena. This would seem to entail that in some way a "resurrecting" took place—probably more than merely a reawakening in the hearts of Jesus' followers. Still, by definition, position 3 disallows prioritizing biblical and theological statements about Jesus' bodily resurrection over philosophical worries about people rising from the dead. Rather, one might claim the resurrection being deeply symbolic or meaningful for today—perhaps even founded on a spiritual (though not literal) raising of Jesus, aiming to correlate the two disciplines for the so-called modern mind.

One other important point should be made about our conceptual Likert scale positions: they may contain subpositions. For instance, we can imagine something like position 3.1, 3.2, and so on, up to 3.9, just shy of position 4.0. So while position 3 may appear to be equalitarian—perhaps even neutral—that's a problem since there is no such thing as an equal or neutral commitment between these two arenas (philosophy and theology). Priority ultimately must be given to one over the other—even if someone diligently works to weigh matters as equally and reasonably as humanly possible. So it probably makes good sense to think more in terms of subpositions—especially when it concerns position 3 on doctrinal matters. In the end, either philosophy or theology takes the lead and has final say. As Christ-followers and philosophers, we ultimately opt for theology maintaining precedence—even as we judiciously philosophize. Just as an atheistic worldview ultimately influences one's perspective, so does a theistic worldview—including as it concerns the resurrection. Thus, one ought to test one's worldview to ensure it is reasonable, livable, and, most important, true.

What has our philosophical theology and Christian philosophical theology discussion shown us to this point? First, philosophical tools, language, and concepts/terms often play important parts for understanding the nature and purpose of theology. Second, using a heuristic device/framework (like a Likert Scale) may help us map and evaluate various philosophical theology positions on important theological claims/doctrines like the resurrection. Third, every philosopher and theologian is powerfully shaped by their worldview, which forms a hierarchy of priorities when approaching and assessing core theological doctrines. Finally, while philosophical theology involves deep and creative reflection, reasoning, and arguments concerning theological issues, Christian philosophical theology concentrates on skillfully using specific philosophical tools for core Christian doctrines.

> The doctrine of the Trinity is not only central to Christianity but one of its most distinctive teachings.
> —Ronald J. Feenstra, "Trinity," *Cambridge Companion to Christian Philosophical Theology*, 3

Bearing all this in mind, we now hope to accomplish our second goal: judiciously applying a faithful Christian philosophical theology approach—involving something like a 3.5 to 4.0 Likert scale philosophy-theology integration—as we consider three additional doctrines central to the Christian faith: the Trinity, the incarnation, and the atonement.

Philosophical Theology Approaches to the Trinity

"I've never understood the Trinity. It's so confusing!" Many of our students have said something like this. Perhaps no other Christian doctrine is more difficult to comprehend or more misunderstood. Theologians discuss the Trinity doctrine as a "threeness-oneness problem"; philosophers call it "the logical problem of the Trinity." This problem challenges Christian philosophical theology advocates to explain the doctrine coherently and faithfully while avoiding heterodox conclusions. (*Heterodoxy* involves notions contrary to *orthodox* doctrinal positions as expressed, for instance, in early church creeds written during the first seven ecumenical councils of the church between 325 and 787 AD).

Among heterodox ideas, three appear especially problematic: (1) the Trinity consists of three gods (tritheism); (2) the Trinity comprises the one God (the Father) plus two related but lesser beings, Jesus Christ and the Holy Spirit (subordinationism); and (3) the one God is manifested in three different ways/modes (modalism): as the Father in ancient Israel, as the Son from the incarnation to the resurrection, and as the Spirit thereafter.

While solutions to the "Trinity problem" have been presented throughout history, none has won total consensus. The problem cannot simply be attributed to the New Testament lacking the term *Trinity*. In fact, several explicit and implicit passages include the "Tri-unity" of Father, Son, and Spirit (e.g., see the Great Commission baptismal formula in Matt. 28:19; Jesus' baptism in Matt. 3:16–17, Mark 1:1–9, Luke 3:21–22, and John 1:32–34; and a benediction in 2 Cor. 13:14). Instead, the Trinity challenge is largely conceptual and linguistic; it involves imagining what terms to use and how to use them in striving to articulate the Three-in-One God for the human mind. Furthermore, virtually all Christian thinkers agree that the Trinity is a mystery; while we can explain the doctrine to some degree, we can never fully understand it since we are discussing God's very being/nature.

Throughout the centuries, two main approaches have been offered to solve the Trinity problem (although the way of dividing up the sides is itself controversial). The Latin approach, generally in the west (Latin culture), is associated with Augustine, and the Greek approach, mainly in the east (Greek culture), is associated with the Cappadocian Fathers: Gregory of Nyssa, Basil of Caesarea, and Gregory of Nazianzus.

The Latin approach takes as basic the unity ("oneness") of God and then attempts to explain the three persons—Father, Son, Spirit—who share the same nature (divinity). The Greek approach takes as basic the diversity ("threeness") of God—distinct and co-equal persons—and then attempts to explain the unity of the one God. One major version of the second approach is *social trinitarianism* (ST), which often argues that each divine person has a distinct mind—a center of consciousness. These three centers of consciousness, volition, and intentionality are necessarily unified and nonconflicting in action and purpose, which some believe is necessary for a loving, internal relationship approximating a "community of divine persons."

Language and good arguments are supremely important to philosophical theology/Christian philosophical theology explorations—especially precise explanations for key terms and concepts. Just consider a few of these for Trinitarianism: divine persons (*hypostases/personas*); substance/essence (*ousia, substantia*); same (*consubstantial*), similar, or different substances (*homoousia, homoiousia, heterousia*); same or identical, inseparability, relationality, and so on.

For introductory purposes, we won't dive too deep into this discussion, but we can note three important points. First, philosophical reflection and discussion on the Trinity is primarily an in-house matter (i.e., of interest to Christian philosophical theology thinkers examining specific Christian doctrines). Second, virtually every Christian philosophical theology approach holds that in some way there is one God (monotheism) who is three-in-one (Triune): one divine substance/nature (*homoousion*) united in action in the three divine Persons

> The Christian doctrine of the Incarnation maintains that the second person of the Trinity became a human being, retaining all attributes necessary for being divine and gaining all attributes necessary for being human.
>
> —Richard Cross, "The Incarnation," *Oxford Handbook of Philosophical Theology*, 452

(*hypostases*). Third, views that deny the second point are likely unsound. Philosophical theologian Stephen Davis helpfully summarizes Trinitarianism: "The doctrine says in sum that the one God exists in three distinct and co-equal Persons—Father, Son, and Holy Spirit. The three Persons are not three Gods, or even three actions or aspects of God, but one God. No Person is subordinate to any other; all are co-equally and co-eternally divine."[7]

Philosophical Theology Approaches to the Incarnation

The doctrine of the incarnation claims that the Son (or Word) of God, one in essence with the Father and the Spirit eternally, became human in the person of Jesus Christ. The Christian Scriptures emphatically claim and support this doctrine (e.g., Phil. 2:5–8; Col. 1:15–20, 2:9). Still, a challenging philosophical question persists: How can one person (*prosopon*)—Jesus—be both divine and human?

Christian philosophical theology scholars throughout history have addressed this issue; we can see it in early Christian creeds (i.e., doctrinal statements), like the Chalcedonian Creed, up to the present day (e.g., in works by C. Stephen Evans, Kathryn Tanner, Thomas V. Morris, Richard Swinburne, and Sarah Coakley).[8] One characteristic explanation has been that the two natures (divine and human) are parts of the whole incarnate second person of the Trinity—each part containing relevant properties for that particular nature. Another view proposes that the incarnation entails "contingent humanity" being added to the essential divinity of the Son/Word of God; thus, Jesus Christ, the God-man, is necessarily divine and contingently human.

Other views, for instance, include (a) *kenotic theories* (the Son/Word of God temporarily "empties himself of" or "sets aside" certain divine attributes during his incarnational time on Earth); (b) the *two-minds solution* (one version says that in Christ, the divine person, there are two distinct-yet-overlapping minds or mental subjects or types of consciousness—divine/eternal and human/earthly [Morris], while another version says the eternal Word gains a contingent body previously lacked [Swinburne]); and (c) the *two-wills theory* (divine and human ways of acting, or having causal capacities, the human will ultimately being subject to the divine will), among others.[9]

While there is significant debate concerning the incarnation, a faithful Christian philosophical theology approach will attempt to (1) incorporate and reasonably explain relevant biblical terms and claims, (2) maintain basic theological consistency with unifying historical Christian statements/creeds while avoiding heterodoxy, and (3) permit diverse Christian philosophical theology approaches and potential solutions (while also avoiding heterodox/heretical views that oppose biblical and credal/historical doctrines).

Philosophical Theology Approaches to the Atonement

Atonement theory "attempts to explain how the Christ-event (the incarnation, life, teachings, and especially death and resurrection of Christ) accomplished or made possible the forgiveness of our sins and our 'at-one-ment' with God."[10] Still, "the nature of the atonement . . . remains a theological conundrum."[11] A faithful Christian philosophical theology approach thus recognizes both the important and challenging nature of the atonement, as well as its being the instrument of redemption/salvation.

> [The atonement] is a central affirmation of Christianity that Christ atoned for the sins of the world and this reconciled a fallen humanity to God.
> —Gordon Graham, "Atonement,"
> *Cambridge Companion to Christian Philosophical Theology*, 124

To begin, we'll briefly mention some major atonement theories, while noting that none has generated unanimous consent. A short list of theories includes ransom, satisfaction, substitution, sacrifice, and moral exemplar/influence—plus subspecies of each—which all draw from Scripture. Various arguments, some better than others, are presented for (and against) each theory. For instance, one *dubious version* of the ransom theory imagines God duping and/or paying off the devil to buy back humans, which seems morally suspect for God. The satisfaction theory includes the idea of God's moral law being broken and God's honor rejected, but then Jesus—the uniquely sinless person—steps in and satisfies/repairs that broken law and relationship, making things right again.

Perhaps by including several stronger atonement theories we may capture a fuller portrait of Jesus Christ's life and work on behalf of sinners. In any case, we think a faithful Christian philosophical theology approach to atonement theory will affirm (at least) these aspects: (1) Jesus' death—and validating resurrection—secures atonement for human sin/sins; (2) sounder atonement theories contain ample biblical and theological support, plus less morally problematic ideas (like Jesus' life/death being merely exemplary or admirable); and (3) philosophical terms/categories should be used to clarify and enhance (rather than confuse) atonement understandings. Thus, a faithful Christian philosophical theology approach may include, for instance, the following types of atonement theories.

Substitution Theory

In some way, Jesus substitutes for humans, who are due just punishment for their sin/sins, by taking their sin/sins upon himself (several substitution subcategories/versions exist, but none are necessary for upholding this general substitution theory). Substitution subtheories often include certain important theological questions (e.g., whether the Atonement is "consequentially necessary" because of the way God made this world; exactly how the penal consequences are transferred to Jesus; whether/how Jesus represents humanity by acting on our behalf).

Satisfaction or Sacrifice Theory

God's nature requires satisfaction for human sins committed against God (i.e., his perfect character and moral law). However, no mere human possesses the ability (i.e., the merit) to pay the debt for such sin; only God (specifically, Jesus Christ, the God-man) is worthy to provide satisfaction for human sin. Some versions focus more on Jesus' willing sacrifice while others emphasize the satisfaction aspect.[12]

How Philosophical Theology May Benefit Your Life

For those interested in going beyond a surface-level knowledge of important theological matters, philosophical theology provides a beneficial way of learning and deepening our understanding by way of philosophical methods, language, and reflection. The philosophy-theology relationship is an important one; throughout the centuries, it has powerfully shaped Christian thought, interpretation and understanding of Scripture, ancient creeds, Christian apologetics, and academic and Christian communities. Engaging Christian philosophical theology helps us better understand central Christian doctrines like the Trinity, the incarnation, the atonement, and the resurrection of Christ, beginning with the biblical text and moving through the history of theological reflection on core doctrines. Staying focused on maintaining vital theological consistency with Scripture and unifying historical creeds may serve at least two important roles: assisting us in avoiding aberrations and heresies, while also encouraging us to understand and appreciate diverse Christian philosophical theology approaches to resolving difficult-yet-crucial questions concerning God, the creation, and our personal lives.

Questions for Reflection

1. Explain one or more similarities and differences between philosophical theology and Christian philosophical theology.
2. Why is it important to understand the role that worldview plays in discussing or even determining central Christian doctrines?
3. Using a Bible-search tool/program, find several passages that you think might be used to support one of the core Christian doctrines studied in the chapter. Create a document or spreadsheet that lists the doctrines and supporting passages for each.

For Further Reading

Allen, Diogenes, and Eric O. Springsted. *Philosophy for Understanding Theology.* 2nd ed. Louisville: Westminster John Knox, 2007.

Crisp, Oliver. *A Reader in Contemporary Philosophical Theology.* London: T&T Clark, 2009.

Davis, Stephen T. *Christian Philosophical Theology.* Oxford: Oxford University Press, 2016.

Flint, Thomas P., and Michael C. Rea. *The Oxford Handbook of Philosophical Theology.* Oxford: Oxford University Press, 2008.

Moreland, J. P., and William Lane Craig. *Philosophical Foundations for a Christian Worldview.* 2nd ed. Downers Grove, IL: IVP Academic, 2017.

Taliaferro, Charles, and Chad Meister. *The Cambridge Companion to Christian Philosophical Theology.* Cambridge: Cambridge University Press, 2010.

Thiselton, Anthony C. *The Hermeneutics of Doctrine.* Grand Rapids: Eerdmans, 2007.

NOTES

1. For instance, see Thomas Aquinas, *Summa Theologica*, trans. Fathers of the English Dominican Province (New York: Benziger Brothers, 1911–1925), which contains the well-known "five ways" (arguments) for God's existence.
2. "Philosophical Theology," www.theopedia.com/philosophical-theology.
3. No one begins with absolute neutrality or objectivity. Moreover, our assumptions may turn out to be true, partly true, or entirely false, but we do have them, regardless!
4. Some suggest a third option, agnosticism, as a viable starting point; however, by its very definition—"Without knowledge" or "ignorance"—agnosticism is more knowledge-oriented (epistemological) than assumption- or belief-oriented. "Agnostic atheism," for example, seeks to combine disbelief with unknowability of God, whereas theism normally unites belief in God with God's knowability.
5. For instance, Christians and other theists typically agree on more general religious doctrines (like God's being the creator of the universe), whereas Christian theists normally disagree

with non-Christian theists about particular Christian doctrines (for instance, Christ's incarnation, atonement, and resurrection).

6. See Stefani McDade, "New Atheism Is Dead. What's the New New Atheism?" *Christianity Today*, August 14, 2023, www.christianitytoday.com/ct/2023/september/new-atheism-is-dead.html.

7. Stephen T. Davis, *Christian Philosophical Theology* (Oxford: Oxford University Press, 2016), 61.

8. An English translation of the Chalcedonian Creed may be accessed online at Theopedia.com. https://www.theopedia.com/chalcedonian-creed.

9. For example, J. P. Moreland and William Lane Craig argue for a creative combination of *enhypostasia* and Christ's "superhuman facets" as largely subliminal, in *Philosophical Foundations for a Christian Worldview*, 2nd ed. (Downers Grove, IL: IVP Academic, 2017), chap. 32.

10. Davis, *Christian Philosophical Theology*, 212.

11. Oliver D. Crisp, "Original Sin and Atonement," in *The Oxford Handbook of Philosophical Theology*, ed. Thomas P. Flint, and Michael Rea (Oxford: University Press, 2009), 430.

12. For more details on these atonement theories (and several others), see ibid., 431–47.

PART 7

Ethics

Theory and Application

CHAPTER 20

What Is Ethics All About?

Imagine a friend asks you if they look good wearing an outfit that you find particularly unflattering. Do you give your honest assessment, or do you lie to avoid relational complication? Or think of a more difficult situation: a soldier is commanded by an officer to detonate a bomb where innocent children may be killed. What does the soldier do? Should he disobey the order so that he can protect innocent children, or should he follow the officer's command?

Difficult scenarios like these help us see what ethics is about. In this chapter, we first look at the theoretical aspects of ethics. We begin with a brief discussion about the purpose and goal of ethics and then discuss some challenges that ethics faces today. We'll finish the chapter by surveying some major ethical theories that people have used in their approach to ethical decision-making.

THE HAPPINESS PARADOX

Achieving "happiness" can be a paradox. On the one hand, those who focus on achieving happiness as the ultimate goal tend to be disappointed when various pleasures of life fall short of perfection. On the other hand, the pleasures in life that tend to bring short-term happiness are often destructive and ultimately lead to unhappiness. Seeking happiness seems to be a self-defeating enterprise. Therefore, it seems that true happiness can be achieved only by focusing on living the good life as the ultimate goal.

Ethics and the Good Life

The term *ethics* comes from the Greek word *ethikos*, meaning "character." Very broadly, ethics is the study about what humans ought to be and how they ought to act, what ought to be valued, and what obligations or duties humans ought to have. It asks questions like, "What is the good we ought to strive for? What should we value? What does it mean to be good? What kinds of actions ought humans do or avoid?"

The goal of ethics has traditionally been understood to answer what it means to live the "good life." In ancient Greek philosophy, the concept of ethics was wed to *eudaimonia*. This word is often loosely translated as "happiness," but the Greeks used it to mean something much more deep, abiding, and excellent than what most people mean when they use that word today. Philosophers, such as Plato, Aristotle, and Epicurus, believed that human action ought to be oriented toward what is good and right, leading to true and lasting happiness. Happiness, however, should not be understood as superficial, immediate self-gratification. Rather, it was believed that *eudaimonia* was obtained through denying temporary gratification in favor of something that was more significant and deeper.

The Christian worldview has also argued that human action ought to be focused upon the good life, or happiness. Happiness from this perspective, however, is focused outwardly, or away from self. For Christians, happiness is obtained only by orienting one's life and actions to glorifying God and loving others. The fifth-century Christian philosopher and theologian Augustine put it this way: "And the happy life is this,—to rejoice unto Thee, in Thee, and for Thee; this it is, and there is no other."[1] The Westminster Shorter Catechism asks, "What is the chief end of man?" It answers, "Man's chief end is to glorify God, and enjoy him forever."[2] These words echo what the apostle Paul states: "Whatever you do, whether in word or deed, do it all in the name of the Lord Jesus, giving thanks to God the Father through him" (Col. 3:17).

Only when humanity pursues the worship and glory of God will personal happiness result. Thus, human happiness is not the goal but the effect of the goal. It is contentment, rest, peace, and joy in the triune Creator of the universe. When someone loves God with their entire being, contentment and fulfillment result, hence reaching the good life. This is the goal of ethics from a Christian perspective.

The study of ethics is typically divided into three subdisciplines: metaethics, normative ethics, and practical (or applied) ethics. Metaethics examines what ethical terms mean, like what is *good*? Normative ethics looks at what is right and wrong and surveys different ethical theories in an attempt to find ethical principles that can be used to guide moral behavior. Finally, applied ethics addresses how to solve specific moral problems, such as abortion, euthanasia, and human sexuality. We will now focus on a few challenges that arise from metaethics, and then we will survey some common normative ethical theories.

Metaethical Challenges

If the purpose of ethics is to help us live the good life, a couple of challenges exist in metaethics that can undermine this purpose. As stated, metaethics deals with the bigger picture: how to interpret ethical claims and what ethical terms mean. Two specific viewpoints in moral philosophy present significant challenges to moral reasoning and in some ways make moral reasoning impossible: nihilism and relativism.

Moral nihilism is the view that moral right and wrong do not exist and that there are no such things as moral values. At first blush, it can be tempting to think there must be more to nihilism than that. Surely, the nihilist will give some qualification to the claim that moral values don't exist, right? After all, isn't it obvious that some things, like racism, injustice, genocide, and torturing innocent children, are wrong? Isn't it obvious that loving people and helping those in need are good? Actually, nihilists insist that none of these things in themselves is either morally right or wrong. Loving your neighbor, the nihilist will say, is neither praiseworthy nor blameworthy; torturing an innocent child is neither good nor evil.

It is undeniable that everyone talks about moral values as if they really do exist and as if good and evil are real. For the nihilist, that is all it is: talk. Some nihilists will interpret moral talk as merely the expression of emotions. On this view, "torturing an innocent child is wrong" means something like, "Yuck! I don't like the idea of torturing an innocent child!" Other nihilists will interpret moral language as the effort to control behavior. For example, if you say, "It is wrong to cheat on your taxes," the nihilist interprets this to mean, "Don't cheat on your taxes!" Either way, whether moral language is interpreted as an expression of emotions or as commands, nihilism insists that no moral right and wrong truly exist.

More common than nihilism is moral relativism. Relativism is a category of different viewpoints which states that moral values are always relative to persons or groups. Moral subjectivism is the idea that moral values depend on the preferences and opinions of individual persons; cultural relativism says that moral right and wrong are determined by a particular culture. Whatever conventions or moral codes are accepted by the culture, that determines right and wrong for that culture.

The core reasoning behind cultural relativism is as follows:

Different cultures have different moral codes.
So there must not be any objective, universal moral values.
Therefore, it is wrong for one culture to interfere with another.

There was a time when cultural relativism seemed to make sense. When travel was more difficult and the flow of information was much more restricted than it is today, a culture was a fairly easy thing to define as a distinct group of people. But when we think about it logically, there are a few obvious problems. First, advocates of cultural relativism are advancing a logical contradiction: there are no objective, universal moral values, and it is wrong for one culture to interfere with another. But the only way it can be wrong for one culture to interfere with another is if it is objectively wrong to do so. This logical contradiction tells us clearly that cultural relativism cannot possibly be correct! But this view has many other problems as well. Since proponents of this view say right and wrong are determined by the culture, this requires a majority rule for determining moral values, which means that all minority viewpoints are treated as immoral. It should be obvious that if the majority opinion is always right (by definition) and the minority is always seen as immoral, societies would never have been able to make the moral progress that they have. Jesus, Gandhi, and Martin Luther King Jr. all would be seen as immoral, because they challenged the status quo. In any case, the long list of problems that cultural relativism has is the main reason why few philosophers take it seriously.[3]

Moral subjectivism is a more common view. Motivated by the belief that matters of morality are entirely and deeply personal, this viewpoint isolates all moral reasoning on the preferences and opinions of individual people. This view says that if you think torture is wrong, then it is wrong for you, but that is as far as it goes. You really can't say what other people should think about it, and you don't have the right to tell other people what is right and wrong for them. Subjectivism is captured in the often-repeated phrase, "No one has the right to judge other people's moral values." On the surface, this seems to promote moral autonomy: we get to engage our own moral reasoning skills to determine what is right and wrong, without interference from others. Subjectivism also seems to promote tolerance: since moral values are determined by the individual person, we should be tolerant of people who have different moral points of view. The problem, of course, is that subjectivism does not actually promote either autonomy or tolerance. If moral values are just matters of personal opinion, then there is nothing stopping me from judging you and interfering in your moral decision-making, and there is nothing telling me that I ought to be tolerant of others. It turns out that we can be morally autonomous and tolerant of others only if autonomy and tolerance (among others) are objectively valuable. So while subjectivism is popular today, and sounds good in some ways, it ends up defeating itself.

Normative Ethical Theories

The evident failure of both the nihilistic and relativistic approaches to ethics leads us to a search for a workable ethical theory, and that is what we now turn to in our discussion. Ethical theories are concerned primarily with "what is the good?" and "how do we achieve it?" The main difference between these ethical theories is in how they answer these questions. The answers are numerous, so our discussion will be limited to giving broad overviews and summarizing major themes of four common theories: utilitarianism, deontology, virtue ethics, and divine command theory.

Utilitarianism

Utilitarianism states that the good is what brings the greatest amount of pleasure to the greatest number of people. Its traditional formulation is best summarized by one of its early proponents, Jeremy Bentham (1748–1832). He stated, "Nature has placed mankind under the governance of two sovereign masters, pain and pleasure, and it is for them alone to point out what we ought to do, as well as what we shall do."[4] The goal, therefore, is to avoid pain and achieve pleasure (or happiness) for the greatest number of people.

Utilitarianism is often categorized as a consequentialist theory. This is because the method by which happiness is obtained does not matter. The only thing that does matter is that happiness is achieved as a consequence of the action. Utilitarianism insists that the end justifies the means. Whether or not the action taken (the means) is morally justifiable depends only on the consequences (the end) that the action achieves. To make a moral decision, the consequentialist thinks about what consequences are desired in that situation, and then does whatever is necessary to bring about those desired consequences. As a result, no action is intrinsically good or evil; every action must be judged on whether the goal of pleasure or happiness is achieved. For example, imagine you saw a friend who needed your assistance to cross the street at a busy intersection. You come alongside and provide the assistance needed because you have good intentions and want to help. But, as you cross the street, a car comes speeding around the corner and hits your friend, resulting in many painful injuries. Since the actual consequences of your action were pain and suffering, then your action is judged to be immoral by utilitarian standards.

Obviously, the consequences of our actions do matter. Everyone seems to be in general agreement on that. However, from a Christian perspective, the consequences are not all that matter, so this theory has numerous problems.

QUANTITATIVE VERSUS QUALITATIVE

There are two primary types of utilitarianism: *quantitative* and *qualitative*. Jeremy Bentham is known for quantitative. He believed that the good was the greatest amount, or quantity, of pleasure for the greatest number of people. Thus, Bentham proposed a "pleasure calculus" to determine which course of action would provide the greatest amount of pleasure. Bentham's pupil John Mill, on the other hand, believed that pleasure differed in kind, or quality. Thus, he thought that the course of action to be chosen ought to be the one which brought the greatest kind of pleasure. Mill illustrated his point by saying, "It is better to be a human being dissatisfied than a *pig satisfied*; better to be Socrates dissatisfied than a *fool satisfied*."[5]

One problem is defining "good" as the greatest amount of pleasure for the greatest number of people. This is ambiguous at best. What is meant by "pleasure"? Beyond the qualitative and quantitative difference, is pleasure physical, psychological, emotional, mental, spiritual, or something else? Also, what is meant by "the greatest number of people"? Are we talking about the number of people in a city, state, country, region, or something else? The basic definition of utilitarianism is too vague to be helpful.

One significant problem with utilitarianism is its notion that the end justifies the means. But if this utilitarian principle is correct, this would force us to accept actions that we ordinarily would believe are immoral. We should also ask ourselves, "What if the majority says that the greatest pleasure would be something that we would consider to be morally wrong?" For example, what if the greatest good for the greatest number of people was to enslave the minority? Surely slavery is morally wrong, but it could easily be justified on utilitarian grounds. Moreover, it is conceivable to argue from a utilitarian perspective that killing an innocent person is morally obligatory if it helps us achieve the greatest happiness for the greatest number. According to the Christian worldview, however, slavery is wrong, and killing innocent people is never morally acceptable (most people call it "murder").

Finally, as a consequentialist theory, we must be able to know in advance the consequences of our actions in order to know which action to take. After all, it isn't the predicted consequences that justify our actions according to consequentialists; it is the actual consequences. This, however, requires us to be able to perfectly predict the future and know for sure both the short-term and long-term consequences that will come from our actions. This is surely impossible. The consequences of our actions don't occur until after we act; but the utilitarian tells us that before we decide on what action we take we must consider the consequences that will come. We might be able to predict accurately what some of the immediate consequences will be; but since none of us can see into the future, we can never truly know what the consequences will be, especially the long-term consequences. Thus, utilitarianism ironically fails to achieve its most basic goal: to tell us what ought to be done in any given situation. It is for these reasons (among others) that utilitarianism ought to be rejected.

Deontology

A second popular approach to ethics is deontology. This theory is associated with the enlightenment philosopher Immanuel Kant (1724–1804). Like utilitarianism, deontology aims to have an objective standard rather than a relativistic one. Rather than basing ethics upon culture or personal feelings, Kant attempts to ground ethics in reason and reason alone. Unlike utilitarianism, however, Kant does not think that we should make ethical decisions based on desired consequences.

Deontology means "the study of duty," particularly human duty. For Kant, human duty is encompassed by what he calls "the categorical imperative." This means that morality should be based upon unconditional duties that always apply in every circumstance apart from a person's desire or inclinations to do otherwise. As such, Kant rejects utilitarianism.

Kant's categorical imperative has three primary characteristics. The first is that the morality of an act ought to justify itself. The consequences of the act are irrelevant. This stands in contrast to utilitarianism's consequentialist ethics. Second, Kant insists that humans ought always to be viewed as an end in themselves—human persons are intrinsically valuable—and never a means to an end or merely instrumentally valuable. An act is immoral, therefore, if it calls for someone to be used to accomplish some goal, without regard for that person's intrinsic worth. Finally, an act is morally right only if it can be willed as a universal moral law. We must ask, "Would I want this act to be considered a universal law that everyone obeys?" If the answer is "no," then the act is immoral.

Kant's deontology has positives and negatives, particularly from a Christian viewpoint. Positively, Kant should be lauded for attempting to put forward ethical objectivism rather than relativism. Christian ethics has historically viewed ethics to be objective, having some divine standard by which to measure human action. Additionally, the idea that acts justify themselves is also agreeable. Acts should always be justifiable apart from the consequences. Moreover, Kant's emphasis on the intrinsic value of humans agrees with the Christian view of ethics. God has made humans in his image, so all persons are valuable and thus never to be used merely as a means to an end.

Negatively, Kant's deontology fails at various points. One failure is basing ethics entirely upon human reason. According to the Christian doctrines of the fall and sin, human reason is incapable of fully discerning what acts ought to be considered morally right or wrong. Although Christian ethics observes that God's law is written on human hearts (ex. Rom. 2:14–15), it is quick to point out that this law was not discovered by human reason (it was placed there by God), is limited, and is distorted by sin. Hence, we cannot expect human reason alone to have the ability to discover all that it needs for ethics. On this point, many non-Christians would agree, obviously. Most people are able to recognize that human reason is often prone to error, so even philosophers who don't believe in the Christian view of sin would be inclined to say that Kant was overconfident in what he thought reason could accomplish.

Another objection from a Christian perspective is that Kant goes too far in refusing to allow actions to have moral value if they are motivated by emotions or feelings and not on reason alone. If we accept Kant's account of moral values, then no one would be able to enjoy doing the right thing or allow positive feelings to serve as a motivation for doing what is right. From a Christian perspective, however, doing the right thing can be seen as desirable and enjoyable. If we are made in God's image, not only are we able to act reasonably but also we should expect to have some degree of affective attraction to what is good. Here again, any non-Christian philosopher who wants to retain an emotional component to moral action would probably agree with the Christian's critique of Kant.

Virtue Theory

The virtue ethics tradition has its heritage in ancient Greek philosophy. We mentioned that the Greek philosophers were concerned with achieving *eudaimonia,* and many prominent thinkers in that tradition believed that the way to *eudaimonia* was through cultivating virtue. This moral tradition focuses on being a certain kind of person rather than performing certain kinds of moral actions.

The word *cultivation* introduces a metaphor that helps us understand morality from a virtue ethics perspective. A farmer works hard to prepare a tract of land for crops, then plants seed, waters, removes weeds and pests, and protects the plants until the time for harvest. Likewise, the virtue ethics tradition emphasizes the cultivation of morality in the life of each person. Parents or moral mentors first require good moral behavior of a child, but this is a kind of preparation for a time when maturity will bring an embrace of the virtue that lies behind that behavior. Another helpful metaphor is that of a marathon runner. This athlete doesn't just wake up one day and decide to run a marathon. In fact, very few people can do such a thing. Instead, the runner forms a lifetime of fitness habits, along with healthy living and rigorous training; eventually, over a long time of disciplined preparation, the person can run a marathon. Likewise, the virtue ethics tradition emphasizes that virtues are moral skills and abilities that are learned deliberately over time by instilling good habits of behavior, patterns of thinking, and dispositions toward others.

Philosophers who take this perspective point out that this account of morality is much more robust than utilitarian or duty-based theories. In those theories, anyone can do the right thing. But the virtue ethicist points out that "doing the right thing" is a thin, weak view of morality. Consider, for example, a police officer who always obeys the law, follows proper procedures, and even occasionally does something heroic. Now, imagine that this police officer would—if he could get away with it—commit extortion and bribery, plant evidence on suspects, and abuse those he places under arrest. He doesn't do those things, but he would if he could get away with it. Would we think that this is a good person? The virtue tradition says that this is not a good person and that morality is more about what kind of person I am rather than what kinds of actions I perform or what consequences come from my actions. Thus, in virtue ethics we have something that we really need in an ethical theory: an account of what it means to be a good person and how to become one.

There are some possible objections to the virtue ethics approach. One of the common ones may be something that occurred to you as you read the previous paragraphs: None of that actually tells us how we should act, morally. After all, this objection says, a good moral theory will be practical and will lead to moral guidance that helps us do things like answer difficult moral questions and solve moral problems, and virtue ethics doesn't do that. In response to this objection, many virtue theorists will reply that there is ample moral guidance that comes from focusing on character formation: as we move toward virtue, we will naturally see that we should avoid vices such as greed, deceit, or injustice and that we should do what is generous, truthful, and just. The complaint might be something like, "Well, yes, but you need to give me moral rules so that I know how to act." The virtue ethicist might say that this is a feature, not a bug.

Another common objection arises from an aspect of virtue ethics we haven't mentioned yet: role models. Historically, virtue ethicists have tended to say that moral role models serve the essential function of helping us see what it looks like to develop a good moral character. The objection here says that this might be correct, but what guidance do we have on who should be our role models and who shouldn't be? It doesn't seem as if there is a clear way to answer this question.

Divine Command Theory

Some philosophers believe that God alone must be the sole source for moral values and moral duties, as God is the one supreme, morally perfect being.

God has given us specific rules of conduct that we must follow, these philosophers say, and these commands create moral duties for us. This perspective is known as *divine command theory*. This theory says that human beings are morally obligated to do whatever God commands and are morally prohibited from doing whatever God prohibits. One important strength of this theory is that it seems obvious that God (the supreme, morally perfect being) is in the best position to reveal to us what is morally good or evil. Another strength of the divine command approach is that it seems to solve all controversy about differences of opinion when it comes to moral judgments: you may be wrong, I may be wrong, but God's moral opinion is never wrong. So God's moral judgment can serve as the objective ground for moral obligation.

The most common objection to divine command theory comes from an adaptation of an ancient dilemma first offered by Plato (c. 400 BC) in a dialogue called *Euthyphro*, named after the main character. The adaptation of Plato's challenge is something like this: Does God command us to do certain things because they are good? Or are those things good because God commands us to do them? The point of this challenge is that no matter how the divine command theorist answers, the answer is unacceptable. If things are good because God commands them, then if God were to command torture, racism, or theft, then those things would be good, and this is certainly not acceptable for the theist because morality isn't arbitrary. On the other hand, if we say that God commands things because they are good, then it seems there must be some standard of goodness that exists independently of God, to which he conforms his commands. Divine command theory has responded to this challenge in various ways, but one basic response is this: God himself is the standard of goodness, so whatever God commands is consistent with his perfect nature. God does command things because those things are good, but this doesn't imply a standard of goodness that is outside of God. Rather, it is simply to say that God commands things in accordance with his morally perfect character, and thus his character (not his commands) is the ultimate foundation of morality.

Summary

In this chapter, we described the goal of ethics: living the good life and achieving true and lasting happiness. We saw that both nihilism and relativism threaten to undermine that entire project, even though they ultimately fail to do so. Recognizing this, philosophers have sought to develop moral theories that help us understand moral good and what we can do to achieve it. We then sketched out four common normative theories that attempt to give just such an account. In our next chapter, we will pick up a theme that we began when we introduced divine command theory: In what way might God be the key to understand what good is and understand how to achieve it? To answer that question, we will examine what is unique about Christian theological ethics.

Questions for Reflection

1. Have you thought about morality as a set of restrictive rules or as a way to achieve a fulfilling and flourishing life? Why?
2. Why do you think it is so tempting for people to want to say that moral values are a matter of personal preference or cultural convention?
3. Among the four normative ethical theories discussed, which do you think has the greatest strengths, and why?

For Further Reading

Holmes, Arthur F. *Ethics: Approaching Moral Decisions*, 2nd ed. in *Contours in Christian Philosophy*. Edited by C. Stephen Evans. Downers Grove, IL: IVP Academic, 2007.

Rachels, James, and Stuart Rachels. *The Elements of Moral Philosophy*, 7th ed. Edited by Stuart Rachels. New York: McGraw Hill, 2012.

Shafer-Landau, Russ. *The Fundamentals of Ethics*, 5th ed. New York: Oxford University Press, 2020.

NOTES

1. Augustine, *Confessions* 10.22.32.
2. Westminster Shorter Catechism, Q1.
3. For a well-known and excellent critique of cultural relativism, see James Rachels, *The Elements of Moral Philosophy*, 7th ed., ed. Stuart Rachels (New York: McGraw-Hill, 2012).
4. Jeremy Bentham, *An Introduction to the Principles of Morals and Legislation*, ed. J. H. Burns and H. L. A. Hart (Oxford: Clarendon, 1970), 11.
5. John Stuart Mill, *Utilitarianism* (London: Parker, Son, and Bourn, 1863), 14.

CHAPTER 21

What Is Unique about Theological Ethics?

In the previous chapter, we surveyed some of the more common ethical systems, most of which (all but divine command theory) attempt to put forward a system of moral philosophy that is nontheistic. These systems approach moral philosophy without reference to God.[1] But now we want to ask an important question that we think everyone should ask and that we want you to ask: How would the project of ethics be different when approached theologically? We will try to begin to formulate an answer to that question in this chapter, and we hope you see that there are some very important ideas that arise from a theological approach. As we seek to describe what is unique about theological ethics, we will focus on a Christian perspective.

The Ontological Foundation of Ethics from a Theological Perspective

When we introduced you to several common systems of ethics in the previous chapter, we mentioned some of the fundamental assumptions that they make about what is good and then how those systems develop a theory of right conduct based on what is good. Against the backdrop of this kind of survey, one might expect that a theological system of ethics begins by assuming the authority of some religious text (like the Bible) or set of religious laws (like the Ten Commandments), but this is not quite correct. While it is essential to address sources of moral authority, a theological approach to ethics does not begin with questions of authority. Rather, it begins with God and the conviction that God himself is the foundation of objective moral values.

All normative ethical systems (except nihilism and relativism, of course) assume that moral values are both objective and universal. Utilitarianism, deontology, virtue ethics, and all other major systems insist that good is not a matter of opinion, nor are right and wrong. Even outside the confines of these major systems, almost everyone thinks that some moral values and duties are objective—values that do not depend on personal preference, opinion, or cultural context. If you think carefully about the moral opinions that you have, we are confident that you will be able to see that you have several moral opinions that you actually believe apply to everyone, everywhere, at all times. A common example in the philosophical literature is "It is morally wrong to torture infants just for the fun of it." Practically no one thinks that this is merely a matter of personal opinion or cultural convention. Torturing an infant for the fun of it is just wrong, and it would still be wrong if there were no laws against it, no religious texts proclaiming it to be wrong, and even if the person doing it didn't think it was wrong. It simply is wrong for everyone, everywhere, always to torture infants for the fun of it. But even after we agree on this, we must immediately consider the obvious question: Why is it wrong? This is the question of moral ontology—considering what it is that makes some things right and other things wrong.

There remains widespread disagreement among nontheist philosophers about this question, and surprisingly few suggestions have been offered that provide appealing answers. Theists, however, think that there is a straightforward answer to this foundational question, and this is one of the main factors that makes a theological approach to ethics unique.

Theological ethics begins with the assertion that God is the foundation for objective moral values. Theists think that in order to have objective moral values—things that really are good or evil—you need a supremely perfect moral being who can ground these values. In this understanding, good is seen as that which is consistent with God's perfectly good moral character, and evil would be whatever is inconsistent with God's perfectly good moral character. Further, God can be the objective basis for our moral duties (what we are morally obligated to do or not to do), revealing to us (in a variety of ways) what moral obligations we have. So why is it wrong to torture an infant just for the fun of it? Because doing so is inconsistent with God's perfectly good moral nature and with the moral values and obligations that God has revealed to us.

Any kind of theist affirms this basic idea: God is the foundation of objective morality. Christian philosophers, however, can go further and affirm a concept of God that can provide an even stronger basis for our experience of objective morality. Based on biblical descriptions of God, particularly in the New Testament, Christians believe that God exists as one single being in three distinct persons. Thus, Christian theology, reflecting on the biblical data, describes God as a Trinity or, sometimes, tri-unity. Theologians use this terminology because the Bible describes God as a single being (there is just one God), and the Bible also teaches that God exists in three persons, using the terms Father, Son, and Holy Spirit to describe these persons. Each of the three persons is distinct and each is properly called God, but they exist together as one single being.[2] The primary reason that this is significant in a discussion of the foundations for morality is that the Trinity introduces the concept of relationships: the persons of the Trinity enjoy perfect loving relationships between each other.

It is often recognized (by theists and atheists alike) that the moral dimension of our existence arises in the context of relationships. The Christian theist has a ready explanation for why this is the case: in the trinitarian God, social relationships are a key component of fundamental reality. If this is what God is like, then it is easy to see how love is thought of as the central Christian virtue. Drawing from the love that is central to God's very being, it can be seen that love for others is objectively good. Further, moral action can be anchored to the biblical concept of human beings made in God's image (the *imago Dei*). What is good and right for humans is to act according to their nature as divine image-bearers. So actions toward others are obligatory to the extent that they reflect the perfect love of God. On the other hand, actions that are inconsistent with God's perfect love are morally impermissible. Returning to our question: Why is it wrong to torture infants just for the fun of it? It is wrong because it is inconsistent with the perfectly loving nature of the triune God, violates God's commands to love, devalues the human person made in God's image, and inhibits human flourishing as God has designed.

How Has God Revealed Morality?

Thus far we have discussed the question of moral ontology from a theistic perspective: God is the ontological foundation for objective values and duties. The next obvious question, however, is the question of moral epistemology: How do we know what is good or evil, right or wrong? This question is complex, and the answer is likely to be multifaceted. Still, in considering a theological approach to ethics, it will be essential to focus in on the idea of revelation. By *revelation*, we mean that God has used a variety of means to reveal moral truth to us, and through this revelation we can acquire moral knowledge.

Traditionally, revelation has been divided into two broad categories: general revelation and special revelation. *General revelation* usually refers to the fact that moral truth is a built-in feature of the created universe, which means that we can simply observe right and wrong, good and evil in the world around us. This revelation is called "general" because it is the revelation of reality and truth to everyone. There are at least two components of this. First, there is the idea that moral qualities are contained within the universe itself. Second, God has made humans to be the kinds of creatures who are able to perceive the moral features of the universe and recognize them as moral.

If God is the creator of everything, as Christians and other theists assert, then the common phrase, "all truth is God's truth," is clearly correct, and this must include moral truths. So we ought to expect to find some instances of near universal consensus on a moral issue. Because God is the loving and wise creator, we should anticipate signposts of objective morality to be pervasive in our world. And we do see such signposts. Returning to our example, virtually everyone agrees that torturing innocent infants just for the fun of it is wrong and evil. Also, just about everyone will also agree that saving a child from running into the street and getting hit by a car is right and good. These kinds of examples provide strong evidence for a general revelation of moral truths existing in our God-designed world. This evidence does not necessitate either total unanimous agreement or absolute certainty. There always will be arguments—however strong or weak—made for and against every moral view, and our own finite nature and imperfections will always keep us from knowing moral truth perfectly. But the moral evidence we see does provide good reasons and plausibility for divinely designed morality.

While general revelation is available to everyone, *special revelation* usually refers to moral principles, standards, and commands that have been directly revealed to specific people at specific times. From a Christian perspective, the Bible is God's revelation of truth to human beings, and that includes moral truth. For simplicity's sake, we can summarize this by saying that God has given us specific moral commands in Scripture. Since morality is founded on God's perfect moral nature, we thus have a moral duty to obey these commands.

From a Christian perspective, God's commands are not arbitrary and therefore morality must be based on something more fundamental than the commands themselves. Instead, as we said, God's very nature stands as the ultimate foundation for all moral values and duties, and that is what serves as the foundation of God's commands. When God commands, "Do not commit murder," this command does not serve as the ultimate foundation for why it is wrong to commit murder, nor is it merely arbitrary.[3] Rather, an aspect of God's nature serves as its foundation. When God issues a command, the command is consistent with his nature. God isn't simply deciding that murder is wrong, as if he could have decided that murder is not wrong. Rather, murder is wrong because it goes against God's nature, and then he decides to issue moral directives that comport with his nature. Thus, God's commands always arise out of his perfectly good moral nature rather than being arbitrary decisions of his will.

DO OUR MORAL DUTIES CONFLICT WITH ONE ANOTHER?

What if you are in a situation in which you have to tell a lie to save someone's life? In a fallen, imperfect world, we are immediately faced with the question of whether we simultaneously have moral obligations that are incompatible with one another. Are we morally obligated to both tell the truth and save the life?

In his book *Christian Ethics*, philosopher Norman Geisler has addressed this question and provided three possible answers.[6] *Unqualified Absolutism* asserts that our moral duties are absolute and unchanging, and they are never in conflict with one another (whether they appear to be in conflict or not). *Conflicting Absolutism* says that our moral obligations do sometimes conflict with one another, and when we make a choice between them, we are inevitably doing wrong. In the scenario described in the previous paragraph, this view would say that it is wrong to tell a lie and it is wrong to fail to save the life. *Graded Absolutism* agrees that there is sometimes conflict between moral duties, but it isn't wrong to choose one over the other. Rather, we are morally obligated to choose the option of the highest value or most morally significant.

In contrast to what we have been saying so far about ethical foundations, some non-Christian theistic systems may attempt to ground all moral values and duties exclusively in God's commands. This is sometimes called *voluntarism*, which generally refers to any system of philosophy that considers the will as the central or most important aspect.[4] Applied to theological ethics, voluntarism would say that nothing is more fundamental than God's will. If this were correct, the only thing that would make murder wrong is that God issued a command prohibiting murder, and had he not issued that command, then murder would not be wrong. Likewise, voluntarists think that God could have decided that adultery, theft, or torture are good and that loving one's neighbor, feeding the poor, or caring for the environment are evil. As suggested, voluntarism (at least as we have described it here) is not compatible with some core features of the Christian perspective on moral philosophy. For example, based on the biblical evidence, Christians believe that God is love.[5] If this is correct, it would be impossible for God to require hate and forbid love, for to do so would be for God to contradict his nature. This is impossible; therefore it cannot be true that God's commands serve as the ultimate foundation for good and evil, right and wrong. Rather, God's character and nature are more fundamental. God's commands arise from and are always founded on God's perfectly good moral character.

Besides moral commands in the Bible, Christians believe that God has also revealed moral truth in the person and work of Jesus Christ. Based on biblical teaching, Christians believe that Jesus Christ is one of the three persons of the triune God. Thus, Jesus is God "in the flesh," and Jesus' entire life, ministry, and moral conduct is a revelation of the perfectly good moral nature of God. This means that Jesus' life serves as a perfect moral example to which we can aspire, and his teachings represent a perfect revelation of moral truth.

Being and Doing: The Christian Moral Life

Even with a correct understanding of both moral ontology (what makes things good or evil, right or wrong) and moral epistemology (how we come to know what is good or evil, right or wrong), the practical moral life is neither automatic nor intuitive. Everyone (whether they are rightly related to God or not) will still go through life being faced with all kinds of moral situations, each of which call for a moral decision. Even among those who agree on everything we have said so far in this chapter, there is some diversity when it comes to the more practical matters of evaluating moral situations, making moral judgments, or deciding what to do. Those differences can be seen in the three primary theological approaches: deliberative, prescriptive, and relational.[7]

Deliberative Approach to Theological Ethics

Much of what we discussed regarding general revelation would be consistent with a *deliberative* approach to ethical decision-making. In this approach, we recognize that human creatures are rational, moral decision-makers made in God's image with the natural ability to perceive moral truth and engage in moral reasoning. This is not merely rationalism (the use of reason alone); rather, in theological ethics it involves a synthesis of moral reasoning and Christian theology. This model combines what naturally and universally occurs in the created world, with reflection on God's perfectly good moral nature, recognizing that human reasoning is imperfect, limited, and fallen (sinful). Nevertheless, redemption and reformation of human reason are made available through Jesus Christ. The deliberative model also normally assumes that moral instruction for the faithful (believers) is ultimately intended for everyone. Moral values and standards may be discerned by reasoning well, including philosophical thinking and other arenas like science, imagination, or intuition—even if Scripture or Christian theology are not explicitly referenced or commended. Thomas Aquinas (thirteenth-century theologian and philosopher) models the deliberative approach, integrating Scripture and Christian theology with Aristotle's philosophy.

One significant strength of this model is that it speaks to all people, including those who don't necessarily accept special divine revelation as (equally or ultimately) authoritative for morality. It also works well for those who find strong connections between Christian norms and philosophical ones. For example, some perceive tight associations between the rightness of "loving your neighbor as yourself" and demonstrating empathy or altruism, or the virtually universal condemnation of murder and adultery. One substantial weakness of this approach is that it may be accompanied by a tendency to minimize or eliminate the important worldview basis for morality. Even if some universal moral norms are revealed in creation, complete consensus across different worldviews on exactly what these norms are generally involves a relatively small number: murder and adultery topping most lists of moral evil, while justice and courage are nearly universally seen as morally good. Furthermore, special revelation is more comprehensive and more specific on particular moral issues. The New Testament alone contains hundreds of explicit moral imperatives—plus many implicit ones—along with numerous principles to draw out from narrative passages and other genres (like parables). It seems to us, then, a "both/and" approach (including both general revelation and special revelation) makes the most sense—with emphasis given to Scripture and Christian theology.

Prescriptive Approach to Theological Ethics

The *prescriptive* approach to ethical decision-making is based on divine revelation and biblical imperatives—especially virtues, principles, and commands—intended to provide theological and practical guidance for human behavior. We described this as special revelation. The Ten Commandments (see Ex. 20:2–17; Deut. 5:6–21) and Jesus' Sermon on the Mount (see Matt. 5–7) reflect a prescriptive approach. It ties directly to a biblical worldview and focuses on specific moral prescriptions for behavior, providing an unchanging standard for moral conduct—regardless of changes in historical and cultural context. Ultimately, God's character and will ground moral decision-making for the individual, the faith community, and (perhaps) society. Some prescriptivists emphasize the life and teachings of Jesus. Others focus mainly on the letters in the New Testament. And some take a more comprehensive approach that encompasses the whole New Testament or entire Bible.

One positive aspect of the prescriptive approach is its commitment to the authority of Scripture. This special divine revelation speaks God's trustworthy word on moral issues—moral truths relevant for today and always. Ultimately, theology and ethics are inseparably linked, revealing God's moral character and will, as well as divine design for human moral flourishing. One negative aspect of this model is that its proponents are sometimes tempted to make the mistake of thinking that Christian ethics equals either moralism (an approach to the ethical life that focuses exclusively on adopting customs or conventions of behavior) or legalism (the belief that we can please God or attain salvation through performing the right kinds or right quantity of morally virtuous actions). Jesus regularly addressed the problems with moralism and legalism that were evident among religious leaders like the Pharisees and Sadducees. (See Matt. 23.) From a Christian perspective, the moral life is not about simply obeying God's commands or trying to adopt Jesus' moral example—the moral life is neither moralism nor legalism. Rather, from a biblical perspective, the Christian life starts with having a proper relationship with God through faith in Jesus Christ, which then enables a person to live a moral life—empowered by the Spirit!

The Bible indicates that each of us is born into a state of relational estrangement with God and thus in need of reconciliation. Each of us is "lost" and needs salvation; we are "dead" and need to be made alive again through a new, spiritual birth. Much of the biblical description of the moral life is provided in a context that is subsequent to this new birth, as God works to transform the heart of the person, which then yields (among other things) good moral conduct as evidence of the transformation. Thus, obeying God's commands is, in many ways, the result of the transforming work that God brings about in the human heart. So to turn moral prescriptions into moralism or legalism is to miss the point of God's moral instructions—to have us flourish in relationship with God and others! God knows—and has divinely designed—what is morally best for humans. We are called to respond to the divine design with good hearts and motives and strive toward the moral life that God has revealed to us, knowing that he has designed it to allow us to flourish.

Relational Approach to Theological Ethics

The *relational* approach to ethical decision-making centers on dynamic interaction with God—the Holy Spirit, in particular. Through this divine encounter, the individual (or faith community) is called to respond appropriately, with both gratitude and obedience, to God's leading on moral matters and situations. Ideally, the person (or group) is motivated by love for God and God's love for humankind. Becoming/being virtuous and having integrity are essential for moral decision-making; learning to do the right thing comes from learning to be the right kind of person (or community) of faith. Morality is essentially based on relationships—with God, with others in the Christian community, and in the world. Depending on the particular individual or faith community, Scripture may be recognized as (1) the ultimate authority by which we can confirm or correct what we experience in our encounters with God in moral situations, (2) a record of how God previously spoke about a moral concern but not necessarily how God may be speaking today, or (3) irrelevant for today. We hold that (1) is the most plausible view from theological, philosophical, and historical standpoints.

One positive characteristic of the relational model is that it holds that moral decisions ought to be impacted by relationships—preeminently, the relationship between a perfectly good and wise God and human persons made in God's image to do right and to be good. Thus, biblical-based relational ethics focuses on God's character, will, and presence meeting human character, will, and response to God in the moral moment. One negative aspect of this model is that it can tend to lead toward subjectivism and relativism—even disconnected from scriptural imperatives or principles—thus undercutting the objectivity of God's universal design of morality. Unfortunately, this mistake is common today. For example, someone (or some group) may claim that "God told me (or us) that divine judgment is just fake news and will never happen because God is pure love," even though Scripture is clear that God is both loving and just, and both of these divine attributes are true and noncontradictory.

Assessing the Models of Moral Decision-Making

Each moral decision-making model we've discussed provides something important to theological ethics: deliberative combines faith and reason; prescriptive focuses on biblically grounded imperatives; relational is centered on encountering God in the moral moment. We believe that, rather than just one of these approaches being sufficient to carry the whole weight of ethical decision-making, a thoughtful synthesis is better: a quality *cumulative approach*. Moral decision-making from a theological perspective ought to consider the strengths and emphases of each model, appropriately weighing/balancing each aspect in light of the others. We note that one aspect likely will outweigh the others, depending on particular variables and situations. This reminds us that no individual or group will achieve perfection in moral decision-making in this lifetime—although always seeking to be faithful and obedient to God's moral will for us is both right and good. Perhaps even more important, our moral weaknesses and failings ought to remind us of our need to call on God's grace and forgiveness, acknowledging our need for divine strength for human moral flourishing

Conclusion

Much more could be said about the ways theologians approach moral philosophy. Here, however, we attempted to introduce you to the basic framework by examining the most important ideas. At the start of the chapter, we suggested that you should ask this question: "How would the project of ethics be different when approached theologically?" Now that we've explained a little bit of how we answer this question, we hope that you understand its significance. Primarily, we hope you see that belief in God cannot be treated as a topic separate from the topic of how moral questions are addressed. Your moral philosophy will be driven by your theology (and worldview). So in one sense, everyone who is engaged in moral philosophy must approach the topic theologically. We noted that God provides the ontological foundation for morality (why things are good or evil, right or wrong), and God is the source of moral epistemology (how we know moral truth). Whether or not you believe God's exists, you must take a hard look at whether your worldview can answer these fundamental questions about the nature of morality. We also discussed several important, practical aspects of moral philosophy, based on a theological starting point. Again, whether a person believes in God's existence or not, all of us need to address these practical questions as we seek to navigate the often-tumultuous waters of ethical decision-making. We think that a theological approach—specifically a Christian approach—provides real, practical answers that other approaches lack and provides a more comprehensive picture of the moral dimension of our lives.

Questions for Reflection

1. How do a person's worldview assumptions, especially about the most fundamental nature of reality, impact how that person understands the foundation of moral values?
2. Why do you think that some moral norms seem to have almost universal agreement across all persons, cultures, and times?
3. Are you surprised that ethical decision-making from a Christian perspective involves more than just following a biblical command? Why or why not?

For Further Reading

Adams, Robert Merrihew. *Finite and Infinite Goods: A Framework for Ethics.* New York: Oxford University Press, 1999.

Geisler, Norman L. *Christian Ethics: Contemporary Issues and Options.* 2nd ed. Grand Rapids: Baker Academic, 2010.

Rae, Scott B. *Moral Choices: An Introduction to Ethics*, 4th ed. Grand Rapids: Zondervan Academic, 2018.

NOTES

1. Kant's philosophy was undergirded by theism, but his system of deontology focuses on human reason, not God.

2. It is not necessary for us to provide a full articulation and defense of this traditional conception of God. Rather, we are simply offering an explanation of how this doctrine can be used by Christian philosophers to develop a more robust account of objective moral values and duties when compared to simple theism.

3. See the previous chapter, on the discussion of the Euthyphro dilemma. For additional helpful discussion on goodness being grounded in God's nature, see Robert Merrihew Adams, *Finite and Infinite Goods: A Framework for Ethics* (New York: Oxford University Press, 1999); and William P. Alston, "What Euthyphro Should Have Said," in *Philosophy of Religion: A Reader and Guide*, ed. William Lane Craig (New Brunswick, NJ: Rutgers University Press, 2002), 283–98.

4. The Latin term for will is *voluntas*, and this serves as the root for the English words *volunteer*, *voluntary*, and *volition*.

5. See, e.g., 1 John 4:8.

6. Norman Geisler, *Christian Ethics: Contemporary Issues and Options*, 2nd ed. (Grand Rapids: Baker Academic, 2010), 66–114.

7. For the following section on approaches to theological ethics, we are deeply indebted to Dennis P. Hollinger, *Choosing the Good: Christian Ethics in a Complex World* (Grand Rapids: Baker Academic, 2002), 128–48.

CHAPTER 22

What Is Bioethics?

Matters of Life and Death

In 1975, Karen Ann Quinlan slipped into a coma while attending a party with friends. Even though some witnesses suggested that she had consumed both alcohol and drugs at the party, the official cause of the coma was never determined. Quinlan suffered from periods of respiratory failure, which led to severe, permanent brain damage. As her condition continued to deteriorate, she entered a persistent vegetative state, and doctors concluded that she would never recover. Quinlan's adoptive parents requested that the ventilator be removed so that she could return to a natural state. Fearing legal repercussions if this action caused Quinlan to die, the hospital refused to remove the ventilator. In a landmark case, the Quinlan family filed suit against the hospital. In March of 1976, the Supreme Court of New Jersey ruled that the hospital was required to honor the request to remove the ventilator.[1] This case has become one of the prime examples cited when dealing with the issue of whether an individual or family has the right to determine the extent of medical treatment taken to prolong life. Since the medical technology existed to keep Quinlan's respiratory system functional indefinitely, should that technology have been employed for the purpose of extending her life?

Difficult questions such as this belong to the field known as *bioethics*. This field of study is related to the work done by many different disciplines. In fact, there isn't firm agreement on exactly what bioethics is or what specific issues fall within its purview. Generally speaking, bioethics is a field of applied ethics dealing with the wide range of moral issues that arise in medicine, biology, biomedical research, biotechnology, healthcare administration, and healthcare law.

This can include a broad range of issues, such as transhumanism, bionics, laboratory-grown human organs, cloning, and biological experimentation on animals. Surely as technology advances, an untold number of as-yet-undiscovered issues will also be included in this field of study. For the purposes of this chapter, however, we will narrow that focus and limit our discussion to moral problems pertaining to the beginning and end stages of human life (what might be called the "margins" of life), with special focus on moral issues pertaining to the application of medical care and medical technology at these stages.

Typically, the moral questions at the margins of life arise as a result of technological advancements in the field of medicine that have brought about new possibilities for creating, extending, or shortening human life and for relieving pain and suffering. At the beginning stages of life, reproductive technologies have afforded aspiring parents the ability to produce children when it would otherwise be impossible. Medical technology can also be used to end life prior to birth through the act of abortion. Additionally, technological advancements have allowed for the creation of human embryos for the purpose of medical or scientific research. At the end stages, life can now be extended far beyond what would be naturally possible in the face of disease or severe injury. Technology can also be employed to end human life earlier than what would naturally occur for the purposes of relieving or preventing suffering. Before examining how some of these issues might be addressed, it is important to first examine some foundational principles for making moral decisions in the area of bioethics.

A Principled Approach to Bioethics

As with all matters of morality, decisions in the area of bioethics are based on fundamental beliefs and assumptions. One's worldview—including beliefs about the nature of reality, the fundamental nature of humanity, and the meaning of life—has a significant influence on the moral principles that are applied to bioethics. There is no doubt that religious commitments will bear significant weight. However, both nonreligious and religious persons alike equally rely on their most fundamental beliefs as they search for answers to complex bioethical questions. Certain nonreligious principles for bioethics have arisen and become standard for addressing problems, and they are often taught to students entering healthcare professions. Philosophers typically focus their discussion on the principles of autonomy, nonmaleficence, beneficence, utility, and justice.[2] These principles are often seen as fundamental and are used to create rules that can be applied in specific cases for making decisions regarding appropriate medical care or the implementation of medical technology.

Autonomy refers to the idea that each person has the inherent right to self-determination, free from coercion or interference from other persons, including medical treatment against her or his will. When autonomy is respected, it places significant restrictions on the ability of persons to make medical decisions on behalf of another person. Respecting autonomy would lead to rules such as a prohibition against medical treatment unless a person has voluntarily consented to that treatment or a rule requiring doctors to provide patients with true and complete information so that patients' decisions are well-informed. While autonomy is often seen as one of the most fundamental and important principles, it has been overridden in some cases in which the patient does not have the capacity to make decisions regarding medical care (such as with Karen Ann Quinlan). It is also widely acknowledged that parents have the authority to make decisions for their immature children, who lack the rational ability to make well-informed decisions.

Nonmaleficence means doing no harm, and it demands avoiding intentional harm to others. This principle is often expressed in the ancient Latin phrase *primum non nocere*, meaning "first, do no harm." While the origins of this phrase are unknown, some form of it has been used in oaths taken by new physicians upon entering their fields of medical practice. This principle is important because it could be that the application of some kind of medical treatment or intervention could actually cause more harm than good or bring about a great risk of harm that is higher than the risk associated with the condition being treated. This principle might lead to specific rules to prevent harm, such as a requirement to ensure that no mistakes are made in the type or dosage of medication when it is administered or the implementation of procedures that would guarantee sanitary conditions in an operating suite.

Beneficence refers to taking actions that help bring about a person's good. All recognize that it isn't enough to simply avoid doing harm. Rather, specific action must be taken to bring about benefit. This is perhaps one of the most obvious principles because it is commonly taken for granted that the goal of medicine and the application of medical technology is to heal or relieve the suffering of those needing care. This principle might lead to a requirement to treat those who are in urgent, dire need of care as a priority over matters such as the patient's ability to pay for the services rendered. This principle might also lead to rules that require physicians to take into consideration the patient's values and life goals and to define the good as the patient would define it, rather than by some impersonal or arbitrary standard.

Utility is sometimes incorporated into the discussions of beneficence and nonmaleficence, but it does represent something unique that can be highlighted. *Utility* refers not just to doing good and avoiding harm but rather to achieving the best balance of good and harm. This principle requires that goods and harms, risks and rewards, be balanced when making treatment decisions. For example, specific medications are known to cause harm in patients. However, these medications are still used because the benefits they bring are thought to outweigh the harms they might cause. Utility might lead to rules designed to help physicians take into consideration as many of the benefits and harms as possible in order to arrive at a proper balance as they administer care to a patient.

Justice, in this context, refers to the fair application of medical care and treatment or the fair distribution of medical resources. This principle tends to be the most difficult to describe, as there are many competing notions of justice. There might be disagreement, for example, about whether a person ought to receive care in proportion to her need or in proportion to her predicted ability to make a positive contribution to society. For example, if two people are equally in need of care, but one is a prison inmate serving a life sentence, should care be applied equally? Or should the priority be given to the person who is not in prison because she could potentially provide a greater benefit to society? What other factors could make one person "deserve" care more than another? Despite the difficulty in defining what justice is and how it can be applied, it is easy to see how some rules derive from this principle. For example, healthcare facilities commonly have specific rules dictating that care must be rendered without regard to a person's ethnicity, sex, or religion because to discriminate based on these factors is thought to be unjust.

These principles are widely accepted, and most philosophers think that they ought to govern moral decisions made in the area of bioethics. While those principles might be good, and we all might agree that they should inform our decision-making, an essential question remains: Why these principles and not others? As philosophers, we must think carefully about what beliefs and assumptions lie behind these principles in order to answer the more fundamental questions in bioethics.

Christian Worldview Considerations

Outside of religious contexts, principles such as those mentioned are often simply acknowledged, adopted, and then applied in the context of creating rules and policies in specific healthcare contexts. Many assume that these principles are fundamental, but they are not. Consider, for example, the principle of autonomy. Perhaps there is universal agreement that autonomy is important and should be respected. Even so, it is still essential to ask the more fundamental question of why autonomy ought to be respected. Indeed, if the deeper why question is not addressed, we are at a much higher risk of autonomy being overshadowed by other concerns that may arise in a stressful, time-sensitive, life-or-death situation. Whether or not the principles we mentioned are correct, any principles that might be adopted must be firmly anchored to deeper worldview commitments, or else they are at risk of being set aside or overlooked.

One relevant foundational aspect of the Christian worldview is that humans are finite and imperfect. From a Christian perspective, humans are not the ultimate source of wisdom, knowledge, or authority over life. God is the creator of all things. God holds ultimate authority over matters of life and death, alone knows all things, and is perfectly wise. Moreover, God's design for creation is for it to reflect his perfectly good character. Christians further believe that God is intimately involved in the day-to-day affairs of humanity and is interested in our ultimate well-being. For these reasons, Christians often pray and ask God for help when faced with difficult moral problems. God responds by providing wisdom and guidance, and he sometimes intervenes supernaturally. (See Prov. 3:5–6; James 1:5.)

Another central component of the Christian worldview is the belief that God has created humans in his image. This has several important implications for bioethics. First, being made in God's image indicates that all human persons are intrinsically valuable and are thus worthy of dignity and respect. This principle demands that we refrain from doing harm to others and that we actively seek to care for others. Second, humans occupy a unique place in God's creation and are thus of greater value than other parts of the created order. Third, all human persons are equally valuable. This means that all human persons have autonomy, in the sense that no person has the proper authority to stand in a superior position over another, for example when making personal decisions regarding medical treatment.

Christians also believe that the brokenness and suffering in the world—including the suffering that comes from disease—is the tragic result of human rebellion against God's good purposes. God's ultimate desire is to bring an end to all suffering. Until that happens, Christians believe that God often works in and through suffering to bring about spiritual growth in the life of the one who is suffering and to bear witness to his desire for all to be finally set free from their personal rebellion and restored to a right relationship with him. (See John 8:31–32; 2 Cor. 5:17–21; 1 Tim. 2:4; 2 Peter 3:9.)

Finally, it is difficult to overstate the significance of the Christian doctrine of salvation for bioethics. This core doctrine reminds us that God is interested in our ultimate destiny far more than our immediate comfort. The doctrine of salvation gives Christians an eternal perspective on all things. Our physical life on this earth is exceedingly valuable, but at the same time we also recognize that life does not end at the grave. God has created us to live forever, so we hold a more reserved perspective on the lengths to which we may reasonably go to relieve suffering or to preserve or extend our physical lives. Christians generally believe that we should seek to provide comfort and relieve suffering whenever possible, but we also recognize that relieving suffering is not the ultimate goal (Matt. 16:26; John 16:33).

Specific Problems in Bioethics

With these principles and worldview considerations in mind, we can now address specific problems in bioethics. For each problem, we will very briefly describe the nature of the problem and make some specific comments on how we can begin to address the problem, with special focus on a Christian perspective for each one. For each one, we encourage you to think through your own worldview commitments, your fundamental beliefs about the nature of humanity and the meaning of life, and how they might impact what moral decisions you would make in each of these areas.

Abortion and the Beginning of Life

Abortion, as we are defining it here, is a deliberate act of intervention to terminate a pregnancy before its natural conclusion by destroying and removing an embryo or fetus. This is sometimes called medical abortion or elective abortion. This is distinguished from spontaneous abortion (often called "miscarriage"), which is the unexpected natural death of the fetus with no deliberate human actions intended to kill the fetus. Elective abortions are performed using chemicals or surgical instruments, at all stages of fetal development, right up through the time when the baby could survive outside the mother's uterus.

Identifying all the moral issues pertaining to abortion is difficult, especially when there is disagreement about what a fetus is and whether the status of the fetus changes throughout its development (for example, does the fetus become something new, or gain rights, at a particular stage in its development). There is near universal agreement that killing an innocent human person is murder and is therefore morally wrong. Because of this, when dealing with a complicated issue like abortion, it can sometimes be helpful to focus on the simple but essential question that tends to shape the entire debate: Is the fetus a human person? There is little doubt that as soon as a human egg is fertilized by a human sperm (the moment of conception), a distinct human organism begins to live.[3] The controversial question, however, is whether that human organism is also a human person. If the answer is no, then the fetus does not have the value, rights, or autonomy that a human person has, and many arguments against abortion tend to become moot. If the answer is yes, then all elective abortions seem to be morally equivalent to murder, and many arguments in favor of abortion likewise become moot.

Nearly everyone agrees that once a baby is born, it is a human person. Many philosophers point out that, while birth is a significant moment, it seems arbitrary to say that the fetus is not a human person immediately prior to birth. After all, there is no fixed moment of biological development that marks when a baby could be born and when it couldn't. In a famous and often-cited essay on this topic, Judith Jarvis Thompson (who argues that abortion is morally permissible) agrees, as she says, "I am inclined to think that we shall probably have to agree that the fetus has already become a human person well before birth."[4] This has led some to suggest that the fetus's ability to survive outside the uterus (sometimes called "viability") is the dividing line, before which the fetus is not a person, and after which it is. But, again, there is no specific moment or stage that marks viability.[5] Others suggest that the key moment occurs when the embryo is implanted in the uterus, when certain kinds of brain activity can be measured, when the fetus is capable of feeling pain, or when there is a detectable heartbeat.[6] It seems clear that any moment that is selected (whether it is viability, heartbeat detection, brain activity, or even birth) is simply another moment in the continuous development of the same human organism. After all, none of these markers occur at the exact same stage of development for each fetus. Thus, it remains to be seen whether it is even possible to clearly define a non-arbitrary moment in development at which point the fetus becomes a person with rights. It seems that the burden of proof would fall to the person who wishes to assert that there is such a non-arbitrary moment. While this will undoubtedly remain a highly controversial point, absent this proof, it seems to us that the most commonsense position to hold is that the human organism is a valuable human person, with rights and dignity, from the moment of conception, through the moments immediately before birth, and onward throughout its natural life.

Some in the debate concede that the fetus may indeed be a human person but that abortion still might be morally justified.[7] In most of these cases, it is presented as a conflict between the autonomy of the mother and the rights of the unborn child. In some cases, it is supposed, the autonomy of the mother and her inherent right of self-determination override any concerns about the value or rights of the fetus. However, if the mother and father knowingly and voluntarily engaged in sexual activity, it seems that they are also voluntarily taking on a moral duty to care for a baby that is created as a direct result of that voluntary activity. Thus, even if a pregnancy is unplanned or the baby is unwanted, the more fundamental moral questions do not change. From a Christian perspective, the virtues of love and self-sacrifice seem to be especially relevant, and while many (rightly) emphasize the unique role of the mother in caring for the child, it seems clear that the father equally shares the moral duties that arise in this situation.

Addressing abortion can also put other issues in bioethics into perspective. For example, birth control methods that are designed to allow fertilization but prevent implantation in the uterus (such as some hormonal birth control pills and some intra-uterine devices—IUDs) seem to be morally problematic for the same reasons that abortion is problematic, since they result in the death of the embryo. Also, fertility treatments (such as in vitro fertilization—IVF) that knowingly create human embryos that are subsequently discarded, frozen, or otherwise prevented from developing into full-term babies are also problematic for the same reasons. Most forms of embryonic research require the creation of living human embryos for purposes that will result in their destruction are similarly problematic. If the human embryo is not a human person, these kinds of activities can be justified on a variety of moral grounds, and indeed some of them may seem to be morally good choices. However, if the embryo is a human person, then any deliberate activity that results in the death of an embryo would seem to carry with it the same moral weight as any other instance of killing any other innocent person. Again, this will remain controversial. From our perspective as Christians, however, we seek to navigate these issues with a keen focus on the inherent sanctity and value of human life and on biblical commands and principles that prohibit murder and require love, care, and respect.

Suffering, Euthanasia, and the End of Life

The case of Karen Ann Quinlan, highlighted at the start of this chapter, brings into focus some of the moral issues involved in caring for those who are suffering or are progressing through the later stages of terminal illness or injury. When Quinlan's adoptive parents asked the hospital to remove life-sustaining medical care, they were asking for what is called *termination of life support* (TLS). As its name implies, this is a deliberate act of removing care that is sustaining the life of the person who is suffering. Whether or not TLS is morally justifiable depends on a wide range of factors, including the wishes that the patient may have expressed regarding measures to prolong life, whether the life sustaining measures are extra-ordinary, and whether there is reasonable hope for recovery. It seems that TLS would be least problematic from a moral perspective if there is no reasonable hope for recovery or the patient has a directive in place indicating that they do not wish to have such life sustaining measures. Removal of life support returns the patient to a natural state, allowing natural processes to run their course.

While TLS can be seen as simply letting the person die, the practice known as euthanasia is the deliberate act of killing a person prior to natural death, usually by the administration of a lethal dosage of some drug. The name of this practice is derived from combining the Greek words *eu thanatos*, meaning "good death," and advocates typically say that euthanasia is necessary to relieve the suffering of a person who is already very near death because of the severity of her condition. While the desire to end a person's pain and suffering can be a powerful motivator for euthanasia, this kind of action is morally problematic for a variety of reasons. First, it is sometimes carried out when the patient is unaware of the actions being taken and therefore cannot give consent. Second, in most cases, alternative treatments that can eliminate or greatly reduce pain are available, such that death is not the only way to relieve suffering. Third, once euthanasia is considered to be an acceptable option to end suffering, it is easy to see that some instances of severe suffering may tempt physicians to carry it out even when there is some reasonable hope of recovery. Despite its name, our perspective on euthanasia is that it is never "good death."

In both TLS and euthanasia, the patient is usually in such dire straits that they are not able to rationally reflect on their condition or their hope of recov-ery. Sometimes, however, a person is suffering from a condition that has not yet reached the more severe stages. Facing the likelihood of future suffering, some patients have sought the assistance of medical professionals in hastening death in a practice commonly known as physician-assisted suicide. Because of the negative stigma associated with the word *suicide*, this procedure is some-times referred to as medical aid in dying. Typically, this is carried out by the physician providing the means of suicide (usually a drug) and the instructions for the person to use these means to commit suicide. In some jurisdictions where this practice is legal, persons can pursue physician-assisted suicide even when their death is not reasonably foreseeable, such as when they are suffering from depression or post-traumatic stress disorder. Even if someone were to try to make a case that a person has the natural right to commit suicide, that isn't precisely what is in view here. Because other persons are involved in bringing about the death, physician-assisted suicide carries with it additional moral impli-cations. Even though the person dying might be thought of as a patient from the perspective of the medical professionals involved, and even though the person dying is actively seeking death, it seems that the process of hastening the person's death, even when done by a medical professional, carries with it many of the same implications as murder.

Conclusion

With rapid advances in medical technology, it seems as if nothing is impossible regarding life and death. What is beyond our imagination today may become a common practice in the future, and with it will arise a host of new moral problems and implications. It is essential for philosophers to anchor their moral judgments in fundamental principles and worldview considerations. If we are able to do this, then (in a sense) we already have the answers to the unknown future questions in bioethics. At the centerpiece of a Christian outlook on bio-ethics, for example, is the virtue of love. If we recognize that every human person, regardless of their physical condition or state of development, is a creature made in God's image, with intrinsic value, this naturally moves us to love. Thus, bioethics is not simply about finding the right moral answers or doing the right thing from a moral perspective. Rather, it is about placing proper value on all persons and doing everything we can to promote their flourishing.

Questions for Reflection

1. To what extent should your own autonomy be the ultimate authority in medical decisions involving your care? Under what circumstances is it justifiable to allow others to overrule your autonomy?
2. Do some people deserve medical care more than others? Why or why not?
3. In the case of Karen Ann Quinlan (based on the limited information provided in this chapter), what would have to be true of her condition for you to say that it would be wrong to remove life support?

For Further Reading

Beauchamp, Tom L., and James F. Childress. *Principles of Biomedical Ethics*. New York: Oxford University Press, 2001.

Foreman, Mark Wesley, and Lindsay C. Leonard. *Christianity and Modern Medicine: Foundations for Bioethics*. Grand Rapids: Kregel Academic, 2022.

Rae, Scott B., and Paul M. Cox. *Bioethics: A Christian Approach in a Pluralistic Age*. Grand Rapids: Eerdmans, 1999.

Rae, Scott B. *Moral Choices: An Introduction to Ethics*, 4th ed. Grand Rapids: Zondervan Academic, 2018.

Vaughn, Lewis. *Bioethics: Principles, Issues, and Cases*. New York: Oxford University Press, 2010.

NOTES

1. For more about Karen Ann Quinlan's story, see www.karenannquinlanhospice.org/about/history/; Joseph Quinlan, Julia Quinlan, and Phyllis Battelle, *Karen Ann: The Quinlans Tell Their Story* (New York: Doubleday, 1977); and Scott B. Rae, *Moral Choices: An Introduction to Ethics*, 4th ed. (Grand Rapids: Zondervan Academic, 2018), 234-35.

2. Most contemporary work on this topic cites Tom L. Beauchamp and James F. Childress, *Principles of Biomedical Ethics* (New York: Oxford University Press, 2001). Beauchamp and Childress omit the principle of utility from their discussion. Lewis Vaughn, *Bioethics: Principles, Issues, and Cases* (New York: Oxford University Press, 2010), addresses the same basic principles but incorporates nonmaleficence into the principle of beneficence and adds utility, which Beauchamp and Childress seem to incorporate into their notion of beneficence.

3. Mary Anne Warren, who argues that abortion is morally permissible, admits that the human organism "if nurtured and allowed to develop . . . may eventually become a person." Mary Anne Warren, "On the Moral and Legal Status of Abortion," in *Exploring Ethics: An Introductory Anthology*, 3rd ed., ed. Steven M. Cahn (New York: Oxford University Press, 2014), 197.

4. Judith Jarvis Johnson, "A Defense of Abortion," *Philosophy and Public Affairs* 1, no. 1 (Fall 1971): 47.

5. See, for example, American College of Obstetricians and Gynecologists, "Facts Are Important: Understanding and Navigating Viability," www.acog.org/advocacy/facts-are-important/understanding-and-navigating-viability. In this work, ACOG sets percentage values representing the average chance of fetal survival at specific weeks of development.

6. Some have attempted to define specific stages in the development of the fetus by indicating the average number of weeks gestation at which the heartbeat is detectible, the fetus has certain kinds of brain activity, or is able to feel pain. These are important factors to consider, but our point here is that each of these markers is on an uninterrupted process of development. Thus, it is arbitrary to attempt to settle on one "defining moment" after which the fetus is a person, but before which it is not.

7. Judith Jarvis Thompson attempts to make one such case. Thompson, "Defense of Abortion," 48.

CHAPTER 23

What Is Sexual Ethics?

Matters of Sexuality, Identity, and Gender

Humans share a lot in common—our struggle with sexuality included! Questions that many of us have include, "How should we understand sexuality in the first place? Do objective standards of right and wrong exist for sex? If so, what or who determines those standards? For people who are single or gay/lesbian/bisexual, is it right or wrong to have sex? Why should marriage matter when it comes to sex—especially since so many unmarried people engage in sex? Are biological sex and gender identity the same thing or different things? Does my worldview have anything to do with how I'm understanding sexuality? And what role does sexuality play in determining personal identity?" In today's hyper-sexed atmosphere, questions like these beg for responses. This chapter is an *introduction* to sexual ethics and therefore can't possibly provide a full-blown treatment of this topic (for book-length works, see our "For Further Reading" suggestions). Moreover, we recognize widespread disagreement exists on this subject matter—across academic, cultural, and religious spheres. Among the reasons for the divergences are differing *worldviews*, *authorities*, and *interpretations*. Because these factors powerfully shape our sexuality views, it's improbable that we'll convince many readers to change their view and support our position. Nonetheless, we hope to explain, support, and encourage you to consider a traditional (or historic) Christian view of sexual ethics, as opposed to alternative viewpoints (whether inside or outside of a Christian framework).

You'll notice our argument centers on belief in divinely intended (or divinely designed) sexuality. We see this communicated preeminently through special revelation (Scripture), as well as through Christian community (the church) and general revelation (creation). Of course, some won't agree with this. Perhaps many theists and most Christian theists will agree, although some will differ on certain issues related to divine intentionality (or design) for sexuality. For instance, those holding an *Affirming View* (or *Revisionist View*) tend to claim that biological, anthropological, psychological, sociological, or other findings undermine certain aspects of the *Traditional View*, especially related to the latter's advocacy of monogamous, male-female marriage as the exclusive context for divinely intended sexual union.[1]

> Ultimately, one's view of sexual ethics depends on whether one believes the triune God has created sexuality (as divinely intended or designed) and has spoken authoritatively (and with the goal of human flourishing) on essential moral/sexual matters through the (infallible and trustworthy) Scriptures.

While we understand the major arguments put forth for the Affirming View, we remain unconvinced. For example, while we may agree with William Loader's interpretation of biblical passages on same-sex attitudes/behaviors (especially Rom. 1:24–27), we disagree with his claim that we now know better (e.g., scientifically) than the apostle Paul concerning same-sex attitudes/behaviors and are thus free to "supplement" (i.e., adjust) for our own time. On the contrary, we affirm Scripture's infallibility and trustworthiness on moral/sexual matters that it affirms or teaches and thus its ultimate authority and objective truth-bearing on these matters. This leads us to maintain the Traditional View on same-sex attitudes/behaviors and related sexual-ethics concerns.[2] Regardless of which view is held, or why, we believe all are called to embody civility and humility amidst advocacy and disagreement—a welcome contrast to many cultural, academic, and church-related trends today.

The historic Christian faith presents a rather distinct sexuality that often contrasts with subjectively centered and culturally derived perspectives. We understand you might disagree with our position, but know that we don't intend to irritate or disappoint you, but rather hope to encourage your thoughtful engagement with this important subject matter.

Approach, Goals, Commitments

Our modest goals for this chapter include (a) defining/explaining sexual ethics and related key concepts/terms—primarily as we understand and use them, recognizing that widespread disagreement, polarization, and politicization over these terms persists; (b) discussing, evaluating, and responding to some major sexual-ethics concerns; and (c) supporting our particular Christian sexual-ethics perspective, utilizing philosophical and theological reasoning alongside our worldview commitments. Three interrelated convictions inform our approach: (1) the Christian Scriptures present/reveal God's moral will for humankind and thus are ultimately authoritative and trustworthy when speaking on matters of sexuality; (2) objective norms and values exist (such as truth, goodness, and rightness) as revealed in God's written word and created world; and (3) the greatest moral "ought" for our lives is to love the Lord our God with all our being and to love our neighbor as ourselves. We understand these two greatest commandments to be non-negotiable for all Christ-followers, whether agreeing or disagreeing on specific sexual issues.[3]

Everyone holds certain philosophical and theological commitments, whether based on theistic, pantheistic, or atheistic frameworks. Moreover, all ethical terms/concepts are understood and interpreted from within particular worldviews, rather than from some supposedly neutral standpoint. We don't mean there are never shared meanings among different worldviews or religions. We do mean often interpretations or illustrations of terms/concepts tend to differ, especially those considered vital (e.g., right, wrong, good, evil, sexuality, gender, identity).[4] So it's important that we define and evaluate key sexual-ethics terms/concepts in connection with our view of reality. Consequently, we've chosen to give significant space to defining/explaining major sexual-ethics terminology and, in select instances, providing additional analysis, background information, claims, and/or arguments that challenge certain views while supporting others.

Definitions and Select Critiques of Key Sexual Ethics Terms and Concepts

Sexual Ethics

The pivotal term, *sexual ethics*, involves everything connected with sexuality from a moral perspective—particularly as to the rightness or wrongness, goodness or badness of thoughts, motivations, and actions. Grenz and Smith define sexual ethics similarly: "The study of the moral framework that pertains to human sexuality, the application of moral considerations to human sexual relationships."[5] Consequently, sexual ethics is highly controversial, intensely debated, and morally significant. No social-cultural context seems exempt from it: families, friendships, social media, entertainment, sports, schools, corporations, politics, courts, medicine, the military, and

> Sexual ethics is the study of the moral framework that pertains to human sexuality, the application of moral considerations to human sexual relationships.
> —Stanley J. Grenz and Jay T. Smith, *Pocket Dictionary of Ethics*, 107

the church. Human biology, psychology, sociology, philosophy, and theology are prime disciplines examining sexual ethics.

We're convinced this topic matters deeply since every human being is inherently a sexual being—whether or not he or she will ever have sex! Many scholars agree that human beings just are sexual beings. Perhaps we are also "connectional beings" as Jonathan Grant argues, which makes caring for people's sexual and relational lives so crucial (particularly for discipleship). Thus, a Christian perspective understands human sexuality as an essential part of our being and therefore irreducible to just sex; sexuality includes sexual desire (*eros*) and is emotional and social, covering "a broad range of human longing."[6] The biblical worldview understands sexuality as "integrated into the total person."[7]

> Sustaining faithful relationships and encouraging the ability to live disciplined sexual lives may be one of the most influential missional tasks of the contemporary church as we witness to the kingdom of God in the midst of a sexually confused and relationally fatalistic culture.
> —Jonathan Grant, *Divine Sex*, 25

Sexuated/Biological Sex/Intersex

Sexuated is a philosophical term describing sexuality as the "state or condition of being biologically sexed as either male or female."[8] Mark Yarhouse (Psy.D., Director of Sexual and Gender Identity Institute at Wheaton College) notes that biological sex may be understood as "male or female (typically with reference to chromosomes, gonads, sex hormones, and internal reproductive anatomy and external genitalia)."[9] Male sperm carries an X or Y chromosome and females carry the X chromosome. Chromosomes are the markers of sex. Thus, XY chromosomes are the chromosomal arrangement typical of human males, and XX chromosomes are the chromosomal arrangement typical of human females. Tomas Bogardus provides further perspective: "[A] male is an organism with the function of producing sperm. When the organism is functioning *properly*—when it is flourishing, fully mature, uninjured, healthy, and so on—this organism will produce sperm. If there's no disorder, no interference, no malfunction, that's what will happen. That's the plan, so to speak. And similarly for females, with regard to ova. That's all it is to be male or to be female. Simple."[10]

Biological sex would appear to be an objective matter.[11] Even so, in rare cases, babies are born intersex.[12] Intersex may be understood as "an umbrella term encompassing a range of conditions that disrupt the development of certain sexual characteristics." According to Abigail Favale, since the term is imprecise and frequently misused, more medically precise terms have been used, such as DSDs, disorders of sexual development, and her preferred term, CCSDs, congenital conditions of sexual development.[13] CCSDs refers to the person having been born with both XX and XY cells because of double fertilization (two different sperm, one carrying an X and one a Y chromosome). Leonard Sax (PhD, MD) claims intersex births are about one in 5,000 (or 0.002).[14] Megan DeFranza (PhD) asserts the number is closer to one in 2,500.

> The bizarre idea that biological sex is "assigned" at birth for everyone is one of several myths about sex that have gained widespread acceptance in our time. These myths tend to cluster together, like one trapdoor that opens into another. Once you accept one myth as true, you quickly freefall down the rabbit hole. The first trapdoor is this idea: sex is not binary but a spectrum.
> —Abigail Favale, *The Genesis of Gender*, 123

DeFranza supports the Affirming View, arguing on the basis of intersex that Adam and Eve, male and female, may be interpreted as the majority kinds rather than exclusive kinds of human beings. Favale rightly disagrees when she argues, "If 'intersex' is used to invoke a category *in between* the sexes, it is a misnomer. However, the label can be accurately used when referring to a biologically based variation *within* maleness or femaleness."[15] DeFranza also states that biblical passages on sexual prohibitions are not addressing consensual, monogamous, same-sex unions.[16] While we do not agree with DeFranza's perspective—on both philosophical and interpretive grounds—we do agree that a proper attitude toward persons born with CCSDs will be the same as toward everyone else: viewing and treating all human beings as intrinsically—therefore equally—valuable, having been made in God's image.

Gender Identity/Gender Sexuality/Gender Dysphoria/Transgender

Gender Identity is traditionally understood as synonymous with biological sex or *gender sexuality*—referring to being a person who is either male or female.[17] Especially since the mid-twentieth century, for many institutions and individuals, gender identity has come to mean one's own psychologically based self-description or personal identity, apart from one's biological/chromosomal sex. More specifically, it is seen by many as how one experiences or thinks of oneself as male or female, including how masculine or feminine one feels.[18] One's subjective thoughts or feelings of being a man, woman, nonbinary, or otherwise are said to "override" one's objective physical body as male (a man) or female (a woman) for defining one's personal identity. *Gender Dysphoria* is a diagnosable mental health condition and refers to the distress associated with incongruence between one's biological sex and perceived gender identity, typically distressing the individual.[19] *Transgender* is a broader umbrella term for many experiences of gender identity that do not align normatively with a person's biological sex.[20]

In her book *The Genesis of Gender*, Abigail Favale traces the historical, sociopolitical, and worldview developments surrounding gender, especially since the latter half of the twentieth century. Her personal and professional experience navigating the various gender "waves" makes Favale's insights particularly compelling. For instance, she explains and laments the effects we are seeing today from the misuse of gender ideology: "Ultimately, the concept of gender has driven a wedge between *body* and *identity*. Sex once referred to a bodily given, a fact of nature. In gender-world, the power of the body to constitute identity is diminished. . . . Once this distance between bodily sex and identity was enabled via gender, it did not take long—merely a few decades—for gender to shift meaning once again, becoming entirely disconnected from sex, which has paved the way for an even more fragmented and unstable understanding of personhood. . . . Unlike sex, 'gender' can be continually altered and redeployed, and we are witnessing in real time the wild proliferation of its meaning."[21] Gender-related issues are complex and controversial. While various Christian approaches to gender and sexuality exist, we lack space here to engage these positions and the challenges involved.[22] Mark Yarhouse proposes a potentially promising "integrated framework" model based on three lenses that institutions and individuals use in assessing gender identity and gender dysphoria: integrity, disability, and diversity.[23] Yarhouse also rightly reminds us to "think about sexuality and gender in the context of God's redemptive plan for creation."[24] This includes remembering that everyone experiences brokenness (e.g., dysphoria), which calls us to compassion, focusing on God's work of redemption, and our responsibility to be in right relationship with God.

Same-Sex Attraction/Same-Sex Orientation/Sexual Minorities/ Sexual Activity/Sexual Perversion

Same-sex attraction refers to an individual's sexual draw toward persons of the same biological sex, whether by internal or external factors or both. *Same-sex orientation* involves a more persistent/consistent attraction, often said to include being oriented toward same-sex sexuality. However, this orientation does not necessarily correspond to an individual's identity, whether or not someone uses identity as a synonym for being same-sex attracted. Moreover, same-sex attracted and same-sex oriented persons might or might not be engaged in sexual acts with same-sex persons. *Sexual minorities* refers to individuals with "same-sex attraction or behavior, regardless of self-identifications."[25]

Some use the terms *gay, lesbian,* or *bisexual* synonymously with same-sex attracted, oriented, or behavior, while others do not; it seems to depend partly on whether such attraction, orientation, or behavior is viewed as essential to one's identity. Is one's core identity ultimately (a) part of one's basic human nature/essence ("who I am") or (b) one's sexual sensations ("what I feel") or practices ("what I do")?[26]

Sexual activity involves any specifically sex-related behavior, whether appropriate or inappropriate. *Sexual perversion* or *distortion* refers to any sex-related behavior that diverges from appropriate sexual activity, encompassing various inappropriate sex encounters.

Two especially helpful scholars (with pastoral wisdom) on these important topics are Wesley Hill and Mark Yarhouse. (Both represent the Traditional View.) Yarhouse discusses sexual identity via a helpful threefold differentiation between attraction, orientation, and behavior.[27] Hill deeply interacts with Scripture's same-sex prohibition passages in conversation with his own self-identified gay Christian celibacy.[28]

Sexual Union/Intercourse/Procreation

Sexual union/intercourse involves the uniting of male and female genitalia—encompassing more than merely physical body parts. Alexander Pruss rightly argues that this sexual union actually involves a "union as one flesh": "not just one mind or one heart . . . crucial to the uniqueness of sexual union among all the unions available to us. . . . In sexuality, the two unite in a totality that involves them not just as persons, but also as animals. We are embodied beings, and sexuality seems one of the most evident features of this embodiment."[29]

Scripture and the historic Christian consensus speak clearly on this: male and female together are quintessential to bearing the image of God and thus flourishing in community—including the marital union.[30] Along these lines, Jonathan Grant argues that "although our culture has sought to 'level the playing field' between maleness and femaleness, there are critical differences between how men and women *generally* relate to each other."[31]

We agree with Nancy Pearcey's argument for the divine purpose of the sexual union. Pearcey states that the "most complete and intimate *physical* union is meant to express the most complete and intimate *personal* union of marriage. Biblical morality is teleological: The purpose of sex is to express the one flesh covenant bond of marriage."[32] If so, then God created (designed) human beings—male and female—for purposes including at least (a) physical union (sex), (b) demonstrating the covenant bond of marriage, and (c) procreation. Regarding point (a), Pearcey insightfully argues that this aspect validates a proper Christian worldview being pro-body (and pro-sex) in contrast with anti-body views that dishonor our biological identity. Yarhouse similarly argues that "Christianity affirms that sexuality in general and genital sex in particular are good things, but it does not reduce human sexuality only to genital sex or behavioral expression. Christianity teaches that lifelong heterosexual relationships are God's revealed will for full genital sexual intimacy, for the specific expression of our sexuality through behavior."[33] Furthermore, this bonding and intimacy, in a life-long union, involves the spiritual dimension—transcending the human marital/sexual relationship to reflect the relationship between God and the people of God: between Jesus Christ and his followers (the church).[34]

We believe this Traditional View ought to be the norm for sexual union/intercourse for Christ-followers. Furthermore, we encourage believers who embrace the claim that "all truth is God's truth" to investigate psychological, sociological, and philosophical arenas for claims, analysis, testimonies, and more. (See "For Further Reading" for some helpful and detailed materials in these areas.)

Nevertheless, we understand there are multiple alternative voices on this issue, both outside and inside the Christian faith. Outside, divergent views abound on questions of the morality and purpose of sexual intercourse. Factors shaping these perspectives may include ultimate-reality beliefs, moral authority, cultural mores, perception of self and others, personal desires, meaning, and purpose. Inside, the two main views of sexual union/intercourse include the Traditional View and the Affirming View.[35]

> Christianity is often accused of being anti-sex and anti-body. But in reality it is the secular ethic that is anti-body. Gay activists [and various others] downplay the body—our biological identity as male or female—and define our true selves by our feelings and desires. They assume that the body gives no reference points for our gender identity or our moral choices. In essence, the secular worldview has revived the ancient Gnostic disdain for the body. It is Christianity that honors the body as male and female, instead of subordinating biological sex to psychological feelings.
> —Nancy R. Pearcey, *Love Thy Body*, 117

It's important to remember that some individuals are called to or choose a life of celibacy (singleness and sexual abstinence); still others may lack the ability to marry or to engage in marital sexual union. These are crucial reminders that marriage is not the ultimate Christian calling—especially since the Lord Jesus himself was celibate, and both he and the apostle Paul taught on this.[36]

Love/Lust

Love involves willing and acting for another's good or benefit or well-being, while refraining from desiring or bringing evil or harm to another. It means valuing the intrinsic nature of persons (uniquely made in God's image) rather than merely their instrumental value (what they can do for me). Love exceeds mere feelings; it indicates heartfelt commitment toward others: generosity, compassion, and affection. Conversely, *lust* comprises self-centered thoughts and behavior toward others, such as pursuing self-satisfaction by using others for one's own ends (instrumentally) rather than valuing others as ends in themselves (intrinsically). Sexually, this may take the form of baiting, coercion, abuse, rape, human trafficking/slavery, or child/adult pornography.[37]

A Christian perspective understands love as a central attribute of God. Since love comes from God, we ought to love (rather than lust after) one another. Sexually, this entails exercising moral integrity (e.g., self-control) for another's good—even at some perceived or actual personal cost—remembering the personal cost involved in God's sending his one and only Son into the world (even to die for us) that we might live through him.[38]

Key Authorities and Other Factors Shaping Our Sexual Ethics Perspectives

Distinguishing moral from nonmoral judgments helps differentiate normative moral acts (the oughts/ought nots) from relative feelings or desires (subjective, personal); this can help guide us toward right actions (and away from wrong ones) amid fleeting emotions and affections. For instance, *moral evaluations* of human trafficking (sexual exploitation or coerced labor) involve judging it as morally good or evil; we believe human trafficking is undoubtedly evil. *Nonmoral evaluations* consider something other than morality, such as pleasure or pain experienced (physical or nonphysical) in judging such an activity (e.g., a nonmoral evil for the victim and a nonmoral good for the perpetrator). Sex-involved acts like rape and adultery are almost universally viewed as moral wrongs/evils—we agree that they are—even if they involve allegedly nonmoral experiences. Ultimately, our evaluation of whether particular sexual thoughts and acts are right/good or wrong/evil hinges on several interrelated factors:

- *Worldviews.* Perspectives on reality shape our "rules" or "codes" for sexuality.
- *Authorities.* Who or what we "authorize" as our ultimate moral authority: God, Scripture, church, family, friends, teachers, heroes, influencers, villains, intuitions, or affections.
- *Relationships and Communities.* Families, friends, churches, cultures, social-media influencers, and more shape/influence our sexual viewpoints.
- *Desires and Affections.* Deep-level wants and loves include sexual passions, hopes, and goals; ethically, what counts is whether or how to seek to fulfill particular desires and affections.
- *Philosophical reasoning and arguments.* These help us assess the validity, plausibility, truth, and soundness of sexual-ethics views.
- *Commitments.* These demonstrate steadfast beliefs and behaviors on matters of sexuality.

Conflicting views on sexual issues may occur within ourselves. Let's illustrate with the topic of nonmarital sexual intercourse. Say you're trying to navigate between your family's view and your best friend's (opposing) view. Assuming you ordinarily respect both your family and friend, the fact that they hold divergent views may produce internal mental or spiritual anxieties: cognitive dissonance, decision-making difficulties, theological/moral doubts. Understanding interrelated factors can help identify why you maintain and act on the views you have, perhaps even helping you to change/correct mistaken sexual perspectives or activities.

While most thinkers agree that sexual ethics ultimately concerns moral oughts/ought nots, viewpoints clash over what qualifies as moral/sexual rights or wrongs. And while virtually everyone desires their own view on sexual matters to be right, perhaps a deeper concern should be, "What grounding, reasons, and assumptions underlie my views?" We should be evaluating (a) whether our views can be supported/justified, and (b) what the logical implications of our views entail. Rigorous evaluation moves us beyond unsupported opinions toward justifiable stances.

Normative and Relative Moral Approaches to Sexuality

Would you say objective moral facts or truths exist, regardless of personal or cultural thoughts or feeling about sexuality? Or would you say morality involves merely subjective or cultural attitudes about sexuality? The view you hold likely indicates either a normative or a relative perspective. Let's look deeper.

Virtually all cultures authorize common "moral codes"—often including expected sexual beliefs and behaviors—which reflect *cultural relativism* (or *conventionalism*). To illustrate, consider a totalitarian government (centralized and dictatorial) ruling a society via a "might makes right" ethic. Its supreme leader decides it's morally acceptable for men in the military to rape female citizens, even asserting, "It's good for morale." Absolute loyalty to the regime equals moral rightness; anything less is moral wrongness. Only the internal governing authorities (those holding power) decide the culture's morality, including sexuality; external authorities get ignored or rejected. Still, some groups and individuals within that society will maintain contrasting moralities—perhaps even normative ethical views (e.g., virtue ethics, objective principles, Christian ethics).

A *normative* approach points beyond cultural-context powers to universal authorities such as God, divine commands, principles, reason, or intuition. Particular sexual beliefs and practices are recognized as either right or wrong—for everyone, at all times, in all places. Moral oughts and ought nots carry *universal* obligations. For example, it may be viewed as morally right for everyone to follow the Golden Rule: "So in everything, do to others what you would have them do to you, for this sums up the Law and the Prophets" (Matt. 7:12). By implication, then, it would never be morally right for military males to rape female citizens—regardless of the totalitarian leader's viewpoint.

> The Golden Rule: "So in everything, do to others what you would have them do to you, for this sums up the Law and the Prophets."
> —Matthew 7:12

Theistic versus Nontheistic Grounding and Criteria for Sexuality and Identity

For many theistic moral philosophers (and virtually all who are Christian), the *source* of sexual ethics matters most. God, who is omniscient, omnipotent, and omnibenevolent is the source of right and good. Consequently, moral/sexual oughts and ought nots are objective rather than relative. Can you see the world of difference—or worldview difference!—this makes? A theistic worldview with a normative ethic contrasts with worldviews adopting merely cultural relativism (conventionalism) or personal feeling or impression (subjectivism). Disagreements persist over whether God has created, willed, and communicated moral/sexual right and wrong to humankind. One's belief about this determines the criteria one accepts for moral/sexual truths and practices. For example, if one excludes God from consideration regarding norms for sexual ethics, one needs some alternative grounding, like lust satisfaction, pleasure seeking, utility, reciprocity, instinct, identity formation, or intimacy. Conversely, if one includes God as the ultimate source and authority for sexual ethics—being the originator/designer of sexuality—one may be compelled to recognize the objective grounding.[39] Ultimately, one's response to the question "Who or what authorizes appropriate sexuality?" likely reveals one's worldview and criteria (norms and conditions). Philosopher Nancey Pearcey rightly sees the importance of criteria in terms of sexuality and personal identity:

> The problem is that when sexual desire is seen as the defining feature of our identity, it becomes rigid and inviolable. To question someone's identity is taken as an attack on their selfhood and worth. If the person refrains from acting on their sexual feelings, they are accused of repression and self-hatred. But why place sexual feelings at the center of our identity? The Bible offers a more compelling script that defines our identity in terms of the image of God, created

to reflect his character. We are loved and redeemed children of God. When we center our lives on these truths, then our identity is secure no matter what our sexual feelings are—and whether they change or don't change.[40]

We again see those key underlying considerations at work: worldview, authority, and context. These factors frequently and repeatedly induce moral conflicts, including in social-political and judicial realms.[41] Of course, not all differences on major or hot-button ethical dilemmas are matters of religious/faith distinctions. Sometimes, people from virtually opposing worldviews join together over some moral concern like abortion, human trafficking, rape, or prostitution.

Theistic Sexual Ethics, Original Intention or Design, and Human Freedom

What emerges from our philosophical approach—founded on a biblically-grounded Christian worldview—are claims and arguments that necessarily assume truth exists: moral and otherwise. Truth may be discovered rather than merely constructed or imagined. While different interpretations of moral and sexual issues exist—even among individual Christ-followers and Christian churches/communities—these differences don't entail each interpretation being equally right or justifiable. Indeed, only one perspective may be the right perspective on many moral issues, sexuality included (e.g., adultery, premarital sex, homosexual/gay/lesbian sex, bestiality, rape). Assuming the law of non-contradiction, we cannot affirm that both the pro and the con view (on any of these issues) are right in the same way and at the same time; our answer to which view is the right view almost certainly depends on our worldview, ultimate authority, and corresponding interpretation.

If our chosen worldview—philosophy of life—embraces distinctly Christian sexual ethics, then we should seek to explain these moral concerns "from the perspective of God's intention for human existence as sexual creatures."[42] This entails embracing objective moral norms. For example, where the written Word speaks on marriage between a man and a woman, we understand Scripture as indicating (a) biologically male and female individuals and (b) the established context for sexual union/intercourse (c) as part of God's originally-intended design. (See Gen. 2:24, Matt. 19:4–6, Eph. 5:21–33.) Such a claim doesn't deny that alternatives to this ideal may provide partners with intimacy and sexual pleasure. For example, consider polygamy. While it was sometimes permitted in ancient Hebrew culture, it was allowed as a concession (or description) rather than as an ideal marital situation (or endorsement). Incest sometimes occurred as well. Nevertheless, neither polygamy nor incest were God's intention, as Old Testament scholar Paul Raabe notes, "When the Creator brings the woman to the man, the man is delighted (Gen. 2:23–25). This is how the Creator designed it, and it was very good. . . . The Creator allowed polygamy, for example Jacob's wives, but it was not the Creator's original good design. The argument of Jesus in Matthew 19:1–9 applies here as well. . . . [T]he laws at Sinai reveal the Creator's strong opposition to sexual immorality, including incest (Leviticus 20). Here incest is put into the same category as adultery and bestiality. . . . Genesis 2 sets forth God's original good design, and both polygamy and incest contradict it."[43]

Prohibited, as well as merely allowed, types of sexual union reflect the *fallen* human condition rather than the divinely intended design.[44] By implication, in our technological age, sex acts with robots, virtual-reality sex, and other forms of "technosexuality" would also amount to misalignment with sexual practices intended by the Creator.

Until relatively recently, virtual consensus was maintained throughout Christian history that sexual intercourse outside of monogamous, male-female marriage was not included as part of God's original intention. This perspective held, even though some such marital unions struggled or dissolved. However, the "sexual revolution" of the 1960s–70s enormously impacted (especially) Western culture. Many (if not most) denominations, fellowships, schools, and individuals connected to Christianity have experienced the moral shift and its effects— whether rejecting, embracing, or trying to mediate revised sexual principles and practices. Responses have varied widely—both from within and without the Christian faith community—over cultural moral shifts and divergent interpretations, particularly within psychological, sociological, biological, ethical, and theological arenas. It's practically impossible to stay up with the latest trends, claims, and understandings (even using AI). While we're definitely not suggesting that "ignorance is bliss" on these crucial moral matters, we should remember that we're finite beings, that diametrically opposite claims cannot both be true (remember the law of non-contradiction), and, all else being relatively equal, our ultimate authority for answering what is true about sexuality (and much more) likely will be decisive for us.

> Mere humans obviously lack perfect character and comprehensive knowledge; any comparison between human virtue and knowledge and divine character and understanding will leave the former in the dust—figuratively and literally!

From our perspective, God's intentional design doesn't seem arbitrary. Divine attributes like intelligence, love, goodness, and wisdom underlie the triune God's beautiful intentionality. Furthermore, the divine character/qualities really matter in terms of justified authority. Plus, God alone possesses total comprehension of who we humans are—individually and relationally. Still, fundamental human nature includes our shared creatureliness: having been made in God's image—including our male/female distinctions.

We also recognize various grey areas within sexual ethics—matters of individual human freedom and conscience (e.g., see 1 Cor. 8) that involve latitude within the overall divine design: for instance, interpretations of modesty or self-control within divinely-intended sexual boundaries. Unfortunately, sometimes grey areas get mixed in with black and white ones, which can lead to legalism or other abuses or injustices.

We believe God created sexuality wisely and purposefully, but tragically, humans tend to disregard this. Sadly, we go astray. The bad news is that we pay the consequences when we do. Going against how something is designed normally leads to negative effects—like driving the wrong way on the freeway! The good news is that our loving Creator understands us perfectly—including our moral failures and sexual struggles. God patiently and graciously calls us to repentance (changing our wrong thinking and behavior). Our Maker desires that his uniquely fashioned and specially loved creatures (that's us!) experience morality as intended—rather than experience moral failure and its consequences—for our own good and well-being.[45]

Furthermore, biblical revelation proclaims—and the historic Christian community worships—God as the creator of life. The Lord Jesus Christ—member of the Holy Trinity (Father, Son, and Spirit)—exemplifies, explains, and elevates divinely-given moral norms. He especially emphasizes heart matters and motives related to morality and sexuality. The Scriptures contain

> The Maker calls us to change our mistaken moral and sexual notions and practices—for our benefit and well-being.

numerous moral imperatives (commands), many involving sexual matters.[46] From the earliest days of Judaism to the time of Jesus' apostles and up to the present, millions have sought to understand and live out their sexuality as they believe God intended. Christ-followers today are called to do the same—recognizing virtuous sexuality as communicated through (a) general revelation (creation) and (b) special revelation (Jesus Christ and inspired Scripture) through the power of the Holy Spirit. Still, no mere human has ever lived a flawless moral life. Christians understand and embrace what the New Testament teaches concerning the only perfectly sinless human, who is also divine, Christ Jesus. "For we do not have a high priest who is unable to empathize with our weaknesses, but we have one who has been tempted in every way, just as we are—yet he did not sin. Let us then approach God's throne of grace with confidence, so that we may receive mercy and find grace to help us in our time of need" (Heb. 4:15–16). We acknowledge our moral/sexual imperfections and need for the Lord's grace and mercy. Still, we believe God has communicated truth on numerous sexual matters. If so, then it's highly likely there is one right/true understanding and expression of sexual union, while perhaps some other sexual matters, especially those not clearly or directly addressed in Scripture, might entail some justifiable diversity or require further qualification (e.g., issues concerning erotic self-stimulation).

The Lord Jesus Christ exemplifies, explains, and elevates divinely-given moral norms. He especially emphasizes heart matters and motives related to morality and sexuality. (See Matt. 5:27; 15:19–20.)

Our broken world—with its innumerable distractions and distortions—tends to muddy our minds, infect our interpretations, and distort God's communicated will on sexual matters. Several plausible reasons for our disagreements may help explain why our views may differ on, say, appropriate sexual union: (1) an understanding of what Scripture actually teaches; (2) the value placed on what Christians have believed and/or practiced historically; (3) the degree that our views and choices have been shaped by historical/cultural influences; (4) our attitudes toward immediate gratification (self-control versus so-called self-expression); (5) the definition and expression of sexual-ethics terms and concepts (e.g., "love" or "lust"); (6) our perspective on the nature of persons (e.g., merely physical beings with bodies/brains or composite beings with bodies/brains and minds/souls); (7) our view of how the sex act should be understood (e.g., merely involving distinct/separate bodies or male and female becoming unitive/united as one-flesh body and soul); and (8) the experience in particular ecclesial (church) traditions and communities (with certain approaches, emphases, and commitments to biblical and other types of authority).

Notwithstanding these significant differences, we think there are good reasons (we've offered some) for maintaining the Traditional View of sexual union as divinely intended for expression within the monogamous male-female marital bond.[47] Grounds for our position ultimately center on the conviction that God has spoken objectively and decisively in Scripture—as well as through humans made male and female, in the image of God—as to divinely-intended/designed sexual union. Correspondingly, we believe the soundest analysis (i.e., exegesis) of pertinent biblical passages leads to the Traditional View rather than its contraries. For sustained analysis of these passages, along with examination of physical, emotional, social, and ecclesial (church-related) implications of certain sexual practices, see Robert A. J. Gagnon's *The Bible and Homosexual Practice: Texts and Hermeneutics*.[48]

We invite you to embrace God's intention/design on important sexual matters—understanding the challenges involved in a "love is love" cultural climate. Much social media significantly clouds the moral/sexual waters, especially within countries allowing more open access. Nancy Pearcey laments all-too-common views of sexual intercourse today, noting this "most intimate of bodily relations has been disconnected from personal relations. Sex is cast as a purely recreational activity that can be enjoyed apart from any hint of love or commitment. All that matters is consent (as though agreeing to perform an act makes it right)."[49] With Pearcey, we grieve over this shallow view of sex, believing that it fails miserably to provide the robust relationality and intimacy God intends. We believe appropriate sexuality can be a way of life for everyone—especially as one follows the way, the truth, and the life, the Lord Jesus Christ (John 14:6).

> Appropriate sexuality can be a way of life for you as you commit to follow the one who is the way (and the truth, and the life): Jesus Christ.

Conclusion

Our view of reality and ultimate authority powerfully shapes our moral life and sexual ethics. The norm for individuals committed to a Christian worldview includes understanding and living out a biblically authorized, God-honoring, Christ-centered, neighbor-valuing, and self-care sexual ethic. If Spirit-inspired Scripture is ultimately authoritative for all matters concerning moral life, then this also includes sexuality. Alternative sources cannot suffice as ultimate guides for morality; still, additional sources for sexual understanding and practice may be consulted and utilized secondarily. Assuming the Triune God has spoken truth regarding moral right/wrong and good/evil, it seems reasonable for us to desire, learn, and embrace divinely revealed truth on all moral/sexual matters—wherever we find it.

Human flourishing is fundamental to God's design, but flourishing necessitates following the divine script—not plotting alternative strategies. It's challenging to stick to the script rather than improvise—especially when widespread hyper-individualism tends to view relationships merely "from the point of view of personal fulfillment and reward."[50] Yet Scripture teaches—and sound theological reflection agrees—that, through trusting God's grace and the Spirit's power, we may be transformed to experience genuine human flourishing—including via the theological virtues of faith, hope, and love.[51] Furthermore, worldview disagreements will continue, including over sexual ethics; thus we recommend patience, persistence, and prudence (wise self-discipline) focused on participating in like-minded communities (e.g., church, college campus chapels and fellowships, and Bible studies, support/recovery groups, and pastoral and professional Christian counseling). Perhaps this way isn't traveled by most people today, but we're convinced the Traditional View continues to carry its own substantial "rewards."[52]

We are grateful for your thoughtful engagement with us throughout this chapter. Allow us to close with a call to a "comprehensive Christian vision of sexuality" that comprises four essential spheres:[53]

1. *Eschatological*: Locates human sexuality within a larger framework—God's unfolding plan for creation—from an eternal, future-destiny perspective.[54]
2. *Metaphysical*: Lines up with reality (how things really are), attuned to the kingdom of God (seen and unseen), which Christ-followers can and should reflect.
3. *Formational*: Forms who we are (our character) in the journeying process toward maturity—especially into the image/reflection of Christ—as a compelling alternative to dominant cultural assumptions.
4. *Missional*: Shapes what we do (our actions), giving purpose to our sexuality that expresses God's character and witnesses to God's world mission.[55]

> When we make sexual decisions, we are not just deciding whether to follow a few rules. We are expressing our view of the cosmos and human nature.
> —Nancy R. Pearcey, *Love Thy Body*, 114

Our vision of sexual ethics recognizes that sexuality is much deeper than mere sexual satisfaction (with its inevitable limits); thus, we imagine that appropriate sexuality ultimately entails commitment to reorienting our desires/affections toward God.

Questions for Reflection

1. How would you explain to a friend the key difference between a *descriptive* and a *normative* approach to sexual ethics?
2. What two or three arguments could be made in support of a biblically based Traditional View of divinely intended sexual union in response to Affirmative View objections?
3. Name several authorities and/or factors that impact your view of sexual ethics. Which authority and/or factor most shapes your perspective, and why?

For Further Reading

Favale, Abigail. *The Genesis of Gender: A Christian Theory*. San Francisco: Ignatius, 2022.

Grant, Jonathan. *Divine Sex: A Compelling Vision for Christian Relationships in a Hypersexualized Age*. Grand Rapids: Brazos, 2015.

Juan, Christopher. *Holy Sexuality and the Gospel: Sex, Desire, and Relationships Shaped by God's Grand Story*. New York: Multnomah, 2018.

Pearcey, Nancy R. *Love Thy Body: Answering Hard Questions about Life and Sexuality*. Grand Rapids: Baker Books, 2018.

Sprinkle, Preston M. *Embodied: Transgender Identities, the Church, and What the Bible Has to Say*. Colorado Springs: David C. Cook, 2021.

Wilson, Todd A. *Mere Sexuality: Rediscovering the Christian Vision of Sexuality*. Grand Rapids: Zondervan, 2017.

Yarhouse, Mark A. *How Should We Think about Homosexuality?* Bellingham, WA: Lexham, 2022.

NOTES

1. See the important dialogue on this issue (and related concerns) between four Christian academics in Preston Sprinkle, ed., *Two Views of Homosexuality, the Bible, and the Church* (Grand Rapids: Zondervan, 2016).

2. Many Christian scholars ably defend the Traditional View. As an introduction we recommend Wesley Hill and Stephen R. Holmes (chaps. 3 and 4, respectively, as well as their responses and rejoinders to affirmative view advocates William Loader and Megan K. DeFranza) in Sprinkle, ed., *Two Views of Homosexuality, the Bible, and the Church*.

3. Admittedly, at times we fail to love as we ought to. Still, we are called—and should endeavor—to love everyone: above all, the Lord. (See Matt. 22:36–39; Mark 12:28–31; Luke 10:27–28.) Christ-followers also should understand the capacity to love others genuinely and fully is not something naturally occurring within us, but rather a fruit of the Spirit being properly realized. (See Gal. 5:22–23.)

4. Some other key moral terms include virtue, vice, truth, grace, justice, mercy, love, and authority.

5. Stanley J. Grenz and Jay T. Smith, *Pocket Dictionary of Ethics* (Downers Grove, IL: IVP, 2003), 107.

6. Jonathan Grant, *Divine Sex: A Compelling Vision for Christian Relationships in a Hyper-sexualized Age* (Grand Rapids: Brazos, 2015), 97.

7. Nancy R. Pearcey, *Love Thy Body: Answering Hard Questions about Life and Sexuality* (Grand Rapids: Baker Books, 2018), 23.

8. Todd A. Wilson, *Mere Sexuality: Rediscovering the Christian Vision of Sexuality* (Grand Rapids: Zondervan, 2017), 33.

9. Mark Yarhouse, *Understanding Gender Dysphoria: Navigating Transgender Issues in a Changing Culture* (Downers Grove, IL: IVP Academic, 2015), 17. (Concerning gender sexuality, see 36.)

10. Tomas Bogardus, "How Our Shoes Can Help Explain the Biology of Sex," Reality's Last Stand,

August 9, 2022, www.realityslaststand.com/p/how-our-shoes-can-help-explain-the. See also Tomas Bogardus, "Evaluating Arguments for the Sex/Gender Distinction," *Philosophia* (January 27, 2020): https://doi.org/10.1007/s11406-019-00157-6.

11. There are rare cases in which those with XY chromosomes present as fully female in their outward appearance. This is called "male pseudohermaphroditism." This is a hormonal condition rather than a condition arising from fertilization abnormalities. There is also "female pseudohermaphroditism." See Robert D. Utiger, "Pseudohermaphroditism: Pathology," revised by Kara Rogers, *Encyclopedia Britannica* online, www.britannica.com /science/pseudohermaphroditism.

12. Instead of the baby being born with either a vagina and two ovaries (female) or a penis and two testicles (male), an individual may have one ovary and one testicle, or a related malformation. For a detailed discussion of intersex and transgender, see Leonard Sax, *Why Gender Matters: What Parents and Teachers Need to Know about the Emerging Science of Sex Differences*, 2nd ed. (New York: Harmony, 2017), chap. 11.

13. Abigail Favale, *The Genesis of Gender: A Christian Theory* (San Francisco: Ignatius, 2022), 125. Some find the term "intersex" or "DSDs" pejorative or stigmatizing, while others do not.

14. See Sax, *Why Gender Matters*, 188; and Megan K. DeFranza, "Journeying from the Bible to Christian Ethics in Search of Common Ground," in *Two Views on Homosexuality, the Bible, and the Church*, ed. Preston Sprinkle (Grand Rapids: Zondervan, 2016), 69–70n1.

15. Favale, *Genesis of Gender*, 125. Evolutionary biologist Richard Dawkins likewise states, "You may argue about 'gender' if you wish (biologists have better things to do) but sex is a true binary, one of rather few in biology." (Richard Dawkins, post on X, @RichardDawkins, January 30, 2024, https://x.com/RichardDawkins/status/1752403995174252724).

16. Megan K. DeFranza, *Sex Differences in Christian Theology: Male, Female, and Intersex in the Image of God* (Grand Rapids: Eerdmans, 2015); and DeFranza, "Journeying," in *Two Views of Homosexuality, the Bible, and the Church*, ed. Preston Sprinkle (Grand Rapids: Zondervan, 2016), chap. 2.

17. For more on gender sexuality, see Yarhouse, *Understanding Gender Dysphoria*, 36.

18. See ibid., 17, and chap. 1 overall.

19. Ibid., 20.

20. See Mark Yarhouse and Julia Sadusky, *Emerging Gender Identities: Understanding the Diverse Experiences of Today's Youth* (Grand Rapids: Brazos, 2020), 12–13. The term *cisgender* is used by some (in contrast to transgender) to indicate congruence between one's psychological and emotional gender identity experience and one's biological sex. At least originally, the term appears to have been invented and used for the purpose of advancing a set of worldview commitments about gender identity in contrast to biological sex. Today, some who hold to biological sex rather than gender identity are utilizing the term as well, but often as a mere descriptor, or for purposes of engaging in dialogue, as opposed to advocating for gender identity. Yarhouse, *Understanding Gender Dysphoria*, 20. Some ideas and language in the definition come from Mark Yarhouse, "Navigating Gender and Sexual Identity Conflicts as a Christian: With Dr. Mark Yarhouse," interview by David Wiedes, *ServingLeaders Podcast*, May 9, 2022, https://podcasts .apple .com /us /podcast /servingleaders -podcast /id1546223308?i=1000560175240.

21. Favale, *Genesis of Gender*, 149–50.

22. We highly recommend that you begin with the "For Further Reading" list at the end of the chapter as a starting point for engaging and exploring discussions, research, and (primarily Christian worldview) approaches to gender and, more broadly, sexual ethics. For transgender-related views and discussion, see James K. Beilby and Paul Rhodes Eddy, *Understanding Transgender Identities: Four Views* (Grand Rapids: Baker Academic, 2019).
23. See Yarhouse, *Understanding Gender Dysphoria*, 46–160.
24. Ibid., 35.
25. Mark A. Yarhouse, *How Should We Think about Homosexuality?* (Bellingham, WA: Lexham, 2022), chap. 3.
26. See Wilson, *Mere Sexuality*, 21–22.
27. Yarhouse, *How Should We Think about Homosexuality?* 41–43.
28. Wesley Hill, *Washed and Waiting: Reflections on Christian Faithfulness and Homosexuality*, 2nd ed. (Grand Rapids: Zondervan, 2016); Wesley Hill, "Christ, Scripture, and Spiritual Friendship," in *Two Views of Homosexuality, the Bible, and the Church*, ed. Preston Sprinkle (Grand Rapids: Zondervan, 2016), chap. 3.
29. Alexander R. Pruss, *One Body: An Essay in Christian Sexual Ethics* (Notre Dame: University of Notre Dame Press, 2012), 131.
30. Wilson, *Mere Sexuality*, 36.
31. Grant, *Divine Sex*, 97.
32. Pearcey, *Love Thy Body*, 23.
33. Yarhouse, *How Should We Think about Homosexuality?* 8.
34. Ibid. See Eph. 5:21–33.
35. See Preston Sprinkle, *Two Views of Homosexuality, the Bible, and the Church* (Grand Rapids: Zondervan, 2016).
36. See Luke 20:34–36 and 1 Cor. 7:25–38.
37. *Voluntary consent* normally involves a "free will" decision, whereas neither coercion nor compulsion do.
38. See 1 John 4:7–9.
39. For instance, we may assert that a "one-flesh" union through marriage and consummation between a biological male (man) and a biological female (woman) uniquely reflects the Creator's design for those choosing to marry. (See Gen. 1:27–28a; 2:20b–25; Matt. 19:4–8; Eph. 5:25–33.)
40. Pearcey, *Love Thy Body*, 123.
41. In the United States, for instance, moral and sexual disagreements regularly occur over religious (especially monotheistic or Christian theism) views contrasting with nontheistic or other alternative views. Consider marriage in the U.S. In 2015, the U.S. Supreme Court (in a 5–4 decision, *Obergefell v. Hodges*) overturned state bans on same-sex marriage and on recognizing such marriages performed in other states. Previously, individual states determined whether to legalize same-sex marriage, with the State of Massachusetts being the first to rule in favor of same-sex marriage (in 2003). Before that, same-sex "civil unions" were recognized in some states, beginning with Vermont (in July 2000). Prior to July 2000, marriage was understood as a union between a man and a woman, based largely on biblical authority and a Christian perspective. Within increasingly non-Christian culture, legislation may reflect worldview changes, including on sexual ethics. Yet this is not a necessity *per se,* especially among those in significant positions of authority or amid grassroots-level

movements, who resist or oppose cultural trends contrary to, say, Christian theism. For instance, in July 2022, *Roe v. Wade* was overturned (in a 5–4 U.S. Supreme Court decision), ending nearly fifty years of abortion being recognized as a constitutional right (via a 1973, 7–2 High Court ruling), which returned to individual states the authority to decide whether to permit, limit, or ban abortion.

42. Grenz, and Smith, *Pocket Dictionary of Ethics*, 108.

43. Paul Raabe, PhD., personal conversation and email correspondence, September 26–28, 2023.

44. Theologian Paul K. Jewett states that "given the monogamous context of Jesus' appeal to this one-flesh union [of Gn. 2:24, constituting "a tacit rejection of polygamy in favor of monogamy"] as an act of the Creator (Mk. 10:9), the Lord, in our judgment, goes beyond a tacit to an explicit approval of monogamy" (Paul K. Jewett, *Who We Are: Our Dignity as Human: A Neo-Evangelical Theology* [Grand Rapids: Eerdmans, 1996], 260, and 260n141 [for internal quote]).

45. For instance, see Ezek. 18:30–32; Acts 2:38–39; Rom. 1:18–32; 2 Cor. 7:9–11; 1 Thess. 1:8–10; Heb. 3:12–14; and 2 Peter 3:9.

46. For instance, in the Old Testament, see Gen. 1:27–28; 2:24; Exod. 20:14, 17; Prov. 5:15–20; 6:23–35; 7:6–27; in the New Testament, see Matt. 5:27–32; 19:3–12; Acts 15:19–20; Rom. 13:13–14; 1 Cor. 5:1–2; 6:18–20; 7:2–6, 8–14, 36–38; Eph. 5:3, 28–33; Col. 3:5; 1 Thess. 4:3–8; 2 Tim. 2:22; Heb. 13:4.

47. Limited space precludes us from considering additional biological, psychological, and sociological arguments supporting our claim.

48. Robert A. J. Gagnon, *The Bible and Homosexual Practice: Texts and Hermeneutics* (Nashville: Abingdon, 2001). We encourage you to seek greater understanding and clarity on these matters—to grow in biblical, theological, and interpretive (i.e., hermeneutical) literacy.

49. Pearcey, *Love Thy Body*, 87.

50. Grant, *Divine Sex*, 139.

51. See 1 Cor. 13:13.

52. Rewards seem connected to being "all in" with a Traditional View of sexual ethics: the peace and joy of knowing God takes pleasure in your commitment/obedience to pursue divinely intended sexuality; possessing a stable, established center (foundation) from which to navigate the challenging cultural views on sexual matters; being empowered by the Spirit to resist sexual temptations outside the boundaries of intended expression; minimizing spiritual and cognitive dissonance in sexual matters; serving as a model/exemplar for others (e.g., family, friends, classmates, coworkers); and potentially benefitting society/culture (perhaps at some personal risk) through actively opposing sexual immorality while promoting divinely intended sexuality.

53. For this section, we are highly indebted to Jonathan Grant, whose material is presented in much greater detail in Grant, *Divine Sex*, 143–64.

54. Marriage and singleness are temporal and relatively equal options as vocations/callings within God's mission since the ultimate horizon is the future (new creation/consummation), focused on a deeper-than-sex social-relational intimate relationship with God and one another. See John 14:2.

55. This includes demonstrating Christian virtues (like fidelity, chastity, courage), vocations (singleness, marriage), and purposes (enriching the faith community and witnessing to God's kingdom).

CHAPTER 24

What about Communication and Information Ethics?

Communication and information are ubiquitous. Almost nothing happens without them. In fact, communication seems to be an essential feature of human beings, relationships, and culture; it happens constantly, whether or not words are being used.[1] Likewise, information is endless, pervading nearly every aspect of our lives. Not surprisingly, then, ethical questions and moral problems saturate these arenas impacting interpersonal, cultural/societal, and global contexts.

Moral philosophy (or ethics) primarily focuses on questions like "What is good?" (character) and "What is right?" (conduct). Communication ethics and information ethics consider these same questions within their respective—and commonly integrated—domains. In this chapter, our main focus will be introducing and examining these major applied-ethics categories (communication ethics and information ethics), as well as certain core subcategories that are especially relevant today (e.g., social media). We'll consider prevalent moral issues within these spheres; exploring several ethical approaches and moral practices in connection with these domains (for instance, smart phone usage and its potential moral impact) along with apparent worldview assumptions and commitments; and presenting an objective-morality approach, rooted in a Christian worldview. We also encourage you to deepen your own study. (See our recommended readings under "For Further Reading.")

Defining Communication Ethics and Information Ethics

Communication ethics is concerned with addressing moral issues involving communication; it seeks to render moral evaluations (i.e., judgments), provide moral guidance, and advocate for particular solutions to communication issues. Thus, communication ethics includes *prescriptive* (what ought to be) rather than merely *descriptive* (what is) assessments. Divergent views concerning ethical "oughts" in communication often stem from underlying worldviews and commitments about right and wrong and/or good and evil.

> Our search for the good life invariably will lead us to be critical of some of our communication habits and informational practices. History shows that every technological advance also delivers us to new moral quandaries.
> —Quentin J. Schultze, *Habits of the High-Tech Heart*, 13

Information ethics concentrates on moral issues involving the use of particular *media* for communicating, including traditional forms such as physical or print media, and newer forms, which are largely digital. (For our purposes, the term *media ethics* will be used synonymously with information ethics.) While communication ethics centers on issues related to the specific communication (e.g., the message to an audience), information ethics examines the particular media through which those messages are disseminated (examples include an individual's voice and/or body language, a presentation technology, or a search engine). Typically, communication ethics and information ethics are integrated and may be best understood as two parts of a whole, like two sides of a coin, so we'll consider these topics together. Let's begin by considering some ethical questions and concerns involving communication and information.

Some Key Questions and Concerns

Are there right and wrong ways to communicate? Does being a good or virtuous person matter when it comes to communicating or when utilizing traditional or new media? Do communicators have moral obligations? What makes a company ethical or unethical? Which stories should the media be presenting to its audience, and why? Should truth-seeking and truth-telling shape what gets communicated publicly and privately, or should some other interest be the determining factor? What ethical standards ought to guide the business world and the political realm? What moral concerns should we have about the online/virtual world? Should social media platforms be held morally responsible for certain content? Are there right ways and wrong ways of using information/media? What ethical parameters should shape or limit the development and use of technologies?

You might already have strong opinions in response to these questions. Further reflection may even help uncover *why* you hold those views—perhaps because of some shaping influences or experiences. The deeper issue, though, may be whether your opinions and responses to these questions are justified.

Historically, a large majority of philosophers have agreed that objective, universal moral good/evil and right/wrong exist, while a minority have rejected this claim. The latter (rejection) view represents *ethical relativism*, whether *conventionalist* or *subjectivist* ethical relativism, which has gained a foothold in some (especially western) cultures since the latter half of the twentieth century. This view might have impacted your own thinking, emotions, and conduct, especially if your morality is driven by the culture or is seemingly self-determined.[2] However, if morality is ultimately objective (as we believe), then right and good answers to applied ethics questions ought to be discoverable—thanks to some greater authority than mere cultural or subjective powers.

What Is Human Communication?

It's hard to imagine something more important than communication, including how and what we communicate. The term *"communication* comes from the same root word underlying *community* and *communion*. Human communication is the act of communing with one another, not merely the business of sending and 'consuming' messages."[3] Types of communication range from intrapersonal (self-communication) to interpersonal (one-on-one to groups) to organizational (e.g., national, international, multinational) across various sectors of society (public, private, and civil). Politics, business, science, health, medicine, technology, and traditional and social media are among the most recognizable and influential communication industries today. For our purposes, we'll be limiting discussion to these three arenas: interpersonal, business, and (traditional and new) media.

> Communication ethics concerns the creation and evaluation of goodness in all aspects and manifestations of communicative interaction.
> —Lisbeth A. Lipari, "Communication Ethics," *Oxford Research Encyclopedia of Communication*

Morality seems built-in to communication. In fact, Lisbeth Lipari states that "because both communication and ethics are tacitly or explicitly inherent in all human interactions, everyday life is fraught with intentional and unintentional ethical questions."[4] Communication ethics, then, focuses on assessing the morality of human attitudes and actions when communicating.

Moreover, communication ethics approaches are grounded in (1) particular worldview assumptions (e.g., theistic or nontheistic) and (2) particular ethical systems (such as virtue ethics, deontological ethics, teleological ethics, or postmodern ethics) and their attributes (e.g., moral realism or antirealism [whether moral facts do or do not exist]).[5] Consequently, we should expect to encounter conflicting communication ethics evaluations (i.e., judgments) involving human communication dispositions and practices.

Moral Communication Components

We suggest that (at a minimum) moral communication ought to include goodness, truthfulness, fairness, and justice. Of course, these concepts (and relevant examples) will be interpreted through particular worldview lenses. Consider truthfulness, for instance. Should truthfulness be understood from an objective or from a relativistic (whether conventionalist or subjectivist) point of view? If understood from an objective perspective, truthfulness is impartial and discoverable: the truth exists about what truthfulness is. One may come to know and/or experience truthfulness through intuition or perception, for instance. It should be noted that the objective view of truthfulness allows and encourages subjective *appropriation*; for instance, personally trusting that truthfulness is morally good and truth-telling is morally right.[6]

If, however, understood from a relativistic perspective, truthfulness is based solely on either personal or social construction: either "we" or "I" create what truthfulness is. Such a merely subjective perspective categorically denies the existence of objective truth.[7] Yet virtually all human beings (rational persons, at least) desire to receive communication free of falsehood, deception, and wrong motives. What view of human nature would disagree with that? Probably none.

Consider this example. All college students anticipate being told/taught the truth about things concerning their educational program, requirements, and expectations. Consequently, no student would be okay with, say, seemingly earning a Bachelor's degree, only to be told just before the graduation ceremony that "it's been discovered that several of your instructors over the past four years have been actors posing as faculty, faking their academic credentials; unfortunately, because of this you won't be able to graduate this year, but instead will need to retake certain courses in order to qualify for graduation at a later date." What a scandal that would be! Each student had been trusting what they have been told by the university administration and staff and taught by the faculty, believing those sources to be truthful. The truth of the matter was assumed to be exactly as it had been printed and spoken by school authorities—including instructor qualifications. Any contrary information, then, would be untrue. We might even say that it would be a matter of moral integrity to see to it that the institution's claims match up with reality. If not, the consequence surely would be enormously destructive. Truthfulness would be undermined!

Obviously, we all want to be able to trust those with appropriate authority to communicate the truth to us—at least the highest probability of something being the case. Trustworthiness matters to us all; it's typically based on qualities of the source, good reasoning, convincing evidence, reliable testimony, and other kinds of credibility. Moreover, we tend to question or reject claims that come from untrustworthy sources and unreliable information or evidence. On this point, ask yourself, "What reasonable person would place her trust in the claim that 'x is true' when the possibility of x being true is extremely remote or virtually impossible, and with no reliable sources or evidence to support the claim?" For example, virtually all rational adults agree that there are many reliable sources, plausible reasons, and abundant evidence that support the claim that "the Earth is round" (or spherical) rather than flat, even if a small group of people continue to promote the Earth being horizontal (e.g., The Flat Earth Society).

Perhaps it's obvious by now that how one answers the question of truthfulness (and other moral concepts) communicates one's view of ultimate reality, including the nature and purpose of human beings in the world. Simply because differing viewpoints get expressed does not necessitate there being no moral facts or objective truths about the nature or value of goodness, truthfulness, fairness, or justice. On the contrary, we think moral truths exist—and for good reasons—although some views of reality won't agree with our own. Let's see how all this pertains to human communication.

Communication and Information in Interpersonal Contexts

Deep down, it's your worldview that ultimately directs (or even determines) what you think is the right moral perspective or practice. For instance, imagine a person being interviewed for a job. Let's say the individual holds a metaphysical view that God exists (theism) and communicates moral truths to humanity, particularly in and through the virtuous character and teachings of Jesus Christ (Christian ethics). In this case, the two Greatest Commandments (first, to love God with all one's being, and second, to love one's neighbor as oneself) and the Golden Rule (to treat others as you would want them to treat you) ought to be followed throughout the job interview. Thus, it seems reasonable to assume that if this job candidate is committed to living accordingly, he or she would tell the truth and be respectful toward the hiring manager. Conversely, consider another person who holds that there are no objective moral goods or truths (ethical relativism) and no greater moral authority than oneself (subjectivism or ethical egoism) and, as a result, is determined to say or do whatever it takes to get the job. In both instances, one's worldview commitment significantly influences one's moral decision-making.

We think this scenario substantiates our point about the existence—and importance—of objective moral goods or truths. Not only does a specifically Christian viewpoint endorse general moral truths but moral truth is specifically embodied in the person of Jesus Christ—the trustworthy Lord and Master—who models true servanthood for his followers.[8] Numerous New Testament teachings concur. Perhaps most directly, the Gospel of John declares that Jesus *is* the truth (as well as the way and the life).[9]

Many other Scripture passages argue for Jesus' moral perfection—even in the midst of his experiencing temptation. For instance, "For we do not have a high priest who is unable to empathize with our weaknesses, but we have one who has been tempted in every way, just as we are—yet he did not sin" (Heb. 4:15). So by implication, we may assume that Jesus always tells the truth. Therefore, we can be confident that (1) objective moral truth exists, (2) such moral truth may be communicated (preferably with humble confidence), and (3) such moral truth may be discovered as true and subsequently incorporated into one's actions.[10] Jacques Ellul adds, "Just as the Word is the way God reveals himself, it also reveals a person to himself. . . . We discover our truth in this Word, which questions us on God's behalf."[11]

Ultimately, then, who or what is most authoritative on moral matters, matters most! If God incarnate (Jesus Christ) is the ultimate authority on all communication matters, then communication ethics should involve sharing information and ideas with others truthfully and graciously, with proper motives and intentions, for the other's sake more than for one's own sake and, above all, in God-honoring ways.

These communication "oughts" also apply when using smart phones and other media, including social media. While it's important to be grateful for technology and acknowledge certain benefits (e.g., instant access to others and information), we also must recognize the media can bring about significant moral challenges. We'll consider information ethics and new media later in the chapter.[12]

Communication and Information Ethics in the Business and Media Worlds

Before joining the academic world as professors, each of us authors were employed in the business world. It would take another book to share with you our many good experiences—along with some horror stories! Higher education and business worlds share many similarities, but also different emphases and priorities. Our experiences in these arenas lead us to conclude that an organization's core worldview and mission—especially as stated and practiced by its leaders—reveals its morality. Of course, when we are speaking of an "organization," necessarily we are referring to the individuals who comprise it. Companies don't actually possess moral thoughts and practices; people do. Nonetheless, we often shorthand this by making claims like "That corporation is so immoral" or "I like that company because it serves the homeless." Certainly, the moral views and actions of its shareholders and stakeholders shape the perceptions of its employees, customers, and others. Whether those perceptions are accurate would seem to matter a lot; unfortunately, mistaken or dishonest practices may lead to people acquiring false beliefs about an organization, sometimes to the point of precipitating an organization's demise. The reverse may happen as well, wherein unscrupulous propaganda tactics of immoral corporate leaders convince people of the organization's commitment to the true and the good. All this calls for us to be diligent and discerning so that any truth claims we make about businesses and their leaders may be supported with good arguments and backing.

So not surprisingly, questions and concerns arise about the ethics and moral practices of particular businesses: What does that organization really stand for? Why does our company treat its employees so well (or so poorly)? How can that pharmaceutical company charge fifty times what it costs to manufacture its product? Why is that fast-food chain restaurant closed on Sundays? Why is everyone who works there so friendly and kind to their customers? Why does that corporation explicitly promote a particular social (or political) agenda? Those two financial institutions conduct business very differently; why is that? What ethical standards and moral practices should guide a company's shareholders and stakeholders?

Consider the business of marketing and advertising. The particular media used to market and advertise a product or service intertwines with communication about that product or service—in some cases, so much so that what is being sold is actually something other than the thing itself (like some alleged status or benefit irrelevant to the product or service being offered). We might call this deceptive or false advertising. Quentin Schultze traces this development and its impact on society: "The commercial media encourage us to form superficial communities of consumption. Beginning in the nineteenth century, first with magazines and later with radio and television, the media connected people across geographic space with consumer products that symbolized attractive lifestyles and the American dream. People began replacing local, ethnic, and religious connections with consumer-oriented lifestyles."[13]

Predictably, the consumerism produced by the commercial media enterprise has resulted in shallow communities of consumption and "many people's substitute for shalom."[14] Something similar may be said about "fake news" creations— stories motivated by some special interest or social-political agenda—misusing or falsifying the actual content or events involved. While we can't go into detail here, it seems evident that moral questions arise about the use of techniques and technology in such cases. Scanning just a few digital news websites can provide some astonishing results. Ethical issues jump off nearly every page. Many such scenarios share similar moral problems: the desire for wealth, power, or control in overriding basic human rights or circumventing responsible action toward people (wrongly disclosed or defrauding them); greed over generosity; selfishness over the interests of others; and harming rather than helping one's neighbor. Injustice is overriding justice, contrary to how things ought to be. Such cases reinforce the need for communication ethics and information ethics to address immoral and detrimental usage of information technologies, which are exceedingly pervasive in the digital world.

This may explain why certain business practices, like those promoting human-trafficking and pornography, are always immoral; they operate outside of God's goodness, design, and will for human flourishing. How so? For one, bosses and managers in those industries characteristically view and treat individuals as mere products or merchandise. They attribute to their victims merely instrumental value (what the injured party can do for the controlling party)[15] rather than intrinsic value or worth (persons having value in and of themselves as human beings) ultimately derived from humans' being made in God's image. In these contexts, vices like greed, lying, deception, and exploitation trump virtues like generosity, truthfulness, kindness, and respect. This explains why many Christian (and other) faith-based organizations lead the fight to free those trapped by human-trafficking,[16] pornography,[17] and other corrupt or categorically evil industries and businesses (regardless of whether such entities operate legally or illegally). Still, Christians—like everyone else—are not immune from these evils; misdirected desires and self-centered freedoms can easily move one into immoral territory—even participating in unethical and criminal industries or activities.

> In a technological society, the very concept of truthful communication is problematic. Deception is built into making technologies and institutional forms of communication.
> —Quentin J. Schultze,
> *Communicating for Life*, 140

Keep in mind that information ethics today is increasingly focused on examining ethical principles and moral practices involving online or digital information—often proposing solutions to unethical foundations and immoral conduct. This arena includes computers, smart phones, the internet/cyberspace, social media, podcasts, blogs, email, apps, digital images, videos, video games, video conferencing, music, film, and television (on demand and/or livestreaming), artificial intelligence (AI), virtual reality (VR), and related new technologies. The ethical debates in this arena range from broad, worldview-level perspectives (e.g., about human nature and its relation to privacy vs. public rights) to specific, practical steps to be implemented (such as allowing free access to information vs. employing some level of censorship). The plurality of worldviews and divergent approaches to these issues makes it extremely challenging to reach consensus on a shared set of assumptions and practices—even though certain organizations and governmental agencies have proposed, and in some cases affirmed, some such commitments.[18]

If we take an objective view of morality, then moral issues in the business and digital realms ought to be evaluated and acted on appropriately—even if beginning with the principle of "innocent until proven guilty." If this is true, then a crucial question might be, "According to what or whose morality should we evaluate and respond?" Of course, this is where worldviews and ethical systems come into play. For instance, would you agree that in the business and media worlds, some character qualities and right actions—like truthfulness/truth-telling—are incumbent on every person, regardless of position, power, feelings, or desires? How you answer this question may reveal whether you embrace an objective and unchanging morality or a subjective and relative one. Shortly, we will consider how an objective-morality approach may be helpful in guiding our thoughts and practical use of new media technologies.

On the one hand, certain benefits of new media seem obvious, particularly smart phones: connecting with loved ones; taking and sending pictures and videos; education-related activities; job searching; attending virtual appointments/meetings; livestreaming events; checking weather, sports, traffic, or news; shopping; finding a restaurant or gas station; booking travel, concerts, and other events and applications. Clearly, then, smart phone users—plus users of other new media—may have good reason to value positive aspects of newer technologies.

On the other hand, it may be just as obvious to everyone participating in the digital world—perhaps especially concerning social media—that information and technologies often get utilized for immoral and evil purposes. Such harmful and evil techniques in technology negatively impact our lives, in some cases contributing toward destroying them. One heartbreaking example is the exponential growth in teen and young-adult anxiety, depression, and suicidal ideation over the past decade—and most tragically, estimates approximate that one in twenty-five suicide attempts are successful. Excessive smart-phone usage and social-media consumption by young people are important contributing factors—particularly considering the ease of access/exposure to cyberbullying, bad news, and, most of all, suicides, including livestreamed. Such negative examples are ubiquitous. Consider this 2020 Pew Research Center study:

> About two-thirds of Americans (64%) say social media have a mostly negative effect on the way things are going in the country today, according to a Pew Research Center survey of U.S. adults conducted July 13–19, 2020. Just one-in-ten Americans say social media sites have a mostly positive effect on the way things are going. . . . Those who have a negative view of the impact of social media mention, in particular, misinformation and the hate and harassment they see on social media. They also have concerns about users believing everything they see or read—or not being sure about what to believe. Additionally, they bemoan social media's role in fomenting partisanship and polarization, the creation of echo chambers.[19]

Rather paradoxically, while many young people rely on social media sources for current events (45 percent), the vast majority don't put a lot of trust in the information they get (only 17 percent do).[20] Trusted sources for news and current events seems to be getting even harder to come by.

Nevertheless, wisdom calls us information-seekers to do our homework to find and utilize reliable, truth-based sources. Even so, we need to keep in mind that particular worldviews—including moral beliefs about information—permeate every organization. As a start, then, we ought to fairly compare and contrast diverse media outlets and their presentation of information, which can help us become wiser, more circumspect consumers of news and current affairs.[21]

What Does All This Mean for Our Lives?

Checking Priorities

A significant challenge we all face—especially in our exploding information age—is keeping focused on the things that really matter. What are some ways we can do so? For one, we can give higher priority to people than to technology. For example, consider when you're face-to-face with another person: Do you give that individual your full attention, or do you keep checking (or keep thinking about checking) your smart phone for messages, the latest online videos or news stories or sports scores, or looking for a way to end the conversation so you can get back to the video game or shopping or scrolling? What really matters most? Craig Detweiler illustrates the expectation of new media that we should be constantly connected or always on—repeatedly raising moral dilemmas and questions of priority:

> We have been swamped by a tsunami of new technologies, without pausing to consider whether they are good or bad, helpful or hurtful. Are they making us more thoughtful, more articulate, more loving? I see the benefits of technology when I can let my family know where I am or send a quick text message of support to a friend. But I also feel pulled away from them in order to check for updates and to respond for requests to information, simply because everything can happen so simultaneously. Our devices demand our attention.[22]

Perhaps Brian Brock's reminder may help us to reconfigure our priorities when navigating the tension between our online and offline worlds. Brock argues that "what the technological imperative promises modern society fits the classic definition of that offered by a god, principality, or power," while in reality it tends to deliver "the tragic electricity of human alienation." Yet there's a silver lining here. Disappointment with these false gods "does provide an opening for a new attentiveness to and cooperation with the true God's work in the world." To enter through that opening, we must (a) "demote the worship of the penultimate [less than ultimate] goods of human ingenuity and work to their proper place before their divine source,"[23] and (b) promote the worship of the ultimate goods of God's creativity (creation) and work (redemption) through Jesus Christ, in the power of the Spirit.

Checking Motives

Keeping focused on the things that really matter requires us to check our motives—and to think about potential consequences—before posting photos, videos, and text messages.[24] Do we take steps to resist the constant barrage from advertisers based on tailored AI-generated algorithms, or do we just allow whatever to happen? Do we wander into open cyber spaces intended to neutralize our morals and values? How is our use of media and information shaping our very being—our soul? Many are awakening to the need for increased ethical reflection and improved moral decision-making in the ever-changing information age.[25]

Checking Self

Finally, keeping focused on the things that really matter calls us to conscientiously consider our responsibility before God and others—for being good and doing right—when we communicate via various media. Do we remain the same self online as when present with others face-to-face? Do we hide out in virtual communities or a virtual world, becoming or expressing a fake self? Permitting oneself to hide out or create a new identity (*persona*)—different from one's offline identity—tends to undermine one's true self, in effect creating a self-contradiction. To live as a coherent self, our thought life must align with our actions (moral practices). There is one who uniquely embodies a fully coherent self, Jesus Christ! The master's own moral life provides his followers with an impeccable model, along with a promise of blessing on those who know and put into practice Jesus' moral teachings (John 13:12–17).

Checking Tech Habits

French philosopher Jacques Ellul (rather prophetically) understood the domination and "totalizing" effects of humanity's growing obsession with methods to bring "absolute efficiency" to everything—using technology to do so. Tech itself becomes a "Master"—humans become enslaved to it—diminishing the quality of life while giving individuals the illusion of freedom. This "technique" includes information and technology being primary "tools" that enslave. Most people are unaware of this.[26] "Wake Up!" reflects Ellul's pressing admonition. Moral issues are at stake. We must resist the total control techniques and technology can gain over our lives.[27]

Ellul likely would have much to communicate about how this situation has progressed (since his passing in 1994). Information and technology developments and inventions have proliferated exponentially—and technique has exploded as well. Algorithms, GPS systems, and health and fitness monitors now track our every move—all with the moral promise to improve our lives while manipulating our minds and decision-making freedoms. Unless we "Wake Up!" soon, technique and technology will continue to outpace ethical reflection and moral actions, further constricting human liberty—perhaps nearing the level of becoming puppets or pawns of the system.

If Ellul is right, then resistance will entail radically altering our habits. It will require subverting the efforts of individuals and institutions aimed at using technology for immoral ends. More important, resistance will compel us to cultivate the kind of character that enables us to see technology's limitations and insidious ways of undermining genuine relationships, communities, and proven ways of nourishing our souls.[28]

Checking Health

Abundant evidence points to various kinds of moral, mental, and physical health problems arising from incessant and addictive overuse of new media such as smart phones and virtual communities. Even before the explosive growth of social media, Richard A. Spinello saw the writing on the wall and the need for *Cyberethics: Morality and Law in Cyberspace*: "The role of morality [in cyberspace] should be quite evident: it must be the ultimate regulator of cyberspace that sets the boundaries for activities and policies. It should direct and harmonize the forces of law, code, the market, and social norms so that interactions and dealings there will be measured, fair, and just."[29]

Checking Principles

Spinello also employs the Golden Rule ("Do to others as you would have them do to you," Luke 6:31), as well as Kant's second version of the Categorical Imperative (to always treat persons as an end, having intrinsic value, and never merely as a means, having only instrumental value). He names these "intermediate ethical principles" coming from the "ultimate good, the human flourishing of ourselves and others" from which "more specific core values about murder, theft, and lying can be derived."[30] We agree with Spinello's main points about morality's "ultimate regulator" role for cyberspace. Moreover, we commend his including Jesus' Golden Rule principle and Kant's absolute imperative. Still, such principles need further normative content—objective directives, commands, and examples to be understood and followed.

Checking Moral Grounds

Biblically based Christian ethics contains such normative content. Among the many benefits of this ethical system are clarity and specificity as to right behavior and good character. Biblically based Christian ethics also rightly rejects implausible systems like ethical relativism, whether of the subjectivist type ("I alone can decide what should be prescribed") or conventionalist sort ("only one's culture decides what is right and wrong"). Although some interpretive differences subsist within Christian ethics, objective moral grounding remains imperative. This grounding is preeminently based in God's character and commands, which guide the interpretive process in recognizing moral truths and moral goods.

If moral truths exist and matter—including goodness, truthfulness, fairness, and justice—then it follows that such truths ought to be employed within communication and information domains. We contend that God has given human beings the capacity to discern/know objective moral truths as revealed via Scripture, Jesus Christ, creation, conscience, intuition, and reason. Moreover, faithful Christian theologians and philosophers have recognized that divinely-revealed moral goods originate from God's good character and moral will, making it both reasonable and right to embrace and obey divinely revealed morality, communally and individually.[31] For Christ-followers, objective moral virtues and practices may be best lived out by emulating the one who is the way, the truth, and the life: the Lord Jesus.[32]

Questions for Reflection

1. What are some ways that you communicate with others that demonstrate certain virtues or vices toward others? Do you think morality matters when communicating with others? Why or why not?

2. What are the greatest moral challenges when it comes to using smart phones, the internet, or social media? List these in order of most to least challenging, and explain how to best meet each challenge.

3. Describe the impact worldviews and ethical systems have on communication, whether interpersonal or via new media. What means may be employed to recognize and evaluate different worldviews and moralities more circumspectly and wisely?

For Further Reading

Brock, Brian. *Christian Ethics in a Technological Age*. Grand Rapids: Eerdmans, 2010.

Detweiler, Craig. *iGods: How Technology Shapes Our Spiritual and Social Lives*. Grand Rapids: Brazos, 2013.

Ellul, Jacques. *The Humiliation of the Word*. Translated by Joyce Main Hanks. Eugene, OR: Wipf and Stock, 2021.

Lipari, Lisbeth A. "Communication Ethics." *Oxford Research Encyclopedia of Communication*. February 27, 2017, https://oxfordre.com/communication/view/10.1093/acrefore/9780190 228613.001.0001/acrefore-9780190228613-e-58.

Spinello, Richard A. *Cyberethics: Morality and Law in Cyberspace*. 4th ed. Sudbury, MA: Jones and Bartlett Learning, LLC., 2011. Cyberethics - Google Books.

Schultze, Quentin J. *Communicating with Grace and Virtue: Learning to Listen, Speak, Text, and Interact as a Christian*. Grand Rapids: Baker Academic, 2020.

Schultze, Quentin J. *Habits of the High-Tech Heart: Living Virtuously in the Information Age*. Grand Rapids: Baker Academic, 2002.

NOTES

1. During interpersonal communication, most of what "communicates" is not the words we use but rather our tonal and nonverbal expressions.

2. For readers who reject categories of moral right/good and evil/wrong, we understand that the suggestions and solutions we present in this chapter may not be convincing to you; we still hope you will give us a fair hearing with an open mind.

3. Quentin J. Schultze, *High-Tech Worship: Using Presentational Technologies Wisely* (Grand Rapids: Baker Books, 2004), 22, emphasis in original.

4. Lisbeth A. Lipari, "Communication Ethics," *Oxford Research Encyclopedia of Communication*, February 27, 2017, https://doi.org/10.1093/acrefore/9780190228613.013.58

5. Each major ethical system contains subsystems; for example, deontological ethics typically includes three primary subsystems: divine command theory (DCT), natural law ethics, and ethical rationalism.

6. In John 14:6a, Jesus claims to be the truth (perhaps meaning embodying it): "I am the way and the truth and the life." Ephesians 4:15 calls its readers to "truth it," translated (in the NIV) as "speaking the truth."

7. Of course, "truth" is a contested term, as is "objective." Even for some thinkers who hold to objective moral facts/truths, the grounding for what is objective varies. We hold that God is the ultimate metaphysical ground for morality, preeminently recognized in the incarnate one, Jesus Christ, as the way, the truth, and the life (John 14:6a).

8. See John 13:14–16, for instance.

9. See John 14:6a.

10. We acknowledge that some extreme situations involving moral dilemmas occur where it may be allowable or appropriate to circumvent truthfulness for an even higher principle or imperative (command), such as saving the lives of individuals by means of deceiving someone

intending to inflict serious injury or death on them. Such extreme cases are viewed by some thinkers as choosing "the lesser of two evils" or choosing "the greater of two moral oughts." Still, it seems plausible that the (rare) exception proves the normative rule of truth-telling. (See Quentin Schultze, *Communicating for Life: Christian Stewardship in Community and Media* [Grand Rapids: Baker Academic, 2000], 139–44.)

11. Jacques Ellul, *The Humiliation of the Word*, trans. Joyce Main Hanks (Eugene, OR: Wipf and Stock, 2021), 52.

12. AI, ChatGPT, and other innovative technologies are constantly being developed, changed, and updated. We acknowledge the need for moral philosophy in these burgeoning areas (and hope to contribute to the critical discussion in some future publications); however, we would not be able to cover this ground sufficiently in this introduction to philosophy.

13. Schultze, *Communicating for Life*, 114.

14. Ibid.

15. Numerous heartbreaking testimonies and evidence confirm this tragic reality.

16. For instance, International Justice Mission (www.ijm.org).

17. For example, Faithful and True (www.faithfulandtrue.com).

18. For instance, see the "Declaration for the Future of the Internet" (www.state.gov/declaration-for-the-future-of-the-internet).

19. Brooke Auxier, "64% of Americans Say Social Media Have a Mostly Negative Effect on the Way Things Are Going in the U.S. Today." Pew Research Center, October 15, 2020, www.pewresearch.org/short-reads/2020/10/15/64-of-americans-say-social-media-have-a-mostly-negative-effect-on-the-way-things-are-going-in-the-u-s-today/.

20. See the 2021 UNICEF-Gallup study, which reached more than 21,000 people, aged 15 to 24 and 40 and older in 21 countries (spanning Africa, Asia, Europe, and North and South America). For a summary, see Julie Ray, "Young People Rely on Social Media, but Don't Trust It," Gallup, November 18, 2021, https://news.gallup.com/opinion/gallup/357446/young-people-rely-social-media-don-trust.aspx.

21. One media company we find helpful toward this goal (of wisely comparing and contrasting media sources) is AllSides (www.allsides.com), whose media philosophy includes moving beyond "filter bubbles" and "highly polarization political and social environment" (endemic to online technologies) and instead providing "balanced news, media bias ratings, diverse perspectives, and real conversation" (see www.allsides.com/about/editorial-philosophy and https://www.allsides.com/about).

22. Craig Detweiler, *iGods: How Technology Shapes Our Spiritual and Social Lives* (Grand Rapids: Brazos Press, 2013), 7.

23. Brian Brock, *Christian Ethics in a Technological Age* (Grand Rapids: Eerdmans, 2010), 379.

24. Engaging with others over controversial topics through social media is not often an environment conducive to civil discourse, given the temptation to perform in front of others rather than work toward better understanding where the disagreement lies or discovering the truth collaboratively in good faith. See Justin Tosi and Brandon Warmke, *Grandstanding: The Use and Abuse of Moral Talk* (Oxford: Oxford University Press, 2020).

25. Book-length treatments on the effects of information, media, and technology on humans, individually and collectively, are proliferating (and will likely continue for the foreseeable future).

26. For an excerpt from Jacques Ellul, *The Search for Ethics in a Technicist Society* (1983), and an excerpt from James Fowler, *A Synopsis and Analysis of the Thought and Writings of Jacques Ellul* (2000), see the International Jacques Ellul Society webpage: https://ellul.org/themes/ellul-and-technique/.

27. Our thanks to Dr. Peter Anderson (assistant dean of the College of Theology at Grand Canyon University, Phoenix, AZ) for important insights into Ellul's project (Ellul was Anderson's primary dissertation interlocutor).

28. Does this "resistance" idea sound like it's from *The Matrix*? In some ways this might not be far from the truth. It's time we take "the red pill" (over the blue one) and wake up to the new reality! (In the film, Morpheus offers Neo a red or blue pill to swallow; the red one symbolizing waking up to reality and the truth, the blue one essentially representing staying "asleep" in the computer-generated simulated world.)

29. Richard A Spinello, *Cyberethics: Morality and Law in Cyberspace*, 4th ed. (Sudbury, MA: Jones and Bartlett Learning, 2011), 7.

30. Spinello, *Cyberethics*, 6.

31. Even so, Christian scholars differ as to what the moral expectations ought to be for non-followers of Jesus. At a minimum, though, most hold that God-designed creation and/or conscience provide all humans with some level of objective moral knowledge. (For instance, many point to Rom. 1:18–32 as a bare minimum moral knowledge.)

32. See John 15:20 (along with the broader context/themes of the chapter).

PART 8

The Meaning of Life

CHAPTER 25

What Does Philosophy Say about the Meaning of Life?

If philosophy is thinking hard about things that matter, then thinking about the meaning of life is an important philosophical practice. Thinking about the meaning of life has significant consequences for one's psychological well-being and outlook on life. The very reasons for getting out of bed in the morning sometimes trace back to how one answers the meaning-of-life question. One of the most significant philosophical questions one can ask, then, is this: "What is the meaning of life?" In this chapter, we will look at what philosophy has to say about the meaning of life.[1] Specifically, we will examine how philosophers have offered better ways of framing the question. This chapter will primarily focus on how to think better about what the meaning-of-life question is asking and how different worldviews provide varying explanatory resources to answer it.

Applying Philosophical Tools to the Meaning-of-Life Question

Meaning-In Life versus Meaning-Of Life

You might think the meaning-of-life topic is something all philosophers spend their time thinking about. After all, if there was ever a philosophical question, surely the meaning-of-life question is one of them. Surprisingly, however, philosophers have only revisited this question with renewed vigor and interest roughly at the beginning of the twenty-first century.[2] But once the meaning-of-life question started receiving the attention it deserves, philosophers soon realized it can be aiming at different targets. For example, is the target of the meaning-of-life question the different ways one can find meaning *in* life? Or is the target of the meaning-of-life question a big bull's-eye—one with the definite article at the center of it? Specifically, what is *the* answer to the meaning *of* life? One of the challenges, then, behind the meaning-of-life question is getting clear about what the question is really asking.

Most philosophers agree that human beings have equal value and worth. Christian philosophers, of course, ground this universal value shared by all humans in the doctrine of the *imago dei*—the belief that humans are created in the image and likeness of God.[3] This is why all humans have intrinsic value and should be treated as ends and never as mere means.[4] The controversy over the meaning-of-life question, however, lies in whether there is an all-encompassing answer to it. Many philosophers deny that an all-encompassing answer to the meaning-of-life question exists. So they instead focus on a related (but different) question: "Can we find meaning in life?"[5] Others think there is an answer to the meaning-of-life question. Philosophers that believe an all-encompassing answer to the meaning-of-life question exists take what Joshua Seachris calls the single-question approach. Philosophers that deny an all-encompassing answer to the meaning-of-life question take what Seachris calls the amalgam approach.[6]

The amalgam approach treats the meaning-of-life question as an umbrella question covering related questions. What things are valuable? What things make life meaningful? What things give life purpose? This approach sees the meaning-of-life question as a project of finding valuable things worth pursuing in efforts to find meaning *in* life. The quantity and quality of relationships, pleasures, and achievements provide countless ways one can find meaning in life. For example, creating families, alleviating pain and suffering, creating beautiful things, experiencing various pleasures, and/or creating goods and services for the benefit of others are often taken as values people pursue to find meaning in life. Indeed, theists and atheists alike can agree that pursuing things of real value can result in a meaningful life.

The single-question approach seeks an answer to the meaning of life; this approach is after something bigger. An all-encompassing answer that applies universally to all humans is what's required for an answer to the meaning of life. Candidate answers to this question appeal to resources usually found in supernatural worldviews. Philosophers taking this approach, according to Seachris and Goetz, seek adequate ways of addressing our "questions and concerns about purpose, significance, value, worth, pain and suffering, [how life and the universe ends], and so on. Contrary to the amalgam [approach], on this view, the question of life's meaning is asking for a single thing—a sense-making explanation."[7]

While Christians agree that there are a variety of valuable projects and activities that provide meaning to one's life, as proponents of the amalgam approach suggest, most Christians believe there is an overarching answer to the meaning-of-life question. The reason is that if God created humans for divine purposes, then many believe the Christian worldview has the right kind of explanatory resources to take the single-question approach.

Understanding "Meaning" in the Meaning-of-Life Question

How can we better understand the meaning-of-life question? Surely, the meaning-of-life question can be stated in different words that seem to get after the same thing or, at least, something in the neighborhood. For example, the following questions seem to share a family resemblance with the meaning-of-life question:

- Why are we here?
- Why does the universe exist?
- What is life all about?
- What is the purpose of life? or Does life have a purpose?
- What's the significance of life?
- How did life originate? or Where did life come from?
- What is the value of life? or What kind of value does life have?

These questions are clearly looking for answers that the meaning-of-life question is looking for, too. They at least address important facets of the meaning-of-life question. But once we include the following questions, we begin filling out what Joshua Seachris calls "existentially charged questions."[8]

- Does God exist?
- Does God personally interact with humans?
- Has God provided special revelation to humans?
- Do objective moral values exist?
- What values should inform how to live life?
- What is justice?
- Who is a good person?
- Can one be genuinely happy?
- Why is there pain and suffering?
- Is there life after death?
- If there is life after death, what happens then?
- Is there a judgment in the afterlife? If so, what kind of punishments and rewards will be meted out?

With this new set of questions, we now have a decent list of existentially charged questions. Many of us have, at some time, thought about such questions. Perhaps you have even spent a significant amount of time wrestling with them. Seachris thinks that at the heart of the meaning-of-life question is a deep-seated desire for a story that narrates to us answers to existentially charged questions.[9] In other words, what motivates the meaning-of-life question is a deep desire and longing for a metanarrative or all-encompassing story that provides answers to existentially charged questions. The metanarrative, then, organizes these answers into a meaningful, coherent whole. Therefore, Seachris says, "When we ask for the meaning for life, we should view ourselves as seeking a wider narrative framework that enables us to make sense of [existentially charged questions] [. . .] [so that the metanarrative] provides practical guidance for leading a flourishing life."[10] Indeed, if there was ever a meaningful life or a life worth living, surely it's a life wherein one is flourishing or is truly happy.

Many philosophers and psychologists alike see value, purpose, and sense-making or coherence as key concepts that, when properly unpacked, provide a greater understanding to what motivates us to ask the meaning-of-life question.[11] Indeed, Goetz and Seachris challenge readers to consider Victor Frankl's position:[12] humanity's greatest motivational drive is neither the will to pleasure (contra Freud)[13] nor the will to power (contra Nietzsche),[14] but rather the will to meaning.[15] They say, "We want the parts of our lives both simultaneously and over time to fit together properly so that our lives as a whole make sense. When this fails to occur, we are haunted by the [pervasiveness] of [life's] meaninglessness."[16]

So what kind of values can provide life with purpose and meaning? What kind of metanarrative can provide answers to existentially charged questions, thereby instructing one on how to thrive at living life well and thus be happy? Answers to these questions require consulting the explanatory resources of one's worldview. One's worldview establishes the existence or non-existence of values and, as we will see, the significance of God and death relative to the meaning-of-life question.

Worldviews and the Meaning-of-Life Question

Worldview Significance to Life's Meaning

We're working with the idea that the meaning-of-life question is roughly asking whether there is a metanarrative that provides answers to existentially charged questions that can help us fit these answers into a meaningful, coherent whole. It's assumed by many that a meaningful life will result in a happy life. But a meaningful life requires practical guidance for knowing what's good for a human being. Knowing what's good for a human requires knowing what good values contribute to human flourishing. Many important, existentially charged questions involve, then, whether key values exist in the world. But not all worldviews have or share the same kind of values.

KINDS OF VALUE

Value, in general, is the worth or significance we attribute to something. Anything that is good or better because of the worth it possesses has value. Things we see as valuable are commonly referred to as "good"; that which lacks, perverts, distorts, or deprives things of goodness we commonly refer to as "bad." Things can have objective value or subjective value. Objective value is anything that has mind-independent goodness that's located in the external world. Subjective value is anything that has mind-dependent goodness that's located in one's mind, usually one's belief. Aesthetic value is when a thing has the property of beauty or elicits a pleasurable experience because of perceived beauty. Intrinsic value is when a thing's value is located inside the thing itself (e.g., the value of human life). Extrinsic value is when a thing's value is dependent upon something outside of it (e.g., the sentimental value of an article of clothing once worn by a loved one). Instrumental value is when a thing's value is located as a means to some end (e.g., money is a means of exchanging it for some product or service). Final value is when the value of something contributes to fulfilling the purpose or design of the thing that has it (e.g., acquiring knowledge or Christ-like virtues contributes to fulfilling the kind of thing a human person was designed to be).

One's worldview and the kind of values it contains informs the metanarrative on how to interpret reality. Recall that the worldview of naturalism has two significant theses: one metaphysical and the other epistemological. The metaphysical thesis is that reality is entirely physical through and through—anything that exists must be physical. According to naturalism, God, angels, demons, souls, and abstract objects do not exist. The epistemic thesis that falls out of this is that the hard sciences (physics, chemistry, neuroscience, astronomy, etc.) are the most (if not only) reliable methods to get epistemic goods like truth, knowledge, and understanding.[17] Other epistemic methods and intellectual disciplines (e.g., philosophy, math, theology, history, psychology, economics, etc.) can discover nonphysical things.

Seachris has divided up the spectrum of worldviews and their implications to the meaning-of-life question into four camps: Objective Naturalism, Subjective Naturalism, Pessimistic Naturalism, and Supernaturalism.[18]

Objective Naturalism

This worldview posits the existence of mind-independent, objective values that are grounded in or emerge from physical matter. God is not needed to ground them, sustain them, nor design human faculties to discover them. According to objective naturalism, Seachris says, "A meaningful life is a function of appropriately connecting with mind-independent realities of objective worth (contra subjectivism), and that are entirely natural (contra supernaturalism)."[19] One can pursue and secure specific pleasures and goals in life and still miss securing the kind of objective values that truly make life meaningful. So a meaningful life will be better to the extent to which one discovers and aligns one's life with objective values furnishing the world.

Subjective Naturalism

This worldview posits the existence of subjective values that one invents—not discovers (contra objective naturalism and supernaturalism). Pursuing a life that aligns with those values one believes are true is a way to find meaning in life, to live a happy life. Like all versions of naturalism, God is not needed to ground, sustain, or design human faculties to discover the kind of values that make life meaningful. According to subjective naturalism, a meaningful life is the result of pursuing whatever an individual believes is good for them. The goals, projects, relationships, and pleasures perceived as valuable—relative to each individual—are a way to make life meaningful.

Pessimistic Naturalism

This worldview feeds a view called nihilism. Nihilism or pessimistic naturalism denies objective values exist. As a result, the prospects for a meaningful life are nil. Nihilism draws from points made by supernaturalism and naturalism: God or some version of supernaturalism is needed to establish the existence of values needed for a meaningful life. But since naturalism is believed to be true, the kind of nonphysical values that can make life meaningful don't exist.[20] According to the pessimistic naturalist, since supernaturalism is false, the implications of death having the last word makes life meaningless. For without God, there is no hope of an afterlife beyond the grave.[21]

Supernaturalism

This worldview posits the existence of mind-independent, objective values that are grounded in a God that sustains them and endows humans with cognitive faculties to discover them. Seachris emphasizes that, according to the Christian tradition, a "meaningful life requires that a person be appropriately related to God, perhaps as expressed in one's beliefs and especially in one's devotion, worship, and the quality of her life lived [amongst others] as, for example, embodied in Jesus' statement of the greatest commandments (cf. Matt. 22:34–40)."[22] Indeed, within the Christian tradition, the meaning of life may be answered, in part, by appealing to Jesus' commands to love the Lord your God with all your heart, soul, mind, and strength, and love your neighbor as yourself (Matt. 22: 37–39). More specifically, within the Reformed tradition of Christianity, the answer to the first question of the Westminster Larger Catechism states, "Man's chief and highest end is to glorify God, and fully enjoy him forever."[23]

Temporal Value and Purpose versus *Ultimate* Value and Purpose

Many philosophers with a supernatural worldview think that objective and subjective naturalists overlook and underappreciate what pessimistic naturalists (or nihilists) infer from a Godless world. Two of the most significant inferences are these: God is the best available explanation for (1) how and why objective values exist and (2) how death need not have the last word. Together, these two conclusions form the basis for seeing an important distinction between *temporal* value and purpose versus *ultimate* value and purpose. Here is how. If God doesn't exist, then (at best) the physical world could possibly (though highly unlikely) bring about objective values, including moral ones. Succeeding at discovering and aligning one's life with these values can indeed make life—to one degree or another—meaningful. Thus, one can live successfully at finding meaning in life.

Be that as it may, the meaning of one's life will not ultimately matter. This is because the forecast of this universe is clear: it will eventually die of a heat loss death once all the stars burn out. Neither advancements in space travel nor memories of one's life continuing to exist in the minds of others will rescue all of humanity from their impending death. Indeed, the universe itself will eventually die. The universe will eventually reach a state of thermodynamic equilibrium—becoming a cold, dark, life-prohibiting, and thus lifeless universe. On naturalism, although a life successfully aligned with things of value can make it better and more meaningful, this life can enjoy only temporal value and purpose.

Naturalism can't provide ultimate value and purpose and, thus, ultimate meaning to one's life. And for the nihilists and others alike, if there's no ultimate meaning in life, then the meaning of life is in serious trouble. Immortality is needed for life to have ultimate meaning. As good, significant, and admirable a life is that's aligned with good values, in the end it is still a life that lacks ultimate meaning and significance. For many people, if death has the last word, then temporal meaning gets swamped by the permanence of death. This distinction casts light on the difference a temporal perspective versus an eternal perspective has on life's meaning.

Endings, Perspective, and Ultimate Meaningfulness

In 1998, Bryce Drew played in the NCAA Men's basketball tournament for Valparaiso, the thirteenth seed team. Their opponent was Ole Miss, the fourth seed. With only 2.5 seconds left in the game, Valpo pulled off an amazing feat for the upset win. It started with an inbound pass from the far end of the court. But this inbound pass was more like a "Hail Mary" pass thrown by Jamie Sykes to Bill Jenkins. Jenkins then receives the ball and successfully tips it to Drew who manages to get off a three-point buzzer-beating shot to win the game.

Now known as "The Shot," Bryce Drew will forever be part of one of the most memorable moments in March Madness. Now consider this: as beautiful and improbable of a play as this was, it would not be remembered as one of the greatest moments in March Madness had Valpo lost the game. Let's be clear: the success of the shot was valuable—indeed, it was valuable in and of itself, as are most successes. But how the game ends determines whether this amazing shot receives additional value. What's more, how the game ends significantly influences how the entire game is evaluated and remembered.

Hopefully this illustrates the profundity of what Seachris calls "the proleptic power of narrative endings" and its relevance to the meaning-of-life question.[24] *Prolepsis* is when something is represented as existing now, before it actually occurs. The idea is this: the way a story ends can retroactively—go back in time— and inject additional value into a prior event. Indeed, think about how some of your favorite stories or movies have ended. I suspect how the story ends makes a significant difference in how you interpret, feel, and understand all the prior scenes leading up to it, as well as the movie as a whole. Again, if Ole Miss won the game, Valpo fans would have felt very different about Bryce Drew's shot and the game overall.

The good news for Christians is that we know how the story ends. Death doesn't have the last word. God will ultimately triumph over evil. God will create a new heaven and earth wherein perfect harmony, justice, and happiness will be enjoyed forever. (See Rev. 21.) The culmination of the Christian metanarrative also includes a time when Jesus will evaluate how we lived our lives on earth.

This future "awards ceremony" (see Matt. 25; 2 Cor. 5:10) can do tremendous work toward helping us discover the hidden values embedded in daily activities—much of which never gets noticed by other humans. Proactively thinking about the temporal value of one's daily decisions and actions, coupled with the ultimate value (the very same action retroactively received), can provide us with countless benefits. For starters, it can significantly increase the value, purpose, meaning, and motivations for performing successful actions. Therefore, it can significantly influence how we think, feel, and interpret our present experiences and circumstances. (All the ultimate value we've accrued will one day be rewarded and experienced!) Indeed, with the right eternal perspective, it can very well increase our degree of happiness experienced throughout life!

Conclusion

In this chapter, we introduced some helpful philosophical distinctions that hopefully will enable you to think better about the meaning-of-life question. Seeing how philosophers disagree over whether there is a true answer to this question explains why philosophers approach the meaning-of-life question differently. We saw that some philosophers take the amalgam approach to find meaning in life, whereas other philosophers believe there is a true answer to the meaning-of-life question and thus take the single-question approach. Finding the answer to the meaning of life rests largely on the explanatory resources made available by one's worldview. Objective naturalism, subjective naturalism, pessimistic naturalism, and supernaturalism address the meaning-of-life question differently, given their metaphysical and epistemic assumptions. Whether there can be ultimate meaning, value, and purpose to life depends on whether death has the last word; if it does, only temporal meaning, purpose, and value is available when addressing the meaning-of-life question. But if death doesn't have the last word, this has significant implications on one's perspective on life's meaning and the kind of additional values and rewards that can be enjoyed. In the next chapter, we build upon this and provide a more substantive Christian answer to the meaning-of-life question.

Questions for Reflection

1. Do you think there is an answer to the meaning of life or many ways of making life meaningful? Do you think there is an important relation between the two approaches?

2. How plausible do you think it is to say that a metanarrative that provides answers to existentially charged questions and fits those answers into a meaningful, coherent whole is what humans are seeking in an answer to the meaning-of-life question?

3. What are some of the costs and benefits of the four different worldviews we've listed insofar as their ability to answer the meaning-of-life question?

4. How significant are ultimate value and purpose in providing a satisfying and coherent answer to the meaning-of-life question?

5. How important do you think an eternal perspective is to making life meaningful?

For Further Reading

General Readers

Craig, William Lane. *Reasonable Faith: Christian Truth and Apologetics*, 3rd ed. Wheaton, IL: Crossway, 2008.

Seachris, Joshua, ed. *Exploring the Meaning of Life: An Anthology and Guide.* New York: Wiley-Blackwell, 2012.

———. "The Meaning of Life: Contemporary Analytic Perspectives," in *Internet Encyclopedia of Philosophy*, ed. James Fieser and Bradely Dowden. URL = Meaning of Life: Contemporary Analytic Perspectives | Internet Encyclopedia of Philosophy (utm.edu).

Seachris, Joshua, and Stewart Goetz. *What Is This Thing Called the Meaning of Life?* New York: Routledge, 2021.

Advanced Readers

Landau, Iddo, ed. *The Oxford Handbook of Meaning in Life*. New York: Oxford University Press, 2022.

Seachris, Joshua W. "Death, Futility, and the Proleptic Power of Narrative Ending." *Religious Studies*, 47 (2011): 141–63.

Seachris, Joshua W., and Steward Goetz, eds. *God and Meaning: New Essays.* New York: Bloomsbury Academic, 2016.

NOTES

1. We're indebted to Joshua Seachris and Stewart Goetz. Their recent work on the meaning of life has been most helpful in preparation for this chapter.

2. This is partly due to academic, analytic philosophy expanding the scope of "acceptable" topics of inquiry. Once disciplines like the philosophy of religion were granted a seat at most

academic tables, naturally the topic of life's meaning began receiving more attention and institutional funding for research.

3. See chapter 14 to consider some unique human characteristics that many think are baked into the idea that humans are image bearers of God.

4. Immanuel Kant (1768–24) famously argued that it's morally wrong to treat rational human beings—at any time and in any circumstance—as a mere means to some end; rather, humans are to be treated as an end-in-itself. In other words, humans have intrinsic value rather than only instrumental value. See the sidebar "Kinds of Value" for brief definitions of different kinds of value. Immanuel Kant, *Groundwork of the Metaphysics of Morals*, trans. Thomas Kingsmill Abbot (1785; Radford, VA: Wilder, 2008), 50.

5. Here is a helpful way of providing clarity to what many have in mind when thinking about what a meaningful life looks like. Seachris and Goetz define a meaningful life as follows: a life that makes sense by structuring one's decisions and choices toward appropriate purposes, activities, and relationships that matter, having positive value (for example, good impacts, not bad ones), and being reliably accompanied by a psychological profile that contains states like well-being, happiness, fullness, and satisfaction. This definition has been slightly modified so the reader can intuitively grasp and apprehend it without having to unpack all the parts of it that get developed in the chapters leading up to it. See Joshua Seachris and Stewart Goetz, *What Is This Thing Called the Meaning of Life?* (New York: Routledge, 2021), 97.

6. Joshua Seachris, "The Meaning of Life: Contemporary Analytic Perspectives," *Internet Encyclopedia of Philosophy*, ed. James Fieser and Bradely Dowden (2022), https://iep.utm.edu/mean-ana/.

7. Seachris and Goetz, *What Is This Thing Called the Meaning of Life?* 11.

8. Joshua Seachris, "The Meaning of Life and Scripture's Redemptive-Historical Narrative: Illuminating Convergences," in *God and Meaning: New Essays*, ed. Joshua Seachris and Stewart Goetz (New York: Bloomsbury Academic, 2016), 18–19.

9. Ibid.

10. Ibid., 20.

11. See William Lane Craig, *Reasonable Faith: Christian Truth and Apologetics*, 3rd ed. (Wheaton, IL: Crossway, 2008), 78–83. Seachris and Goetz, *What Is This Thing Called the Meaning of Life?* 93.

12. Victor Frankl (1905–97) was a psychiatrist, philosopher, and Holocaust survivor. His psychological theory, Logotherapy, takes the desire for life's meaning to be the strongest motivational force driving human behavior.

13. Sigmund Freud (1856–1939) took sexual desire or desire for pleasure to be the strongest motivational force driving human behavior.

14. Friedrich Nietzsche (1844–1900) took the desire for power, dominance, and strength over the world, including humans and human relationships, to be the strongest motivational force driving human behavior.

15. Goetz and Seachris, *What Is This Thing Called the Meaning of Life?* 93.

16. Ibid.

17. See chapter 17 for the problems of this epistemic method known as scientism.

18. See Seachris, "The Meaning of Life," in *Internet Encyclopedia of Philosophy*, https://iep.utm.edu/mean-ana/. Seachris includes a fifth category, namely, hybrid naturalism, which aims

to capture the merits of both subjective and objective accounts. But for the purposes of this chapter, we omit it to focus on the metaphysical and epistemological claims made by different worldviews. Hybrid naturalism is more flexible and can even be adopted into supernatural worldviews.

19. Ibid.

20. Indeed, philosopher J. L. Mackie (1917–81) famously says in the first sentence of *Ethics: Inventing Right and Wrong* that "there are no objective values [in the world]." See J. L. Mackie, *Ethics: Inventing Right and Wrong* (Harmondsworth, UK: Penguin, 1977), 15; quoted in David A. Horner and J. P. Moreland, *Metaethics: A Short Companion*, ed. C. Ben Mitchell and Jason Thacker (Brentwood, TN: B&H Academic, 2024).

21. Ibid.

22. Ibid.

23. Seachris, "The Meaning of Life and Scripture's Redemptive-Historical Narrative," 22.

24. See Joshua Seachris, "Death, Futility, and the Proleptic Power of Narrative Ending," *Religious Studies* 47 (2011): 141–63.

CHAPTER 26

What Is a Christian Philosophy of Life?

Chapter 25 addressed some of the philosophical fruit recent scholarship has produced on the meaning-of-life question. Making sense of what the meaning-of-life question is even asking is a challenge. Using the meaning in life versus meaning of life distinction provides a helpful framework; it explains why some philosophers emphasize the amalgam approach over the single-question approach. Many theists and atheists alike agree that pursuing valuable things makes life meaningful. Depending on one's worldview, however, the kind of explanatory resources one can use determines whether there is only temporal value and purpose or also ultimate value and purpose. Ultimate value and purpose get supported by how one's metanarrative ends, in addition to countless resources provided by God while the narrative unfolds. Does death have the last word or not? How the story ends determines whether events here and now can receive additional value and purpose in the life hereafter. In this chapter, we attempt to provide a Christian answer to the meaning-of-life question. But before developing this answer, it is important to first consider a plausible naturalist response. By doing so, we can compare how the Christian answer is arguably better by enhancing, enriching, and ultimately delivering on many of the commonly held values, desires, and hopes shared by many atheists and theists alike.[1]

Worldview, Metanarrative, and Existentially Charged Questions

The meaning-of-life question can be plausibly interpreted as a deep-seated desire for a metanarrative that provides answers to existentially charged questions.

These answers, then, get organized into a meaningful, coherent whole which allows us to find our true home within it. A metanarrative, then, narrates over life events while also providing an eternal perspective on them (depending, of course, on how the story ends).

> *Metanarrative:* A story with built-in metaphysical and epistemological assumptions that provides a way to interpret reality and answer existentially charged questions. Answers to existentially charged questions are then better understood and located within the story's temporal framework and further understood by considering how the story ultimately ends, thereby offering a temporal or eternal perspective (or both).[2]

Let's now consider a significant existentially charged question: Why are we here? Any metanarrative inevitably must address this question. But recall that one's worldview provides the kind of assumptions, commitments, norms, standards, values, principles, beliefs, and theories needed to fill out the plot of the metanarrative.[3]

Versions of subjective naturalism and pessimistic naturalism provide some unsatisfying and strange answers, given the explanatory resources of each worldview. Take, for example, the famous Harvard paleontologist and evolutionary biologist Stephen Jay Gould's answer to why humans are here: "We are here because one odd group of fishes had peculiar fin anatomy that could transform into legs for terrestrial creatures; because the earth never froze entirely during an ice age; because a small and tenuous species, arising in Africa a quarter of a million years ago, has managed, so far, to survive by hook and by crook. We may yearn for a 'higher' answer—but none exists."[4]

The reason why Gould's answer falls flat to the ears of many is that subjective and pessimistic naturalism are worldviews lacking teleology.[5] *Teleology* is a kind of cause or principle that explains the goal, aim, or purpose of some entity or event. Teleology provides an answer to the why question. But in a Godless world, it is difficult to account for how mindless, purposeless causes and events can be happening for genuine goals, aims, or purposes. Because Gould's worldview lacks teleology, he appeals to a mechanistic (or scientific) explanation for why humans are here; it's certainly not a personal explanation or one invoking God's purposes.

Richard Dawkins, a scientist known for publicly defending atheism, echoes Gould's answer by emphasizing the role that genes play in explaining human existence. Dawkins takes why questions, let alone the meaning-of-life question, to be akin to "What does the color blue taste like?" Why questions make a category mistake; there are no answers because the universe lacks teleology.[6] Indeed, he says, "Only the scientifically illiterate" continue asking why questions about living creatures. The scientifically literate know better.[7] He says, "Presumably there is indeed *no purpose* in the ultimate fate of the cosmos."[8] The purpose of human life is to propagate our DNA. He says, "We are survival machines—robot vehicles *blindly* programmed to preserve the selfish molecules known as genes."[9]

Some subjective naturalists like Jean-Paul Sartre (1905–1980) think a universe lacking teleology is good news. Instead of God imposing upon humanity an essence or nature that determines what's good for them, humans get to decide for themselves. Indeed, Sartre says a godless world allows humans to create their own essence, which is where we get the famous phrase "existence precedes essence."[10] Since humans can create their own essence, they can invent new purposes for a meaningful life that are grounded in whatever one feels or wants to be true. This grounds what some people mean when they say they are living out their "authentic self."[11]

But can humans really invent their own purposes for a meaningful life? Presumably a meaningful life entails doing good things that are beneficial to the individual and others. But can one be confident in knowing what's good for a person without knowing what kind of thing a person is? Submersion in water is good for a fish, but not for a computer. Most electric devices don't work well underwater given the kind of things they are. So unless we know the essence or nature of humans, can we say with any confidence that we know what is good for them, and thus, what their true purpose is?

Mechanistic explanations cite the relevant matter and laws that deterministically or probabilistically bring about some effect. Personal explanations cite the relevant beliefs and reasons for why a person intends to act in a certain way for the purpose of achieving a specific goal. For example, if we're trying to explain why the kitchen table is set a certain way—which includes your favorite meal and dessert—we can give a mechanistic explanation or a personal explanation. The former will appeal to physical causes evaluated at different levels of reality through the disciplines of physics, chemistry, and biology. Citing prior physical causes governed by certain laws of nature will explain why event A deterministically or probabilistically caused event B. The latter will appeal to intentions, motivations, beliefs, reasons, and purposes an agent uses to cause an event. So we can explain the ordering of the kitchen table by appealing to, say, events analyzed at the level of physics, or we can explain it by appealing to your spouse intending to surprise you for the purpose of celebrating your birthday with your favorite meal.[12]

What Is the Purpose of Human Life?

Parents often get asked what they want for their child. They typically reply with one of two answers: happiness or goodness. A parent might say, "I don't care what my child ends up doing—I just want them to be happy."[13] Or a parent might answer this way: "I want my child to be good." Might it be the case that happiness and goodness are two sides of the same meaning-of-life coin? Aristotle seemed to think so.[14]

Aristotle had a powerful answer to the why questions addressing the purpose of life. When children ask, "Why are you doing X?" and you respond, "I'm doing X because Y," most children follow up with another why question. For example, consider the following exchange:

Child: "Dad, why are you lacing up your sneakers?"
Father: "Because I want to exercise."
Child: "Why do you want to exercise?"
Father: "Because it promotes health."
Child: "Why do you want to be healthy?"

To stop this line of questioning or any iterative why-questioner you may encounter, Aristotle said the ultimate purpose for why humans perform activities is ultimately to be happy. Happiness is the question-stopper! Indeed, were someone to ask, "Why do you want to be happy?" do we even have to answer? (Responding with an incredulous stare might even be appropriate.) After all, who doesn't want to be happy? Happiness is a good thing, a very good thing, perhaps even the best thing—period!—end of discussion![15] So the purpose of life as being happy rings true to many theists and atheists alike. But what does it mean to be happy?

Who Is the Happy Person?

Aristotle says the happy person is one who thrives at living well. Happiness is virtuous activity.[16] And virtuous activity is intrinsically valuable (valuable in and of itself) and has final value (contributes to fulfilling one's nature and purpose).[17] From the moment one wakes up to the time one goes back to sleep—the happy person successfully lives all facets of life well. A genuinely successful life will not be lacking anything; indeed, you won't trade it for anything else the world has to offer.

We can conceive of cases involving people—indeed, we may even know people—who have tried to find meaning in life by pursuing what Aristotle would call counterfeit candidates for happiness: pleasure, honor, and wealth. Let's call this person Consumer-Joe. Each meal, drug, sex-act, performance, and purchase leaves Consumer-Joe emptier.[18] Aristotle says that counterfeit candidates for happiness have the wrong kind of value. Specifically, they lack intrinsic and final value; moreover, they aren't self-sustaining. It isn't until Consumer-Joe starts putting himself together that he will, according to Aristotle, begin tasting real, authentic Aristotelean-happiness. Once Consumer-Joe starts cultivating good character, he will be able to reason better (intellectual virtue) and act better (moral virtue). He will begin changing from Consumer-Joe to Virtuous-Joe, which will enable him to succeed in virtuous activity. Virtuous-Joe is engaging in successful activities involving the good, true, and beautiful.[19] More exactly, he's developing healthier relationships, thereby fulfilling his purpose to will the betterment of others (the good); developing his mind, thereby fulfilling his purpose to acquire epistemic goods (the true); and cultivating the passion and skill to make beautiful things, thereby fulfilling his purpose to create (the beautiful). Aristotle would say Virtuous-Joe is happy because his virtuous character enables him to fulfill his purpose of knowing what the right thing to do is and successfully do it—thrive at living life well.

What Is a Meaningful Life?

So far, we have said that a reasonable answer to the purpose of life is to be happy. We then provided an Aristotelean account of happiness.[20] Accordingly, happiness is virtuous activity—successfully living all facets of life well for the purpose of achieving the good, true, and beautiful. (On this account, the good, true, and beautiful are objective values and, thus, can be adopted *to one degree or another* by objective naturalists and supernaturalists.) Living life well because of virtuous activity seems like a good recipe for a meaningful life. Earlier, we endorsed Seachris's definition of a meaningful life, which many theists and atheists presumably will agree with, namely:

Meaningful Life: One's life is meaningful to the *degree* that it is oriented around that which matters (mattering that is of positive rather than negative value), which in turn fuels the purposive activity one pursues to give one's life direction, and, therefore allows one's life to make sense and exhibit proper fit with reality—a fitting place within the whole of what is true, good, and beautiful. Someone who lives such a life will tend to be *happier,* more *fulfilled,* satisfied, and engaged.[21]

Notice this definition allows for a meaningful life to come in degrees. Clearly, someone like Virtuous-Joe can be living a more meaningful life than someone spending all day counting grains of sand, playing video games, or eating bonbons.

Wisdom is a proper appreciation of the most important things. Some of these things include excellences, first principles, or values that contribute to human flourishing/happiness. Traditionally, there is a distinction between practical wisdom (*phronesis*) and theoretical wisdom (*sophia*). Theoretical wisdom is having the ability to discover those facts about reality that contribute to human flourishing/happiness. Practical wisdom is the ability to know, given the context and circumstances, how to appropriately execute the right action.

Atheists and theists alike can agree that pursuing objectively valuable things provides one's life with purpose, thereby making it a meaningful one. It takes theoretical wisdom to truly see what "valuable things" really do have the kind and degree of objective value needed to provide a more accurate understanding of the true, good, and beautiful. A wise person will also have practical wisdom—the kind of character needed—to successfully acquire them and consistently live them out.

The Christian conception of wisdom also absorbs the "wisdom" in Proverbs 9:10: "The fear of the Lord is the beginning of wisdom, and knowledge of the Holy One is understanding." So not only must one have the wisdom to know which versions of the good, true, and beautiful contribute to human flourishing/happiness, one also must see how these objective values fit together into a coherent whole. The good news for Christians is that fellowship with the Trinity can provide the kind of wisdom needed to properly orient oneself to both God and reality. Special revelation clarifies that God is the most important thing in this world, in addition to a proper appreciation and orientation toward God, which includes an attitude of reverence, holy fear. What's more, this kind of wisdom recognizes that one's dependency and cooperation with God is needed both to discover objective excellences, first principles, and values (*sophia*) and to have the power and resources to acquire them (*phronesis*) for the purpose of achieving Christian flourishing/happiness.

Virtuous-Joe's virtuous activity enables him to succeed at obtaining degrees of the good, true, and beautiful.[22] Indeed, two of the leading experts on the meaning of life—Seachris (a Christian theist) and Metz (an objective naturalist) agree on the following points regarding the meaning-of-life question:[23]

- Aligning one's life with discovered objective values (as opposed to mere invented subjective values) makes life meaningful—specifically, values that have both intrinsic and final value.
- Objective values are wanted for their own sake and not for the sake of something else (i.e., instrumental value).

- Meaning entails a plurality of purposes and values that make life meaningful.
- Objective values (e.g., the good, true, and beautiful) exist and successfully orienting one's life toward them makes life meaningful to one degree or another.
- Atheists and theists can live meaningful lives by orienting their lives around objective values.
- A meaningless life is proportionate to the lack of orientation toward and success at acquiring objective values.

It is not uncommon, then, to discover theists and atheists alike agreeing that pursuing objective values gives purpose to life. A purposeful life acquires and experiences objective values. So pursuing objective values and allowing those values to give one's life purpose is what makes life meaningful—it is what makes a person happy.

Why the Christian Prescription for a Meaningful Life Is Better

The first thing to point out is that the Christian tradition doesn't just appeal to happiness as the ultimate purpose for human life.[24] Rather, it is perfect happiness—an eternal, blessed state—what Aquinas calls *beatitudo*.[25] Aquinas says that perfect happiness is acquired "through union with God . . . which alone [humanity's] happiness consists."[26] Almost a century before Aquinas, Saint Augustine famously said of God: "You have made us for yourself, and our heart is restless until it rests in you."[27]

As impressive as the Aristotelean account of happiness is for objective naturalists, someone like Virtuous-Joe is still lacking two of the most important objective values he was designed to enjoy: a loving, reconciling relation with God and fellowship with God's community, the church. If Christianity is true, then Jesus' diagnosis of the human condition is true, and humans are in desperate need of God to rescue them from malevolent powers at work. What's more, the human heart, mind, soul, and body need supernatural repair. Therefore, according to the Christian worldview, Virtuous-Joe is not feasting on the main course of happiness for several reasons.

First, Aristotle and objective naturalists don't adequately address the human condition. If Christianity is true, then humans are created in the image and likeness of God (Gen. 1:26). But given the effects of sin (see, e.g., Rom. 5), the human condition has been corrupted. It's not hard to justify the claim that humans are imperfect with conclusive evidence. Recall G. K. Chesterton's point about the doctrine of original sin as the only part of Christian theology that can be empirically proven.[28] Further, the noetic capacities responsible for making God's presence as obvious as the noses on our face have been damaged by sin, thereby making God's presence hidden (Ps. 89:46; Isa. 59:2; Mic. 3:4). This missed diagnosis from biblical anthropology is critical because if Christianity is true, then humans were created to live in daily communion and fellowship with God. Any conception of happiness that excludes a reconciling relationship with God—made possible through the sacrificial act of love Jesus personified in his life, death, and resurrection—falls short of the kind and degree of happiness that God created humans to enjoy. So despite the degree of happiness obtained by Virtuous-Joe, he was created to enjoy a far superior kind and degree of happiness.

Second, Aristotle and objective naturalists assume that humans have the wherewithal to cultivate the virtuous character needed to flourish. But if Christianity is true, then the corrupted human condition lacks the power and resources to cultivate the kind of character needed to consistently flourish which, again, is a kind of flourishing that involves an orientation toward God, God's kingdom, and dependence on God. Even having the wisdom needed to know what one should and shouldn't do isn't enough (cf. Rom. 7).[29] Human beings were created to live in dependence upon God, which is how human agency was originally designed to function.[30] Just because Virtuous-Joe can put together a solid day of living, it doesn't mean he couldn't have lived even better, having the power and resources to do it consistently and enjoy it (even more) because of God's presence and involvement. If Christianity is true, humans were designed to be informed and empowered by God to fulfill their true function, purpose, and capacity for happiness. This entails a union, communion, and dependency upon God, who is worthy of worship. Indeed, acknowledgement and cooperation with God's will results in a life wherein one worships, glorifies, and loves God and others, including one's enemies.[31] This is part of the Christian design plan for how humans experience the best kind of happiness.

Third, if Christianity is true, then Jesus is the standard by which all moral exemplars are to be judged. Since God is necessarily morally perfect and perfectly loving, God alone is the moral standard. Lacking knowledge of the way Jesus lived the regenerative life leaves important gaps one needs to fill and blind spots in need of correction. Aristotle's and objective naturalist's description of the moral and intellectual virtues can cover important ground. But without emulating Jesus' dependency upon the Father and the Holy Spirit (and now, for Christians, their dependence upon Jesus, the Holy Spirit, and the Father), one will not live life consistently well and qualitatively well (John 15:1–5).

Many objective naturalists, drawing from Aristotle's conception of happiness, assume both too much and too little. They assume too much because humans—left to their own resources—are powerless to consistently succeed at flourishing a certain kind of way—that is, getting right how to live in dependence on and fellowship with God, in addition to loving God and others, including one's enemy. They assume too little because succeeding in different areas of life will never fill the God-shaped hole in human hearts which can be filled only by becoming an adopted child of God, indwelt by the Holy Spirit (Rom. 6 and 8; Eph. 1:13–14; 1 John 1:1–3). The greatest kind of happiness on offer comes from being forgiven by God of one's sin and errant actions and being reconciled as an adopted child of God, thereby becoming a new creation in Christ (2 Cor. 5:17) with love and power to overcome the powers of sin and vice (Rom. 6 and 8). This happiness continues as one lives out the regenerative life. It transforms one's corrupt character into Christlike character (Rom. 5:5; Gal. 2:20; Eph. 3:14–19; 1 Corinthians 13; 1 John 4:7–8).[32] This kind of character informs, enables, and empowers one to live life the way God designed humans to flourish—to be truly happy.

Counterfeit candidates for happiness are morally impotent and powerless to provide the kind of love, power, peace, contentment, and joy that only knowing the Triune God—accompanied by the internally dwelling Holy Spirit—can provide the human soul. Indeed, as the psalmist testifies: "Taste and see that the LORD is good; blessed is the one who takes refuge in him" (Ps. 34:8).

The Christian Metanarrative Provides the Way to Understand the Meaning of Life

One does not have to live very long before existentially charged questions begin to form. Even if one discovered some plausible (perhaps, even true) answer to each existentially charged question, one would still lack an important epistemic good: understanding.[33] Now one would be in possession of some very good things if they had knowledge of true answers to existentially charged questions. But one would be in possession of something much greater if one could see how all these answers fit together into a coherent whole. That is to say, if one had understanding of how these bits of knowledge fit into a coherent story, then one can better comprehend the significance and meaning of them. This provides a greater sense of purpose since one will better understand the story being written within the metanarrative. Indeed, one will understand oneself as a protagonist in life, having specific roles to play within this epic drama playing out—a true, divine authoritative call to adventure! Having a true metanarrative enables one to have a degree of understanding about the meaning of life. The following are some main chapters structuring the plot of the Christian metanarrative.

Ultimate Origins: In the Beginning Was . . .

Every metanarrative has an account of ultimate origins.[34] Since necessary existence seems, for many, to be a divine-like attribute, many worldviews function like religious ones by postulating the existence of something whose existence doesn't depend upon anything else. Throughout history there have been only a few candidates: Mind/Nous/God/gods (Supernaturalism), matter (Naturalism), or abstract objects (quasi-supernaturalism; Platonism).[35] Whatever exists necessarily will somehow ground the existence of contingent things; contingent things will have dependency relations to that which has always existed. According to the Christian metanarrative, "In the beginning God created the heavens and the earth" (Gen. 1:1). In the beginning, there was a supernatural Mind/Nous/Consciousness, and contingent things like matter and abstract objects, as well as the rest of creation, are dependent upon it (cf. John 1:1; Col. 1:17).

The Diagnosis: The Fall Affects All

Nothing is immune to the effects from the fall. It doesn't take long to figure out that things are not the way they are supposed to be.[36] Viruses, cancers, tornadoes, and hurricanes are just some of the natural evils that cause pain, suffering, and death. Lying, stealing, betraying, harming, and murdering are some moral evils causing much pain, suffering, and death. Even the human heart, soul, body, and mind have been damaged. These parts of the human person continue to become less healthy and less reliable given the consequences of choices influenced by the fall. From individuals destroying lives, families, and communities to nations systematically destroying groups, other nations, and parts of creation, the fall affects the quantity and quality of evil in this world. Something much deeper at the heart of humanity and creation needs rescuing, and no advancement in science, medicine, social policy, or government will ever be able to deliver.[37] For they are all versions of the metaphorical "bread," which are good, but as Jesus taught, humans don't live on bread alone (Matt. 4:4).

The Remedy: God's Redemptive Plan

Many theists and atheists alike agree that pursuing valuable things (like creating families, alleviating pain and suffering, acquiring epistemic goods, cultivating virtuous character, creating beautiful things, experiencing various pleasures, creating goods and services for the benefit of others, and assisting others to do likewise) makes life meaningful. But without knowing God, pursuing these objective values can end up missing the true target. The Christian metanarrative includes specific ways of defining these objective values (especially when special revelation addresses them).

Objective naturalists and Christians, for example, may agree that objective values exist. But when we start carefully defining these objective values, there is sometimes significant disagreement. What's more, the way humans pursue the good, true, and beautiful will look different. God sent Jesus to rescue humans from the powers of sin, selfishness, and idolatry; Jesus is the exemplar that showed humanity how to participate, cooperate, and yield one's will to God's will (Matt. 26:39; Mark 14:36; Luke 22:42; John 6:38) through his dependence upon the Holy Spirit. This transformation was foretold by the prophets Ezekiel (36:36) and Jeremiah (31:33); part of the remedy for the fall will be a new covenant with God wherein God will give humans a new heart—the core of our being will be infused by a new kind of love, power, and orientation toward God, others, and reality. This is an eternal kind of life. This kind of divinely assisted human agency enables one to fully participate in the kingdom of God that Jesus taught about. By successfully loving God and others through the power provided by the indwelling Holy Spirit, and discipling others to do likewise (Matt. 28:16–20), true happiness can be experienced, which is a very different prescription than what the objective naturalist's metanarrative offers.[38]

The Prognosis: Perfect Happiness (*Beatitudo*) through a New Heaven and New Earth

The apostle Paul's letter to the church at Corinth says, "For our light momentary troubles are achieving for us an eternal weight of glory that far outweighs them all" (2 Cor. 4:17). The prognosis for humans within the Christian metanarrative is indescribably good—beyond what our finite minds can imagine and appreciate. But we do have some clues. The resurrection of Jesus with a new glorified body is an indication of new things to come. First, death doesn't have the last word. Second, humans will receive new glorified bodies that are no longer subject to sickness; disease; suffering; torment; distorted or perverted desires, passions, feelings, and emotions; sinful habits; deterioration; and the noetic effects of sin. Third, Revelation 21 speaks of a New Heaven and a New Earth.[39]

This new creation will lack natural and moral evils. Therefore, the effects of the fall will no longer affect our bodies, environment, and life. Those obstacles between us and the good, true, and beautiful will finally be removed. Seachris eloquently addresses the new creation this way: it is about "peace, justice, reconciliation, restoration, the reign of God's glorious kingdom, and the defeat of darkness being brought to all aspects of the cosmos to the glory of God. This final blessed state, anchored in and resulting from Jesus' resurrection, is, as the prophet Isaiah depicts, something of a return to the Garden of Eden, where deep harmony between humanity, creation, and God comes to full fruition, and where sin in all its manifestations, disease, and death are abolished forever (cf. Isa. 11:1–9)." [40] Indeed, the apostle John says, "Look! God's dwelling place is now among the people, and he will dwell with them. They will be his people, and he will dwell with them. They will be his people, and God himself will be with them and be their God. 'He will wipe every tear from their eyes. There will be no more death' or mourning or crying or pain, for the old order of things has passed away" (Rev. 21:3–4).

Conclusion

In this book we covered topics intended to assist you in developing a better worldview than the one you currently have. Recall that a worldview is a mental map that we use to interpret evidence and form beliefs to help us better navigate through reality. More specifically, a worldview consists of existing assumptions, commitments, and beliefs about rules, standards, and principles that filter evidence and process it when forming beliefs about the nature of reality and answers to life's most profound questions.[41] Some of these questions include existentially charged questions. We think one important way of addressing the meaning-of-life question is to think hard about it (i.e., practice philosophy) with the hope of discovering a true metanarrative. This metanarrative can then organize existentially charged questions into a meaningful, coherent whole; moreover, it can narrate over life events, while also providing an eternal perspective on them. We believe the Christian metanarrative provides a true account of ultimate origins and provides an accurate human diagnosis, remedy, and prognosis. Even if you deny the human prognosis, we hope that you, at least, hope it's true—recognize how beautiful a story it is.[42] If so, we sincerely invite you to explore it more deeply—specifically, the claims of Jesus and the life he offers as the remedy to the human condition. We believe the prognosis of a new heaven, earth, and glorified bodies we will receive further contributes toward satisfying the deep longing we have for perfect happiness. Furthermore, we hope you will continue studying philosophy so that, as your worldview becomes more accurate, you will improve your ability to succeed at acquiring the good, true, and beautiful.

Questions for Reflection

1. Do you think final causation (teleology) is a real cause, even if science can't account for it by appealing to prior physical events governed by the laws of nature? If so, what evidence and reasons can you use to support your answer? If not, explain why and how personal explanations are inferior to mechanistic/scientific ones?

2. What are the arguments against the idea of reducing happiness to pleasure? What do you think is the strongest argument in favor of reducing happiness to merely stimulating one's nervous system?

3. Is the Aristotelean version of happiness better than an Epicurean view of happiness? Explain what the merits are supporting your answer.

4. Why might someone argue for why the Christian version of happiness is arguably better than the Aristotelean version of happiness? What alleged correctives does it offer, assuming Christianity is true?

5. What do you find attractive, desirable, and/or beautiful about the Christian metanarrative, even if you don't currently believe that it is true?

For Further Reading

Budziszewski, J. *How and How Not to Be Happy*. Washington, D.C: Regnery Gateway, 2022.

Ganssle, Gregory E. *Our Deepest Desires: How the Christian Story Fulfills Human Aspirations*. Downers Grove, IL: IVP Academic, 2017.

Gould, Paul M. *A Good and True Story: Eleven Clues to Understanding Our Universe and Your Place in It*. Grand Rapids: Brazos, 2022.

Metz, Thaddeus, and Joshua W. Seachris. *What Makes Life Meaningful? A Debate*. New York: Rutledge, forthcoming.

Moreland, J. P., and Klaus Issler. *The God Question: An Invitation to a Life of Meaning*. 2nd ed. Downers Grove, IL: IVP Academic, 2021.

Moreland, J. P., and Klaus Issler. *The Lost Virtue of Happiness: Discovering the Disciplines of the Good Life*. Colorado Springs: NavPress, 2006.

Seachris, Joshua W., and Stewart Goetz, eds. *God and Meaning: New Essays*. New York: Bloomsbury, 2016.

Seachris, Joshua W., and Stewart Goetz. *What Is This Thing Called the Meaning of Life?* New York: Routledge, 2021.

NOTES

1. We're indebted to Joshua Seachris for his recent work on the meaning of life. This chapter greatly benefitted from the work of both Seachris and Thaddeus Metz in their debate over

the meaning of life, which was done in a book format. Any strengths this chapter possesses is the result of being better informed by their contributions and Seachris's essay "The Meaning of Life and Scripture's Redemptive-Historical Narrative: Illuminating Convergences," in *God and Meaning: New Essays*, ed. Joshua W. Seachris and Steward Goetz (New York: Bloomsbury, 2016). See Thaddeus Metz and Joshua W. Seachris, *What Makes Life Meaningful? A Debate* (New York: Rutledge, 2024).

2. This is inspired by Joshua Seachris's definition of what he calls a "candidate meaning of life narrative," which he defines as "one that narrates across some existentially relevant threshold of life aspects and accompanying questions largely captured by the category of EC_Q by adding an ultimate metanarrative framework that helps us make sense of EC_Q and that provides practical guidance for leading a flourishing life." See Seachris, "The Meaning of Life and Scripture's Redemptive-Historical Narrative," 20.

3. Recall back to chapter 1, wherein we said a worldview influences the way one processes information, interprets reality, and forms beliefs. A worldview is comprised of specific assumptions, commitments, norms, standards, values, principles, beliefs, and theories that filter and process evidence and/or information. Sometimes we are even unaware of the ways in which our worldview is filtering, processing, coloring, and assisting us when forming beliefs and interpreting reality. In chapter 26, we looked at four different worldviews: objective naturalism, subjective naturalism, pessimistic naturalism, and supernaturalism.

4. Stephen Jay Gould, "The Meaning of Life," *Life*, December 1988, 84. We borrow this point and quotation of Gould from J. P. Moreland—specifically, the idea that naturalism lacks teleology, which prevents why-questions from being answered, that is, providing answers that appeal to objective purposes, aims, or goals. See J. P. Moreland, *Kingdom Triangle* (Grand Rapids: Zondervan, 2007), 56.

5. Because teleology seems to be such a necessary explanatory resource to explain certain things (e.g., consciousness, agency, moral values, and reason), some naturalists try to devise a naturalist worldview that is hospitable to teleology. For example, see Thomas Nagel, *Mind and Cosmos: Why the Materialist Neo-Darwinian Conception of Nature Is Almost Certainly False* (Oxford: Oxford University Press, 2012).

6. Dawkins says, "In a universe of *blind* physical forces and genetic replication, some people are going to get hurt, other people are going to get lucky, and you won't find any rhyme or reason in it, nor any justice. The universe we observe has precisely the properties we should expect if there is, at bottom, no design, no *purpose*, no evil and no good, nothing but blind, pitiless indifference." See Richard Dawkins, *River out of Eden: A Darwinian View of Life* (New York: Basic Books, 1996), 133, emphasis ours.

7. Ibid., 98.

8. Richard Dawkins, *The Selfish Gene* (Oxford: Oxford University Press, 2006), xiii, emphasis ours. Dawkins still uses the term "purpose," but it is only a helpful metaphor—indeed, "a fruitful metaphor" in the case of explaining the function of genes (196).

9. Ibid., xxi, emphasis ours.

10. Jean-Paul Sartre, *Existentialism Is a Humanism* (New Haven: Yale University Press, 2007), 24.

11. See Carl R. Trueman, *The Rise and Triumph of the Modern Self: Cultural Amnesia, Expressive Individualism, and the Road to Sexual Revolution* (Weaton, IL: Crossway, 2020). Trueman delineates some of the philosophical and intellectual influences of the past three hundred

years (e.g., Rousseau, Nietzsche, Marx, Darwin, Freud, Marcuse) to set the stage for a view of the individual self, culminating in the sexual revolution and evolving today with the rise of personal identity debates, fads, and political trends.

12. See Richard Swinburne, "God as the Simplest Explanation of the Universe," *European Journal of Philosophy of Religion* (2010), 2–4.

13. Some people think of happiness in terms of pleasurable feelings, emotions, and/or sensations. So, wanting one's child to be happy is to want the child to experience as much pleasure as possible—not having to experience pain. This is not the kind of happiness we're considering here. We are simply acknowledging that some parents may have this version of happiness in mind when answering the question.

14. David McPherson identifies happiness with a meaningful life. See David McPherson, *Virtue and Meaning: A Neo-Aristotelian Perspective* (Cambridge: Cambridge University Press, 2020), 47.

15. Aristotle says, "happiness appears to be one of the most divine things, since the prize and goal of virtue appears to be the best good, something divine and blessed." See Aristotle, *Nicomachean Ethics*, 1.9, 1099b16–18.

16. Contrary to Aristotle's view of happiness as virtuous activity, Stoics and Epicureans take happiness to be a state of virtue and pleasure, respectively. We reject the thin, shallow view of happiness as reduced to mere pleasure, despite its popularity amongst many in contemporary culture.

17. Intrinsic value is when a thing's value is located inside the thing itself (e.g., the value of human life). Final value is when the value of something contributes to fulfilling the purpose or design of the thing that has it (e.g., acquiring knowledge or Christ-like virtues contributes to fulfilling the kind of thing a human person was designed to be). See the sidebar "Kinds of Value" in chapter 26 for descriptions of different kinds of value.

18. A movie that captures pretty well this idea of Aristotelian-happiness is *Groundhog Day*, directed by Harold Ramis, featuring Bill Murray, Andie MacDowell, and Chris Elliot, motion picture (Columbia Pictures, 1993).

19. The good, true, and beautiful have interested philosophers dating all the way back to, roughly, 500 BC (e.g., Parmenides). Sometimes called the *transcendentals*, the good, true, and beautiful is a common triad used to refer to those things humans naturally desire and are attracted toward. The values and meaning possessed by this triad are believed by some to transcend the value and meaning one can infer from merely studying physical things and events. Or this triad transcends education and socialization because of their universal appeal to humans given humanity's natural desires, curiosities, and moral concerns.

20. We are assuming that happiness is not reducible to mere pleasurable feelings or desire satisfaction. There may be pleasurable feelings accompanying the moments lived by the happy person, but they are not necessary. The happy person acts virtuously, thereby succeeding at acquiring epistemic goods (the true), healthy relationships (the good), creating beautiful things and services, including character (the beautiful), and assisting others to do likewise (the good). An Aristotelean version of happiness captures this kind of happiness to an impressive degree. But below we will discuss a Christian version of happiness which exceeds what an Aristotelean account can achieve.

21. Metz and Seachris, *What Makes Life Meaningful?* 7, emphasis ours.

22. We're assuming the good, true, and beautiful are objective values that furnish the world.

Furthermore, we agree with objective naturalists that pleasure alone is inadequate for a meaningful life for reasons given by the likes of John Stuart Mill and Robert Nozick. Mill took there to be an objective hierarchy of pleasures, contrary to Jeremy Bentham's subjectivist view of pleasures as the good right actions aim to secure. Indeed, Mill says, "It is better to be a human dissatisfied than a pig satisfied; better to be Socrates dissatisfied than a fool satisfied." Intellectual pleasures are superior to base pleasures that satisfy one's appetites. Nozick appeals to one's intuitions by painting a picture of one's nervous system connected to a pleasure machine—a life lived in a virtual reality of one's own making. Many intuitively see that a life disconnected from reality is striped of truth—real people, places, and success—despite the fact one's nervous system is stimulated to the max. Thus, pleasure alone is taken as an inadequate way to account for happiness.

23. Metz and Seachris, *What Makes Life Meaningful?* 141--43, emphasis ours.

24. We're indebted to Joshua Seachris for providing this list of Christian thinkers discussing Christian happiness as the purpose for human life. See Thaddeus Metz and Joshua W. Seachris, *What Makes Life Meaningful?* 60–61. Saint Augustine (354–430): "[W]e wish to be happy, do we not? [. . .] Everyone who possesses what he wants is happy. . . . Therefore, [. . .] whoever possesses God is happy." Boethius (480–524): "[T]he whole concern of men [. . .] strives to arrive at one and the same end, that of happiness. . . . In all of these things it is obviously happiness alone that is desired; for whatever a man seeks above all else, that he reckons the highest good. But we have defined the highest good as happiness; wherefore each man judges that state to be happy which he desires above all others. . . ." Saint Anselm (1033–1109): "It ought not to be doubted that the nature of rational beings was created by God . . . in order that, through rejoicing in him, it might be blessedly happy. . . . Man, being rational by nature, was created . . . to the end that, through rejoicing in God, he might be blessedly happy. . . . God . . . [made man] for the purpose of eternal happiness." Thomas Aquinas (1224–74): "[T]he ultimate [purpose] of man . . . is called felicity or happiness, because this is what every intellectual substance desires as an ultimate end, and for its own sake alone." John Calvin (1509–46): The "holy patriarchs expected a happy life from the hand of God (and it is indubitable that they did), they viewed and contemplated a different happiness from that of a terrestrial life." C. S. Lewis (1898–1963): A Christian "believes that men are going to live forever, [and] that they were created by God and so built that they can find their true and lasting happiness only by being united to God. . . ."

25. Aquinas says Christians can experience imperfect happiness (i.e., *felicity*) this side of heaven despite the impediments of the world, flesh, and devil. It's not until we are finally home, in heaven, seeing God face-to-face, that we will experience perfect happiness (i.e., *beatitudo*). See Aquinas, *Summa Contra Gentiles*, I-II, Q5. A3.

26. Thomas Aquinas, *Summa Theologica* I-II. Q3. A8.

27. Saint Augustine, *The Confessions of Saint Augustine*, trans. John K. Ryan (New York: Doubleday, 1960), 43.

28. G. K. Chesterton's famous line went like this: "Certain new theologians dispute original sin, which is the only part of Christian theology which can really be proved." See G. K. Chesterton, *Orthodoxy* (1908; New York: Image Books, 2001), 8–9; thanks to J. Budziszewski for reminding me of this quote in his wonderful book *How and How Not to Be Happy* (Washington, D.C.: Regnery Gateway, 2022), 173.

29. This is unfortunately a problem for many people who have left Christianity because the moral standard prescribed is too hard to live up to. The problem, however, is not prescribing what can't be consistently lived out; rather, the problem is trying to live life well and in obedience to God's commands without daily dependency, cooperation, and yielding of one's will to the power and resources God provides through the ministry of the Holy Spirit. Far too many people have attempted to live "the moral life" relying solely upon their own resources, rather than the Christian way of life and, as a result, have succumbed to the vices they wanted to be free from.

30. For a proposed model that explains what this dependency might look like, see Gary Osmundsen, "Sanctification as Joint Agency with the Triune God: An Aristotelian Causal Model," *Philosophia Christi* 21, no. 2 (2019): 325–54.

31. If Christianity is true, then God is the creator and sustainer of all things, especially all good things. Love is one of those good things; thankfully, many theists and atheists draw from it, act in it, and allow it to inform their intentions and/or motivate their actions. But if Christianity is true, then unacknowledging the source of love, the Gift-giver of this gift, fails at satisfying greater degrees of the cultivation of virtue—specifically, humility and gratitude. Such humility and gratitude can increase one's achieved degree of happiness and enhance one's character. Failure to see God as the provider of this power—this gift—results in too much self-credit. This only adds to the common tendency of unacknowledging our inability to self-create our existence, bodies, and world in which we get to perform these successful achievements.

32. Romans 5:5 speaks to the supernatural love God infuses into humans in and through the indwelling and ministry of the Holy Spirit. This kind of divine love immediately begins transforming human character into degrees and levels of Christlike character.

33. Recall from chapter 10 that understanding is another kind of epistemic good that should not be confused with knowledge. For example, one can know that a particular event, E, occurred, but lack knowledge of why or how E occurred, which requires understanding. Similarly, one can know that object X is a chair. But one may not understand (1) what the chair is made of; (2) why the chair is shaped that way; (3) how the wood changed into that shape; (4) and the purpose of the chair (why the chair was made). An adequate account of understanding requires knowing the four causes of a thing, which answer many of the "how" and "why" questions. Understanding allows one to see how many independent pieces of knowledge fit together into a coherent whole. Aristotle named these four causes the material, formal, efficient, and final cause. The material cause answers the question, "What is the physical material of something?" The efficient cause answers the question, "What caused the events that changed the physical material?" The formal cause answers the question, "Why does the physical material have that shape, structure, or framework?" The final cause answers the question, "What is the purpose of this thing or why was this thing made?" See Aristotle's *Physics* 194b21–22, and *Metaphysics* 1044a32-b1.

34. Roy Clouser has shown that whatever one takes to exist necessarily functions within the metanarrative as that which is divine. See Roy Clouser, *The Myth of Religious Neutrality: An Essay on the Hidden Role of Religious Belief in Theories* (Notre Dame: Notre Dame University Press, 1991).

35. Carl Sagan famously coined the phrase, "The cosmos is all that is or was or ever will be."

Sagan is a naturalist and, like many naturalists, matter is taken to exist necessarily, making it the thing all other contingent things depend upon for its existence.

36. For a classic treatment that diagnoses the effects of the Fall, see Cornelius Plantinga, *Not the Way It's Supposed to Be: A Breviary of Sin* (Grand Rapids: Eerdmans, 1996).

37. Aleksandr Solzhenitsyn famously said, "The line separating good and evil passes not through states, nor between classes, nor between political parties either—but right through every human heart—and through all human hearts. This line shifts. Inside us, it oscillates with the years. And even within hearts overwhelmed by evil, one small bridgehead of good is retained." See Aleksandr Solzhenitsyn, *The Gulag Archipelago: An Experiment in Literary Investigation*, vol. 2, trans. Thomas P. Whitney (New York: HarperPerennial, 2007 [1973]), part 4, chap. 1.

38. See Dallas Willard, *The Spirit of the Disciplines: Understanding How God Changes Lives* (New York: HarperCollins, 1988); Dallas Willard, *Renovation of the Heart* (Colorado Springs: NavPress, 2002); Richard Foster, *Celebration of Discipline: The Path to Spiritual Growth* (New York: HarperCollins, 1978).

39. To see why a dynamic view of heaven is arguably better than a static view, see Eric J. Silverman, "Conceiving Heaven as a Dynamic Rather Than Static Existence?" in *Paradise Understood: New Philosophical Essays about Heaven*, ed. T. Ryan Byerly and Eric J. Silverman (Oxford: Oxford University Press, 2017).

40. Joshua Seachris, "The Meaning of Life and Scripture's Redemptive-Historical Narrative," in Seachris and Goetz, *God and Meaning*, 32.

41. Some profound questions are these: Does God exist? Does God personally interact with humans? Do objective moral values exist? What is the meaning of life? How did life originate? Do humans have free will? Is there life after death? What is knowledge and can humans get it? What happens when humans die? Who is a good person?

42. For an excellent attempt at showcasing the many beautiful facets of the Christian metanarrative, see Paul M. Gould, *A Good and True Story: Eleven Clues to Understanding Our Universe and Your Place in It* (Grand Rapids: Brazos, 2022).

Glossary

abduction. A method of reasoning that attempts to infer the best explanation for observations made in an inquiry.

abortion. A deliberate act of intervention to terminate a pregnancy by destroying and removing an embryo or fetus.

ad hominem. A type of informal fallacy in which it is suggested that a person's claim must be false because of some undesirable character trait of that person.

ad populum. A type of informal fallacy in which it is suggested that the popularity of a claim shows that the claim is true.

agent-causation. An event is caused by a person exercising causal powers to bring about the event as an originating source; the event is not caused by some prior physical state within a person, but rather, the person—the agent—acting as an uncaused first cause.

amalgam approach. A philosophical approach to the meaning-of-life question that seeks various ways of making life meaningful, as opposed to seeking one definitive answer to the question.

antirealism. In the philosophy of science, antirealism is the view that science does not explain or reflect the natural world. In metaphysics, antirealism maintains skepticism about the existence of the world, whether it is held that (a) nothing exists or (b) nothing can be known or accessed outside the mind.

applied ethics. The branch of ethics concerned with correct and consistent application of principles and theories across a range of specific moral problems.

argument. A set of logically connected reasons (called premises) that are presented in order to support the truth of a claim (called the conclusion).

Aristotelean happiness. The kind of human flourishing achieved through virtuous activity that succeeds at living all facets of life well and, thus, does not lack anything.

atomism. The metaphysical view that everything is comprised of some set of atoms arranged a certain way.

atoms. The very tiny basic moving particles that make up physical reality.

autonomy. A person's inherent right to self-determination, free from coercion.

basic belief. A belief that is justified, but not because of an argument or additional beliefs supporting it.

Beatitudo. Blessedness or perfect happiness—the most complete, satisfying state for humanity, which comes through union with God.

begging the question. Circular reasoning; this fallacy occurs when the truth of the conclusion is assumed in a premise of the argument.

behind the text. Author-centered attempt to find the meaning of a text by discovering the intention or mind of the writer/author (e.g., biblical), combined with the historical/cultural context of the writing.

beneficence. Taking actions to help bring about a person's good.

biological sex. Indicates male or female in terms of sperm-producing (male) or ova-producing (female) capacity chromosomes (if functioning properly), typically serving as the markers of sex.

Christian philosophical theology. From a Christian perspective, attempts to utilize the methods, concepts, and language of philosophy for application to theological issues by employing rigorous and creative reflection, reasoning, and arguments that examine the intelligibility, consistency, and coherency of theological concepts, claims, and truths preeminently concerned with central Christian doctrines such as the Trinity, incarnation, atonement, and resurrection for seeking to achieve a deeper understanding of Christian teachings.

Christlike character. The degree to which one has both the kind and integration of virtues, dispositions, abilities, intentions, motivations, affective states, thoughts, beliefs, values, and orientation toward God and reality that the incarnate second person of the Trinity possesses.

cogito ergo sum. Latin phrase meaning "I think, therefore, I am," coined by Descartes.

cognitive dissonance. A mental state of anguish that comes from discovering that two mental states (i.e., beliefs, thoughts, or ideas) are in tension with each other.

cognitive distortions. Unreasonable, fallacious, or irrational patterns of thought that typically result in beliefs that are unreliably formed and commonly contribute to levels of stress, anxiety, and/or depression.

coherence theory of truth. A statement is true exactly when a subject sees how that statement coheres with other existing beliefs that are taken as true. It denies the correspondence theory of truth, which says that a statement is true when it corresponds with reality.

communication ethics. Addresses moral issues involving communication (e.g., messages), focused on rendering moral evaluations, guidance, and solutions generally based on underlying worldviews and commitments about right and wrong and/or good and evil.

compatibilism. The view that says determinism and free will can coexist because one doesn't entail the falsity of the other, and vice versa.

confirmation bias. Engaging in activities aimed to further justify and confirm a belief one wants to be true, and resisting evidence, testimony, and arguments that suggest the contrary.

consciousness. Subjective awareness of mental experiences like thoughts, beliefs, desires, sensations, choosing, and reasoning, including self-awareness.

control principle. Humans can be morally evaluated only according to those factors that are under the agent's control.

correspondence theory of truth. A statement is true exactly when the content of that statement corresponds with the relevant facts about reality.

cosmological arguments. Arguments for God's existence based on the existence of the universe.

cultural relativism. The view that moral right and wrong are determined by the accepted standards within a particular culture or society.

deduction. A method of reasoning that seeks to conclude what must be true, given that certain premises are true.

defeater. A doubt, belief, reason, or experience indicating that one's justification for a belief is suspect (undercutting defeater) or the belief itself is false (rebutting defeater).

demarcation problem. In the philosophy of science, this problem arises from the fact that there are no necessary or sufficient conditions by which to define science.

deontology. A normative ethical system based on moral duty. Immanuel Kant's version of deontology is focused on human reason.

descriptive analysis. Analyzing something by listing the relevant properties, facts, statistics, and/or patterns that explain why something is the case.

determinism. The metaphysical view that says every event has a prior cause that guarantees the subsequent event must happen—every event in the universe (including one's decisions and actions) is fixed by prior events, states, or objects that are governing them to only one possible outcome.

dialectic. A conversation that continually asks questions to ascertain the exact definition of words and come to a definitive answer to a philosophical question.

divine command theory (DCT). The view that moral duties and obligations are created on account of God's commands. Various versions of DCT exist, differing mainly on the particular focus on attributes, motivations, or purposes of God.

divine hiddenness. An epistemic interest in why there is an absence of experiential evidence for God's existence. This interest elicits questions like these: "Why isn't God's presence more obvious?" Or, if one has a perceptual awareness of God's presence, then "Why doesn't God provide this kind of experiential evidence equally to others?"

dualism. The philosophical view that mental states are not physical (property dualism) or the thing that has non-physical mental states is not physical (substance dualism). Property dualism says there is only one physical substance (i.e., the brain), but this physical substance possesses both physical and nonphysical mental properties. Substance dualism emphasizes that minds and brains are categorically two different kinds of things—they exist independently from each other but can causally interact with each other.

empiricism. The epistemological view that knowledge is gained exclusively (or at least preeminently) by the five human senses.

epistemic circularity. Unlike logical circularity, this kind of circularity involves using cognitive faculties to justify the reliability of one's cognitive faculties. For instance, using the faculty of perception to justify the reliability of beliefs formed from perception. This kind of circularity is arguably permissible given our epistemic situation and because it's not reinserting the conclusion of an argument again as one of its premises, like logical circularity does.

epistemology. The subdiscipline of philosophy that attempts to explain how our minds can connect to reality to get truth and knowledge; it analyzes and attempts to explain *epistemic goods* such as evidence, justification, truth, knowledge, understanding, and wisdom.

ethics. A subdiscipline of philosophy that investigates moral values, moral evaluations, and moral theories, aimed at what humans ought to be and how they ought to act, morally.

eudaimonia. Often translated "happiness," this term from ancient Greek philosophy refers to living the good life because of right reason and virtue or simply flourishing as a human.

euthanasia. An act that hastens the death of a person who is believed to be suffering greatly or hopelessly and/or near death. Euthansia is often classified as either active (via the administration of a lethal dosage of some drug) or passive (by withholding life-sustaining treatment), which involves either the person's voluntary consent (conscious decision) or, if unavailable, nonvoluntary (another person's decision) or involuntary (against the person's will) action.

event-event causation. Any event is the result of preceding physical events or physical states that are causally connected to the event. These preceding physical events or states are sufficient to bring about the event.

evidence. Relevant facts or information that can be used in the context of an inductive argument to show that the conclusion of the argument is likely or probably true.

evidentialist objection. The claim that, in order for a belief to be reasonable, rational, or justified, it must be supported by an argument with premises that represent strong, disclosable evidence.

existentially charged questions. Big-ticket questions many humans yearn for answers to about evil, pain, suffering, God's existence, morality, the afterlife, and life's meaning, purpose, and value.

externalism. An epistemic view of justification. What justifies a belief includes all the facts about its origin, the faculties involved, and the relationship between the subject's mind and reality, incorporating both first-person and third-person perspectives.

fallacy. A mistake in reasoning. An argument that contains a fallacy cannot support its conclusion, even if the premises are true.

falsificationism. In the philosophy of science, this is the view that in order to be ranked as scientific, statements must be capable of being falsified by observation.

fideism. The philosophical view that religious faith is something that does not require evidence, reason, or argument in order for it to be rational. One can rationally believe religious statements based on faith alone without needing to have additional justification.

fine-tuning argument. A teleological argument for God's existence based largely on scientific constants that appear to demonstrate a finely-tuned universe in order for life as we know it to exist.

form. A universal, non-physical ideal of an object or idea.

free will defense. Alvin Plantinga's theistic response to the problem of evil. Plantinga argues it's logically possible for an all-powerful, all-loving, all-knowing God to coexist with evil. Since the creation of free will is such a good thing—making possible moral goodness and loving relationships—God endowed persons with it even though free will can also be used by persons to choose wrong actions and bring about evil.

free will. The ability to make a choice from a set of alternatives that are under one's control. It is an essential capacity that enables the kind of agency needed for a human person to be the proper object of moral evaluations; without free will, morally evaluating actions deserving of judgments like "good," "bad," "right," "wrong," "praiseworthy," and "blameworthy" would be irrational.

gender dysphoria. A recognized mental health condition that involves the distress related to incongruence between an individual's biological sex and perceived gender identity.

gender identity. Traditionally understood as synonymous with biological sex or gender sexuality, referring to being a person who is either male or female. Increasingly understood today (by many institutions and individuals) as one's own psychologically based self-description or personal identity, apart from one's biological/chromosomal sex.

general revelation. The term used to describe the idea that God has revealed truth as a built-in feature of the universe.

generalization. The use of inductive methods of reasoning to draw general conclusions from particular examples.

genetic fallacy. Suggesting that a belief is false based on its origin.

golden mean. The way to describe that the morally right action, or that which will bring happiness, is the one that avoids the two extremes of deficiency or excess.

hermeneutical circle or spiral. Constructive and upward process of moving from prior understanding toward fuller understanding (especially of texts), examining and relating parts to the whole in a back-and-forth interaction, recognizing that grasping the whole requires getting the parts, and grasping the parts requires understanding how they work as part of the whole, while also allowing for reconsideration, modification, and correction of interpretation in light of further learning and fresh insights.

hermeneutics. Primarily focused on the theory, practice, science, and art of interpretation, particularly via exploring ways of reading, understanding, and handling texts; critically reflecting on presuppositional, situational, motivational, and related factors involved in the interpretive process; seeking the meaning of things while working to understand others, and trying to be understood.

heterodoxy. Wrong opinion, deviation, or opposition as to sound orthodox doctrine pertaining to the Christian faith as articulated via the historic Christian tradition; inconsistent with the apostolic faith and fundamental truths regarding the identity, mission, and teachings of Jesus Christ.

human communication. Encompasses the exchange of verbal, tonal, and/or nonverbal information or messages, typically focused on gaining or sharing meaning or understanding by various methods such as speech, writing, and gestures, involving intrapersonal, interpersonal, or organizational levels.

hypothesis. The explanatory starting point that someone might use to explain the available evidence.

idealism. The metaphysical view that says reality is fundamentally mental or immaterial. It says the only things that exist are minds and ideas. This view rejects the existence of independent physical objects; rather, what is perceived as a physical object is really dependent on or reducible to immaterial minds.

in front of the text. Reader-centered attempt to gain the meaning or understanding of a text as produced by its recipients, combined with the historical/cultural context of the readers.

incarnation. The second person of the Trinity, the eternal Son or Word, one in essence with the Father and the Spirit, who took on a human body through the union of perfect human nature (born of the Virgin Mary) with the divine (by the Holy Spirit), one divine-human person, Jesus Christ, for our salvation.

incompatibilism. The view that says if determinism is true, then humans lack free will because free will and determinism cannot coexist—that is, free will and determinism cannot both be true at the same time. A core claim held by incompatibilists is that determinism violates a person's ability to have acted differently or the ability to have done otherwise, which is known as the principle of alternative possibilities (PAP). PAP is often considered a necessary condition for free will.

induction. Using inductive reasoning to draw conclusions.

inductive. A method of reasoning that uses the accumulation of evidence to suggest that a conclusion is probably or likely to be true.

informal fallacy. Mistakes in reasoning related to the content of the argument, rather than related to the form or structure of a deductive inference.

information ethics. Examines moral issues involving the use of particular media for communicating (traditional and newer forms), and increasingly centers on investigating ethical principles and moral practices involving online or digital information, often proposing solutions to unethical foundations and immoral conduct therein.

innate ideas. Ideas (or knowledge) are in the human intellect inherently. This idea is often associated with the epistemology of rationalism.

instrumentalism. In the philosophy of science, this is the view that scientific theories are merely tools useful for predicting and explaining human observations.

intellectual virtues. Certain abilities and skills that enable one to better succeed at acquiring truth, knowledge, and understanding. Examples of intellectual virtues are intellectual curiosity, intellectual humility, intellectual conscientiousness, intellectual perseverance, intellectual charity, intellectual autonomy, intellectual courage, intellectual firmness, and intellectual open-mindedness.

intentionality. A philosophy-of-mind term capturing how mental states are about things like persons, places, propositions, and other kinds of content.

internalism. An epistemic view of justification, specifically, the idea that what justifies a belief is going to be—to one degree or another—accessible to the subject from the first-person point of view.

interpretation. Process or performance of explaining or understanding the meaning of a text (verb); a result of the interpretive process (noun).

justice. The fair application of care.

justified true belief (JTB) account of knowledge. A person knows some fact about reality exactly when that person believes the truth because of this person's justification—that is, because this person has sufficient evidence and/or reasons supporting the true belief.

kafkatrapping. When denying guilt is used as evidence of guilt.

knowledge. When one successfully gets the truth because of justification, a reliable faculty, or an intellectual virtue. To know something, one must have a true belief and the subject must have acquired the true belief because of sufficient justification, or because a reliable faculty is responsible for bringing the true belief about, or because the true belief was brought by intellectual virtues or virtuous character and not because of dumb luck or accident.

law of identity. The principle of reasoning that whatever something is, that is what it is, and it is not something else.

law of noncontradiction. The principle of reasoning that two statements that contradict one another cannot both be true at the same time and in the same sense.

law of the excluded middle. The principle of reasoning that any clearly articulated statement is either true or false.

legalism. The belief that we need to please God by performing the right kinds or quantities of morally virtuous actions in order to earn salvation.

logic. The branch of philosophy that focuses on proper reasoning, including the evaluation of arguments.

logical circularity. When one assumes to be true in a premise or premises what the argument aims to support in the conclusion.

materialism. The view that all that exists is physical or material. It denies the existence of anything immaterial or spiritual (such as God, angels, or human souls).

mental hygiene. Self-monitoring and attentiveness toward the kind of vices, invalid inferences, passions, emotions, impulses, and patterns of reasoning that distort one's interpretation of reality and prevent one from reliably forming true beliefs, especially about oneself.

metaethics. The branch of ethics that focuses on the meaning, nature, and justification of ethical terms and judgments.

metanarrative. A story with built-in metaphysical and epistemological assumptions that provides a way to interpret reality and answer existentially charged questions. Answers to these questions are then better understood and located within the story's temporal framework and further understood by considering how the story ultimately ends, thereby offering a temporal or eternal perspective (or both).

metaphysics. The subdiscipline of philosophy that studies the fundamental nature of reality and categories that comprise the world.

methodic doubt. The method of doubting every knowledge claim by which Descartes attempted to find certitude of knowledge.

methodological naturalism. A method of scientific inquiry that holds that naturalism must be assumed when approaching the study of science.

modernism. The philosophical movement focused on finding the exact method to ascertain total certainty (rationalism) or near-total certainty (empiricism) of knowledge.

monism. The metaphysical view that says there is only one physical substance/reality, and everything else is a property of it or a collection of its parts.

moral arguments. Arguments for the existence of God that are based on the revelation of, and/or observation of, objective moral values and duties.

moral subjectivism. The view that moral right and wrong depend on the preferences of individual people and apply only to those individuals.

moral virtues. Certain abilities and skills that enable one to better succeed at acquiring truth and knowledge about morally right actions and having the motivation, power, and ability to perform the morally right action given one's circumstance. Examples of moral virtues are love, temperance, courage, wisdom, justice, generosity, compassion, chastity, kindness, diligence, and humility.

moralism. An approach to the ethical life that focuses exclusively on adopting customs or conventions of behavior. This approach is adopted by some for religious purposes, such as attempting to please a deity or to earn salvation (in contrast to receiving God's grace through faith in Christ and the enabling power of the Spirit for moral living).

naturalism. The metaphysical view of reality that takes there to be nothing over and above physical matter—a rejection of the existence of any non-physical thing, including God, angels, demons, souls, moral values, abstract objects, etc.

naturalistic explanation for belief in God. An attempt to explain belief in God by suggesting that such belief is grounded in something natural, rather than supernatural (e.g., God's existence).

necessary condition. A condition that must be present in order for something else to occur. (Condition P is necessary for B, if and only if B cannot possibly occur without P.) A condition that must be met for a statement to be true.

new media. Digital communication technologies, often involving interactive or customizable two-way or many-to-many processes using computers, smartphones, and other electronic devices connected to the internet and engaged in various online interests, such as social media communities, content creation, video and audio streaming, podcasts, email, blogs, hypertexting/linking to information sources, online work and education, career development, virtual networks and simulation or virtual worlds, etc.

nihilism. The view that moral right and wrong do not exist; that there is no such thing as objective moral values.

nominalism. The metaphysical view that rejects the existence of universals and/or abstract objects. This metaphysical view takes concrete, physical objects as existing entities while rejecting the existence of non-physical entities that can exist in more than one place at the same time (i.e., universals). Nominalists reduce universals to linguistic conventions, useful fictions, or conceptual tools, which entails abstract objects and universals lack existence in the world.

non-basic belief. A belief that is justified by argument or supported by additional beliefs.

nonmaleficence. Refraining from doing harm.

normative analysis. Analyzing something in order to determine what ought to be the case or why something should be the case by appealing to morally and/or epistemically correct criteria, reasons, principles, methods, and/or sources.

normative ethics. The branch of ethics that focuses on various theories of moral conduct, especially concerned with the question of moral "ought" (e.g., right actions, good character).

objective morality. Moral truths and goods exist in reality and apply universally for all persons and civilizations, regardless of beliefs or practices (since such moral truth and goods originate with God).

objective naturalism. The metaphysical view of reality that takes there to be nothing over and above physical matter; however, the physical world also includes objective values and moral values humans can discover and can align their lives to.

ontological arguments. Arguments for God's existence based only on the concept of God, that use reason alone, rather than observed evidence.

orthodoxy. Right opinion and sound and trustworthy doctrine concerning the Christian faith as articulated via the historic Christian tradition; consistent with the apostolic faith and fundamental truths regarding the identity, mission, and teachings of Jesus Christ.

personal identity. A philosophy-of-mind term referring to what it is that makes a person numerically the same over time (i.e., what makes a person what that person is as a unique individual). Personal identity addresses the ontological conditions that need to be satisfied in order for Past-you, Present-you, and Future-you to be the same exact person despite various changes that have taken place to one's body, brain, and psychology. Outside of philosophy and the philosophy of mind, personal identity may reference certain functional roles that some refer to as their identity. Familial roles (e.g., "I am the spouse of"), vocational roles (e.g., "I am an electrician"), community roles (e.g., "I'm a volunteer for organization X"), future perceived roles (e.g., "I'm going to be the next president of the United States"), and, for Christians, their new relation to the Trinity as an adopted child of God, indwelt by the Holy Spirit (ontology), thereby making them a new creation in Christ and, thus, identifying as a Chirstian or disciple of Jesus (e.g., "I am a follower of Jesus").

person. A subject of experience that has the powers and capacities for consciousness (necessary for sensations, thoughts, beliefs, desires, reason, language, deliberating, etc.), agency (necessary for ability to act for reasons, enter into relationships with others, and be the proper object of moral responsibility and evaluations), having a body (e.g., human person) or not (e.g., angels, demons, God) to express countless intentions and ways of interacting with other persons and the world, and typically retains the same identity over time despite undergoing various changes.

pessimistic naturalism. The metaphysical view of reality that takes there to be nothing over and above physical matter and, unlike objective naturalism, denies the existence of objective values and moral values.

philosophical theology. Attempts to utilize the methods, concepts, and language of philosophy for application to theological issues, often involving rigorous and creative reflection, reasoning, and arguments that examine the intelligibility, consistency, and coherency of theological claims, helping to provide careful distinctions and achieve greater clarity; addressing such topics as the existence of God, divine attributes, religious epistemology, the problem of evil, and the doctrines and practices of specific religious traditions.

philosophy of religion. The subdiscipline in philosophy that addresses theoretical topics of religious belief, such as the nature of religious claims, the relationship between faith and reason, and arguments for the existence of God.

physicalism. The metaphysical view that everything that exists has extension in space and/or depends on the physical. It typically denies the existence of any non-physical entities or properties.

physician-assisted suicide. A person's taking action to end their own life through the assistance of a medical professional.

pragmatic theory of truth. A belief or statement that something is true if and only if it brings about the right kind of beneficial results over the long haul.

presocratics. Ancient Greek philosophers who preceded the Greek philosopher Socrates.

proper function account of knowledge. A person knows a statement exactly when that person believes the statement is true because this person's belief is produced by properly functioning cognitive faculties in an appropriate environment according to a design plan aimed at reliably getting the truth.

properly basic beliefs. A belief that is justified, but not justified because of an argument or additional beliefs supporting it, and the source from which the belief derived is a reliable one.

quale. A philosophy-of-mind term that captures the felt subjective experience of what it's like to have a mental state.

rationalism. The epistemological view that knowledge is exclusively (strong form) or predominantly (weak form) acquired by human reason.

realism. In metaphysics, realism is the view that there exists a mind-independent reality—that is, a world that exists independently of one's subjective experiences, perceptions, and beliefs. In epistemology, realism is the view that a mind-independent reality exists that human minds can cognitively connect with to get true beliefs, knowledge, and degrees of understanding. In moral epistemology, realism refers to the idea that objective moral values exist and that humans can both access these values and form true beliefs about them, as well as acquire knowledge of them. In the philosophy of science, realism refers to the idea that there is a physical world that is, in principle, discoverable and that the methods of science can, in principle, reliably represent facts about reality.

reformed epistemology/reformed view. A model of justification and/or knowledge that doesn't require that a subject's belief needs to be supported by an argument. Epistemologists like Alvin Plantinga and William Alston built on a tradition tracing back to Thomas Reid (1710–1796) emphasizing that a justified religious belief need not have to be inferred from premise-beliefs (relying upon sharable evidence) to a conclusion-belief. Religious beliefs can be justified (and even an instance of knowledge) because of a reliable faculty producing it (e.g., Plantinga's *sensus divinitatis* producing a properly basic belief about God and statements about "the Good News") and/or a non-inferential, perceptual belief of God (e.g., Alston's use of parallel reasoning between sensory experience grounding perceptual beliefs of physical objects and sensory experience grounding perceptual beliefs of God guiding, strengthening, comforting, communicating audibly or through conscience to a human being).

relativism. The view that moral right and wrong are relative to the preferences or customs of people or groups.

relativist theory of truth. A belief or statement that something is true if and only if it is determined to be true relative to whatever invented standard is used by an individual or group.

reliabilist account of knowledge. A person knows a statement exactly when that person believes the statement is true because this person's belief was produced by reliable belief-forming processes.

religious experience. Having experiential evidence in support of some kind of supernaturalism (in general). In particular, it is sometimes evidence for the existence of God that can come by way of either indirect evidence (e.g., inferring God's existence from data or information in nature, personal events, historical events, personal transformation, etc.) or direct evidence (e.g., encountering God via a divine manifestation through nature, conscience, other persons, or having a direct, perceptual awareness of God's presence empowering, guiding, communicating, or comforting a person).

resurrection. Event in which the exalted Lord Jesus Christ was raised bodily from the dead, demonstrating the completed work of redemption and victory over death itself, finalizing and vindicating Christ's saving activity; together, the cross and resurrection (as a single event) are viewed by Christians as the most important in and for all of history, illuminating God's plan of salvation and allowing humans through faith to partake of the divine nature, attain future resurrection, and enjoy everlasting life with the triune God.

sanctification. The supernatural state or process of becoming set apart via God's grace—cultivating Christ-like character, empowered by the Spirit—in order to fulfill one's purposes in life.

scientific realism. In the philosophy of science, this view suggests that scientific theories reflect how the real world actually operates.

scientism. The view that the sciences are the best, or only, valuable and authoritative means by which humans can gain knowledge.

self-refuting. The characteristic of a theory whereby merely asserting it shows that it is false, because it fails to live up to its own standards of acceptability. For example, the statement "all statements have exactly three words in them" is self-refuting. This is a statement that makes a claim about what condition "all statements" must meet, but it fails to meet that condition.

sensus divinitatis **("sensing the divine").** A faculty some Christians believe God has endowed humans with to be able to have a perceptual awareness of God and his influence, testimony, and witness, in addition to forming true, properly basic beliefs about God and his purposes for humanity.

sexual ethics. Encompasses the study of concepts and practices pertaining to human sexuality from a moral standpoint.

sexual union. The uniting of male and female genitalia, divinely intended to express the one-flesh covenant bond of marriage, transcending the human marital/sexual relationship to reflect the spiritual dimension: relationship between God and the people of God, between Jesus Christ and his church.

sexuality. Essential part of our whole being, not reducible to merely sex, covering a panorama of human desiring.

single-question approach. A philosophical approach to the meaning-of-life question that takes the question as a legitimate one and thus seeks an objective answer that applies universally to all human persons.

skepticism. A family of critical attitudes toward the acquisition of knowledge (in general) or specific kinds of knowledge (e.g., moral knowledge) because evidence is insufficient to rule out doubt and/or fail to achieve certainty.

socractic method. Named for the manner in which Socrates investigated philosophical questions. See *dialetic.*

sound argument. Describes an argument that is both valid and has true premises.

special revelation. The term used to describe the idea that God has communicated some specific truths directly to humans. From a Christian perspective, special revelation is understood to include both Scripture and the person of Jesus Christ.

strong scientism. The view that something is true or rationally justified only if it is a scientific claim that has been tested using scientific methods.

subjective naturalism. The metaphysical view of reality that takes there to be nothing over and above physical matter, and values and moral values exist only as subjective states in the minds of persons.

substance. An individual entity that has and organizes its properties, parts, powers, dispositions, and capacities.

sufficient condition. A condition that guarantees the occurrence or existence of something else. S is a sufficient condition for Q if and only if the occurrence of S guarantees the occurrence of Q.

supernaturalism. A worldview that posits the existence of mind-independent, objective values that are grounded in a God that sustains them and endows humans with cognitive faculties to discover them.

tabula rasa. Latin phrase meaning "blank slate" and associated with John Locke's concept of the human mind as it begins to obtain knowledge from perceptions or experiences.

teleological arguments. A family of arguments for God's existence based on observed design in the universe.

teleology. A kind of cause or principle that explains the goal, aim, or purpose of some entity or event; it provides an answer to why questions.

termination of life support. A deliberate act of removing care that is sustaining the life of a person who is suffering.

theological virtues. Certain abilities and skills given by God via grace that enable one's character to be good and, thus, better equipped to know and love God and others, including one's enemies. Examples of theological virtues are faith, hope, and (*agape*) love.

Thomas's Five Ways. Five arguments for God's existence put forth by medieval theologian and philosopher Thomas Aquinas.

traditional media. Long-established forms of mass communication such as newspapers, magazines, film, and radio and TV broadcasting and programs, typically involving one-way information flowing from the sender to the receiver.

Trinity. The central Christian view that God exists as one being in three persons: Father, Son, and Holy Spirit.

truthfulness. Habitual moral virtues or qualities such as honesty, integrity, authenticity, sincerity, and fidelity, in contrast to vices like deceit, hypocrisy, duplicity, pretense, and betrayal; communicating the actual facts of the matter that are true to life.

truth. There are many different theories of truth (e.g., correspondence, coherence, pragmatic, postmodernist, etc.). They all attempt to explain what truth is and what it means when people utter the term *true* or *truth*. The commonsense view of truth is the correspondence view, which says that a statement, thought, belief, or judgment is true exactly when it corresponds to and/or accurately represents reality. For example, what makes the statement "the milk is in the fridge" true is that the content of the statement accurately corresponds to facts about reality—namely, a milk container is inside the refrigerator. If there is no milk in the refrigerator, then the statement is false.

two-realm theory of truth. The view that there are two realms of truth: an upper story that is non-rational and subjective, populated only by personal beliefs and values, but not knowledge; and a lower story that is rational and objective, made up of scientific knowledge.

ultimate purpose. The powers, capacities, and/or abilities a thing or person has to bring about good ends (final, intrinsic, instrumental, or extrinsic values) that continue existing for a potentially infinite amount of time because natural death or the death of the universe doesn't eliminate them.

ultimate value. People and things that have various kinds and combinations of final, intrinsic, instrumental, and/or extrinsic values that continue existing for a potential infinite amount of time because natural death or the death of the universe doesn't eliminate them.

understanding. When one sees various relationships, dependency relations, and/or causes shared between knowledge of independent things and/or true statements. Grasping the dependency relations within things such as stories, systems, aggregates, or models is to see how all the relevant information fits together into a coherent whole.

unity of consciousness. A philosophy-of-mind term referring to how multiple mental states can be bound together and experienced at the same time by a subject experiencing them.

universal. The metaphysical view that says that the exact same properties or kinds or relations can be had by multiple things at the same time. For example, the very same properties of love, joy, peace, patience, kindness, goodness, faithfulness, gentleness, and temperance that the apostle Paul speaks about in Galatians 5 can be had by multiple people at the same time, in different places, during different times, throughout history.

utilitarianism. The normative moral theory that states that the good is that which brings the greatest pleasure or happiness for the greatest number of people.

utility. In ethics, utility refers to a specific approach to moral reasoning that prioritizes achieving the best balance of good and harm.

valid. Logically correct. A valid argument is one that does not commit a mistake in reasoning, such that the premises are properly connected to each other and the conclusion.

virtue account of knowledge. A person knows that a statement is true exactly when that person forms a true belief because this person's belief is produced by intellectual abilities and/or intellectually virtuous activities.

virtue theory. The moral theory that focuses on the cultivation of moral virtues in the character of the person, rather than on moral duties or the consequences of action.

voluntarism. Any viewpoint that considers the will as the central or most important aspect. In the context of theological ethics, voluntarism insists that God's commands alone determine moral right and wrong.

warfare thesis. Another term for the conflict view, which states that faith and reason are always in conflict or at war with one another.

weak scientism. The view that science is the most authoritative and best way to gain knowledge, but not the only way.

within the text. Text-centered attempt to find the meaning of the text from within the text itself, including its literary aspects (language, genre, structure, narrative, quality, etc.).

worldview. A mental map we use to interpret evidence and form beliefs to help us better navigate through reality; more specifically, it consists of existing assumptions, commitments, and beliefs about rules, standards, and principles that filter evidence and process it when forming beliefs about the nature of reality and answers to life's most profound questions. These beliefs, then, inform the decisions and commitments we make and orient us toward reality in a certain way.

Index

Page numbers with an *n* include footnote numbers.